Market-Based Governance

Visions of Governance in the 21st Century

Why People Don't Trust Government
Joseph S. Nye Jr., Philip Zelikow, and David King, editors
(1997)

Governance in a Globalizing World
Joseph S. Nye Jr. and John D. Donahue, editors
(2000)

Governance amid Bigger, Better Markets
John D. Donahue, and Joseph S. Nye Jr., editors
(2001)

Governance.com: Democracy in the Information Age
Elaine Ciulla Kamarck and Joseph S. Nye Jr., editors
(2002)

Market-Based Governance

Supply Side, Demand Side, Upside, and Downside

John D. Donahue
Joseph S. Nye Jr.
Editors

VISIONS OF GOVERNANCE
IN THE 21ST CENTURY
Cambridge, Massachusetts

BROOKINGS INSTITUTION PRESS
Washington, D.C.

ABOUT BROOKINGS

The Brookings Institution is a private nonprofit organization devoted to research, education, and publication on important issues of domestic and foreign policy. Its principal purpose is to bring knowledge to bear on current and emerging policy problems. The Institution maintains a position of neutrality on issues of public policy. Interpretations or conclusions in Brookings publications should be understood to be solely those of the authors.

Copyright © 2002
Visions of Governance in the 21st Century

All rights reserved. No part of this publication may be reproduced or transmitted in any form or by any means without permission in writing from the Brookings Institution Press, 1775 Massachusetts Avenue, N.W., Washington, D.C. 20036 (www.brookings.edu).

Library of Congress Cataloging-in-Publication data
Market-based governance : supply side, demand side, upside, and downside / John D. Donahue, Joseph S. Nye Jr., editors; Visions of Governance in the 21st Century.
   p.   cm.
Includes bibliographical references and index.
  ISBN 0-8157-0628-6 (cloth : alk. paper)
  ISBN 0-8157-0627-8 (pbk. : alk. paper)
  1. Government business enterprises. 2. Privatization. I. Donahue, John D. II. Nye, Joseph S. III. Visions of Governance in the 21st Century (Program)
    HD3850 .M3195 2002
    352.3'4—dc21   2002005446

9 8 7 6 5 4 3 2 1

The paper used in this publication meets minimum requirements of the American National Standard for Information Sciences—Permanence of Paper for Printed Library Materials: ANSI Z39.48-1992.

Typeset in Adobe Garamond

Composition by R. Lynn Rivenbark
Macon, Georgia

Printed by R. R. Donnelley and Sons
Harrisonburg, Virginia

Contents

Preface ix

Acknowledgments xi

1 Market-Based Governance and the Architecture of Accountability 1
John D. Donahue

PART ONE
Demand Side

2 Government Contracting for Health Care 29
Karen Eggleston and Richard Zeckhauser

3 Service Contracting with Nonprofit and For-Profit Providers: On Preserving a Mixed Organizational Ecology 66
Peter Frumkin

4 Strategic Contracting Management   88
   Steven Kelman

PART TWO
Supply Side

5 Market and State Provision of Old-Age Security:
   An International Perspective   105
   Georges de Menil

6 Bundling, Boundary Setting, and the Privatization
   of Legal Information   128
   Frederick Schauer and Virginia J. Wise

PART THREE
Inside and Outside

7 Making Social Markets:
   Dispersed Governance and Corporate Accountability   145
   Archon Fung

8 Lessons from the American Experiment
   with Market-Based Environmental Policies   173
   Robert N. Stavins

9 Management-Based Regulatory Strategies   201
   Cary Coglianese and David Lazer

PART FOUR
Upside and Downside

10 The End of Government as We Know It   227
   Elaine Ciulla Kamarck

11 The Problem of Public Jobs *John D. Donahue*	264
12 Privatizing Public Management *Mark H. Moore*	296
13 Government Performance and the Conundrum of Public Trust *Robert D. Behn*	323
Contributors	349
Index	351

Preface

TWO ATROCITIES FORM the bookends for the work assembled here. The bombing of the Murrah Federal Building in Oklahoma City led me to accept the deanship of Harvard's John F. Kennedy School Government and to launch Visions of Governance in the 21st Century, an effort to harness the Kennedy School's scholarly resources to an exploration of the problems and possibilities of modern democratic governance. The attacks of September 11, 2001, occurred as the chapters in this book—the fifth Visions of Governance collected volume—were taking their final shape. The first atrocity demonstrated the depths that alienation from government could reach. The second may mark a turning point in attitudes toward the public sector and could enable a more open-minded assessment of what had been a contentious topic—the employment of market means to advance public goals.

It is hazardous to predict the implications of so vast an event, to be sure. But it seems likely that one effect of September 11 will be to dampen the fires of antigovernment sentiment that flared so searingly at Oklahoma City. The language of contempt and hostility toward the public sector that had become commonplace in the late twentieth century suddenly seemed irresponsible in America's altered context. The targets, after all, were public buildings. The indispensability of public safety workers was vividly on display. And in the edgy aftermath of the attacks, Americans, and people around the world, gained a new sense of their shared stakes in effective governance. Polls showed rising trust in government after decades of low standing in the public's eyes, and indeed the greater short-run risk may be an excessive retreat from the American tradition of prudent wariness about public authority.

A rebalancing of attitudes toward governance is welcome for a great many reasons, but somewhere on the list is an improvement in the intellectual climate for this book. Dispassionate analysis about the virtues and dangers of market-based governance had been overshadowed and distorted by the dominant narrative about a struggle between government and its critics. This environment nurtured the simplistic view that markets and governance are inherently conflicting and mutually exclusive principles. Those who sought to bridle an over-ambitious public sector often instinctively endorsed market-oriented models of governance as the next best thing to shrinking the public realm. Government's defenders—often just as instinctively—generally took a dim view of market means, lest conceding their potential be seen as surrendering ground to a formidable foe.

If September 11 does indeed rid us of the less reflective and more extreme manifestations of antigovernment sentiment, we can discuss market-based governance more calmly and candidly. As the level of ideological ardor ebbs, even those most enamored of the market's deft precision in private exchange will concede that the invisible hand deals clumsily with some collective tasks. And as their confidence grows about the renewed legitimacy of collective purposes, those committed to public missions will recognize that the true dedication to a cause requires openness to any promising tactic in its pursuit. Neither governments nor markets provide all the answers for good governance, but each model has something to contribute. This is the spirit in which this inquiry into markets as means for public ends has been written, and the spirit in which we hope it will be read.

JOSEPH S. NYE JR.

Acknowledgments

HARVARD'S JOHN F. KENNEDY School of Government launched the Visions of Governance in the 21st Century project in 1996, in order to better anticipate, account for, accommodate, and appropriately influence major trends in the missions and in the means of governance. The Visions project concentrates the school's scholarly resources on the large medium-term questions of governance, with the proximate goals of better understanding and more effective teaching, and the ultimate goal of better professional practice. The project has shaped courses and executive sessions, informed many participants' articles and books, and produced five volumes—of which this is the latest—on particular aspects of the changing challenge of governance.

Support for the work from which these essays grew has been generously provided by the Ash Fund for Research on Democratic Governance, the Christian A. Johnson Endeavor Foundation, and the Smith Richardson Foundation. We gratefully acknowledge their assistance. We also thank the participants in the 2001 Visions of Governance faculty symposium and seminars in which these chapters were first presented and discussed, including Graham Allison, Arthur Applbaum, Robert Blendon, Iris Bohnet, Nolan Bowie, Carol Chetkovich, Akash Deep, Mickey Edwards, Jane Fountain, Jeffrey Frankel, Steven Goldsmith, Joan Goodman Williamson, Deborah Hurley, Ira Jackson, Nancy Katz, Barbara Kellerman, Sanjeev

Khagram, Taeku Lee, Jeffrey Liebman, Richard Light, Brian Mandell, Ernest May, Jerry Mechling, Shelley Metzenbaum, Joseph Newhouse, Bonnie Newman, Pippa Norris, Paul Peterson, David Pryor, Dani Rodrik, Monica Toft, John White, and Richard Zeckhauser.

As our publishing partnership with Brookings Institution Press matures, we have gained an abiding appreciation for the talents of Christopher Kelaher, Janet Walker, Janet Schilling Mowery, and Susan Woollen. For the present volume, we acknowledge the gimlet eye of copy editor Katherine Kimball, as well as the proofreading of Ingrid Lockwood and the indexing of Enid Zafran. And we continue to rely on the formidable skills of Visions of Governance project coordinator Lynn Akin, whose innumerable contributions to this book span the enterprise from the very start (organizing the seminars at which the first unformed ideas were floated) to the very end (finding references, checking page proofs, and advising us on cover art).

JOHN D. DONAHUE
Raymond Vernon Lecturer in Public Policy
Director, Visions of Governance in the 21st Century

JOSEPH S. NYE JR.
Don K. Price Professor of Public Policy
Dean, John F. Kennedy School of Government

Market-Based Governance

1

JOHN D. DONAHUE

Market-Based Governance and the Architecture of Accountability

Accountability underpins civilization. It defines a virtual nervous system for an interdependent community composed of discrete individuals. Separate minds conceive and carry out actions with shared consequences. Thus any prospect for something better than solitude, subjugation, or chronic conflict depends upon and has always depended upon devices for taking into account the interests of others. We manage interdependence through mechanisms of accountability.

There are a great many such mechanisms. Some (such as family, friendship, and empathy) are elemental antecedents of organized society, not its constructs. Some (such as religion) are partly constructed, partly not. Still other mechanisms of accountability are clear-cut artifacts, rather than preconditions, of civilized life. One broad model of accountability is governance—the rules and institutions for the authoritative organization of collective life. Another is the market—cooperation arising out of voluntary exchange based on individual assessments of value. Each of these generic models has taken on countless different forms through human history ranging from primitive to intricate in their construction, from crude to sophisticated in their operation, and from calamitous to triumphant in their consequences.

Governance and markets also tend (to varying degrees and with varying results) to be entangled with each other. History displays the two generic mechanisms in a nearly infinite array of hybrids, alloys, and combinations. In this book we are concerned with one particular kind of entanglement—the use of the market as a means for pursuing the goals of governance. There is nothing new about market-based governance. When a Wall Street broker was elected mayor of Jersey City in the 1990s and launched a purportedly unprecedented tax-collecting partnership with private firms, he was merely reprising (in essence, and in many of the details) arrangements that were routine in the Roman Empire.[1] Mercenary soldiers (who kill and die for the state not out of a sense of obligation or patriotism but for a fee) antedate Rome and are with us still.

The final quarter of the twentieth century, however, was marked by a surge of experimentation with new forms of market-based governance (especially, but not only, in the English-speaking world). The administrations of Margaret Thatcher in Great Britain and Ronald Reagan in the United States provided sharply etched mileposts for the trend's early stages. Openness to market-oriented styles of governance both endured and diffused, however, until by century's end it was an unremarkable mainstream sentiment. It may have been George W. Bush (Reagan's would-be political heir) who bluntly declared that "government should be market-based," but Bill Clinton's views were only slightly less sweeping.[2]

This burgeoning enthusiasm for the market as a means toward public ends has two sources, each displaying both sounder and shallower manifestations. One source is the comparative performance of markets and government; the other is change in the perceived legitimacy (among both élites and the general public) of market-based arrangements. The two are related, of course, as perceptions of relative performance reshape relative legitimacy. Babe Ruth, asked why he should earn more for hitting baseballs than Herbert Hoover earned for leading the country, explained, "I had a better year than he did."[3] It is hard to deny that markets have had a better half century or so than governments. In the United States and in most other Western economies, the period after World War II witnessed a preponderance of success in the market realm. Incomes rose. Wealth grew. Technology advanced. Corporations expanded and evolved.[4]

There were failures, too (and, just as important, sharply uneven rewards from market success), but compared with the first half of the century, the market stood in triumph. Over the same period, communism—perceived, fairly or not, as one extreme on a market-to-government spectrum—was unmasked as an apocalyptically bad idea. Even Western democratic governments, meanwhile, seemed plagued by scandal, sclerosis, misjudgment, and lame performance. As trust in government decayed, the market gained legitimacy (at least in relative terms).[5] Especially in the interval bracketed (at its start) by the fall of the Berlin Wall and (at its end) by the dot-com collapse and the September 11 attacks, the reverence for markets and disdain for collectivism that has always figured in America's weltanschauung was at full flood tide.

Four cautionary observations are warranted, though, before any further inquiry into the potential and limits of market-based governance. First, the lessons of the late twentieth century are considerably more complex than simply "the more market, the better." A good deal of the market's gratifying performance (in the United States and elsewhere) can be attributed to astute public policy. Government's contributions to economic success have been pervasive (if admittedly hit-and-miss), including interventions as esoteric as nurturing technological progress and fine-tuning the macroeconomy and as elementary as building roads and maintaining the rule of law. By century's end, several countries (including Russia) were demonstrating that too light a governing hand—not just too heavy—could have regrettable consequences.

Second, a prudent respect for the market can degenerate into sterile orthodoxy. Ideological fashion sometimes inspires a universal and unreflective faith in market solutions, rather like the enthusiasm for speaking French among nineteenth-century Russian aristocrats—not because of any reasoned assessment of the merits but because it has become de rigeur among right-thinking people. This phenomenon may have reached its apotheosis (if that is the right word) in the first of "Armey's Axioms" promulgated by Representative Dick Armey: "The market is rational and the government is dumb."[6] When the case for market-based approaches rests on axioms rather than analysis, the conversation becomes at once dull and dangerous.

Third, turn-of-the-century enthusiasm for market approaches has been largely informed by performance on the market's home turf—the production of goods and services paid for by and tuned to the tastes of individual consumers. It requires a daunting logical leap to extend into the public realm the advantages markets display in private production. The evidence is decidedly more mixed about the merits of markets as a means to public ends—consider Nixon-era experiments with education contracting; federal sales of timber, grazing rights, and electromagnetic spectrum; or any number of sobering stories from military procurement. There are more ways to fail in the public realm or (put differently) a larger and more demanding set of things that must go right if market means are to efficiently serve public ends.

Fourth, market ascendancy may prove fleeting. At least some of the factors behind the growing legitimacy of market solutions will turn out to be cyclical, not secular, and we may have already reached the trend's inflection point. It is too early, as of this writing, for any confident predictions about the impact of new economic tensions, the events of September 11, 2001, or Enron's abrupt implosion. Most of this book's chapters were drafted in sunnier times, and we have not asked authors to hastily speculate about the shifting context for market-based governance. There are some signs, however, of a turning tide. Railtrack, a major component of Great Britain's privatized railroad system, suffered financial collapse in 2001 and went into receivership.[7] Airport security in the United States has been wrenched from a heavily market-based system to one closely controlled by classic instruments of governance. The American public's level of trust in government has sharply (albeit perhaps temporarily) spiked. A *Washington Post* survey taken two weeks after the attacks found that nearly two-thirds of respondents trusted "the government in Washington" to do the right thing most of the time or nearly always—more than double the levels of trust prevailing in recent years.[8]

Yet whether the reigning predisposition toward market-based approaches proves enduring or ephemeral, it is our task, as analysts of public policy, to separate the promise from the perils of market means toward public ends. How can we engineer the most favorable balance between the upside and downside of market-based governance? Which collective missions are best pursued by market means? Where, in short, does engaging the market offer the most promising blueprint for accountability in the pursuit of particular public goals? For some purchase on these questions, and as the overture to the coming chapters, consider the distinction between two dimensions of accountability, which we can label intensive and extensive.

Intensive accountability is circumscribed but concentrated—in terms of the spectrum of values that must be taken into account or the constituencies whose interests must be taken into account or both. A type specimen of intensive accountability is described, interestingly enough, in the New Testament. Jesus tells of three stewards, each entrusted with a quantity of capital to manage for their traveling master. On his return, the master demands an account of each steward's investment. The two who report healthy returns are handsomely rewarded; the last we hear of the third involves "wailing and gnashing of teeth."[9] This parable illustrates a highly intensive form of accountability. There is a single entity to whom the stewards are answerable—the master. There is a single metric of accountability—return on capital. (This was a parable, not a case study, and abstracts from complications like tax treatment, environmental rules, or compliance with the Aramaeans with Disabilities Act.)

In its simplest and most stripped-down form, capitalism is constructed on this blueprint of highly intensive accountability. The metric of faithful stewardship is the growth of capital value through adroit commercial moves. The steward is answerable only to owners—and if he is the sole owner, only to himself. Success and failure are unambiguous. This clarity allows for simple, sturdy measures to manipulate agents' motivation and to invoke whatever consequences their performance merits. Deviations—a lost contract, a surge in costs, a dip in profits, a slip in capital value—are rightly seen (absent a compelling excuse) as conclusive evidence of bad performance.

Extensive accountability, by contrast, involves multiple metrics or multiple masters or both. For an illustrative example here, consider the principal of my children's elementary school. He is answerable to the children, to their parents, to the teachers and administrators, to the school board, the selectmen, members of the town meeting, the town manager, a large cluster of state agencies, a larger cluster of federal agencies, neighbors upset about traffic, and so on. Not all constituencies have equal standing, to be sure, nor are all goals equally important. It is reasonably clear that teaching the children well while using taxpayers' resources efficiently is the basic idea. Notice, however, that neither of these goals—good education and parsimony—is clearly subordinate to, or instrumental of, the other. There is no simplifying story like "customer satisfaction equals shareholder value." The mission is (at the least) bipolar, not unipolar.

Neither pole, moreover, is cleanly defined. There are many plausible versions of "teach the children well." (Think of the trade-offs between mainstream and special-needs kids; between social and academic development; between math and reading; between kindergarten—where the leverage may be greatest—and the upper grades—where the stakes are higher.) Even if the definition of good education is reduced to standardized test scores and nothing else, it matters greatly whether the metric of success has to do with the mean, the median, or the range of student scores. Nor are taxpayers' interests unidimensional. Some voices call for minimizing local taxes by keeping costs as low as possible; others call for maximizing property values by maintaining excellent schools; still others play down economics and emphasize one generation's duty to the next. Meanwhile, constituencies aside from families and taxpayers—teachers, staff, public officials at local, state, and federal levels, neighbors, unions, and all the rest—cast their own interests, with a fair degree of sincerity, as instrumental to advancing some version of either, or both, of the central goals. This is not a particularly complicated example of public stewardship. Nor does the principal seem daunted by the thicket of criteria he confronts; it goes with the territory. Compared with almost any business leader running a similarly scaled operation, however, he operates within a strikingly extensive structure of accountability.

We rarely—indeed, never—encounter in practice either exclusively intensive or exclusively extensive accountability. The closest approach to a pure form of intensive accountability may be the commodities trader scrambling in the pit to get the best price for her client, and even she is bound by constraints of law and custom, must worry about her reputation and that of her firm, and cannot seek a trading advantage by slipping a stiletto into a competitor. The purest real-world example of extensive accountability may be the secretary general of the United Nations, who is answerable (at least in principle, and in a mediated way) to most people on the planet. Yet even he puts a different weight on the concerns of members of the Security Council, and he owes no allegiance to stateless people.

In a perfect world, all human relationships would feature full measures of both intensive and extensive accountability. In the same perfect world, of course, everyone would reach full wisdom in robust youth and never misplace keys. Given the imperfections of the world we inhabit, there is typically a trade-off between intensive and extensive accountability. This is not always so, of course; a truly broken structure of accountability can be made both more intensive and more extensive simultaneously. In general, however, we must be ready to sacrifice some extensive accountability to obtain more intensive accountability (and vice versa).

Intensive accountability requires sturdy measures to induce fidelity to some goals and (less obviously) also requires shields and filters that make it possible to ignore or grant lower priority to other desiderata. Extensive accountability requires, as an ineluctable entailment of multiple missions, continuous balancing of obligations and the capacity to grant something short of maximum fulfillment to any claim so as to give due weight to all. The central design challenge, for institutions of accountability, involves this trade-off between extensiveness and intensity. Mechanisms of accountability that tilt toward extensiveness we tend to call "governance." Mechanisms of accountability that tilt toward intensity we tend to call "markets."

To be clear, extensiveness and intensity are only characteristic of, not exclusive to, the public and private spheres respectively. Every market institution has concerns beyond the bottom line—not just the general constraints of law, custom, and conscience but sometimes deliberately structured measures such as the "balanced scorecard," social investment criteria, and some of the innovations discussed in this book. The public sector has pockets of accountability at least as intensive as anything in the private sector; consider, for example, the tight focus that characterizes a healthy military organization.[10] Nevertheless, the statement of general tendency holds up reasonably well.

Each model of accountability can fail. A critical tradition going back at least to Adolph Berle and Gardiner Means charges that the capitalist story of intensive accountability to owners has become a sham and a shield for stewards' self-dealing.[11] Similarly, an influential school of economic thought holds that breakdowns in governments' extensive accountability are the norm, not the exception. Politicians and bureaucrats invoke obligations to Peter to evade obligations to Paul, in this argument, and exploit the confusing multiplicity of goals to dodge accountability entirely. The failure-proneness of particular structures of accountability is an important matter that arises in several chapters of this book. Beyond the debate about the probability and consequences of design failure, however—and in some ways logically prior to that debate—there is an important conversation about design fit. For each particular task, at some particular time, within some particular context, what is the best-suited structure of accountability?

"Market-based governance" can be characterized (at a high level of generalization) as engineering into public undertakings a greater degree of the intensive accountability that typifies markets. It succeeds where it makes possible a better balance of the two styles, delivering an increment of intensity without an undue sacrifice in extensiveness. This basic logic of market-based governance—surrendering some extensive accountability to gain some intensive accountability—clarifies analysts' obsession with the precision and "tightness" of public mandates delegated to market agents. Intensive accountability is both narrow and powerful. Any uncertainty surrounding the relation between market means and public ends, any range of discretion or ambiguity, will result, we must anticipate, in effort gravitating toward the focus of intensity—where profit is the driving motive, for example, toward higher net revenues.

This is not because market actors disdain broader goals; as individuals, they may honor other dimensions of value as much as or more than do public officials. Nor is this to predict crude opportunism in every case of discretion. Arrangements that take reputation and past performance into account can and do motivate private actors to employ discretion and resolve ambiguities in ways that are extensively accountable, even if profit is their only ultimate motive. (Such arrangements, indeed, are classic examples of good contractual architecture.) Intensive accountability, however, tends to subordinate everything—not just waste and muddle but also the personal values of agents and any dimensions of public value that are not explicitly and deliberately built into the relationship—to the pursuit of the primary goal. That is what structures of intensive accountability are *supposed* to do.

The chapters of this book explore—from varying perspectives, in varying ways, with varying alloys of generality and specificity—the merits of market-based governance. When is it advantageous to ramp up the intensity of accountability for a collective endeavor, whether by revising the structures of stewardship within the public sector or by delegating duties to agents already enmeshed in systems of intensive accountability? When can restructuring the architecture of accountability make the pursuit of public missions more flexible, or more transparent, or defter, or more parsimonious? When, conversely, is it too hard to harness the potent instruments of intensive accountability? When does a diminution of extensive accountability necessarily entail (or clearly threaten) the unwarranted surrender of shared value, masquerading as a simple shift in means?

The first cluster of chapters deals with the "demand side" of market-based governance, with issues surrounding government's role as a customer. Karen Eggleston and Richard J. Zeckhauser set the tone with an inquiry into health care. They stipulate (for present purposes) that health care will be largely paid for collectively. The question is how it should be delivered—publicly or privately and (when private) by for-profit or nonprofit suppliers. To clarify this question, they weave an analytical fugue of ideas and evidence featuring three central themes. The first is a general answer about the private sector's proper role in delivering health care: It depends. The second is the good news: We can say, with some precision, on what it depends. The third is the bad news: There is little reason to think we will stumble by accident onto the right pattern of market-based health care.

What makes their work both rewarding with respect to health care specifically and of more general relevance as well is their disciplined examination of incomplete contracts and their consequences. Suppose contracts were always complete—in other words, that we could routinely build structures of accountability that are at once sturdy, clear, and richly detailed, specifying the agent's duty to every legitimate stakeholder in every possible contingency. Accountability could be both fully intensive and fully extensive, with no impediments to reaping the benefits (focused incentives, competition, flexibility) of market-based delivery. As economists have long recognized, however, such complete contracts are vanishingly rare. In practice, contractual architecture (in health care and elsewhere) tends to be marred by gaps and flaws, forcing a choice between intensity and extensiveness. The crucial point, for Eggleston and Zeckhauser, is that tasks differ in both the nature and the gravity of contractual incompleteness. Providers differ, too—public, nonprofit, and for-profit institutions should vary in the way they respond to incomplete contracts. These two observations define the context for an intricate, high-stakes matching game, for which Eggleston and Zeckhauser lay out the rules.

They first review the evidence on the behavior of public, nonprofit, and for-profit health-care providers, finding it generally consistent with (but considerably less tidy than) what theory would predict. Next they elaborate their analytical framework, which hinges on the incentives hard-wired into an organization's structure by the way property rights are defined. They develop decision rules for which category of provider, and which kind of contractual structure, is the best match for particular types of functions. Their focus, significantly, is *comparative* advantage. They sidestep the fervent and murky debate about the overall role of the market in health care and anchor on a seemingly humbler but far more productive question: "In what order should services be placed in the for-profit, nonprofit, and government sectors? In theory, Republicans and Democrats, Labourites and Conservatives, Socialists and Christian Democrats should be able roughly to agree on this question, even though they might be bitterly divided on the amounts they would like to place in each of the three sectors."

Although they are fully aware that historical accidents, inertia, ideology, and the interplay of interests exercise considerable leverage over the division of labor in any health-care system, analysis plays a role as well. They distill from their analysis some quite clear-cut guidelines for matching tasks to providers. The intensive accountability that characterizes private providers, for example, serves best for services that are readily contractible, easy to monitor, susceptible to competition and for which innovation is especially valuable. "Examples include elective surgery and most dental care, as well as the provision of drugs and many aspects of primary care." Conversely, the extensive accountability of public (and, in some cases, non-profit) providers has a comparative advantages for services that are difficult to define in advance, offer benefits beyond those received by the patient, or have aspects of quality that are hard for patients to monitor (among other features.) Examples here include care for severe mental illness, blood banks, and long-term elder care.

Beyond the insightful observations about health care they offer, Eggleston and Zeckhauser earn the lead-off slot in this book for their elegant analytic structure, their liberating focus on comparative (rather than absolute) advantages for different delivery models, and (not the least) the accuracy and the significance of the simple sentence that ends their chapter: Although they may be derived from the health-care sector, "most of the principles set forth apply to a wide range of services."

Peter Frumkin develops a similar theme of complexity and contingency in the proper matching of tasks to agents. His point of departure, though, is the observation that government not only selects from a roster of potential suppliers but often also powerfully shapes that roster. Frumkin's focus is on human services, an arena in which government tends to be the dominant (and sometimes sole) source of demand. For a private firm this can be a happy position (though a tricky one to play to best advantage) as leverage over sellers leads to lower prices and other benefits. For a public sector purchaser with an extensive list of criteria for human services—including flexibility, cultural fit with client populations, reliability even when oversight is weak, and other factors beyond cost and readily defined quality measures—the right choice of providers can require thinking several steps ahead. A supplier (or set of suppliers) spurned today might not survive to be an option tomorrow; the chosen model is apt to prosper and expand.

This would be a minor matter if the right allocation of human services to public, for-profit, and nonprofit delivery was clear cut and well understood. Suppose we had a well-developed body of theory and evidence, along the lines of the Eggleston and Zeckhauser analysis of health care, offering guidelines for the proper assignment of every human service. Then the withering away of rejected models would be no loss, just healthy evolution within the organizational ecology. Frumkin suggests, however, that the state of the art in this domain remains lamentably primitive, as "evaluation research on the comparative performance of agencies across sectors is slim and contradictory." In many cases, he argues, we simply cannot say with much confidence which delivery model works best.

To complicate matters further, Frumkin contends, the for-profit players within the human services ecology are systematically more robust. Absent deliberate efforts to preserve the diversity of the system, he fears, nonprofits will be crowded out of many of their accustomed niches. Especially if the apparent advantages of for-profit suppliers prove illusory, a short-term focus on the part of the public purchaser risks degrading the organizational gene pool. Frumkin urges those who make decisions about the purchase of human services to maintain "an appreciation of the effects these decisions have on the long-term evolution of the ecology of service providers in the many fields of human services for which government funding represents a critical source of agency finance."

In short, he argues, "preserving room for both nonprofit and for-profit service providers across a range of fields, at least for now, must be viewed as a managerial imperative, given the generally poor state of current knowledge." There is a tacit subtext to this conclusion: Ignorance is expensive. The downside of an impoverished organizational ecology, and the substantial insurance premium implicit in sustaining a diversity of suppliers that may or may not turn out to be optimal, highlight the payoff to research and analysis.

The first two chapters illuminate the debate over whether and when government should opt for market-based alternatives. Steven Kelman next raises the salient but often neglected question of *how*. Delivering services directly, through the extensively accountable option of employing people and situating them in a formal government agency, imposes a fairly familiar set of public management worries. However, "though the decision to contract [for services] changes the nature of government's worries," Kelman warns, "it does not eliminate them." The management of contracting relationships is a demanding and distinctive craft.

Especially for those agencies that already outsource much of their operations (including the U.S. Departments of Defense and Energy and the National Aeronautics and Space Administration), but also for any governing entity that embraces market-based demand strategies, "the ability to manage contracting must be considered a core competency." Federal procurement reforms in the second half of the 1990s widened the range of discretion and inspired agencies to think anew about what to make and what to buy and how to choose the best outside providers. However, "the third element of strategic contracting management, the administration of contracts once they have been signed, has been the neglected stepchild of these efforts." Kelman's chapter (and the larger effort from which it is drawn)[12] marks an attempt to give the neglected stepchild the attention it merits.

Kelman clears the ground by challenging the view (common among both academics and the general public) that government is peculiarly bad at managing contracts and systematically outwitted by nimbler, better-motivated private counterparts. Cost overruns in large defense projects are standard illustrations for the contention that mismanaging contracts is the norm. However, Kelman cites evidence that comparably large development projects in the private sector suffer to an equal or greater degree from cost escalation. Nor do financial data show richer returns for firms or units contracting with government, as should be the case if it were true that the public sector offers predictably easy pickings for shrewd private sellers.

Even if federal contract management is far better than the folktales suggest, according to Kelman, it is not as good as it needs to be. The implicit view that the real work of public management involves employees, not contracts, is at odds with reality in many agencies and invites a perverse underemphasis on the trade craft required to manage contracts well. Although contract management is often considered a mechanical matter to be handled by junior officials, "the most important responsibilities . . . are not just managerial in general: they are analogous to those of a senior executive, not a first-line supervisor or middle manager." Kelman outlines a fine-grained, pragmatic agenda for upgrading the profession, organized around three kinds of reforms: "properly [defining] and [providing] training for the job, [splitting off] lower-level tasks from executive-type tasks, and [making] an investment in performance measurement as a discipline."

From his privileged perspective as an architect of earlier rounds of federal procurement reform, Kelman argues that the changes required to render contract management an appropriately central part of strategic public management are at once necessary and feasible. He ends, though, with the cautionary note that this next stage of reform involves surmounting different kinds of hurdles. Whereas the 1990s reform campaigns "were in the first instance institutional design challenges," reshaping the profession of contract administration, by contrast, involves "predominantly challenges of human resources management—of people and job design." It thus requires grappling with larger issues concerning the quality, deployment, and motivation of federal personnel.

The next two chapters take up the "supply side" of market-based governance, examining unsettled questions about government's role as a provider (rather than a purchaser) within the market system. Georges de Menil considers the balance between market and government in ensuring adequate retirement income. This is by no means a neglected topic—oceans of ink have been spilled on the subject in recent years, along with no small quantity of vitriol—but it remains far from settled. Although he does not expect to still the debate, de Menil calmly sorts out the arguments and sets them in historical and international context.

He starts by calibrating the stakes. If accountability, generically, is civilization's underpinning, the duties owed to the aged are among the most salient specific forms: "The provision of old age security is, like the organization of exchange or the maintenance of law and order, one of society's central functions. . . . A community in which the young were structurally incapable of providing for their old age, and the old were regularly abandoned by the collectivity, would be unlikely to survive for long." Yet in principle, at least, there is an abundance of alternative formulas for old-age income security, with all-but-infinitely varying alloys of traditional governance and market-based means. In practice, a healthy fraction of those imaginable alternatives have been tried at some time and in some place.

The chapter begins with an overview of the history of old-age income practices in the United States and Western Europe, tracing the origins of what developed into the rival paradigms of individual insurance through the market versus collective provision through government. Next, de Menil provides a compressed but illuminating summary of the logic by which the two paradigms can be assessed. Finally, he surveys recent experience with altered blueprints for old-age income security in both developed and developing countries. He ends with cautious optimism about an emerging synthesis of market and governance, while underscoring the need for both deftly designed transactional architecture and difficult political choices for any community considering such an approach.

Information is a special kind of commodity. Whatever effort may be entailed in generating a piece of information, the incremental cost of disseminating it to an additional person—its marginal unit cost—tends to be low. One person's possession of a bit of data, moreover, does not diminish its value for any other possessor (with exceptions that include competitive or strategic data). Indeed, information often grows in value as it is shared (think of technical standards, or product ratings). For these and other reasons, economists have generally looked more benignly on public provision of information than on other cases of governmental supply. Information about the law is a special case of the special case, because its wide dissemination is not just desirable but essential to almost any definition of accountable governance. Unless those who are subject to the law are well informed about their obligations, Frederick Schauer and Virginia Wise suggest, "there is perhaps no law at all." A naive observer, then, might predict a dominant role for formal government in the supply of legal information. Yet, at least with respect to the United States, that naive observer would guess wrong. Government turns out to be a secondary and shrinking player in the market for legal information. Schauer and Wise probe the reasons for this curious fact and assess its implications.

They trace the shifting mix over time of public and private supply. During a century or so of parallel provision, both supply channels for legal information flowed briskly. Official alternatives tended to be cheaper; private alternatives tended to be more artfully organized. The private advantage in value-added information services gradually widened, as the proprietary organizing scheme of the leading commercial purveyor became the de facto standard for citations and legal education. As the private channel grew dominant, the public channel of supply dried up for many types of data. Much legal information can no longer be obtained—either in a convenient form or at all—from government, and three foreign corporations dominate the U.S. market for legal data.

The government's retreat from the supply of legal information could be a harmless curiosity, rather than a source of anxiety. Schauer and Wise suggest several reasons—some straightforward, and others quite subtle—for concern, however. The market power of a concentrated industry implies the risk of costs that are higher, or product offerings that are less finely tuned to users' preferences, than the competitive market ideal. Beyond this generic defect of concentrated markets is the fact that "the bundling of legal information to make it available to users reflects the financial incentives and internal structures" of the private suppliers. The most widely used data on American court rulings comes in separate packages for each of seven geographic regions, in an accidental artifact of decisions made long ago by an early market leader. Evidence assembled by Schauer and Wise hints that this bundling affects how the law works and how it evolves. For example, because "when seen from California, Kansas and Nebraska are quite legally similar, there appears a substantial possibility that the bundling of opinions from Kansas but not from Nebraska courts within the set of law books that most California lawyers and judges own may have played a significant role" in Californians' disproportionate reference to Kansas precedent.

Similarly, legal publishers increasingly bundle legal information with other product lines offered by their conglomerate parents. Schauer and Wise find reason to believe that this has promoted the "substitution of nonlegal secondary information for legal secondary information, a substitution that has potentially profound implications for the nature of legal education, the nature of legal argument, the nature of legal practice, and the nature of law itself."

The tilt toward market supply has occurred with remarkably little analysis or controversy. At one level, this shift can be seen as simply one more example of the emergence through evolution of the lowest-cost, best-performing supply model—the sifting and sorting that market economies do so well. However, if "legal information is best seen as constituting law rather than just describing it," Schauer and Wise suggest, "a transformation that on its face may have looked technical and inconsequential" may be quietly reshaping something quite central to governance.

The third cluster of chapters explores experiments with market-based arrangements for orchestrating accountability outside government by altering the incentives that operate inside market institutions. Archon Fung starts the section with a provocative topic—the prospects for rendering commerce itself more extensively accountable through the creation of "social markets." This term simply refers to market settings in which investors and consumers apply their social values to the choices they make. "To the extent that consumption and investment decisions depend not only on preferences about the price, quality, or features of products or about the risk and return characteristics of securities but also on preferences about the labor and environmental consequences of production processes and corporate policies, social values become important components of economic markets." In such settings, "corporate officers must advance notions of social responsibility in order to make money for their shareholders." The goals conventionally pursued by authoritative mandates and regulation may thus be advanced by utterly different means, in a marriage of intensive and extensive accountability.

Fung urges both openness to the potential value of such approaches and alertness to their characteristic risks and limits. To serve both ends, he starts by describing the ideal of social markets in a counterfactually transparent and orderly world. He then gradually backs away from the ideal and toward the messy realities of our own world, gaining perspective (at the price of complexity) with each step. This method lets him distinguish accidental defects of social markets that can, in principle, be remedied from their fundamental drawbacks, including the generalization that "wealthy consumers will have more voice than poor ones." Once his conceptual lens is ground, Fung applies it to some of the evidence on emerging social markets. These include a range of initiatives, both organized and diffuse, to promote "ethical consumerism." They include as well the attempts of some corporations to portray themselves (on capital markets or consumer markets or both) as differentially attentive to particular social concerns. They include efforts to organize associations of firms pledging allegiance to explicit codes of conduct that serve as clear and coherent signals of their social practices. They include as well deliberate moves by policymakers to structure and catalyze social markets as adjuncts or alternatives to more conventional regulation.

Fung notes that social markets are still in their infancy, and he synthesizes from his chapter three criteria to guide their growth. Social markets offer a particularly promising blueprint for accountability when public sentiment is reasonably coherent; when firms are sufficiently vulnerable to diffuse public preferences; and where conventional alternatives—authoritative incentives, mandates, and regulation—are comparatively weak. Without suggesting that social markets will (or should) sweep away more traditional methods for engineering extensive accountability into the market realm, Fung predicts that they will remain an area of lively innovation in market-based governance.

It was only in the final decade or so of the twentieth century that a market-based approach to environmental protection made its break from the world of abstract theory to become a practical bipartisan policy initiative in the United States. Robert Stavins, an intellectual midwife of this movement, observes that "as more and more market-based environmental policy instruments have been proposed and implemented, the concept of harnessing market forces to protect the environment has evolved from political anathema to political correctness." He marks the highlights of this transformation and extracts the main lessons.

Market-based approaches to environmental policy deploy a range of devices including tradable permits (which incorporate into firms' production costs a price for harmful emissions) and pollution charges that use fees (rather than fiats) to discourage environmental damage. When these and similar instruments "are well designed and implemented, they encourage firms or individuals to undertake pollution control efforts that are in their own interests and that collectively meet policy goals." The traditional "command-and-control" approach, by contrast, overlays onto conventional market motives a separate structure of public accountability that is in tension with, rather than integrated into, firms' economic incentives. Stavins distills from his long experience as an analyst and advocate some hard-won and quite specific lessons about the advantages of market-based alternatives (and how to recognize and reap those advantages) in particular environmental policy settings.

Stavins then broadens the frame to take in the "positive political economy" puzzle of why the breakthrough on market-based environmental policy approaches occurred in the late twentieth century (instead of earlier, or not at all). The defects of command-and-control regulation, after all—irrational uniformity, uneven and often random relationships between the costs and benefits of particular protective measures, rigidity, weak or even perverse incentives for firms to extend the technological frontier for clean production—had long been recognized. Why, before 1988, had these been seen by everyone except a few economists as an unavoidable and acceptable price to be paid for sound environmental stewardship? Why, by century's end, had the notion of doing better through market-based approaches become a new orthodoxy (albeit still not the norm in practice)?

Stavins describes a stable though suboptimal equilibrium, lasting from the surge of new environmental laws in the 1970s to the end of the 1980s, in which "command-and-control instruments have dominated because all of the main parties involved—affected firms, environmental advocacy groups, organized labor, legislators, and bureaucrats—have had reasons to favor them." What disrupted that equilibrium, he suggests, was not (as scholars might fondly dream) an improvement in prevailing levels of conceptual sophistication among practitioners. Stavins advances as a "refutable hypothesis" that a study of shifting views on market-based instruments among relevant congressional staffers over the past twenty years "would find increased support from Republicans and greatly increased support from Democrats but insufficient improvements in understanding to explain these changes." Instead, he attributes the shift to rising regulatory costs, the embrace of market approaches by a few pioneering environmental advocates (inspired in part by initiatives that clearly cast market-based tools as ways to reduce pollution), and the emergence of previously uncontrolled pollution challenges—including sulfur dioxide and chlorofluorocarbons—where there was no command-and-control status quo to overcome. He also describes the ideological equivalent of slow tectonic shifts, as markets generally rose in public favor. Finally, "a healthy dose of chance" placed a few open-minded incumbents into key policy positions.

Yet the environmental area, he suggests, does afford a heartening case in which analysis and evidence have won a round against inertia and orthodoxy. "There is clearly no policy panacea," he concludes, in words that could be inserted into every chapter of this book. Rather, "the real challenge for bureaucrats, elected officials, and other participants in the environmental policy process comes in analyzing and then selecting the best instrument for each situation that arises."

Cary Coglianese and David Lazer follow with a related inquiry into melding extensive accountability onto the market motivations of private actors. They offer an account of a class of innovations they term "management-based regulation." This approach is generically distinct from conventional regulation in that it eschews the imposition of specific obligations and instead requires firms "to engage in the planning and decisionmaking required to identify both technologies and performance targets needed to achieve socially desired goals." They identify the potential advantages of this approach: it situates "regulatory decisionmaking at the level at which the most information about processes and potential control methods is available." If firms believe their own standards are more "reasonable and legitimate" than external mandates, they may be "less resistant to compliance." Not least important, "by giving firms flexibility to create their own regulatory approaches, management-based approaches can promote innovation and social learning."

Coglianese and Lazer dodge the sterile debate over whether this approach is superior or hazardous *in general* and structure an exploration of the conditions under which such a regulatory strategy makes sense. Their prudent starting point is "not always." Performance-based regulation, which mandates some particular result, "dominates the alternatives" when it is easy to measure those results. Technology-based regulation, which mandates some particular means, is indicated when "the regulated sector is homogeneous" and it is possible to develop "a technological standard based on 'best practices.'" The most promising domain for management-based regulation covers cases for which there is a "general understanding of how to achieve social objectives, but the appropriate response in particular situations depends on contextual factors." Here there is no substitute for managers' intimate understanding of their own operations and a high payoff from enlisting managers' aid in drafting the terms of their broader accountability.

Eliciting candor and ensuring fidelity when the managerial imperatives of extensive and intensive accountability collide, of course, present serious challenges. Coglianese and Lazer move to a rigorous review of the conditions that must hold for management-based regulation to succeed in practice. They then illustrate their model by showing how those conditions have held tolerably well in an important and otherwise troublesome regulatory area: food safety. The dispersed and diverse food industry is ill suited to either technological or performance standards. Recognizing this, food safety experts in government and industry quietly improvised what came to be called the Hazards Analysis and Critical Control Points system. This system, which has been used for decades but became mandatory (in the United States) only in the 1990s, features "mandates that require firms to evaluate, monitor, and control potential dangers in the food-handling process." Coglianese and Lazer document the respectable, though incomplete, accomplishments of this prototypical management-based regulatory approach.

They reach an appropriately nuanced conclusion: Management-based strategies "still require a governmental enforcement presence to ensure that firms conduct the necessary planning and implement their plans effectively." Even so, these strategies appear particularly suited to a number of increasingly salient issues, including "worker fatigue, chemical accidents, ergonomic injuries, and contamination of food." Coglianese and Lazer stress that even if "management-based regulation proves to be only an imperfect strategy, it may well be useful to remember that the alternatives . . . have imperfections of their own." The emerging management-based model, in short, "increasingly competes in the regulatory toolbox with technology-based and performance-based" approaches. Regulating well is not easy; aligning extensive with intensive accountability is an endlessly diverse challenge; expanding the regulatory repertoire is generally good news.

The final set of chapters examines the upside and downside of market-based governance. Elaine Ciulla Kamarck leads off with an enthusiastic, though not undiscriminating, overview of transformations under way in the governance zeitgeist. She samples particularly telling instances of a global "revolt against bureaucracy" that dominated the final quarter of the twentieth century. These include the repudiation of "big government" not just by the American Democrat Bill Clinton and the British Labourite Tony Blair but also, to take just some of the cases she cites, by former (and even current) Marxists in the developing world.

Kamarck distinguishes three subspecies of new-style government, each one a bit more distant than the last from the classic midcentury model. The first is "entrepreneurial government," in which familiar structures remain in place but practices are radically altered. "Entrepreneurial governments go out of their way to hide the fact that they are government organizations, and for that reason they are the last, best hope of the traditional public sector." Next is "networked government," in which "the formal state is but one actor in an informal network of organizations." The other nodes in the network can include for-profit firms, structured nonprofit organizations, interest groups, governments at different levels or in different countries, trade associations, ad hoc clusters of civic concerns and energies, and a dizzying range of other entities. Formal government may have a privileged role in setting the agenda and providing funding for a particular mission (easing the transition from welfare to work, say), but it is not, in any familiar sense, in control of the network. The third variant, and the sharpest departure from the classic model, is "market government." This model "operates with almost no government as we know it." The function of formal authority is "to place costs on things that contribute—positively or negatively—to the public good," then step back and let the market do the rest. Here (to use the terminology of this introduction) extensive accountability has no visible presence at all but operates solely through manipulating the terms of intensive accountability.

Kamarck offers a rich menu of examples of each model's application in settings around the world. She sketches some principles to mark the most promising terrain for each of the three. She turns to the public-management literature to underscore the risks and limitations of such startlingly heterodox approaches to governance. Although Kamarck may be a Ph.D. political scientist, she is also a savvy and scarred veteran of real-world policymaking at the very highest levels. She has learned that a pungent sound bite can trump a penetrating study. So she urges her scholarly colleagues to continue their efforts to deepen our understanding of the downside of market-based governance. She puts them on notice, however, that (incomplete research notwithstanding) "the capacity of these new forms of government to answer public needs while continuing to shrink the size of the state will make experimentation with them irresistible for politicians."

In the following chapter, my contribution to this volume, I consider the implications of market-based reforms for the governmental workforce. I suggest that the application of criteria discussed elsewhere (in this book and in my previous work)[13] are likely to yield a reasonably long list of collective functions that could be shifted out of formal government. What would this imply for public workers? Should employees' interests have standing in the debate over market-based governance?

Plumbing a range of data sources and employing several different metrics, I show that, contrary to the perception of rampant outsourcing common among both critics and advocates, government employment has by no means withered away in the United States. Market-based approaches, so far, have only nibbled at the edges of the conventional model of public workers delivering public services. By the most comprehensive available metric, "at century's end as at midcentury, roughly two-thirds of the government's work was still being done by public employees." There have clearly been instances of aggressive market-based reforms, but even in the aggregate they fall short, so far, of a revolution in governance. A fundamental shift in the means by which public missions are pursued, then, "is not a fait accompli to be accommodated" but rather "a choice to be weighed."

The choice matters, I argue, because government jobs are distinctive. The research literature suggests that America's public sector has resisted the broader economy's tilt, during recent decades, toward relentless meritocracy. This means that though "public service may be financially unattractive to élites, it is quite the opposite for many workers who lack the high-level skills that the private economy increasingly rewards and demands." So a major shift toward market-style public management and market-based supply would at once widen government's access to top talent and squeeze the less-skilled workers sheltering in public jobs from an inhospitable economic climate.

I admit to "a quite uncomfortable degree of ambivalence" about this prospect. Income disparities may be corroding Americans' sense of commonwealth; but the public payroll is an exceedingly clumsy weapon against economic inequality. Denying other citizens the advantages they might reap from market-based reforms, moreover, is hard to justify in the name of protecting the interests of government workers. I present a few recommendations for softening the conflict but conclude that inequality must be confronted economy-wide rather than by fighting a rearguard campaign through public employment. "So long as labor policy remains the tacit subtext of the debate, . . . it will be hard to think clearly, or to talk honestly, about market-based government."

Whereas I am at least implicitly sanguine—labor's stakes aside—that some significant common missions can be better pursued through market means, Mark Moore's misgivings are more fundamental. Governance and the market, he suggests, hinge on models of accountability that are more profoundly distinctive than is commonly recognized, and attempts to breed market traits into public management carry hidden hazards.

Moore starts with a challenge to the reigning enthusiasm for making "customer service" a watchword for improving governance. The idea of a customer is not merely an imperfect metaphor for the citizen's relationship to government, it is a perniciously illusory one. Those positioned "at the tail end of the production process" in the public sector, analogous to the customer's position in the private sector, seldom pay all costs of the services they receive; they have no legitimate monopoly on the criteria by which services are assessed; and they receive obligations and sanctions as well as benefits. Although there are cases in which citizens are, in essence, government's customers and in which good customer service entails real public value, Moore argues that these cases are by no means typical, and the term is mischievously misleading.

Similarly, Moore rejects the idea that good governance can or should be guided by a single bottom line. His objections here go beyond the common observation that government's goals are hard to measure; they are similar to (but deeper than) the notion of extensive accountability employed in this chapter. Financial measures are irredeemably flawed gauges of net value-added for government; nor is it logically (let alone practically) possible to define any other unidimensional metric. There is no alternative to basing both public management and public decisions on "multiple measures covering costs, processes, and outputs as well as outcomes."

Finally, Moore takes up issues raised by outsourcing public tasks to private suppliers. Previous work on the topic stresses that sound privatization decisions require (among other things) that the work to be done can be clearly defined. In the public realm, however, as Moore observes, this is an exceedingly tall order. It has always been "difficult for a collective to reach agreement about the precise attributes of public value that it wants to see produced." To suggest that privatization might boost performance, once goals have been specified, is to shirk the real work, Moore contends. "The problem in government management continues to be the difficulty of organizing politics to give a clear mandate of what is to be produced." Debates over means, he suggests, are both simpler than and inherently subordinate to this core challenge of defining public value.

The conversation about market-based governance (unlike the conversation about markets, *not* government) occurs chiefly among people who endorse a relatively ambitious definition of the public purpose. Their openness to market means is instrumental rather than fundamental—a tactic for improving the performance of public work and restoring citizens' confidence that common goals can be pursued effectively. Robert Behn's chapter both honors the appeal of this logic and highlights its hazards. "One of the implicit promises of market-based governance is that it will not only directly improve the performance of government but also, as a result, indirectly improve the public's trust of government." He sets about assessing what needs to occur for this sequence—market-based reforms improving performance, better performance increasing trust—to work out in practice.

First, he observes that there are at least four distinguishable grounds for distrust of government: corruption, abuse, flawed choices, and poor performance. Behn explores each of these and contends that they are separate indictments, not just different manifestations of an underlying disaffection. Market-based reforms, even at their best, have leverage against only part of citizens' complaints.

Even if we were convinced that perceived performance shortfalls were the most important explanation for distrust of government, Behn warns, public perceptions of performance are loosely linked to actual performance. So market-based reforms could boost the effectiveness with which public work is done and still have only a delayed and diluted impact on perceived performance. Moreover, performance gains achieved through market means may be viewed not as a victory for government but as the practical admission of its weakness.

Yet though Behn urges us "to be a little less giddy about what improved performance can do for public trust," he concludes by endorsing well-considered market-based reforms (along with any other promising strategies for boosting performance)—but with realistic expectations about the payoff in citizens' esteem.

Behn's themes provide the appropriate segue to what is as close to a concluding lesson as can be distilled from so diverse a set of perspectives on so sprawling a topic: It would be irresponsible to squander any opportunity for using market mechanisms to expand the repertoire by which, and to improve the efficiency with which, the work of governance gets done. This admonition applies with special force to those committed to an expansive collective agenda, however wary they may be about market solutions. It would be equally irresponsible to ignore the risk that market-based governance can distort public missions or introduce its own brand of waste into public undertakings. *This* admonition applies with special force to those concerned about operational efficiency and the integrity of public choice, however inclined they may be to look with favor on market principles.

Analysts of public policy have a responsibility to help society economize, insofar as it can, on learning by trial and error. Experimenting with alternative architectures of accountability to find out which stand, which collapse, and which warp common work in unpredicted ways can be an effective means of gaining wisdom, but often it is an expensive and traumatic one. By assessing evidence from analogous efforts, extrapolating from past experience, and thinking through the likely trajectory of alternatives still untried, analysts can narrow the range of alternatives that must be tested out in real life, with the fates of real people at stake. This is a duty that the authors of the chapters assembled here clearly recognize and admirably fulfill.

Notes

1. The tax-lien sale plan engineered by Mayor Bret D. Schundler is described in David M. Halbfinger, "Schundler's Record in Running Jersey City," *New York Times*, October 19, 2001, p. A17.

2. Office of Management and Budget, *The President's Management Agenda* (Executive Office of the President, August 2001), p. 17.

3. This quotation appears (among other places) in the *Baseball Almanac*, online version (www.baseball-almanac.com/quotes/quoruth.shtml [October 15, 2001]).

4. John D. Donahue and Joseph S. Nye Jr., eds., *Governance amid Bigger, Better Markets* (Brookings, 2001).

5. Joseph S. Nye, Philip D. Zelikow, and David C. King, eds., *Why People Don't Trust Government* (Harvard University Press, 1997).

6. "Armey's Axioms," from homepage of Representative Richard Armey (R-Tex. 26th) (armey.house.gov/axioms.htm [November 14, 2001]).

7. Juliette Jowit, "How the Rail Privatisation Experience Went Wrong" *Financial Times*, October 7, 2001.

8. The *Post* results for September 2001, April 2000, and February 1999—as well as longer time series for comparable, though not identical, questions—are from the *Polling Report* website (www.pollingreport.com/institut.htm#Government [November 16, 2001]).

9. Matt. 25:14–30.

10. See David S. C. Chu and John P. White, "Ensuring Quality People in Defense," in Ashton B. Carter and John P. White, eds., *Keeping the Edge: Managing Defense for the Future* (Cambridge: MIT Press, 2000).

11. Adolph A. Berle and Gardiner C. Means, *The Modern Corporation and Private Property* (New York: Macmillan, 1933).

12. Steven Kelman, "Remaking Federal Procurement," Working Paper 3 (Cambridge, Mass.: Harvard University, John F. Kennedy School of Government, Visions of Governance for the Twenty-First Century Project, July 2001).

13. John D. Donahue, *The Privatization Decision: Public Ends, Private Means* (Basic Books, 1989).

PART I

Demand Side

2

KAREN EGGLESTON
RICHARD ZECKHAUSER

Government Contracting for Health Care

Around the world the governments of industrialized nations finance health services. Such financing is justified or rationalized on efficiency grounds in some instances; in other contexts distributional or political considerations play the major role. Health-care services are sometimes provided directly by government, sometimes through government-financed enterprises in both the public and private sectors. Although the focus in this chapter is on health care, the analytic framework should prove useful for other contracting contexts as well.

In this discussion we draw upon the property rights theory of ownership.[1] This theory, based on a framework of incomplete contracting, is helpful because it tells us that ownership structure matters, but only when contracts are incomplete.[2] Contract incompleteness is an inherent institutional feature of health care.[3] Uncertainty and its delinquent nephew, asymmetry of information, are extraordinarily important for health care. Together they produce problems of moral hazard, adverse selection, noncontractible quality, and costly consumer search. These factors accompany

We are grateful to participants in the 2001 Visions of Governance in the Twenty-First Century Project, particularly Robert Blendon, Jack Donahue, Minah Kim, Robert Lawrence, Georges de Menil, Joseph Newhouse, Paul Peterson, and Guy Stuart, for many useful suggestions.

the supply-side market power wielded by highly trained medical professionals, with their monopoly license, and by hospitals and provider networks in some markets.[4] These features sour the economist's dream of paying for health services through an efficient contingent-claims market or through complete ex ante contracts that specify the efficient quantity and quality of medical services for each possible medical condition for each consumer. The incomplete contract theory of ownership highlights the link between incentives for innovation and contractual incompleteness, a linkage that bestows power upon those with residual control rights. This spotlight on innovation is particularly helpful given the undisputed importance of rapid technological advance in modern health care.[5]

A purchaser of health care must take account of the health-care triad of patient, insurer, and provider. For simplicity, our analysis abstracts from this distinction between insurer and provider on the supply side, implicitly assuming that government contracts with an integrated insurer-provider such as a managed care organization (for example, a health maintenance organization [HMO] or preferred provider organization [PPO]). This formulation illustrates the distinctive institutional features of contracting for health care, many of which stem from the fact that health care, even when totally government financed, is overwhelmingly privately consumed. It is thus a salient example of a directed good, as is education.[6] Such goods differ in important ways from public goods (national defense or basic research, for example) and limited or local public goods (local police services or road repairs, for example). Although they may involve a limited element of externalities and public goods, their benefits flow overwhelmingly to individual consumers. All directed goods are by their nature redistributional.[7]

Any analysis of the optimal division of production responsibilities in the health-care sector among services financed by government must address two questions. First, what fraction of services should be produced by the government directly, by the for-profit sector, and the nonprofit sector? Second, taking as given these three fractions, which services should be in which sector?

The first is a question of absolute advantage—which ownership form delivers health services most effectively?—and it is the issue that generates the most intense political debate. The second is a question of the comparative advantage of different ownership structures for different health-care services, and it is the focus of this chapter. If the final allocation of expenditure levels across sectors is not in conflict, in what order should services be placed in the for-profit, nonprofit, and government sectors? In theory, Republicans and Democrats, Labourites and Conservatives, Socialists and

Christian Democrats should be able roughly to agree on this question, even though they might be bitterly divided on the amounts they would like to place in each of the three sectors. Suppose economists agreed, for example, that public and private providers had a comparative advantage for severe mental and regular dental health services, respectively. Then even if policy advisers (for example, advisers to postsocialist economies) disagreed regarding what overall share of hospitals and clinics should be public or private, they could nevertheless agree that any privatization program should apply first to dentists and last to inpatient mental health facilities.

After identifying the comparative advantages of public, private nonprofit, and investor-owned (for-profit) providers, we then briefly consider the markets that bear and incentives that act on these structures. We argue that for health care, just as important as ownership in itself are such factors as competition, payment incentives, and hardness of budget constraints. This implies that *how* to contract out, or how one is able to contract out, matters as much as whether or not to do so and to whom.

Our analysis is informed primarily by two sets of experiences. The first is that of the United States (and, to a lesser extent, other established market economies), both because it is familiar and because it receives plentiful coverage in the health economics literature. The second is that of the nations of eastern Europe, where the health-care sector has been swept along with the broader economic forces unleashed by the transition from planned to market economies. We focus on this region partly because arguments from comparative advantage are most relevant for systems undergoing the changes that occur when the status quo dictated by history and ideology is eroding. Although the experiences of eastern European nations are far from uniform, and the differences between the United States and eastern Europe are dramatic, these disparities make the similarities identified—the importance of payment incentives, competition, and hard budget constraints as much as ownership form—all the more striking.

These similarities seem broadly applicable. Table 2-1 lists the health-care systems in the twenty-nine member countries of the Organization for Economic Cooperation and Development and their performance rankings as assessed by the World Health Organization (WHO).[8] The twenty highest-ranked countries worldwide include countries with public shares of financing both well above (Luxembourg, United Kingdom) and well below (Portugal, Greece) the average of the European Monetary Union (about 75 percent; see table 2-2), as well as countries in which the private share of inpatient beds ranges from minimal (Norway, United Kingdom)

Table 2-1. *Public Financing of Health Care in OECD Countries, Private Share of Inpatient Beds, and WHO Health System Performance Rankings*
Percent, except as indicated

Country	Health expenditure as share of GDP	Public share of total health expenditure	Private share of total inpatient care beds	WHO Health System Performance ranking (out of 191)
Luxembourg	7.0	91.8	n.a.	16
United States	13.9	46.4	66.8	37
Norway	7.5	82.2	0.1	11
Switzerland	10.0	69.9	n.a.	20
Denmark	8.0	83.8	0.7	34
Iceland	7.9	83.8	n.a.	15
Japan	7.2	79.9	65.2	10
Canada	9.2	69.8	0.9	30
Belgium	7.6	87.6	61.9	21
Austria	8.3	73.0	30.3	9
The Netherlands	8.5	72.6	85.0	17
Australia	8.4	66.7	56.6	32
Germany	10.7	77.1	51.5	25
France	9.6	74.2	35.2	1
Italy	7.6	69.9	21.9	2
Finland	7.4	76.0	4.7	31
Ireland	6.3	76.7	n.a.	19
United Kingdom	6.8	84.6	3.7	18
Sweden	8.6	83.3	23.6	23
New Zealand	7.6	77.3	0.1	41
Spain	7.4	76.1	32.5	7
Portugal	7.9	60.0	21.7	12
Korea	6.0	45.5	90.3	58
Greece	8.6	57.7	29.6	14
Czech Republic	7.2	91.7	9.1	48
Hungary	6.5	69.1	n.a.	66
Mexico	4.7	60.0	25.6	61
Poland	5.2	90.4	0.2	50
Turkey	4.0	72.8	5.2	70

Sources: Organization for Economic Cooperation and Development, *OECD Health Data 99: A Comparative Analysis of Twenty-nine Countries* (Paris, 1999); World Health Organization, *World Health Report 2000, Health Systems: Improving Performance* (Geneva, 2000).

Note: Countries are listed from highest to lowest 1997 per capita GDP (measured in purchasing-power parity terms). Data for first three columns are for 1997; data for last column are for 2000.

Table 2-2. *Public Financing of Health Care, by World Region*
Percent

Region	Total health expenditure as share of GDP	Public health expenditure As share of GDP	As share of total health expenditure
Low-income countries	4.20	1.30	30.95
Middle-income countries	5.70	3.10	54.39
High-income countries	9.80	6.20	63.27
East Asia and Pacific	4.10	1.70	41.46
Latin America and Caribbean	6.60	3.30	50.00
Middle East and North Africa	4.80	2.40	50.00
South Asia	4.80	0.80	16.67
Sub-Saharan Africa	3.20	1.50	46.88
European Monetary Union	8.90	6.60	74.16

Source: Data from World Bank, *World Development Indicators 2000* (World Bank, 2000), pp. 90–92.

Note: Public health expenditure includes compulsory social insurance contributions. Data are for most recent year available from 1990 to 1998.

to dominant (Japan, the Netherlands).[9] Postsocialist Slovenia ranks neck-and-neck with the always capitalist United States in overall health system performance (United States thirty-seventh, Slovenia thirty-eighth; data not shown), according to the WHO study.[10] Although the appropriateness and accuracy of the WHO assessment rankings are debatable, these comparisons nevertheless highlight the heterogeneity of purchasing and delivery systems—even among established market economies—and the widespread importance of government contracting for health care.[11]

We focus on government purchasers of health care and assume that the purchaser's sole goal is to maximize social welfare. The conceptual framework of comparative advantage should nevertheless be useful to other purchasers, such as employers, and can be adapted to different goals.[12] The focus on comparative advantage suggests that the purchaser may wish to contract with multiple ownership forms simultaneously. However, the administrative complications that may arise from such contracting and the potential efficiency benefits of a mixed delivery system largely lie outside the scope of the analysis.[13]

A final caveat needs mention. Although we focus on comparative advantage and government contracting, we recognize that the development of a nation's health-care system more closely resembles a dynamic ecosystem, with public and private agents interacting over time within the social and political context to shape the delivery system. Our hypothesis is that the allocation of health-care services across ownership forms tends to reflect patterns of comparative advantage, except where there are impediments to its function. At times such impediments—such as regulatory barriers, the political economy of reforms, lack of access to capital for nonprofits, or other important social and ideological factors—may overpower comparative advantage in determining a system's historic trajectory.

Performance Differences by Ownership Type

Although some studies find performance differences between public and private providers, the evidence is far from conclusive. Frank Sloan notes some troubling results showing lower quality of care in public hospitals, although findings are mixed regarding efficiency despite clear differences in mission.[14] Using 1980s Medicare data, E. B. Keeler and colleagues report that on average the quality of care is lower in public hospitals than in private hospitals. However, "public teaching hospitals in 1986 had better process [quality] than private hospitals, and the city-county hospitals had generally high quality, perhaps because most were large and teaching hospitals."[15] A recent study finds that heart attack patients treated in Veterans Health Administration hospitals had more coexisting conditions than Medicare patients, though there was no significant difference in mortality, suggesting at least equivalent quality of care.[16]

The paucity of definitive differences between public and private providers could be considered surprising, given the myriad constraints imposed on public facilities. Government-owned hospitals usually have less autonomy than private hospitals, especially with regard to employment and compensation, a fact that can hamper efforts to attract and retain the most capable clinicians and managers. Public hospitals also usually cannot turn away patients.[17]

Many studies of ownership effects examine differences in community benefit—defined to include such unprofitable services as charity care and bad debt, care for public program beneficiaries, community services such as twenty-four-hour trauma centers, programs for special needs populations, and teaching and research.[18] Public hospitals, along with major teaching hospitals, provide a disproportionate share of community benefits according to virtually all definitions of that term.[19] Public facilities clearly form the backbone of the U.S. hospital "safety net."

Studying short-term acute-care hospitals in California and Florida, Richard Zeckhauser, Jayendu Patel, and Jack Needleman find significant evidence of "sloughing" by private providers—that is, a reduction in the rates of uncompensated care when public hospital beds are abundant.[20] More recent studies find similar results.[21] Such evidence suggests that government health-care facilities act as "providers of last resort" for uninsured, low-income, or otherwise disadvantaged patients. Studies of privatization of U.S. public hospitals confirm that conversions often lead to reductions in uncompensated care.[22]

Much of the U.S. literature on health-care ownership sets aside public hospitals to focus on for-profit and nonprofit providers. Some scattered evidence seems to support the view that nonprofits attend more to nonpecuniary aspects of health care, such as community benefits, than do their for-profit counterparts. "For-profit hospitals," for example, "are more likely than nonprofits to pressure physicians not to admit uninsured and Medicaid patients, and physicians report conflict over the treatment of indigent persons more often in for-profit than in nonprofit hospitals."[23] For-profit providers also have been shown to engage in higher average levels of "upcoding" to maximize government reimbursement—by coding treatment for pneumonia as respiratory infection, for example, which pays 50 percent more.[24] These results reinforce anecdotes about for-profits' exploiting opportunities for fraud.[25]

Nonprofit organizations often provide more charity care and other community benefits than for-profit providers, although whether nonprofits provide community benefits in excess of the value of their tax exemptions is a controversial question.[26] Part of the difference arises from systematic differences in location. Within the same market, nonprofits and for-profits seem to behave similarly, perhaps driven by competition or by the tendency for organizations to mimic one another's success—what Paul DiMaggio and Walter Powell call "mimetic isomorphism"; but for-profits tend to locate in communities that are more profitably served, so that comparisons based on national aggregate data can be misleading.[27]

Few studies find any consistent evidence of differences in cost, efficiency, or quality between nonprofits and for-profits or in their provision of charity care or public goods.[28] Zeckhauser and colleagues find for-profit and nonprofit hospitals to be of similar efficiency and to offer similar services (including "noncore" unprofitable services), with local market norms and historical presence or absence of nonprofits also important in explaining local variations.[29] Daniel Kessler and Mark McClellan, analyzing longitudinal data on nonrural Medicare beneficiaries hospitalized for heart attacks, find that within a market, for-profit and nonprofit behavior is similar.[30] Even the provision of goods and services that are (local and general) public goods, such as teaching and research, does not seem to differ systematically between investor-owned (for-profit) and non-investor-owned (nonprofit) private hospitals.[31] Most experts would agree that "two decades of research has failed to provide definitive empirical evidence on the differences between for-profit and nonprofit health-care facilities and on the social consequences of changes in ownership."[32] "Overall, the evidence suggests that for-profit and private not-for-profit hospitals are far more alike than different."[33]

Simple Conceptual Framework

A government purchaser of health care must decide whether to provide services "in-house" (that is, through vertically integrated public facilities) or by contracting out to a private health plan, hospital, or physician group. Our analysis focuses on the contract between the government and the manager of the delivery institution.[34]

Throughout the analysis, we assume that all providers are a priori equally productive. We first illustrate the potential importance of different preference trade-offs regarding cost and quality, using quantitative data. In the remainder of the analysis, however, we abstract from initial differences and focus instead on providers with identical, or at least similar, preferences.[35] Thus, in this framework, comparative advantage arises endogenously from the property rights structure of different ownership forms, not from an assumption that public and private providers innately differ in their production capabilities or in their preferences regarding cost and quality.

Benefits, Costs, and the Purchaser's Objectives

Assume that a provider of a health service can provide patients with treatment benefits (or quality), B. B is measured in dollar units—for example, through willingness to pay. The cost of producing B is $C(B)$. Costs and marginal costs are both increasing in B.

The purchaser seeks to maximize social surplus—that is, benefits minus costs, or $B - C(B)$. If contracts were complete, the purchaser would contract

Figure 2-1. *The Social Optimum*

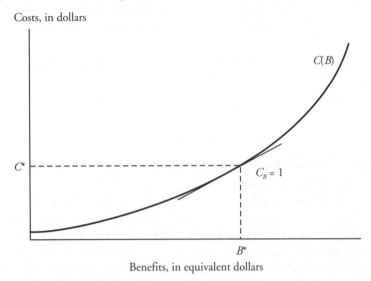

Benefits, in equivalent dollars

for optimal quality B in exchange for payment R, where $R \geq C(B)$. B is the level at which an additional dollar's worth of benefits costs just a dollar to produce or, in the language of economics, the point at which marginal benefit equals marginal cost. Figure 2-1 illustrates this result.

Assuming that public and private providers are equally competent and therefore have the same initial cost function, $C(B)$, the contract could be with a public provider or a for-profit or nonprofit private provider, with exactly the same result. If patient benefits fall short of B^*, the provider has to return some or all of the prepayment R.

The great challenge is that many aspects of quality for a health service are not contractible. Suppose instead that only minimum quality B_{min} is contractible—because, for example, B_{min} is readily observable or is a widely accepted norm. The purchaser would like to contract with the provider to choose quality B^* greater than B_{min}. However, the purchaser cannot enforce a breach of such a contract—by firing the employee or "firing" the independent contractor by switching to an alternative provider—unless quality falls below the level of B_{min}.[36] The provider therefore has a default option of always providing the basic service at the minimum acceptable level B_{min} at corresponding minimum cost $C(B_{min})$. Under this scenario, the purchaser will face the same contracting challenges of motivating B^* for both public and private providers. Ownership in terms of control rights over the health service facility once again does not affect the outcome unless we assume that different ownership forms foster a different preference trade-off between *B* and *C*. Preference differences are explored in the next subsection. A second possibility, examined in the remainder of the chapter, is that purchasing takes place in a multiperiod context in which postcontractual innovations are important.

Different Preference Trade-offs Regarding Benefits and Costs

Providers with the same cost function but different preferences will choose to produce different levels of benefits, as illustrated in figure 2-2. The figure considers three idealized types, which may or may not correspond to ownership forms (government, nonprofit, and for-profit). Consider first a provider who values only net revenue, $R - C(B)$, as an economics text might posit. The indifference curves of such a provider would be horizontal, representing the desire to minimize cost under prepayment (U^{minC}). Such a provider would choose barely to fulfill the letter of the contract by providing minimum quality.

In contrast, if a provider were altruistic, valuing quality as well as net revenue, the positive marginal rate of substitution between *B* and *C* would encourage the provider to choose higher (and costlier) points on the cost curve. In the figure, a provider with preference U^{trade} is willing to trade off between *B* and *C*. Depending on the level of altruism and concern with cost, the chosen combination of cost and quality could be below, equal to, or above the socially desired level.

A third class of providers may actually wish to maximize benefits, perhaps owing to strong altruism or because it reaps prestige from offering high-quality services. In figure 2-2, such a provider has preferences $U^{maxB,K}$, implying that it would like to maximize benefits subject to a break-even constraint *K*. Such a "gold plater" would have an indifference curve that is steeply sloped before the break-even constraint binds (that is, the point at which $C < R$), indicating willingness to increase cost considerably to achieve higher benefits. At the constraint, there is a downward kink in the indifference curve. Beyond this kink, at which point extra spending connotes negative net revenue, the provider continues to value quality but is willing to pay much less per unit to provide it. Others have posited similar behavior by health-care providers.[37]

Figure 2-2. *Examples of Provider Preferences*

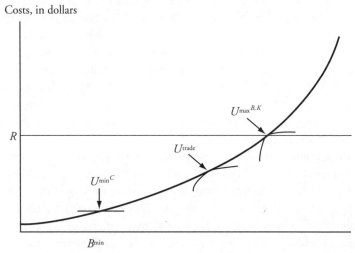

The purpose of figure 2-2 is not to characterize the preferences of different provider types; that would be of limited use, particularly given the significant variability within types. It is, rather, to stress the importance of considering provider preferences when contracting capabilities are limited. However, we do not focus on differences in provider preferences or production capabilities in the remainder of the analysis, for at least two reasons. First, no ownership form has a monopoly on altruism. Second, a useful theory of ownership should explain why differences in efficiency arise. It seems unsatisfying to base a theory of the comparative advantage of public, private for-profit, and private nonprofit providers on exogenous assumptions about how provider preferences and altruism correlate with ownership status or how initial production capabilities differ across ownership types.

Endogenous Differences Emerging across Ownership Types

A useful theory of differences between public and private ownership should start by asking whether a single provider would act differently as a government employee or as an independent contractor, given the same human capital, productive efficiency, and altruistic concern for patients. The property rights theory of ownership, based on incomplete contracts, suggests an affirmative answer. In this theory, ownership matters to the extent that changes over time in the way a good or service is delivered, such as innovations in quality improvement and cost control, cannot be spelled out explicitly in a contract ex ante. Important opportunities for innovation will therefore arise after a contract has been negotiated, drawn up, and signed. Incentives for such innovations will depend crucially on who has control rights to implement, and will thereby capture the benefits from, those innovations.

In the incomplete contracting approach, ownership is defined as the allocation of residual control rights over a nonhuman asset, such as a hospital. Oliver Hart, Andrei Shleifer, and Robert Vishny develop this framework and apply it to prisons.[38] The service (prison management) is assumed to be a public good. The manager receives a fixed payment, either a salary or a contracted price, contingent on delivery of the basic service for a specified period of time. In the model, private owners typically have stronger incentives to invest in cost and quality innovations but may overinvest in cost reduction because they ignore the adverse impact on noncontractible quality. The theory presented by Hart, Shleifer, and Vishny suggests that costs are always lower under private ownership, but quality may be higher or lower. The authors presume prepayment. They do not explicitly model competition, choice of quantity of treatment per consumer, differences between for-profit and nonprofit providers, soft budget constraints, or the contracting challenges arising from consumer heterogeneity.

Postcontractual Innovations

Suppose that a health service provider faces two choices, each of which affects cost and quality: the level of up-front cost-reducing investment, e, to be undertaken and the intensity of treatment, q, to be delivered to each patient. An up-front investment in cost reduction costs the provider e but decreases the marginal cost of producing quality (in effect, the cost curve $C[.]$ is shifted downward). The provider must incur an observable but not verifiable cost per patient treatment episode of $C(e,q)$. This cost is decreasing in e, with decreasing marginal returns, and increasing in q, with increasing marginal costs. Patient benefits from treatment, $B(e,q)$, may be adversely affected by the quality-damaging side effects of cost reduction and are increasing and concave in intensity of treatment over the relevant range.

Assume that the contract between the government and the provider is incomplete in the sense that only minimum quantity per patient, q_{min}, is contractible. Treatment costs, quantity above q_{min}, and cost innovations are noncontractible, albeit mutually observable. Implementation of innovations requires approval from the facility owner and may not be forthcoming unless the purchaser agrees to pay additionally for them. The purchaser would like to encourage innovations but does not want excessive cost control at the expense of (noncontractible) quality.

The Performance of Government, For-Profit, and Nonprofit Forms

Consider the likely outcome under direct government provision. The government purchases a health service for its beneficiaries by employing a provider G to run a public facility, such as a hospital or a clinic. By choosing to provide the health service in-house, the government retains control rights over the nonhuman assets (the hospital or clinic). The job description of the provider G specifies provision of the basic service. The public provider may take initiative to control costs in ways not specified in the original contract, which may affect service quality. As a civil servant, however, G must obtain approval from his or her supervisor or other relevant authority before innovations can be implemented.

The government seeks to maximize benefits to patients, less prepayment R and any payments made when renegotiating for changes not specified in the initial contract. Without renegotiation to obtain approval and compensate G, innovations are not forthcoming. With renegotiation, the net benefit from the improved service is split between government and G. We illustrate the effects of renegotiation assuming that net gains are shared equally.

The public provider G is assumed to seek to maximize payment, including compensation for innovation, less the cost per case and the effort costs of developing innovations. Without renegotiation for permission from government supervisors, the public provider cannot implement investment e and therefore would not want to invest in cost reduction. Moreover, because the provider bears the cost of treatment q but receives no extra compensation for additional treatment, G would choose to provide minimum intensity of treatment.

However, because the government purchaser can benefit from encouraging an appropriate amount of cost control and intensity of treatment, renegotiation will almost surely take place. By anticipating the surplus from renegotiation, G implicitly takes some account of how his or her choices of e and q will affect the benefits the patient receives from use of the service. However, G cannot reap the full rewards of his or her cost-control initiatives; indeed, given the constraints on government employee compensation, G may be able to reap no more than a tiny fraction of them.[39] As a result, despite having internalized the quality-damaging side effects of cost control, G may have stunted incentives for cost innovations. The latter is a cause for concern, especially in light of rapid advances in health technology. In a dynamic setting, even a slightly stunted incentive for innovation would lead to cumulatively low levels of innovation, so that such a provider would end up considerably behind the technological frontier. Because lack of control rights, and therefore stunted incentives for innovation, seems inherent to public ownership, a government purchaser of health services may wish to consider alternative purchasing strategies, such as contracting out to a private provider.

The likely outcome under for-profit ownership is quite different. Assume a for-profit private provider Π seeks to maximize net revenues—prepayment less the costs incurred in treating patients and in developing cost-control innovations. As the owner of the facility, Π can implement e without seeking the purchaser's permission. Π therefore has maximum incentives to reduce cost, both by investing in cost-reduction innovations and by skimping on treatment, irrespective of the negative impact on patient benefits.

From the purchaser's perspective, although the goal of cost-control innovation is furthered by contracting out to Π, there is a significant mismatch in goals that may lead to excessive cost cutting, thereby damaging quality. The private provider has stronger incentives to invest in cost control; hence e^Π will be greater than e^G, and the cost curve of the for-profit provider will lie below that of the public provider. In this case, contracting out is potentially much more efficient. Nevertheless, by retaining residual control rights over the facility under G, the government can achieve greater fidelity to purchaser goals—that is, more of the payment will flow into patient benefits rather than provider net revenue.[40] Even with identical preferences, public and private providers will make different investment choices because they have different claims on the returns from those investments.

This model suggests that the optimal ownership structure depends on the relative trade-off between higher fidelity under public ownership and greater productive efficiency under private for-profit ownership. Public providers have a comparative advantage for delivering services for which large adverse side effects may accompany aggressive cost control. By contrast, for-profit providers have a comparative advantage for services for which the quality damage from cost control is slight to nonexistent, or cost control enhances quality, or policies are available that ameliorate the incentives for or consequences of excessive cost control.

QUALITY INNOVATIONS. The basic framework presented above extends readily to allow for providers to invest in quality-enhancement innovations, i, as well as cost-control innovations, e. Assume that quality-improvement investments increase benefits from treatment but add to costs of care. Renegotiation occurs in the same way as it does for cost-control innovations. Thus, as is the case with cost-control innovation, a public provider will have stunted incentives for quality innovations. Indeed, public providers are not known for being on the cutting edge of either medical quality-improving or cost-reducing innovations.[41]

A for-profit provider, by contrast, can reap the entire surplus from implementing innovations because Π has sole control over the relevant nonhuman assets. However, quality-enhancement investments, unlike cost-cutting innovations, do not increase Π's net revenue unless additional payment is forthcoming, either from the purchaser or from additional patients seeking care from that provider. The purchaser will in general find it optimal to negotiate with a single-source private provider to enhance quality in exchange for additional payment. We assume that the bargain is struck so that half the surplus value generated from the quality innovation goes to the provider and half to the purchaser. This produces an outcome in which, as Hart, Shleifer, and Vishny have found in prison management, quality is higher than it would otherwise be because Π anticipates renegotiation.[42] However, because Π receives only half the surplus, Π's chosen level of quality enhancement, i, will typically still be less than is socially optimal and may be no higher than that of public providers. This shows that private ownership, despite Π's greater control rights over the surplus from innovation, does not always lead to high levels of innovation.

COMPARATIVE ADVANTAGES OF PUBLIC AND PRIVATE FOR-PROFIT OWNERSHIP. The foregoing analysis comparing public to for-profit private ownership does not yield an unambiguous ranking of ownership forms. A for-profit private provider will always have greater incentive for cost control and thus lower cost for a given quality. However, a for-profit's excessive cost control may lead to large adverse impacts on noncontractible quality, counteracting the advantage of higher incentive for quality-improvement innovations. A public provider's incentives for innovations will generally be stunted compared with those of a for-profit private provider. Nevertheless, these stunted incentives are sometimes efficient (for example, limiting quality-damaging cost control and skimping on intensity of treatment). The public provider will be less responsive than a private contractor—with less risk of overzealous cost cutting but also less incentive to pioneer quality breakthroughs and creative cost-control methods. Whether in-house provision is preferable to contracting out to a for-profit provider will depend on several issues: the characteristics of the health services in question, the ability to specify desired quality and treatment intensity in the contract, the availability of complementary purchasing strategies (such as allowing patient choice of provider to motivate investment in quality enhancement), and similar factors.

This comparison still leaves out an important option for many purchasers, the possibility of contracting out to a not-for-profit (nonprofit) private provider. Does the nonprofit ownership option present distinct advantages? Any attempt to answer that question requires a conceptual framework for distinguishing and analyzing nonprofit ownership.

ALTRUISM, COST CONTROL, AND NONPROFIT OWNERSHIP. The theory of nonprofit behavior stirs controversy.[43] Because of their prevalence in the health sector, the behavior of nonprofits has been the focus of considerable theoretical work by health economists.[44] The framework used here, based on the property rights theory of ownership, focuses on residual rights of control. Although residual control rights and residual income rights are often bundled together on a one-to-one basis, they need not be;[45] and they are not bundled in nonprofit enterprises. Arguably, nonprofits also seek to maximize net revenues, or "profits," but instead of distributing those funds to shareholders, nonprofits allocate them to uses that firm insiders select, such as community benefit programs, "contingency funds," or higher employee perks. This suggests that nonprofit providers have control rights similar to those of for-profit private providers but have murkier claims to residual income and may even have to distort surplus to channel it into forms they can appropriate (for example, perks, such as attractive offices, rather than dividends).[46]

At least two characteristics of nonprofit providers are important for health-care purchasers: first, nonprofit ownership may develop as a signal of trustworthiness to consumers; second, incentives for cost control may be diminished because residual income cannot flow directly into a nonprofit provider's pocket (the celebrated "nondistribution constraint").[47] In this analysis we capture the first characteristic by assuming that nonprofit ownership is associated with a degree of altruism, or agency on behalf of patients, that is at least as great on average as in for-profits. In other words, agency problems between patients and nonprofit providers are no greater, and are sometimes less, than those between patients and for-profit providers.

Our hypothesis is consistent not only with Henry Hansmann's idea of nonprofit status as a signal of trust but also with previous theory and empirical evidence, as discussed in the foregoing section on performance differences by ownership type.[48] Two important caveats should be noted, however. First, a higher degree of fealty to patient desires is not always socially desirable from an ex ante point of view: altruistic providers indulge patient moral hazard more than their less altruistic counterparts, resulting in inefficient overutilization of services.[49] Second, there is no inevitable link between nonprofit status and high fidelity to patients. Competition may change the "mission" of nonprofits so that they resemble for-profits in all but name.[50] This factor could help to explain the overall similarity of nonprofit and for-profit providers in competitive settings.

Recent empirical evidence lends credibility to the idea that nonprofit and for-profit behavior is closest in competitive environments. For example, in his examination of how hospitals respond to financial incentives to treat low-income patients, Mark Duggan finds that nonprofit hospitals in areas with many for-profit competitors are significantly more responsive to financial incentives than other nonprofits.[51] This finding is consistent with the idea that competitive pressure makes nonprofits more profit oriented. Richard Arnold, Marianne Bertrand, and Kevin Hallock find that nonprofit hospitals compensate top executives more according to profitability as HMO penetration in the hospital's market increases.[52] Studying the tendency of hospitals to "upcode" Medicare reimbursements to obtain greater revenue, Elaine Silverman and Jonathan Skinner find that nonprofits operating in heavily for-profit markets upcoded at rates similar to those of their for-profit competitors.[53]

Applying the property rights theory to nonprofit providers, assume that the objective of the nonprofit provider, N, is to maximize utility from net compensation and from altruistic pleasure associated with patient benefits. Further assume that for a nonprofit provider to reap benefit from the firm's net revenue, surplus must be distorted slightly (for example, from cash to perks), implying that a fraction of the surplus gets dissipated. Altruism on the part of a provider increases the incentive to provide socially optimal cost and quality innovations and combats incentives to skimp on treatment. The provider with a high regard for altruism takes full account of the impact of innovations and treatment intensity on patient benefits and hence internalizes the full social marginal benefit. As Kenneth Arrow suggests, a "perfect agent" can balance the interests of patients and society.[54] However, excess identification with patient interests can lead to overemphasis on quality at the expense of cost, encouraging moral hazard and wasteful overuse.

The nonprofit provider's lack of direct access to residual income can also lead to distortions. Unable to capitalize on the net revenue benefits of cost control and quality investment, N may overemphasize quality (high i and q) at the expense of cost (low e). This problem may be acute in medical care, where quality is often associated with prestige and there is ample latitude to overprovide services.[55] The framework suggests that N has diminished incentives to invest in cost control because he or she can reap only a fraction of the benefit generated by that investment. Therefore, a nonprofit, like a government provider, may invest too little in cost-reducing innovations. Renegotiation with the purchaser can move toward a socially preferred outcome but cannot fully restore efficiency if the original incentives were distorted, because the provider receives only half the gain in surplus from renegotiation.

If this model of altruism and nonprofit behavior reasonably approximates reality, then the comparative advantage of nonprofits lies in their ability to combine the flexibility of private ownership with the patient-centered concerns of the public purchaser. In a sense, nonprofits lie "in between" public and for-profit private ownership, with concomitant strengths and weaknesses. However, to pin down the full comparative advantages of different ownership forms, we must go beyond the simple setting used so far.

The Effect of Institutional Characteristics

A purchaser must decide not only with whom to contract for health services but also how to structure the contract to offset the limitations of public and private ownership. Contract structure implies questions regarding the additional instruments available to purchasers (for example, payment incentives and competition) and their interaction with additional contracting challenges inherent in purchasing quality health care (for example, patient heterogeneity, patient selection concerns, and soft budget constraints).[56]

PAYMENT INCENTIVES. Different payment structures may be useful for aligning provider incentives with purchaser goals. For example, whereas prepayment systems such as capitation (in which a uniform per capita fee is paid) encourage limiting q (for example, to q_{min}), fee-for-service payment systems reward high utilization. Indeed, fee-for-service reimbursement may result in excessive utilization stemming from providers' indulging patient moral hazard or even from "supplier-induced demand."[57]

The correlation between disaggregated (fee-for-service) payment and higher cost emerges empirically both at the broadest (national) and narrower (organization and individual physician) levels. For example, Ulf Gerdtham and Bengt Jönsson, controlling for an array of economic and institutional factors, find a 17 to 21 percent higher average expenditure in fee-for-service payment systems as compared with capitation systems in member countries of the Organization for Economic Cooperation and Development.[58] At the level of the individual clinician, capitation or salary payment is associated with less service use. In the United States, after the prospective payment system (PPS) was introduced for hospitals, admissions generally declined, average lengths of stay fell, and some patients got dumped to non-PPS facilities, consistent with the incentives of case-based payment.[59]

Eastern European countries as well have seen significant reactions to payment incentives, although the evidence to date is mostly anecdotal. In Hungary, provider reimbursement reforms introducing aggregated prepayment (capitation payment for family doctors and case payment for hospitals) "have had a much greater impact on the character of service delivery than earlier changes in ownership."[60] Real health-care spending in the Czech Republic increased by almost 40 percent in the two years following the introduction of an open-ended fee-for-service system.[61] Physicians in private practice who were paid on a fee-for-service basis billed significantly more in every category of service than did state (primarily salaried) providers.[62] The expenditure-increasing effects of the fee-for-service system proved so powerful that in 1997 Czech policymakers chose to revert to a global-budget method of payment.

How will provider response to payment incentives differ systematically by ownership form? Scant empirical evidence speaks to this issue. The framework presented here suggests that by retaining residual control rights, government stunts a public provider's incentives for innovations compared with those of a for-profit private provider. Efficiency must be lost. These stunted incentives sometimes produce the second-best outcome achievable, however. Moreover, incentives can be adjusted by payment method. A prepaid public provider may prove to be considerably less costly than a fee-for-service private provider, with little difference in patient health outcomes. A public or nonprofit provider's responsiveness to payment will be less extreme than that of a for-profit private contractor—with less risk of overzealous cost cutting under prepayment or aggressive "demand inducement" under a fee-for-service system but also less incentive for generally efficiency-enhancing initiatives.

MULTIDIMENSIONAL QUALITY. When the multidimensionality of quality is acknowledged, the ability of patients to monitor the quality of their care becomes a significant concern. If patients can discern some aspects of quality better than others, providers have the incentive to invest primarily in those aspects of quality that patients can recognize (for example, amenities of care such as pretty waiting rooms or shorter waiting times) at the expense of those that they cannot (technical quality of care, for example). This provider behavior resembles the problem of "teaching to the test" in standards-based educational reform. Provider professionalism and altruistic concern for patients can ameliorate these inefficiencies. For example, a highly altruistic nonprofit would not exploit patients' imperfect monitorability to curb quality along less visible dimensions.[63]

Some empirical evidence supports this conclusion. In their study of the adoption of quality-enhancing technologies by kidney dialysis units, for example, R. A. Hirth, M. E. Chernew, and S. M. Orzol find that nonprofit and for-profit facilities differed in the cost-saving trade-offs made when adopting the new technologies.[64] Nonprofits were less likely to lower technical quality of care, whereas for-profits tended to deliver lower technical quality of care but also offer more amenities (for example, more dialysis stations). This behavior is consistent with our theoretical prediction that of the three ownership forms, for-profits are most likely to respond to the incentive to exploit patients' imperfect monitorability of health services by curbing quality along less visible dimensions and promoting quality along those that are more easily observed.

COMPETITION AND SELECTION BY PATIENTS. Can consumer choice promote appropriate outcomes in the health-care marketplace? Consider, first, an ideal situation, with a homogeneous group of well-informed patients and perfect competition. Suppose that there is perfect monitorability, so that only providers offering efficient quantity and quality attract consumers. In other words, consumer choices of exit, voice, and loyalty are perfectly capable of guiding and disciplining providers to offer quality care at reasonable cost. In this case, performance under all ownership forms would tend to converge.[65]

Unfortunately, such ideal conditions are rare for health services. Competition bolsters financial incentives for patient-observable quality improvement (for example, shorter waiting times) and tempers the incentive for cost-cutting measures that might damage patient-observable quality, especially among for-profit providers. Competition also bolsters the incentive to skimp on nonmonitorable dimensions of quality and to cut costs in ways that are unobservable to patients (for example, lower technical quality). The effect of competition on public and nonprofit private providers is analogous, and these incentives can conflict with the altruism or role of backstop provider often associated with these ownership forms.

These results suggest that when patients effectively monitor providers by observing and reacting to differences along all relevant dimensions (perhaps through the provider's reputation), competition for patients can have welfare-improving effects regardless of ownership form. In many cases the most effective way for a public purchaser to harness competitive forces on behalf of beneficiaries is by contracting out to competitive private providers, both investor owned and nonprofit. Yet not all health services are equally suitable for informed patient decisionmaking about treatment options.

HETEROGENEITY AND SELECTION OF PATIENTS. Even if all services could be monitored perfectly, mere competition for customers might not be efficient, because not all patients can be served equally profitably. Competition might push providers to engage in sorting and discrimination—an inefficient process known as "cream skimming" or "risk selection"—to attract those who will be served more profitably. One way to ameliorate incentives for creaming and dumping is to make selection partially contractible by adjusting prepayments—case-based, capitation, or premium payments—for observable and verifiable characteristics of enrollees (for example, age, gender, diagnoses, or past treatment expenditures). This process is known as risk adjustment. Accurate risk adjustment would allow a purchaser to contract out to competing private providers without fear of selection inefficiencies. However, risk adjustment is currently not widespread, and where it does exist it is limited in accuracy.[66] The incentives for risk selection can also be reduced by tempering payment incentives.[67]

Nonprofit and public providers are not immune to incentives for profitable patient sorting. Indeed, many transitional economies have discovered their susceptibility. For example, preliminary analysis documents significant risk segmentation among competing Czech nonprofit, for-profit, and government insurers, although to what extent this reflects a welfare loss remains a question for further research.[68] The Czech Republic was the first country in eastern Europe to implement a (simple demographic) risk adjustment system. Experience from other transitional economies suggests that selection is a concern even when virtually all insurers and providers remain government owned.[69] Such entities still have revenue concerns, especially if they face a relatively hard budget constraint; but public ownership, by retaining ultimate control in the hands of state authorities, constrains public providers in their opportunities and flexibility to engage in risk selection.[70] Attention to these issues of heterogeneity and selection is critical for accurate analysis of the distributional and efficiency effects of ownership structure and competition, not only in health-care markets but in any market in which the cost of service depends on the individual served.[71]

SOFT BUDGET CONSTRAINTS. An organization enjoys a soft budget constraint if some institution (such as the government) will finance its deficit, enabling it to continue to operate despite consistently exceeding its budget.[72] Anticipation of soft budget constraints can seriously damage efficiency: a firm that expects a bailout can slack on its performance. In such a situation a purchaser that fails to impose a hard budget constraint will end up with the wrong producers or the wrong consumption bundle or both—in effect subsidizing inefficiency.

The combination of a government commitment to serve as a provider of last resort and the lack of control rights of government facility managers suggests that soft budget constraints may present particular challenges to vertically integrated government provision of services. Indeed, empirical evidence supports the view that public health-care providers face soft budget constraints. For example, in his study of the response of public, private for-profit, and nonprofit hospitals to a change in financing, Duggan finds that "the critical difference between the three types of hospitals is caused by the soft budget constraint of government-owned institutions."[73]

In eastern Europe, the legacy of soft budget constraints for government-owned providers continues to plague the reforming health-care systems, including newly established social insurance institutions. In several nations (Hungary and Croatia, for example), any deficit in the social insurance fund is the legal responsibility of the government. It is no surprise that this soft budget constraint has lead to sustained and sizable deficits in social insurance funds in those countries, in contrast with others, such as Slovenia, that lack similar guarantees. In 1998, the Polish Finance Ministry carried out an extensive bailout of the Polish health sector, which had amassed debts equivalent to several billion dollars.[74]

The tendency of government health-care providers to operate with soft budget constraints suggests that for-profit and nonprofit private providers have a comparative advantage in providing services for which the inefficiencies of persistent refinancing of deficits outweigh the benefits of reduced incentives for both quality-damaging cost control and inefficient sorting of patients. However, it is important to note that the susceptibility of public providers to soft budget constraints does not mean that public delivery systems will generally have higher expenditures than private delivery systems; in fact, quite the opposite is true. Public providers in many contexts (for example, in several eastern European countries) must operate under a chronic shortage of funding, even if a soft budget constraint precludes closure. A vertically integrated delivery system such as the United Kingdom's National Health Service must compete with other sectors in the political arena for public revenues and is frequently associated with a lower percentage of gross domestic product (GDP) allocated to health care (see table 2-1). By contrast, contracted private providers may become adept at political lobbying for additional funding (for example, for expensive high technology), effectively softening the budget constraint on overall health spending.[75]

Government Purchase and Pluralistic Delivery: Suggestive Evidence on Patterns of Comparative Advantage

To what extent do allocations of services across ownership forms in health-care delivery systems correspond to the patterns of comparative advantage suggested by the analysis presented in this chapter? This is an important area for future research. We do not attempt any formal "test" of the theory here, but we can offer some suggestive evidence that contracting out is an important policy question and that the comparative advantage framework can be a useful guide for analysis of specific health sectors.

Government Purchase of Health Care

Almost half of total spending on health services in the United States comes from public sources, and governments in most other industrialized countries finance a significantly larger percentage of health spending, if (as is standard) compulsory social insurance contributions are counted as public financing (see table 2-1). Public funds finance more than three-fifths of total health expenditures in high-income countries.[76] The public share of health spending averages almost three-quarters in the countries of the European Monetary Union and comprises an average of 6.6 percent of gross domestic product. These averages hide significant variation in the public share of national health expenditures, even across western European nations (see table 2-2).[77]

The starting point for the countries of eastern Europe before 1990 was public financing and public delivery of almost all health care, in line with the model of the Soviet Union. During the past decade of postsocialist transition, state budget financing was being replaced by compulsory social insurance, supplemented by private financing. The latter, including formal out-of-pocket payments, private insurance, and under-the-table payments, represents a small but probably underestimated share of health spending.[78]

Pluralistic Delivery

Ownership structures of health sectors are diverse, though public and nonprofit providers are prevalent. In the United States, almost every segment of the health-care sector includes a mix of public, private for-profit, and private not-for-profit providers, although the mix varies considerably by medical service (see table 2-3). The private sector dominates, except for psychiatric hospitals. Nonprofits play a particularly important role in the health sector, especially for hospitals, hospices, and blood banks. For-profits represent only about 16 percent of community hospitals and account for less than 12 percent of all hospital admissions.[79] Investor-owned firms represent about two-thirds of the nursing home market and 68 percent of non-hospital-based dialysis centers.[80] For-profit organizations are also prevalent in managed care. The majority of HMO enrollees belong to for-profit organizations.[81]

Ownership in the U.S. health sector suggests a moderate pattern of comparative advantage. A government role in provision has been particularly strong for services with elements of a public good or with large externalities; examples include control of communicable diseases (tuberculosis and venereal diseases) and provision of substance abuse and severe mental health services, partly because of public safety concerns.[82] Private ownership is common for services consumers can readily judge and for which they plan, such as health insurance and dental care, and for much outpatient care.

Table 2-3. *Ownership Composition of the U.S. Health Sector, Various Years, 1990–97*
Percent

Service, unit, and year	Private Nonprofit	Private For-profit	Government Federal	Government State and local
All Hospitals				
Admissions, 1997	68.1	11.8	3.7	14.0
Outpatient visits, 1997	63.4	7.9	11.7	15.2
Community hospitals				
Facilities, 1997	59.3	15.8	0	24.9
Beds, 1997	69.2	13.5	0	17.3
Admissions, 1997	72.5	12.5	0	15.0
Outpatient visits, 1997	73.4	9.1	0	17.6
Psychiatric hospitals				
Facilities, 1991	11	21		67
Beds, 1991	3	6		91
HMO enrollment, 1995	42	58		~0
PPO plans, 1995	20	80		~0
Blood bank facilities, 1990s	~100	~0		~0
Home health care				
Agencies, 1991	36.7	40.6		22.5
Clients, 1991	55.3	28.0		15.9
Nursing homes				
Homes, 1996	26.2	65.9		7.9
Beds, 1996	24.1	66.7		9.2
Hospices				
Facilities, 1991	88.1	5.0		5.4
Clients, 1991	77.6	16.1		5.9

Sources: National Center for Health Statistics, *Health, United States, 1999, with Health and Aging Chartbook* (Hyattsville, Md., 1999); for home health agencies and hospices, see the 1991 National Health Provider Inventory, as summarized in Renee Delfosse, "Hospice and Home Health Agency Characteristics: United States, 1991," *Vital and Health Statistics* (of the National Center for Health Statistics), vol. 13 (April 1995), pp. 1–33; for nursing homes, see the 1996 Nursing Home Component of the Medical Expenditure Panel Survey, as summarized in Jeffrey Rhoades, D. E. B. Potter, and Nancy Krauss, *Nursing Homes: Structure and Selected Characteristics, 1996,* MEPS Research Findings 4, AHCPR Pub. 98-0006 (Rockville, Md.: Agency for Health Care Policy and Research, 1998); for psychiatric hospital beds, see Susan Rose-Ackerman, "Altruism, Nonprofits, and Economic Theory," *Journal of Economic Literature*, vol. 34 (June 1996), pp. 701–28, table 4, p. 710; for PPOs, see Gary Claxton, Judith Feder, David Shactman, and Stuart Altman, "Public Policy Issues in Nonprofit Conversions: An Overview," *Health Affairs*, vol. 16 (March–April 1997), pp. 9–28, p. 12; for HMO enrollment, see Jon R. Gabel, "Ten Ways HMOs Have Changed during the 1990s," *Health Affairs*, vol. 16 (May–June 1997), pp. 134–45, p. 135.

Note: Numbers may not sum to 100 percent if a small "other" category cannot be attributed to one of these ownership forms. Community hospitals are short-term hospitals excluding hospital units in institutions such as prison and college infirmaries, facilities for the mentally retarded, and alcoholism and chemical dependency hospitals.

Nonprofits fall in between public and for-profit private provision, dominating in areas, such as blood banks, in which market failures are rife (in the form of asymmetry of information about the quality and safety of a donor's blood and problems of adverse selection if paying for donations) or the profit motive is symbolically objectionable (owing to a distaste for market allocation of God-given resources, such as blood).

This is not to suggest, however, that the ownership structure of the United States approximates the ideal, even the ideal understood from a comparative advantage point of view. One may wonder, for example, how appropriate it is to have for-profit organizations dominate among nursing home providers, given the vulnerability of the residents, mostly frail elderly, and hence the opportunities for unobserved quality-damaging cost cutting in the provision of this service.[83] For-profits have an advantage in access to capital and are much more responsive to its demands; this fact helps to explain their dominance in nursing homes (which came upon the scene quite suddenly once the government agreed to pay for their services under Medicaid and Medicare) and their general willingness to undertake transitions (for example, to eliminate surplus hospital beds).[84] Nonprofit providers will thrive only in supportive regulatory and capital market environments (for example, under the Hill-Burton federal grant program for nonprofit hospitals in the United States, a program not replicated for nursing homes).[85]

In eastern Europe, private sector delivery has begun to develop, although its share of health service volume generally remains in the low single digits.[86] The pace of reforms has varied across the region, partly for ideological reasons.[87] Privatization has been most extensive for dentists and pharmacies, whereas most inpatient care is delivered by public entities (table 2-4). Entry by private providers has generally been allowed since the early 1990s, leading to the rapid growth of private individual and small group practices. A growing share of eastern European clinicians practice in both the public and private sectors.[88] Spending on private insurance is trivial except in Slovenia, where it constitutes 12 percent of total health expenditures.

Although a convergence to equilibrium in eastern Europe may take many years, the emerging ownership pattern seems to be broadly in line with comparative advantage. The private sector share has increased most markedly for those services in which patients can discern quality and make informed choices among competing providers (such as dentistry and pharmacies); public ownership continues to dominate other parts of the delivery system (such as inpatient facilities and public health services). Caution

Table 2-4. *Share of Private Health-Care Providers in Eastern Europe, 1997*
Percent

Country	Inpatient beds	Primary care physicians	Dentists	Pharmacies	Private insurance as share of total health expenditure
Bulgaria	~0	Minor	82	70	<1
Croatia	~0	Minor	96	~100	<1
Czech Republic	9.4	95	~100	~100	<1
Hungary	~0	76	40[a]	~100[a]	<1
Poland	~0	Minor	~100[a]	93	<1
Romania	~0	Minor	~100	75	<1
Slovakia	~0	98	~100	100	1[b]
Slovenia[a]	~0	14	37	68	12

Source: János Kornai and Karen Eggleston, *Welfare, Choice, and Solidarity in Transition: Reforming the Health Sector in Eastern Europe* (Cambridge University Press, 2001).
a. 1998.
b. 1995.

is warranted, however, as there is considerable historical path dependency in health sector development, and privatized delivery or financing can easily become institutionally entrenched even if it deviates considerably from principles of comparative advantage.[89]

Conclusion

The distribution of public, private for-profit, and private nonprofit health-care providers in any given country reveals the tracings of history and ideology, with the evolution of ownership patterns heavily path dependent.[90] However, economic analysis of relative efficiency can and should play a role, at least in determining the comparative advantage of different ownership forms for delivery of different health services. Our application of the property rights theory of ownership to the distinctive features of health-care contracting supports the following conclusions:

—Public (or sometimes private nonprofit) providers have a comparative advantage for health services that exhibit some combination of the following characteristics: they are hard to contract;[91] they involve pure public goods or high externalities; they are not monitorable by patients, in the sense that patients can discern provider quality distortions; and they are highly susceptible to inefficient patient sorting. Examples might include care for the severely mentally ill, population-based health initiatives, blood banks, and long-term care for elderly.

—Private providers have a comparative advantage for services that combine one or more of the following features: they are readily contractible; quality is monitorable by patients (directly or through provider reputation); they are susceptible to competition; they are not amenable to dumping of unprofitable patients, or risk adjustment of payment is feasible and reasonably accurate; and incentives for rapid quality innovation are more valuable than low-powered incentives for quality-damaging cost control. Examples include elective surgery and most dental care, as well as the provision of drugs and many aspects of primary care.

—The profit status of a private provider is another key consideration. Our model supports prior analyses in the general view that nonprofits have a comparative advantage over for-profits where expensive monitoring hampers competition as a device for quality assurance and where contracting is not possible on variables critical in determining quality.[92]

—For health care, ownership form can be important, but other factors are also critical, including competition, payment incentives, and hardness of budget constraints (for both public and private providers). How to contract out matters as much as whether, and to whom, to do so.

—The sorting of health-care facilities among ownership forms in many nations appears to a considerable extent to respect principles of comparative advantage. Factors such as history and access to capital may impede this process. Focusing on comparative advantage and policy mechanisms that facilitate its operation can be effective and beneficial.

Our analysis in this chapter has focused on health care. However, most of the principles set forth apply to a wide range of services.

Notes

1. See Oliver Hart and John Moore, "Property Rights and the Nature of the Firm," *Journal of Political Economy*, vol. 98 (1990), pp. 1119–58; Oliver Hart, *Firms, Contracts, and Financial Structure* (Oxford University Press, 1995); Oliver Hart, Andrei Shleifer, and Robert Vishny, "The Proper Scope of Government: Theory and an Application to Prisons," *Quarterly Journal of Economics* (November 1997), pp. 1127–61.

2. Oliver E. Williamson, *The Economic Institutions of Capitalism* (Free Press, 1985); Sandy Grossman and Oliver Hart, "The Costs and Benefits of Ownership: A Theory of Vertical and Lateral Integration," *Journal of Political Economy*, vol. 94 (1986), p. 691. The incomplete contracting approach recognizes that contracts are difficult to write in sufficient detail to cover all possible contingencies, so any contract will contain gaps or ambiguities. This contract incompleteness bestows power on owners, who enjoy the right to control the relevant asset in any circumstance not explicitly delegated to others by contract. See the discussion in Hart, *Firms, Contracts, and Financial Structure*.

3. Kenneth J. Arrow, "Uncertainty and the Welfare Economics of Medical Care," *American Economic Review*, vol. 53 (December 1963), pp. 941–73; Ching-to Albert Ma and Thomas G. McGuire, "Optimal Health Insurance and Provider Payment," *American Economic Review*, vol. 87 (September 1997), pp. 685–704.

4. David Dranove and Mark A. Satterthwaite, "The Industrial Organization of Health Care Markets," in Anthony J. Culyer and Joseph P. Newhouse, eds., *Handbook of Health Economics*, vol. 1B (Amsterdam: Elsevier Science, North Holland, 2000), pp. 1093–139; Arrow, "Uncertainty and the Welfare Economics of Medical Care."

5. In a recent survey of fifty leading U.S. health economists, 81 percent agreed with the statement that "the primary reason for the increase in the health sector's share of GDP over the past 30 years is technological change in medicine" (Victor R. Fuchs, "Economics, Values, and Health Care Reform," *American Economic Review*, vol. 86 [March 1996], pp. 1–24, p. 227).

6. Richard Zeckhauser, "Directed Goods," memorandum, May 1990, Harvard University, John F. Kennedy School of Government.

7. The redistribution, of course, need not go to the poor. The monies could go to the schools, helping the young; to hospital services, helping the sick; or to "high culture," providing benefits to artistically inclined consumers—who are disproportionately represented among high-income individuals. Ordinary income transfers are a special and important case of directed goods.

8. Twenty-nine members in 1999, at the time the data for table 2-1 were published. The Slovak Republic became the thirtieth member in September 2001.

9. Drawing upon the experiences of the 191 member countries of the World Health Organization, the report emphasizes the importance of strategic purchasing, payment incentives, and risk pooling and discusses the organization of health service delivery without explicitly attending to, or making recommendations regarding, public versus private ownership. The WHO's assessment system is based on five indicators: the overall level of population health, health disparities within the population, the overall level and the overall distribution of health system responsiveness (including patient satisfaction), and the distribution of the health system's financial burden within the population (World Health Organization, *World Health Report 2000, Health Systems: Improving Performance* [Geneva, 2000]).

10. The poor showing of the United States is attributable to low ratings on some measures—for example, equity in distribution of health status and fairness of financial contribution—despite advanced medical capabilities and high health expenditures.

11. See, for example, Robert Blendon, Minah Kim, and John M. Benson, "The Public versus the World Health Organization on Health System Performance," *Health Affairs*, vol. 20, no. 3 (2001), pp. 10–20.

12. Private employers may place a higher value on cost control than does the government, or they may be less concerned about access and inefficient sorting of patients (because they can "free ride" on public insurance programs and may wish to attract or retain only relatively healthy employees). An employer might also wish to encourage an employee to seek coverage through a spouse's employer (David Dranove, Kathryn E. Spier, and Laurence Baker, "'Competition' among Employers Offering Health Insurance," *Journal of Health Economics,* vol. 19, no. 1 [2000], pp. 121–40).

13. For example, "yardstick competition" among ownership forms provides valuable information to the purchaser as well as incentives for the providers, as we discuss briefly under the section on competition for patients. A purchaser may find having a mixed for-profit and nonprofit hospital sector useful for measuring the amount of community benefits a nonprofit should provide to justify tax exemption (see Sean Nicholson, Mark V. Pauly, Lawton R. Burns, Agnieshka Baumritter, and David A. Asch, "Measuring Community Benefits Provided by For-Profit and Nonprofit Hospitals," *Health Affairs,* vol. 19, no. 6 [2000], pp. 168–77). R. A. Hirth, "Consumer Information and Competition between Nonprofit and For-Profit Nursing Homes," *Journal of Health Economics,* vol. 18, no. 2 (1999), pp. 219–40, emphasizes quality spillovers from nonprofits operating in mixed industries. A mix of public and private providers may also be important for issues of legal accountability; John L. Akula, "Sovereign Immunity and Health Care: Can Government Be Trusted?" *Health Affairs,* vol. 19, no. 6 (2000), pp. 152–67, suggests that "when government is regulator and a major player but the delivery system is primarily private, accountability at the point of delivery remains high. The 'tone' of the relatively small public delivery system is perhaps best maintained by the spillover of standards and expectations shaped by the private system" (p. 165). This latter point is closely related to professionalization and normative pressures for institutional isomorphism (Paul J. DiMaggio and Walter W. Powell, "The Iron Cage Revisited: Institutional Isomorphism and Collective Rationality in Organizational Fields," *American Sociological Review,* vol. 48, no. 2 [1983], pp. 147–60).

14. Frank A. Sloan, "Not-for-Profit Ownership and Hospital Behavior," in Anthony J. Culyer and Joseph P. Newhouse, eds., *Handbook of Health Economics,* vol. 1B (Amsterdam: Elsevier Science, North Holland, 2000), pp. 1141–74.

15. E. B. Keeler, L. V. Rubenstein, K. L. Kahn, D. Draper, E. R. Harrison, M. J. McGinty, W. H. Rogers, and R. H. Brook, "Hospital Characteristics and Quality of Care," *Journal of the American Medical Association,* vol. 268, no. 13 (1992), pp. 1709–14.

16. Laura A. Peterson, Sharon-Lise T. Normand, Jennifer Daley, and Barbara McNeil, "Outcome of Myocardial Infarction in Veterans Health Administration Patients as Compared with Medicare Patients," *New England Journal of Medicine,* vol. 343 (December 28, 2000), pp. 1934–41.

17. Sloan, "Not-for-Profit Ownership and Hospital Behavior."

18. To what extent knowledge itself constitutes a community benefit (as opposed to a broader public good) is less clear.

19. For example, Medicare Payment Advisory Commission (MedPAC), "A Data Book on Hospital Financial Performance," in *Report to the Congress: Selected Medicare Issues,* June 2000, appendix C, pp. 175–92 (available at www.medpac.gov [August 1, 2001]), reports that the ratio of uncompensated care to cost in 1998 was 9.8 percent for urban government hospitals and 4.7 percent for rural government hospitals, compared with 4.5 percent for voluntary and 4.2 percent for proprietary hospitals (p. 190). The largest single category for

provision of uncompensated care is public major teaching hospitals (12 percent, compared with 5 percent for private major teaching hospitals).

20. Richard Zeckhauser, Jayendu Patel, and Jack Needleman, *The Economic Behavior of For-Profit and Nonprofit Hospitals: The Impact of Ownership on Responses to Changing Reimbursement and Market Environments*, report prepared for the Robert Wood Johnson Foundation (Harvard University, John F. Kennedy School of Government, March 1995), p. 107.

21. Janet Currie and John Fahr, "Managed Care and Hospital Provision of Charity Care: The Case of California," *RAND Journal of Economics* (forthcoming, 2002). Looking at charity care provided by California hospitals between 1988 and 1996, Currie and Fahr find that in response to higher managed-care penetration, public hospitals end up with higher shares of uninsured patients and higher fractions of the charity caseload admitted from the emergency room (suggesting sicker patients).

22. Jack Needleman, Deborah J. Chollet, and Joann Lamphere, "Uncompensated Care and Hospital Conversions in Florida," *Health Affairs*, vol. 18, no. 4 (1999), pp. 125–33. The authors studied hospital conversions in Florida between 1981 and 1996. After controlling for year, number of beds, teaching status, and metropolitan location, they find that public hospitals had substantially higher levels of uncompensated care than their private counterparts, and privatization to for-profit status of four public hospitals led to a large decline in uncompensated care. Kamal Desai, Carol VanDeusen Lukas, and Gary J. Young, "Public Hospitals: Privatization and Uncompensated Care," *Health Affairs*, vol. 19, no. 2 (2000), pp. 167–72, examines care in fifty-two privatized hospitals in three states (California, Florida, and Texas) between 1981 and 1995 (fifteen were changed to for-profit status and thirty-seven to nonprofit status). They find that "public hospitals that privatized provided significantly less uncompensated care before privatization than did other public hospitals, both before and after privatization," suggesting some sorting by ownership form; "public hospitals that converted to nonprofit status generally sustained their levels of uncompensated care," but "public hospitals that converted to for-profit status showed a significant decline in the level of uncompensated care they provided" (p. 170).

23. Bradford H. Gray, "Conversions of HMOs and Hospitals: What's at Stake?" *Health Affairs*, vol. 16, no. 2 (1997), pp. 29–47, p. 40.

24. Elaine Silverman and Jonathan Skinner, "Are For-Profit Hospitals Really Different? Medicare 'Upcoding' and Market Structure," *RAND Journal of Economics* (forthcoming, 2002).

25. For example, the largest U.S. hospital company, the for-profit Healthcare Company (HCA), will pay criminal and civil penalties totaling more than $800 million for submitting inflated bills to the government and paying kickbacks to doctors for referrals (Kurt Eichenwald, "HCA to Pay $95 Million in Fraud Case," *New York Times*, December 15, 2000).

26. Some studies suggest that nonprofits provide community benefits in excess of the value of their tax exemptions, but there are wide variations, and "if [for-profits were to] include the amount of tax they pay as community benefits, they generally would be found to provide more community benefits than [nonprofits]" (David Shactman and Stuart H. Altman, "The Impact of Hospital Conversions on the Healthcare Safety Net," in Stuart Altman, Uwe Reinhardt, and Alexandra Shields, eds., *The Future U.S. Healthcare System:*

Who Will Care for the Poor and Uninsured? [Chicago: Health Administration Press, 1998], pp. 189–206, 199). Other recent studies find nonprofits seem to be falling short of expected levels of community benefits (Nicholson et al., "Measuring Community Benefits Provided by For-Profit and Nonprofit Hospitals").

27. DiMaggio and Powell, "The Iron Cage Revisited: Institutional Isomorphism and Collective Rationality in Organizational Fields"; Edward C. Norton and Douglas O. Staiger, "How Hospital Ownership Affects Access to Care for the Uninsured," *RAND Journal of Economics*, vol. 25 (Spring 1994), pp. 171–85; for discussion of the latter point, see, for example, Shactman and Altman, "The Impact of Hospital Conversions on the Healthcare Safety Net."

28. See, for example, Mark V. Pauly, "Nonprofit Firms in Medical Markets," *AEA Papers and Proceedings*, vol. 77 (May 1987), pp. 257–62; Frank A. Sloan, G. A. Picone, D. H. Taylor Jr., and S.-Y. Chou, "Hospital Ownership and Cost and Quality of Care: Is There a Dime's Worth of Difference?" *Journal of Health Economics*, vol. 20, no. 1 (2001), pp. 1–21; Susan L. Ettner and Richard C. Hermann, "The Role of Profit Status under Imperfect Information: Evidence from the Treatment Patterns of Elderly Medicare Beneficiaries Hospitalized for Psychiatric Diagnoses," *Journal of Health Economics*, vol. 20, no. 1 (2001), pp. 23–49.

29. Zeckhauser, Patel, and Needleman, *The Economic Behavior of For-Profit and Nonprofit Hospitals: The Impact of Ownership on Responses to Changing Reimbursement and Market Environments*.

30. Daniel P. Kessler and Mark B. McClellan, "The Effects of Hospital Ownership on Medical Productivity," *RAND Journal of Economics* (forthcoming, 2002).

31. David Blumenthal and Joel S. Weissman, "Selling Teaching Hospitals to Investor-Owned Hospital Chains: Three Case Studies," *Health Affairs*, vol. 19, no. 2 (2000), pp. 158–66. In this study of three teaching hospitals sold to investor-owned hospital chains, the authors find, for example, no measurable adverse impact of the ownership change on the hospitals' social missions, including teaching, research, and indigent care.

32. Ibid., p. 158.

33. Sloan, "Not-for-Profit Ownership and Hospital Behavior," p. 1168.

34. For simplicity, we abstract from the multiple layers of relationships between principal and agent within the delivery institution, although similar incentive and contracting problems are likely to arise between each layer (for example, between a health plan and its physicians).

35. The statement is qualified because our model of nonprofits does posit a different preference structure, albeit with for-profit preferences as a special case.

36. B. R. Klein and Armen A. Alchian, "Vertical Integration, Appropriable Rents, and the Competitive Contracting Process," *Journal of Law and Economics*, vol. 21, no. 2 (1978), pp. 297–326.

37. See, for example, the pioneering work of Joseph P. Newhouse, "Toward a Theory of Nonprofit Institutions," *American Economic Review*, vol. 60 (March 1970), pp. 64–74. More recently, Randall Ellis, "Creaming, Skimping, and Dumping: Provider Competition on the Intensive and Extensive Margins," *Journal of Health Economics*, vol. 17, no. 5 (1998), pp. 537–55, analyzes the incentive for competing hospitals to "dump" unprofitable patients by assuming that hospitals dump patients in relation to overall hospital profitability (not the profitability of individual patients) and must reach a minimum level of profit. Such a hos-

pital would exhibit a kinked indifference curve, with extreme reluctance to incur costs beyond the break-even point.

38. See Hart, Shleifer, and Vishny, "The Proper Scope of Government: Theory and an Application to Prisons."

39. This may be in part a function of the government budgeting process, wherein money G saves by coming in under budget one year is usually returned to the treasury. Although multiyear budgeting may help to alleviate the loss of cost control incentives associated with this phenomenon (as Guy Stuart has suggested), lack of longer-term control rights for government managers seems to be a fundamental characteristic of public sector provision.

40. Note that the fidelity of G arises from lack of control rights, not from an assumption of innately differing preferences.

41. The empirical literature is briefly reviewed in the previous discussion on performance differences by ownership type. Commenting on quality, the General Accounting Office notes in a report to Congress that the "VA was slow to take advantage of changes in medical technology"; assessing cost reduction, the General Accounting Office observes that "between 1975 and 1995, the number of community hospitals decreased by about 12 percent. During the same 20-year period, VA did not close any hospitals because of declining utilization" (*VA Hospitals: Issues and Challenges for the Future,* GAO/HEHS-98-32 [U.S. General Accounting Office, April 1998], pp. 5–6).

42. See Hart, Shleifer, and Vishny, "The Proper Scope of Government: Theory and an Application to Prisons."

43. See, for example, Burton A. Weisbrod, *The Voluntary Non-Profit Sector: Economic Theory and Public Policy* (Lexington, Mass.: Lexington Books, 1977); Henry Hansmann, "The Role of Non-Profit Enterprise," *Yale Law Journal,* vol. 91 (November 1980), pp. 54–100; and Susan Rose-Ackerman, "Altruism, Nonprofits, and Economic Theory," *Journal of Economic Literature,* vol. 34 (June 1996), pp. 701–28.

44. See, for example, Newhouse, "Toward a Theory of Nonprofit Institutions"; Mark V. Pauly and Michael Redisch, "The Non-Profit Hospital as a Physician Cooperative," *American Economic Review,* vol. 63 (March 1973), pp. 87–100; Sloan, "Not-for-Profit Ownership and Hospital Behavior."

45. Hart, *Firms, Contracts, and Financial Structure.*

46. In many nonprofits, it is not clear who the principals are; the obvious candidates include the board, employees, donors, and clients.

47. Hansmann, "The Role of Non-Profit Enterprise."

48. See, for example, Newhouse, "Toward a Theory of Nonprofit Institutions."

49. Moral hazard refers to the tendency of (typically well-insured) patients and their providers to utilize medical services even if the health improvement benefit they offer does not justify their cost.

50. The nonprofit label in fact may constitute a social loss, in that society forgoes the services that could be purchased with tax revenues from the nonprofit, and the nonprofit, by avoiding taxes, may gain an unfair market advantage over for-profit competitors.

51. Mark G. Duggan, "Hospital Market Structure and the Behavior of Not-for-Profit Hospitals: Evidence from Responses to California's Disproportionate Share Program," Working Paper 7966 (Cambridge, Mass.: National Bureau of Economic Research, October 2000).

52. Richard Arnold, Marianne Bertrand, and Kevin F. Hallock, "Does Managed Care Change the Mission of Nonprofit Hospitals? Evidence from the Managerial Labor Market," *RAND Journal of Economics* (forthcoming, 2002).

53. Silverman and Skinner, "Are For-Profit Hospitals Really Different? Medicare 'Upcoding' and Market Structure."

54. Arrow, "Uncertainty and the Welfare Economics of Medical Care."

55. Monitorable and prestigious aspects of quality are often associated with technology, such as magnetic resonance imaging (MRI) machines and other cutting-edge equipment, rather than lower-tech aspects, such as time spent interpreting tests for each patient.

56. These issues are discussed in considerably more detail in Karen Eggleston and Richard Zeckhauser, "Ownership and Purchase of Health Care: An Incomplete Contracting Approach," Harvard University, John F. Kennedy School of Government, April 1, 2001, mimeographed.

57. See discussion in Thomas G. McGuire, "Physician Agency," in Anthony J. Culyer and Joseph P. Newhouse, eds., *Handbook of Health Economics*, vol. 1A (Amsterdam: Elsevier Science, North Holland, 2000), pp. 461–536; and David M. Cutler and Richard J. Zeckhauser, "The Anatomy of Health Insurance," in Anthony J. Culyer and Joseph P. Newhouse, eds., *Handbook of Health Economics*, vol. 1A (Amsterdam: Elsevier Science, North Holland, 2000), pp. 563–643.

58. Ulf G. Gerdtham and Bengt Jönsson, "International Comparisons of Health Expenditure: Theory, Data, and Econometric Analysis," in Anthony J. Culyer and Joseph P. Newhouse, eds., *Handbook of Health Economics*, vol. 1A (Amsterdam: Elsevier Science, North Holland, 2000), pp. 11–53.

59. Cutler and Zeckhauser, "The Anatomy of Health Insurance," table 7.

60. Alexander Preker and Richard Feacham, "Market Mechanisms and the Health Sector in Central and Eastern Europe," Technical Paper 293 (World Bank, February 1996), p. 35.

61. Jorgen Marree and Peter Groenewegen, *Back to Bismarck: Eastern European Health Care Systems in Transition* (Aldershot, England: Avebury, Ashgate Publishing, 1997), p. 64.

62. Thomas A. Massaro, Jiri Nemec, and Ivan Kalman, "Health System Reform in the Czech Republic: Policy Lessons from the Initial Experience of the General Health Insurance Company," *Journal of the American Medical Association*, vol. 271 (June 15, 1994), pp. 1870–74.

63. Indeed, a "perfectly altruistic" provider might choose the same package of quality innovations among services that it would choose if there were perfect monitoring by patients. Such an outcome would be infeasible if losing patients to competing providers would compromise the nonprofit's viability.

64. R. A. Hirth, M. E. Chernew, and S. M. Orzol, "Ownership, Competition, and Adoption of New Technologies and Cost-Saving Practices in a Fixed Price Environment," *Inquiry*, vol. 37 (Fall 2000), pp. 282–94.

65. Albert O. Hirschman, *Exit, Voice, and Loyalty: Responses to Decline in Firms, Organizations, and States* (Harvard University Press, 1970).

66. Patricia Seliger Keenan, Melinda J. Beeuwkes Buntin, Thomas G. McGuire, and Joseph P. Newhouse, "The Prevalence of Formal Risk Adjustment in Health Plan Purchasing," *Inquiry*, vol. 38 (Fall 2001), pp. 245–59.

67. Examples include extra payment for high-cost conditions or treatments and fee-for-service reimbursement for a share of all patients' expenditures (see Joseph P. Newhouse, "Reimbursing Health Plans and Health Providers: Efficiency in Production versus Selection," *Journal of Economic Literature*, vol. 34 [September 1996], pp. 1236–63).

68. Ágnes Benedict, "A Cseh Egészségügyi Reformról" (On the reform of the health sector in the Czech Republic), *Egészségügyi Gazdasági Szemle*, vol. 38 (2000), pp. 83–98.

69. For example, anecdotal evidence indicates that fixed payment systems have led providers in China to refer costly patients elsewhere: "administrators of a primary hospital openly admitted that they refused admission to patients who were seriously ill and referred them to secondary and tertiary hospitals" (Winnie Yip and William Hsiao, "Medical Savings Accounts: Lessons from China," *Health Affairs*, vol. 16, no. 6 [1997], pp. 244–51, p. 249).

70. In the United States, for example, "both VA's strategic goals and the incentives it is creating through some of its restructuring efforts suggest that VA, like many community hospitals, is focusing its marketing efforts on attracting revenue-generating patients" (*VA Hospitals: Issues and Challenges for the Future*, p. 5). Congressional concerns that the VA was not appropriately maintaining its level of certain high-cost specialized services—such as treatment for spinal cord dysfunction, blindness, amputation, and severe mental illness—fostered legislation to ensure that the volume of these services did not decline below 1996 levels (see the statement for the record by Stephen P. Backus, director of veterans' affairs and military health care issues, Health, Education, and Human Services Division, in *Veterans' Affairs: Progress and Challenges in Transforming Health Care*, GAO/Y-HEHS-99-109 [U.S. General Accounting Office, April 15, 1999], p. 13).

71. An analogy can be drawn to educational policy, in which concerns regarding market sorting—by student ability and income, similar to patient sorting—gives pause to policymakers otherwise eager to harness the benefits of privatization and competition—through vouchers, for example—to increase productivity, choice, accountability, and quality.

72. János Kornai, *Economics of Shortage* (Amsterdam: Elsevier Science, North Holland, 1980); János Kornai, "The Softness of the Budget Constraint," *Kyklos*, vol. 39, no. 1 (1986), pp. 3–30; János Kornai, "Legal Obligation, Non-compliance, and Soft Budget Constraint," in Peter Newman, ed., *New Palgrave Dictionary of Economics and the Law* (New York: Macmillan, 1998), pp. 533–39; Eric S. Maskin, "Theories of the Soft Budget-Constraint," *Japan and the World Economy*, vol. 8, no. 2 (1996), pp. 125–33.

73. Mark G. Duggan, "Hospital Ownership and Public Medical Spending," *Quarterly Journal of Economics* (November 2000), pp. 1343–73, p. 1343. See Karen Eggleston, Nolan Miller, and Richard Zeckhauser, "Ownership Structure and Provider Behavior," paper prepared for the 2001 conference of the International Health Economics Association, York, England, July 25, 2001, p. 1343, for a theoretical model of provider behavior that explicitly includes the phenomenon of the soft budget constraint.

74. János Kornai and Karen Eggleston, *Welfare, Choice, and Solidarity in Transition: Reforming the Health Sector in Eastern Europe* (Cambridge University Press, 2001).

75. Robert Blendon and Minah Kim, "Comments on the Eggleston and Zeckhauser Paper on Government Contracting for Health Care," Harvard University, John F. Kennedy School of Government, June 2001, mimeographed.

76. High-income countries are those whose per capita income in 1998 exceeded roughly nine thousand dollars.

77. Ideological factors presumably play a large role in determining this variation. There is little correlation between total health spending and the public share—that is, between the first and second columns of table 2-1 (a correlation coefficient of 0.01). There is a more significant, and negative, correlation between public share of financing and private share of inpatient beds (–0.4); we omit the United States in both calculations because it is an extreme outlier. János Kornai and John McHale analyze the trends in public financing of health expenditures in OECD countries from the 1970s to the 1990s. Their fixed-effect model finds significantly positive relationships among per capita public health expenditure, income, and the elderly share of the population. Although the public share has been fairly stable, this consistency hides conflicting trends—an increasing public sector role, associated with aging populations, offset by a decreasing time trend, which the authors speculate reflects "a long-lasting attempt to shrink the welfare state" (Kornai and John McHale, "Income, Technology, or Demographics? An Accounting for Trends in International Health Spending," Harvard University, Department of Economics, July 1999, p. 17).

78. Semilegal "gratuity" payments to physicians are both prevalent and of significant magnitude, especially in Hungary, Romania, Poland, and Bulgaria (see Kornai and Eggleston, *Welfare, Choice, and Solidarity in Transition: Reforming the Health Sector in Eastern Europe*). Including such payments would increase doctors' incomes by 100 percent or more in Poland (Mukesh Chawla, Tomasz Tomasik, Marzena Kulis, Adam Windak, and Deirdre A. Rogers, "Enrollment Procedures and Self-selection by Patients: Evidence from a Family Practice in Krakow, Poland," Discussion Paper 66 [Harvard University, School of Public Health, 1999]) and by 150 percent in Hungary (Géza Bognár, Róbert Iván Gál, and János Kornai, "Hálapénz a Magyar Egészségügyben" [Gratuity money in the Hungarian health sector], *Közgazdasági Szemle*, vol. 47 [April 2000], pp. 293–320), and even these estimates are likely to be conservative. The prevalence of under-the-table payments is consistent with health care as a directed good, one for which the government pays but a single individual is the overwhelming beneficiary. Given this property, it is to be expected that individuals will wish to voice their preferences and that some governments will grant them latitude, even if they speak through semilegal or illegal payments.

79. "If one includes the approximately 400 psychiatric, alcohol and chemical dependency, and rehabilitation hospitals owned by for-profit companies and the 350 nonprofit and public hospitals that these companies manage, the [for-profit] sector accounts for almost 32 percent of U.S. nonfederal hospitals and approximately 23 percent of the beds" (Bradford H. Gray, "Hospital Ownership Form and Care for the Uninsured," in Stuart Altman, Uwe Reinhardt, and Alexandra Shields, eds., *The Future U.S. Healthcare System: Who Will Care for the Poor and Uninsured?* [Chicago: Health Administration Press, 1998], pp. 207–22, p. 208).

80. MedPAC, "A Data Book on Hospital Financial Performance," p. 137.

81. Although table 2-3 lists the public share of HMOs as ~0 percent, there are public managed-care organizations, if initiatives of the Department of Defense and some other public purchasers are counted.

82. Richard G. Frank and Thomas G. McGuire, "Economics and Mental Health," in Anthony J. Culyer and Joseph P. Newhouse, eds., *Handbook of Health Economics*, vol. 1B (Amsterdam: Elsevier Science, North Holland, 2000), pp. 893–954.

83. Hansmann, "The Role of Non-Profit Enterprise."

84. Hirth, "Consumer Information and Competition between Nonprofit and For-Profit Nursing Homes." "Areas in which demand is growing rapidly are likely to have high for-profit market shares because the capital market constraints faced by [nonprofits] make rapid expansion difficult" (p. 235). Hirth therefore suggests using demand growth in a market as an instrumental variable for for-profit market share when studying ownership effects.

85. We are grateful to Robert Blendon and Minah Kim for this point.

86. Blendon and Kim, "Comments on the Eggleston and Zeckhauser Paper on Government Contracting for Health Care."

87. In some cases—primary care, dental and outpatient specialist practices in the Czech Republic, and individual practices in Slovakia and Croatia—privatization campaigns have specified deadlines for privatization of providers in certain categories.

88. For example, according to a survey conducted in Krakow (Chawla et al., "Enrollment Procedures and Self-selection by Patients: Evidence from a Family Practice in Krakow, Poland," p. 10), 1,096 specialists employed in the public sector also spent an average of 10.8 hours a week on private practice.

89. One example is the U.S. Medigap system of supplementary private insurance for Medicare, a system that has high administrative costs and would be more appropriately included in Medicare yet is politically and institutionally difficult to change. We are grateful for Joseph Newhouse for this point.

90. Eastern European countries, for example, are likely to continue to see a larger presence of state ownership in the health sector than economies that were never socialist.

91. For some goods and services, "the government cannot fully anticipate, describe, stipulate, regulate, and enforce exactly what it wants" (Andrei Shleifer, "State versus Private Ownership," *Journal of Economic Perspectives*, vol. 12, no. 4 [1998], pp. 137).

92. Hansmann, "The Role of Non-Profit Enterprise."

3

PETER FRUMKIN

Service Contracting with Nonprofit and For-Profit Providers: On Preserving a Mixed Organizational Ecology

SEEKING GREATER PROGRAMMATIC effectiveness and lower costs, government agencies have long contracted with both nonprofit and for-profit providers for the delivery of a broad range of human services.[1] In recent years, however, the stakes involved in many service-contracting decisions have changed. Public managers today are increasingly having to make judgments about the current and future structure of the provider marketplace that will have far-reaching implications for the organizations that deliver services, the clients who rely on these services, and the public that ultimately finances them. In many fields of human service delivery, the delicate population ecology of nonprofit and for-profit service providers is profoundly shaped by government contracting decisions because public funding represents a large and critical source of agency finance.[2] Thus, when public managers make decisions about the kind of organizations with which they will contract—nonprofit or for-profit—they simultaneously make choices not just about ways to achieve particular policy objectives but

The author gratefully acknowledges the support of Harvard's John F. Kennedy School of Government's Program on Innovations in American Government in the preparation of this chapter.

also about the nature and composition of the population of service providers that will emerge at the end of the process.

The ecology of nonprofit and for-profit service providers has proved over time to be far from stable. Business activity has expanded in many fields long dominated by nonprofit organizations.[3] Large for-profit corporations are now providing job training, child care, and rehabilitation services at ever greater levels. In health care, for-profit hospitals and health maintenance organizations are buying out nonprofit institutions and moving into new markets. In education, publicly traded firms have actively staked out a significant portion of the expanding charter-school market in states from Arizona to Florida. In welfare-to-work services, several large defense contractors have begun to compete for and win contracts. As these and many other sectoral boundary incursions have occurred and as for-profit providers have gained ground, nonprofit advocates have argued that it is now necessary to counter some of the real advantages that business firms possess to allow both nonprofit and for-profit providers to take part in the delivery of complex human services. All of this raises the difficult question of how to preserve a human service marketplace that includes both nonprofit and for-profit organizations.

Sorting out—through the allocation of government contracts—the division of labor between nonprofit and for-profit service providers ultimately requires an appreciation of the advantages and limitations of for-profit and nonprofit organizational forms and the careful balancing of competing values and priorities across a vast range of contexts.[4] In principle, at least, some important public services may be better delegated to for-profit than to nonprofit organizations. Equally true is the proposition that other services may well be handled best by nonprofit organizations. The central argument of this chapter is that preserving room for both nonprofit and for-profit service providers across a range of fields, at least for now, must be viewed as a managerial imperative, given the generally poor state of current knowledge about when and under what circumstances one kind of provider is likely to serve the public interest better than the other. Although significant differences in capacity and culture may allow business firms to beat out nonprofits for service contracts, especially in situations in which cost is a central concern, service contracting inevitably involves complex decisions about competing priorities—decisions that go well beyond the bottom line. The potential short-term gains generated by exclusive for-profit provision may not always be large enough to justify the wholesale—and potentially irreversible—shifts in the long-term organizational ecology of human service fields that may be fueled by government service contracting that prioritizes one kind of provider over another.

Nonprofit and For-Profit Provision of Services

As nonprofit managers survey the terrain of service contracting, many believe that the rise of for-profit providers of human services poses major strategic challenges and questions, not the least of which is how to hold on to the nonprofit sector's traditionally large market share and client base. Some nonprofit organizations, viewing the entry of business firms as a major threat, have attempted to respond to the new competition by becoming more businesslike in their own operations. This has sometimes led to the unreflective adoption of management tools such as total quality management, benchmarking, reengineering, and other techniques that promise to improve operations.[5] Other nonprofits have fallen back on the values and commitments that make the character and quality of their services unique. As a consequence, some nonprofits emphasize the commitment of their staff, the underlying values or faith guiding the organization, and the unique community connections that many small organizations possess.[6] Although these emphases may help some nonprofits manage their service delivery operations better in the short run, they are unlikely to be sufficient to stop the trend toward greater levels of for-profit service provision and the erosion of many nonprofits' position in the contracting regime.

In key areas, nonprofits appear to face substantial structural obstacles to competing successfully with business in the market for government contracts. Data on the relative growth of nonprofit and for-profit provision of human services suggest that business may be capitalizing on its advantages to capture a greater share of the human service markets that nonprofits have traditionally dominated. The data indicate that the number of for-profit providers of individual and family services, job training and vocational rehabilitation, day care for children, and residential care for the elderly and the infirm increased by 202 percent between 1977 and 1997, far faster than the number of nonprofit providers. During the same period, the workforce of for-profit human service providers increased by 273 percent, more than twice the growth rate within nonprofit establishments. Even the receipts of for-profit providers have increased at a faster pace than

Table 3-1. *Nonprofit and For-Profit Provision of Social Services, 1977 and 1997*
Units as indicated

Category	Nonprofit	For-profit
Number of establishments		
1977	40,983	23,104
1997	92,156	69,713
Change (percent)	124.9	201.7
Number of employees		
1977	676,473	177,449
1997	1,586,186	662,201
Change (percent)	134.5	273.2
Receipts (millions of dollars)		
1977	9,415	2,038
1997	75,683	18,894
Change (percent)	703.9	827.1

Source: U.S. Bureau of the Census, *Census of Service Industries* (1977, 1997).
Note: Social services include individual and family services, job training and vocational rehabilitation, day care for children, and residential care. Data for receipts not inflation adjusted.

those of nonprofits. Although in 1997 nonprofits still managed to capture a substantial portion of the overall growth in the fields, the success of for-profit activity has raised the question whether the division of labor between the sectors is beginning to undergo a reordering (see table 3-1).[7]

When the competition between sectors comes down to the cost, speed, and quantity of otherwise similar services, nonprofit human service providers face at least five serious competitive disadvantages compared with business firms.[8] Public managers seeking to understand the ecology of service providers must recognize that some of the disadvantages detailed below lend themselves to government action, whereas others clearly do not. The main task facing public sector service contractors in the years ahead will be to fashion a response that is sensitive to the need to preserve the mixed organizational ecology that now characterizes most human service fields.

Scale and Complexity Limitations

One of the most common concerns of nonprofit service providers is the scale limitations inherent in nonprofit enterprise. The financial and human resources of most nonprofit organizations limit their ability to mount complex, large-scale programs with the speed and ease possible for for-profit firms. Aside from a few highly visible national charities, nonprofit organizations are for the most part poorly financed and understaffed. They often are run on tight budgets, with narrow fund balances carrying them from year to year. In addition, small nonprofits, which make up much of the organizational population, lack experience with complex information technology and management systems, skills that are needed if they are to handle large caseloads and complex administrative requirements.[9]

The size problem confronting many nonprofits puts business firms in a strong position within the emerging human services contracting arena. In some instances the scale of human service contracts is simply enormous and requires a mastery of complex information technology. A grassroots or informal nonprofit organization that has focused its entire history on delivering quality services to a small community seems almost certain to flounder under some of the substantial management demands placed on organizations seeking large public contracts. Although some nonprofits may seek to create opportunities for themselves by pursuing smaller contracts at lower levels of government—contracts that include only direct client services and leave information-intensive reporting work to for-profit firms—coordinating such a division of labor over the long term will have substantial costs. Many nonprofit organizations simply lack the operational capacity to tackle large-scale contracts, including many of those recently put out for bid by states under U.S. welfare reform.

Availability of Capital

Simple undercapitalization can be a serious problem for nonprofit organizations, given that some government contracts often withhold part of the service fees until the client has been served or some documented outcome has been achieved.[10] In the rehabilitation services field, for example, a growing number of contracts pay providers small up-front fees for each client served and deliver the balance of the payment only after the client has completed his or her rehabilitation.[11] A contractor who receives payment only months after assisting a client must find a way to pay the up-front costs of delivering services while waiting for payment to arrive. Moreover, many contracted services require facilities that the service provider must either be able to acquire or already have in its possession. This can put substantial capital demands on nonprofit organizations.[12]

In terms of raising the funds needed to meet capital expenses, the positions of nonprofits and business firms could not be more different. Business has long been able to raise millions of dollars through a range of financial transactions. By contrast, most nonprofit officials concede that their firms are undercapitalized by charitable supporters, and few have revenue-generating operations large enough to support major capital outlays. Moreover, even if nonprofit managers could raise operating capital through loans or other means, they might well be subject to criticism from watchdog groups who accuse them of assuming too much risk and exposing their organizations to financial stress.[13]

Business firms have several tools at their disposal with which to raise capital. If they are just starting out, they may seek large amounts of funding and a long-term commitment from venture capital investors in exchange for a stake in the firm. Often this funding comes with the added bonus of an in-depth relationship in which investors lend management assistance to the firms in which they have a stake. Once a business firm reaches a certain level of operation, it has a second opportunity to raise capital in the equity markets. Through initial public offerings and routine stock offerings, business firms can command resources on a substantial scale. Through both venture capital and equities, business sells ownership stakes to outside parties. Businesses that do not want to relinquish ownership can raise funds through the bond market. These funds must eventually be repaid, but firms receive the benefit of being able to spread out major capital and research expenses over long periods of time.

Nonprofit organizations, on the other hand, cannot sell ownership stakes and are not in a position to take part in equity markets.[14] They can, however, and to a limited extent already do, use bonds to fund major capital projects. Most bond offerings to date have been confined to major institutions like hospitals, universities, and museums.[15] Few midsize nonprofits have been able to take part in the bond market and use these instruments to launch major expansion efforts. One reason bonds have not been a popular instrument of finance is the high transaction costs associated with evaluating, underwriting, and servicing them. In addition, few existing banks are willing to invest the effort to establish lending criteria in areas that lack an observable track record. As a consequence, only the largest nonprofits are able to meet the threshold at which a bond offering represents a viable option. Because many underwriters look not just at real estate in making decisions but also at reliable sources of income, nonprofits face a real challenge in convincing the lending community that their multiple revenue streams are sufficiently reliable and their assets sufficiently valuable to justify major financial commitments.[16]

Access to Power

Unlike business firms, public-serving nonprofits are somewhat limited in their ability to engage in lobbying, and this presents another stumbling block for nonprofits. Significant differences in style are obvious between the sectors in terms of the political messages they convey. Lobbyists for businesses often try to educate and inform government officials about the advantages of outsourcing and permitting for-profit competition in the human services. In some cases business firms have intervened in the design of the contracting systems under which their firms would eventually operate. One reason for this comfortable relationship is that business is able to present a message of efficiency to government. Nonprofits, on the other hand, often convey a message of equity and caring. Armed with political connections reinforced through campaign contributions and the potent claim of a strict bottom line, the capacity of business to shape the political and funding environment is more formidable than that of 501(c)(3) nonprofits, which face real limits on lobbying and political activity.[17]

Congress placed limits on the political activities of nonprofit service providers in 1976, though it took the Internal Revenue Service (IRS) fourteen years to issue final regulations.[18] Nonprofits that elect to come under the law agree to certain limits on the expenditure of money to influence legislation. The regulations differentiate between direct lobbying, which aims to shape legislation through communication with legislators, and grassroots lobbying, which is targeted at shaping public opinion. The 1976 law establishes ceilings on total lobbying expenditures, ranging from 20 percent of expenditures for tax-exempt purposes for smaller organizations up to a flat $1 million for organizations with budgets in excess of $17 million. One of the most widely acknowledged flaws in the current rules of government lobbying by public charities is that lobbying simply is not understood by nonprofit managers, who are often confused about how much lobbying activity is allowed before the 501(c)(3) status of a nonprofit becomes threatened. As a result, they tend to avoid lobbying entirely or to conduct it under the umbrella of a 501(c)(4) social welfare or advocacy organization, which does not offer contributors a tax deduction and faces no limits on political activities.

Compensation and Human Resources

Major corporations have been able to gain a competitive advantage by attracting and hiring—sometimes with lucrative offers—prominent and well-respected human service officials from both the public and nonprofit sectors for management positions in their growing for-profit human service divisions. High-profile expertise is more likely to go to for-profit human services providers, for the simple reason that an undercapitalized nonprofit can rarely offer a salary comparable to what large corporations can pay. As long as business can attract the best talent, as it has recently in the job training and welfare-to-work fields, nonprofit organizations are likely to face tough questions about whether they have the knowledge and expertise to compete at the highest levels.[19] Over time, if disparities between the sectors become too great, nonprofit organizations may face a real talent drain that will weaken the sector's competitive position.

For years government largely turned a blind eye to the difficult issues raised by compensation levels within the nonprofit sector. However, the IRS has recently set in place a new regulatory framework to guide compensation in public charities, along with a system of sanctions that government can now impose on organizations that fail to comply. The U.S. government has taken a position on the subject of how much nonprofit managers earn and attempted to regulate compensation levels in the sector for a number of reasons: because existing disclosure mechanisms are thought to be flawed and unreliable, because nonprofit boards have weak incentives to monitor, because several categories of nonprofits are substantially insulated from any market test, and because, even if stakeholders monitor diligently, compensation regulation may be necessary to ensure that charitable dollars are dedicated to public purposes. New regulations were finally enacted as part of the Taxpayer Bill of Rights in July 1996. In August 1998, the IRS released the details of its plan, and after receiving public comments it revised these regulations.[20] Rather than setting meaningful limits on nonprofit compensation, as was intended, the regulations are likely to have the exact opposite effect, allowing nonprofits to pay higher and higher salaries.

The new regulations define excessive compensation as that which "exceeds what is reasonable under all the circumstances." Compensation is reasonable "if it is only such amount as would ordinarily be paid for like services by like enterprises under like circumstances."[21] On the surface, this sounds like a fairly loose and porous standard, given the challenge to interpret "like enterprise" and "like circumstances." Because there is little case law in this area, the reasonable compensation definition by itself leaves organizations with little notice as to what is required of them and offers little protection to their expert judgment. To allow nonprofits to exercise this judgment with greater certainty, Congress placed a "rebuttable presumption" in the legislative history, a clause that the IRS adopted in its regulations. Charities may rely on a rebuttable presumption that their compensation decision was reasonable if the board that approved it was made up entirely of individuals unrelated to, and not subject to the control of, the applicant; obtains and relies on appropriate comparability of compensation data; and adequately documents the basis for its salary decision. Relevant data for demonstrating reasonableness include, among other things, compensation levels paid by similarly situated nonprofit and for-profit organizations for positions that are functionally comparable.

Although these new rules are not well understood by nonprofit organizations, over time, as the idea of constructing a rebuttable presumption using data on compensation at other nonprofit and for-profit firms takes hold, the lid will effectively be removed on nonprofit compensation. The intermediate sanctions regulations were initially designed to give government an alternative to simply closing down nonprofit organizations guilty of financial mismanagement. However, the protections built into the system effectively make it possible for nonprofits to pay their executives salaries equivalent to those of workers in the corporate sector. Of course, whether nonprofits will have the resources to do this and the extent to which their boards and donors will go along with such an approach remain uncertain.

Normative Constraints

Perhaps the most important obstacle that nonprofits face when attempting to compete with for-profit firms is the absence of both a profit motive and a willingness to cut corners when the bottom line so dictates. Some observers worry about the consequences of contracted payment systems that require specified reductions in the size of the welfare caseload or dictate payment of a fee whenever a client is successfully rehabilitated. One danger is that business firms will "cream" or "cherry-pick" clients by electing to work only with the most job-ready or least disabled clients while writing off those who face multiple barriers to employment. For-profit firms may be tempted to reduce caseloads by cutting off eligible recipients or by taking other steps to achieve performance standards without helping clients become better prepared to function in the work world.

The trend toward outcome funding and performance pay raises all kinds of challenges for nonprofits that want to provide services but have strong social missions and commitments.[22] Over time, increased competition with business firms for performance-based contracts will quite likely strain the identity of nonprofit agencies or lead to the slow erosion of funding. Faced with a choice between competition and capitulation, many nonprofits may reexamine their service delivery systems and look for ways to increase efficiency and effectiveness. Although this work may lead to improved nonprofit operations, it also risks cutting into the "low-return" charity work that nonprofit service organizations have traditionally undertaken. Special-needs clients, particularly in the fields of education, health care, and social services, may find changes in the quality and availability of their often higher-cost services as cross-sector competition and outcome-based funding take root.

It may be unwise to tamper with the cultural and ethical constraints that are part of the nonprofit sector's identity. Although nonprofits—particularly value- and faith-based organizations—may face real disadvantages in competing with for-profits in a market in which outcome funding emphasizes quick and frequent case closures, in many arenas the focus of nonprofits on human needs and long-term personal development are integral to program success. In many nonprofits the willingness to bend rules, the ability to make decisions that are related to mission not margin, and the dedication of staff allow these organizations to offer unique services.

Growing competition between nonprofits and businesses is significant because it ultimately risks narrowing the scope and vision of nonprofit organizations. As they become locked into increasingly fierce competitive struggles with businesses, nonprofit organizations risk becoming ever more instrumental in their approach. When nonprofit organizations are simply efficient intermediaries through which services are produced—efficient enough that differences in methods between the nonprofit sector and business become obscured—questions naturally arise as to why these organizations should be granted tax exemption. The competitive drive in some parts of the nonprofit sector to produce services at low cost is an important challenge to the sector's traditional charitable orientation.

Conceptual Needs for Service Contracting across Sectors

The differences between the for-profit and nonprofit forms of organization suggest that as government continues to shift a substantial portion of the responsibility for service delivery to providers outside of government, the ecology of for-profit and nonprofit organizations is likely to continue to shift over the coming decades, especially if business is able to capture the most lucrative and large-scale contracts that federal, state, and local governments make available. As a consequence, interpreting and reacting appropriately to the changing dynamics of the service-contracting landscape is likely to be a central challenge for governance. Given the importance of public funds in most human service fields, it is increasingly hard to avoid the conclusion that as public managers make difficult decisions about the criteria to use in making contracting decisions they will simultaneously be making decisions about the landscape of providers that is likely to emerge at the end of the process. What considerations should public managers therefore have in mind as they make these critical service-contracting decisions? The answer given here is that traditional, short-term considerations must be expanded to include an appreciation of the effects these decisions have on the long-term evolution of the ecology of service providers in the many fields of human services for which government funding represents a critical source of agency finance.

At first blush it might be tempting to deny that the issue of contracting needs to be complicated at all. Some might view the trend toward greater levels of for-profit provision as a sign that business firms not only enjoy competitive advantages over nonprofits but also offer better services. One might also conclude by looking at the growth of for-profit activity that clients simply find corporate forms of human service delivery superior to traditional nonprofit forms of assistance. These conclusions would be misplaced, however. Although a fair amount of evidence supports the contention that business firms have a competitive edge over nonprofits, there is almost no evidence that the services they render are of higher quality than those offered by nonprofit organizations. Indeed, evaluation research on the comparative performance of agencies across sectors is slim and contradictory.

Differences between nonprofit and for-profit forms of production have been analyzed in a select number of fields to determine whether substantial differences in service quality and cost can be located. Beyond some basic intuitions, the actual evidence is utterly conflicting and inconclusive.[23] Some studies have shown that nonprofit child care is of higher quality than for-profit alternatives; other studies have shown high levels of parental satisfaction with for-profit providers. Some studies have detected differences in the levels of uncompensated care in nonprofit as against for-profit hospitals, whereas others have not. Several studies have differed in their findings as to the comparable efficiency of for-profit and nonprofit hospitals.[24] Early evidence on the comparative performance of nonprofit and for-profit charter schools is not yet conclusive, though parent interest in and satisfaction with some for-profit schools appears strong. Government satisfaction with for-profit providers of job training has been sufficiently high to drive substantial growth in this field while at the same time raising concerns in some areas about the long-term effectiveness of these programs.[25]

In light of this confused trickle of evidence, the current capacity of public managers to speak authoritatively about the desired organizational ecology of different human services fields is minimal. As a consequence, the shifting presence of for-profit and nonprofit providers can hardly be interpreted in many fields as the result of careful planning or strategy. Moreover, the effects of some of the unplanned and unanticipated ecological shifts have not always been positive. Anecdotal evidence suggests that there may be a fair amount of concern about the expansion of for-profit human services. In the area of health insurance, there is a growing chorus of criticism about the effects of for-profit health maintenance organizations on the quality and accessibility of health services, a trend that has fueled calls for a bill of rights to protect patients. In the nursing home field, which has come to be dominated by for-profit firms, grave doubts have emerged about the capacity of the system to care compassionately for the coming tidal wave of elderly that the retirement of the baby-boom generation will create. Similar concerns have emerged in the area of welfare-to-work services, in which large corporations have established a significant presence. As corporations like Lockheed and Electronic Data Systems (EDS) have secured large state contracts, many community activists have questioned the degree to which these companies are able to provide the kind of help that is needed in the diverse communities in which clients reside, especially to those individuals who face multiple barriers to employment and who need long-term psychological and vocational support.

The paucity of good data on the comparative performance of nonprofit and for-profit service providers has led public managers to focus on the one area for which data is available, namely, cost. Many managers are drawn to the idea that cost should be the central factor in contracting decisions because measuring and comparing costs across proposals is far easier than making tough judgments about the quality of underlying service models or the qualifications of the providers. Political pressures and demands for fairness in the allocation of contracts also tend to push public managers to focus on service cost as the critical criterion in contract allocation. To focus entirely on the cost of service provision is, however, to set up a contracting system that will have the inevitable effect of favoring business firms over nonprofit organizations.

Without a more complex and sophisticated set of criteria, the long-term consequences of such an unreflective approach to contracting is likely to be the slow squeezing out of nonprofit providers from certain fields. This sort of ecological shift might seem to be a small price to pay for the ability of the public sector to economize on the costs of service delivery. However, there may well be unforeseen consequences to this kind of reorganization of sectoral responsibilities. Chief among these is the permanent disappearance of the "nonprofit option." In fields such as nursing home care, in which for-profit market penetration has been deep and complete, it is hard to imagine how a mixed ecology can ever be restored. The sectoral shift in the nursing home arena was accomplished to achieve economies, but it ultimately has had the effect of driving out nonprofit providers. Once a field has been purged of nonprofits, even if consumers want to restore a nonprofit option, policymakers may be unable to take meaningful action because the barriers to reentry for nonprofits are high and play into the sector's weaknesses in mobilizing large blocks of capital.

Because of the difficulty in reversing major ecological shifts in the organizational population, public managers need to radically expand the quality and breadth of their conceptual frameworks for thinking about large contracting decisions. This can be accomplished by developing a set of analytic tools for understanding when and why either nonprofit or for-profit provision is likely to work best, based on the characteristics of providers, the needs of consumers, and the nature of the underlying service. Until a compelling conceptual framework for deciding the division of labor across sectors emerges from the slow accretion of reliable data, protecting the mixed ecology of service providers will require a shift in the underlying criteria used by many public managers in the awarding of contracts.

Among the many possible public sector criteria for the awarding of service contracts, three stand out. First, government may continue to seek to use cost-effectiveness as a measuring stick for choosing between providers.

Second, government contractors may choose to focus on program effectiveness in awarding contracts to service providers; by looking at an organization's track record in achieving meaningful client outcomes, government funders should be able, in principle at least, to focus resources on organizations that have proved they can deliver quality results in their chosen field. Finally, government may seek to emphasize innovation and methodological diversity as prime factors in the awarding of contracts, especially in fields in which knowledge is not settled and further experimentation is needed. In so doing, public managers affirm the value of pluralism and its many dimensions and implications. A good case can be made for shifting toward the third criterion while still taking seriously the first two.

In the face of considerable uncertainty about the relative performance of nonprofit and for-profit providers, the wisest course of action today is the affirmation of the value of pluralism and provider diversity. Although it may well be possible to fuel a race to the bottom by allowing for-profit service providers to bid down contracts to the lowest possible margin, such an approach may alienate clients and consumers, especially in many areas in which the quality of care is critical. Similarly, though it may be possible to structure a market made up only of nonprofit providers in which competition centers principally on programmatic quality and responsiveness, this route would quite likely raise concerns about cost containment. Given the difficulty of ever reversing major ecological shifts, public managers must tread carefully: with cost and quality considerations in mind, a sensible and practical policy objective for the public sector is the preservation of a mixed market of service providers in which for-profit and nonprofit providers compete along multiple dimensions.

Policy Options for Managing the Complex Organizational Ecology

As public managers and policymakers consider the task of preserving in many fields a mixed organizational ecology of nonprofit and for-profit service providers, some modest steps can be taken to ensure that nonprofits are not unduly disadvantaged in the competition for service contracts. Two of the five nonprofit competitive disadvantages described earlier—limitations of scale and access to capital—can be addressed through modest policy changes.

Modest Measures

In the area of helping nonprofits to overcome some of the limitations they face in terms of meeting the scale and financing demands of large public contracts, one possible solution is to require that major public contracts be structured so as to explicitly encourage or require the use of local subcontractors. In many fields in which direct client services are rendered, neighborhood knowledge and legitimacy are critical and require community connections established over a long period of time. To capture this knowledge and to help nonprofits bid on contracts that may seem too large for any single organization to handle, public managers may want to consider structuring service contracts so as to reward bidders that propose to rely on experienced subcontractors. In so doing, government might have to trade away some efficiency for the benefits that smaller, more locally connected organizations might bring. By breaking large projects into smaller, more manageable projects, public managers could take a critical step toward removing an emerging barrier to nonprofit participation.

A different option for overcoming the scale limitations of many nonprofit organizations is the facilitation of mergers.[26] At present, large numbers of nonprofit organizations operate without much grasp of the organizational landscape around them. Often, several nonprofits provide services in a relatively narrow geographical territory while other areas are left untouched. To help nonprofits compete for contracts that require a heightened level of integration and scale, proposals at the state level have been put forward to create "consolidation funds" that would reward nonprofits that merge operations and reduce some of the overlap and inefficiency. Because much of the law bearing on the disposition of charitable assets is administered by state attorneys general, any such reform effort would have to proceed incrementally on a state-by-state basis. Although the idea of achieving scale through state-aided consolidation appeals to some nonprofit managers, to others the idea is fraught with problems, including the incompatibility of nonprofit missions, the culture of decentralization within many organizations, and the resistance of managers and boards to surrendering control.

Some action is also possible in the area of capitalization. Beyond opening up opportunities to secure tax-exempt bonds, government can play a role in improving nonprofits' access to capital by creating pools of public funds that can be used by enterprising nonprofits to overcome some of the barriers to entry present in certain contracting areas. In the arena of charter schools, for example, the U.S. Department of Education recently established a fund to help new charter schools locate the start-up resources necessary to plan and open a school. This fund was created in response to a serious cash-flow problem: the only funds available to many charter schools were per pupil allocations payable at the start of the school year, and many cities and states found that the charters they had issued were going unclaimed because few nonprofit entrepreneurs could figure out how to acquire a school building and overcome the initial costs associated with creating a new school. The solution, though simple, has relevance in the many service fields in which government payments are keyed either to program enrollment or to the achievement of specified client outcomes. To be able to compete with business firms that are not subject to these short-term cash flow challenges, nonprofits may need an array of start-up funding sources that will enable managers to cover the costs associated with entering a field in which government service delivery contracts are available.[27]

Some nonprofit managers have recently begun to explore the possibility of securitizing accounts receivable. Nonprofits might be able to acquire working capital not by using real estate and buildings as collateral but by securing funds with accounts receivable—most likely, renewable government contracts. This idea has remained on the drawing table largely because few government contracts are of a sufficiently long term to satisfy lenders and because of a general sense that government contracts can be revoked if the nonprofits fail to perform as expected. Thus one way public managers could assist nonprofits in securing financing, be it through the securitization of accounts receivable or through conventional loans, is by making their contracts longer and more dependable. Of course, any change in this direction would remove some of the government's flexibility in contracting for services.[28]

Seeking Balance

As public managers look out at the changing service-contracting landscape and work to address some of the challenges that nonprofit organizations face to full and fair participation in the service-contracting marketplace, a bit of balance may well be in order. Although many human service nonprofit organizations now portray themselves as David facing the corporate Goliath, the moral basis of the nonprofit sector's plea for help is weakened to some extent by the range of advantages that nonprofit organizations enjoy, from their exemption from corporate taxation and their ability to offer contributors a deduction for their contributions to their exemption from property taxes and the subsidized postal rates they enjoy. Although many of these special privileges do not bear directly on the ability of nonprofits to secure government service contracts, the subsidies they receive do allow nonprofits to conduct commercial activities that generate additional revenues that can be used to reduce the costs of service delivery.

As a consequence, business lobbies have argued that nonprofit organizations require a far more differentiated tax treatment than they presently receive. One approach that has been considered is the granting of a sliding scale of tax benefits to nonprofits, geared to the level of public service they deliver. Under such a plan, donors to soup kitchens might receive full tax deductions for their gifts, while supporters of more commercialized nonprofits, such as hospitals, would receive only partial deductions. Similarly, some nonprofits would enjoy the full postage discount, while others would be forced to pay rates closer to the market rate. The problem, however, with any such arrangement designed to differentiate between nonprofits based on the social benefits generated is that it puts government in the awkward position of judging the social value of the missions of public charities, a responsibility that would be hard to discharge fairly.

Business groups have recently been joined by local municipalities in questioning why all nonprofit organizations enjoy exemption from property taxes. From the perspective of business, the ability of nonprofits to avoid contributing to local tax receipts imposes on local businesses an unreasonable and unfair burden, one that can render the playing field less than balanced. The ability of large institutions and highly commercial nonprofits to operate free from property taxes has led many cities to investigate ways to ensure that financially successful nonprofits are not allowed to enjoy a free ride at the expense of other taxpayers. One option that is now being explored in Baltimore, Maryland, is a sliding scale that would seek payments in lieu of taxes—ranging from nothing to several million dollars, depending on the resources of the nonprofit organization.

The high ground of nonprofits has also been eroded by another significant recent trend: the sharp and continuing rise in unrelated business income activity within nonprofits and the meager amounts of taxes paid on these revenues. A growing number of nonprofit organizations have established ventures or enterprises that bear no real connection to their core charitable missions but nevertheless generate a stream of income that can be used for social purposes. The regulation of these "unrelated businesses" has increased in recent years as competitors in the business world have raised complaints about unfair competition. When revenues are derived from an enterprise that is "not substantially related to the mission" of the nonprofit, a tax in principle is applied by the IRS. The "unrelated business income tax" is intended to limit the expansion of nonprofit enterprise into areas that businesses occupy or at least to level the playing field. The range of unrelated businesses operated by nonprofits is enormous and can include everything from a bakery operated by a youth center to a real estate development firm operated by a university.

As unrelated commercial activity by nonprofits has increased in recent years, a difficult problem has arisen related to the enforcement of rules designed to protect fair competition. Although nonprofits have been engaging in increasingly greater levels of commercial ventures, each year the amount of profit they report remains very low, and hence the taxes they pay on their unrelated business has stayed relatively low. The best explanation for this phenomenon lies in the clever accounting techniques employed by nonprofits, which allow these organizations to report minimal gains or even losses related to the generation of the unrelated income. This is accomplished by shifting costs from program-related activities to commercial ventures. In other words, as nonprofits have created flows of income from ventures that sometimes compete directly with for-profit firms, they have learned to move staff, overhead, and capital expenses from the charitable side of the balance sheet to the commercial side. As this cost shifting occurs, any profits generated by unrelated business activity are quickly turned into losses,[29] and the nonprofit's tax liability is thereby often reduced or eliminated. The IRS has grown suspicious of this practice, challenging nonprofits as to why they continually engage in activities that lead to losses.[30] The answer, of course, is that often these activities lead to profits, not losses, but the organizations behind them have discovered a way to skirt the rules designed to level the playing field between business and nonprofit enterprises.[31]

To counter this trend, greater enforcement of the regulations governing the unrelated business income tax and higher levels of oversight by the IRS may be needed to ensure that nonprofit organizations report their financial results accurately. One way to accomplish this would be to bring greater order to nonprofit reporting by improving the generally poor standards guiding nonprofit financial accounting.[32] Today, only nonprofits receiving a total of $300,000 or more in government grants and contracts are subject to A-133 audits.[33] For nonprofits below this threshold, the level of oversight over their financial statements is extremely low. Building a stronger, more reliable accountability system would go a long way to satisfying business that nonprofit organizations are not taking undue advantage of their tax-exempt status.[34]

Conclusion

In the end, as the division of labor between the public and private sectors works itself out, policymakers can take a few steps toward ensuring that the nonprofit option is not lost and that pluralism as a value in service delivery is protected. Helping nonprofits access capital and opening service contracts to subcontractors might well help ensure that nonprofits are not shut out of contracts that require large-scale operations and technical capacity. In fields such as the transition from welfare to work, in which the scale of some of the contracts can be immense, the vast universe of community-based nonprofit providers is at a real disadvantage. Without some appropriate action the public sector may ultimately lose out on the special skills and local contacts that many of these small service providers possess. On the business side, clarification of the line between related and unrelated income would be welcome by almost everyone, as would a more effective oversight of the financial reporting of nonprofits. The lack of clarity in nonprofit financial reporting practices, if left unattended for much longer, will lead to an erosion of public confidence in nonprofit organizations.

The calm and peaceful world that may once have existed for nonprofit service providers is now long gone. Market pressures have entered the nonprofit sector in ways that cannot help but change the sector and the way government purchases human services. As these changes take hold, it is clear that should nonprofits continue to lose out as the trend continues toward greater and greater business activity in fields traditionally dominated by nonprofits, the scope and character of human services will be impoverished. Although data on the comparative performance of the sectors is inconclusive in many fields, almost everyone should be able to agree that in fields like early childhood education, community health, and job training—fields in which knowledge about what works remains highly contested—it remains desirable to invest in a plurality of approaches across sectors. With their unique commitments and value-based missions, nonprofit service providers have the ability to continue to offer innovative approaches to public problems that are linked to community needs and standards. With their strong commitments to results and the bottom line, business firms also have something valuable to bring to the market for government service contracts. Until greater data and conceptual clarity emerge about the comparative advantages of nonprofit and for-profit service delivery, government at the federal, state, and local levels should work to preserve a mixed organizational ecology in which both nonprofit and for-profit providers play a role in the changing landscape of human service provision.

Notes

1. For good accounts of the trend toward greater public funding of nonprofits, see Steven Rathgeb Smith and Michael Lipsky, *Nonprofits for Hire: The Welfare State in the Age of Contracting* (Harvard University Press, 1993); Ralph M. Kramer, *Voluntary Agencies in the Welfare State* (University of California Press, 1981); Susan Bernstein, *Managing Contracted Services in the Nonprofit Agency* (Temple University Press, 1991); and Jennifer Wolch, *The Shadow State: Government and the Voluntary Sector in Transition* (New York: Foundation Center, 1990).

2. See H. Brinton Milward and Keith Provan, "The Hollow State: Private Provision of Public Services," in Helen Ingram and Steven Rathgeb Smith, eds., *Public Policy for Democracy* (Brookings, 1993), pp. 222–40; and Elizabeth T. Boris and C. Eugene Steuerle, eds., *Nonprofits and Government* (Washington: Urban Institute Press, 1999).

3. William Ryan, "The New Landscape for Nonprofits," *Harvard Business Review* (January–February 1999), pp. 127–36.

4. On the distinctive capacities of nonprofits, see Burton A. Weisbrod, *The Nonprofit Economy* (Harvard University Press, 1988), and Burton A. Weisbrod, "The Future of the Nonprofit Sector: Its Entwining with Private Enterprise and Government," *Journal of Policy Analysis and Management,* vol. 16 (Fall 1997), pp. 541–55.

5. For examples of the application of business ideas to nonprofit management, see Alceste Pappas, *Reengineering Your Nonprofit Organization* (Wiley and Sons, 1995); and Paul Firstenberg, *The Twenty-First-Century Nonprofit: Remaking the Organization in the Post-Government Era* (New York: Foundation Center, 1996). For an overview of this trend, see Paul S. Light, *Making Nonprofits Work: A Report on the Tides of Nonprofit Management Reform* (Brookings, 2000).

6. On the place of values and commitments in nonprofit activity, see David E. Mason, *Leading and Managing the Expressive Dimension* (San Francisco: Jossey-Bass, 1996); and Richard C. Cornuelle, *Reclaiming the American Dream: The Role of Private Individuals and Voluntary Associations* (New Brunswick, N.J.: Transaction Publishers, 1993).

7. It is useful to note the Census Bureau data here is presented by "enterprise," not by "establishment." Because many for-profit enterprises tend to have many establishments or sites, whereas nonprofit enterprises tend to be single establishment, the relative number and size of nonprofit and for-profit establishments may not be captured fully in these data.

8. See Peter Frumkin and Alice Andre-Clark, "When Missions, Markets, and Politics Collide: Values and Strategy in the Nonprofit Human Services," *Nonprofit and Voluntary Sector Quarterly,* vol. 29, no. 1 (Supplement 2000), pp. 141–64.

9. On the skewed distribution of nonprofits tending toward small and financially weak organizations, see William G. Bowen, Thomas I. Nygren, Sarah E. Turner, and Elizabeth A. Duffy, *The Charitable Nonprofits* (San Francisco: Jossey-Bass, 1994).

10. For an overview of outcome funding from the perspective of the funder, see United Way of America, *Measuring Program Outcomes: A Practical Guide* (Alexandria, Va.: United Way of America, 1995).

11. Mark Abramson, *Managing for Results* (Lanham, Md.: Rowman and Littlefield, 2001).

12. Some believe that outcome funding, though it may impose some financial hardships, actually helps a nonprofit to focus on its mission and improve its ability to execute its programs (see Natalie Buckmaster, "Associations between Outcome Measurement, Accountability, and Learning for Non-Profit Organizations," *International Journal of Public Sector Management*, vol. 12, no. 2 [1999], pp. 186–97).

13. See Reid Lifset, "Cash Cows or Sacred Cows: The Politics of the Commercialization Movement," in Virginia A. Hodgkinson and Richard Lyman and Associates, *The Future of the Nonprofit Sector* (San Francisco: Jossey-Bass, 1989), pp. 140–67.

14. On the distinctive nature of nonprofit organizations, see Henry Hansmann, "The Role of Nonprofit Enterprise," *Yale Law Journal*, vol. 89 (April 1980), pp. 835–98; and Henry Hansmann, *The Ownership of Enterprise* (Harvard University Press, 1996).

15. The Smithsonian Institution recently issued $41 million in bonds, backed by a $600 million endowment, sixteen museum buildings, a successful catalog business, and a large annual federal appropriation.

16. See Howard P. Tuckman, "How and Why Nonprofit Organizations Obtain Capital," in David C. Hammack and Dennis R. Young, eds., *Nonprofit Organizations in a Market Economy* (San Francisco: Jossey-Bass, 1993), pp. 203–32.

17. Elizabeth J. Reid, "Nonprofit Advocacy and Political Participation," in Elizabeth T. Boris and C. Eugene Steuerle, eds., *Nonprofits and Government* (Washington: Urban Institute Press, 1999), pp. 291–328.

18. The Tax Reform Act of 1976, P.L. 94-455, led to IRS Code sections 4911 and 501(h), which define the limits on lobbying; see Bob Smucker, *The Nonprofit Lobbying Guide* (Washington: Independent Sector, 1999), for a full discussion of these provisions.

19. Large firms, like EDS and Lockheed, have paid former state human service commissioners generous salaries to head their new job training and welfare-to-work divisions.

20. Peter Frumkin and Alice Andre-Clark, "Nonprofit Compensation and the Market," *University of Hawaii Law Review*, vol. 21 (Winter 1999), pp. 425–85.

21. "Failure by Certain Charitable Organizations to Meet Certain Qualification Requirements: Taxes on Excess Benefit Transactions," *Federal Register* 63, no. 41, 486–501 (1999).

22. Harold S. Williams, Arthur Y. Webb, and William J. Phillips, *Outcome Funding: A New Approach to Targeted Grantmaking* (Rensselaerville, N.Y.: Rensselaerville Institute, 1995).

23. Part of the problem in drawing conclusions about the comparative performance of social programs stems from the difficulty both of defining and of measuring meaningful client outcomes.

24. See Mark McClellan and Douglas Staiger, "Comparing Hospital Quality at For-Profit and Not-for-Profit Hospitals," in David Cutler, ed., *The Changing Hospital Industry:*

Comparing Nonprofit and For-Profit Institutions (University of Chicago Press, 2000), pp. 93–112; Elaine M. Silverman, Jonathan S. Skinner, and Elliot S. Fischer, "The Association between For-Profit Hospital Ownership and Increased Medicare Spending," *New England Journal of Medicine*, vol. 341 (August 5, 1999), pp. 420–25; and Mark G. Duggan, "Hospital Ownership and Public Medical Spending," *Quarterly Journal of Economics*, vol. 115 (November 2000), pp. 1343–73.

25. William Ryan, "The New Landscape for Nonprofits," *Harvard Business Review* (January–February 1999), pp. 127–36.

26. Kevin P. Kearns, *Private Sector Strategies for Social Sector Success* (San Francisco: Jossey-Bass, 2000).

27. For a good overview of the multiple sources and consequences of nonprofit agency finance, see Kirsten A. Gronbjerg, *Understanding Nonprofit Funding: Managing Revenues in Social Service and Community Development Agencies* (San Francisco: Jossey-Bass, 1993).

28. On the need for flexibility in contracting, see Vincent Gooden, "Contracting and Negotiation: Effective Practices of Successful Human Service Contract Managers," *Public Administration Review*, vol. 58 (November–December 1998), pp. 499–509.

29. See Joseph J. Cordes and Burton A. Weisbrod, "Differential Taxation of Nonprofits and the Commercialization of Nonprofit Revenues," in Burton A. Weisbrod, ed., *To Profit or Not to Profit* (Cambridge University Press, 1998), pp. 83–104. One recent report notes that more than a quarter of all nonprofits receiving $500,000 or more in private contributions reported no fund-raising expenses on their tax forms (Harvy Lipman, "Charities' Zero-Sum Filing Game," *Chronicle of Philanthropy* [May 18, 2000], p. 1).

30. See Margaret Riley, "Unrelated Business Income of Nonprofit Organizations: Highlights of 1995 and a Review of 1991–1995," *SOI Bulletin* (Spring 1999), pp. 80–112; and James R. Hines Jr., "Non-Profit Business Activity and the Unrelated Business Income Tax," in James S. Poterba, ed., *Tax Policy and the Economy*, vol. 13 (MIT Press, 1999), pp. 57–84; Richard Sansing, "The Unrelated Business Income Tax, Cost Allocation, and Productive Efficiency," *National Tax Journal*, vol. 51 (June 1998), pp. 291–302.

31. One reason nonprofits are able to get away with cost shifting is that the IRS is able to audit only a small number of nonprofits each year (see Jennifer Moore and Grant Williams, "Taxing Times for the Tax Agency," *Chronicle of Philanthropy* [October 17, 1996], p. 1).

32. See Regina Herzlinger, "Can Public Trust in Government and Nonprofits Be Restored?" *Harvard Business Review* (March–April 1996), pp. 97–107.

33. Earl R. Wilson, Leon E. Hays, and Susan C. Kattelus, *Accounting for Government and Nonprofit Entities* (New York: Irwin McGraw-Hill, 1999).

34. On the need for a more reliable accountability system, see Kevin P. Kearns, "The Strategic Management of Accountability in Nonprofit Organizations: An Analytic Framework," *Public Administration Review*, vol. 54 (March–April 1994), pp. 185–92.

4
STEVEN KELMAN

Strategic Contracting Management

GOVERNMENTS CONTRACT BOTH for products and services that are inputs into what government produces (ranging from office supplies or computers on the desks of government employees to fighter aircraft or cost-benefit studies of a proposed regulation) and for actual government outputs (including debt collection for delinquent college student loans, operation of customer service hotlines, garbage collection, and delivery of job training). In all, the U.S. federal government spends about $200 billion a year buying goods and services, an amount equivalent to about 30 percent of discretionary spending.[1]

It is tempting to believe that when government makes the decision that something for which it is paying should be provided by private organizations, it has removed one item from its agenda of worries. No longer, one might imagine, need government worry about how to make computers if it buys them from Dell or Compaq; no longer need it worry about how to educate kids, or get jobs for the unemployed, if it contracts with a private organization to run a school or a job training program.

A moment's reflection will suffice to remind any who might hold such fond hopes that though the decision to contract changes the nature of government's worries, it does not eliminate them. When government contracts for computers, schools, or job training, it need not know how to produce the products or services in question. It does, however, need to be able to do three things well: develop a business strategy (specifying requirements for what will be bought and choosing an appropriate contract arrangement and incentives), select the right suppliers, and administer the contract once it has been signed. These skills are different from those required to produce computers, schools, or job training. These tasks have traditionally been the province of the government's procurement system.[2]

Almost a decade ago, Donald F. Kettl argued that if contracting is to work well to achieve public purposes, government must be a "smart buyer."[3] I would go further. Because so much of what many agencies do and deliver has increasingly come to depend on contracts with third parties, successful contracting has become a central part of agency success. A number of agencies, such as the Department of Defense, the Department of Energy, and the National Aeronautics and Space Administration, spend much of their budgets on contracted products and services—46, 94, and 78 percent, respectively. Most agencies contract out development of information technology applications that are crucial to running their organizations, as well as other central activities such as scientific research. For such agencies and functions, the ability to manage contracting must be considered a core competency of the organization.

For this reason I believe that agencies need to think about the strategic management of contracting: contracting should be used aggressively to promote central agency goals. My view is quite different from a traditional view that regards contracting as a subsidiary administrative function that rightly receives little attention from senior agency leadership. In the twenty-first century, in many agencies, strategic contracting management needs to become a central concern of senior agency political and career executives, like other organizational core competencies.[4] In particular, the business strategy part of contracting—the stage in the process at which an organization decides what it will be buying and how the business arrangement will be structured—should, for important contracts, receive the personal attention of senior career and political general management.

Over the past decade, significant changes have taken place in the U.S. federal government's procurement system, changes designed to improve the system's performance through a strategy of making procurement less rule bound.[5] Concentrated in the areas of business strategy and source selection, these changes provide a good foundation upon which to build strategic contracting management. The third element of strategic contracting management, the administration of contracts once they have been signed, has been the neglected stepchild of these efforts. This chapter seeks to address what needs to happen in the area of contract administration.[6]

A word is first in order about the current state of the world with regard to contract administration. A coalition of government employee unions, opposed to contracting out jobs that might otherwise be filled by their own members, and journalists and politicians ever eager to uncover the unholy trinity of waste, fraud, and abuse has promoted an image of contract administration that suggests an environment in which government is "asleep at the switch" and nobody is "minding the store"—and in which, therefore, contractors run roughshod over the public and hapless agencies. This is a world of cost overruns and performance failures. Academic concerns about a "hollow state" in which government contracts out rather than producing have sounded a parallel alarm, sometimes citing similar journalistic accounts of contracting problems.[7]

Such images should be taken with a grain of salt. Surely, to take the best-known exhibits for the prosecution, there are "cost overruns" in many weapons and technology projects; but these should not be seen simply, or even mostly, as owing to sloth or fraud. Some result from changes in project specifications, so that what government ends up buying includes performance features not present in the original contract. Some cost growth results from unrealistically low initial cost estimates used to garner political support for a project. (To be sure, such gaming is problematic for other reasons, but it suggests skepticism about any assumption that the original cost estimate is what the project "should" have cost and that any final figure over that estimate means government is paying "too much.")

Moreover, many of these projects involve complex, first-time tasks that go beyond the current state of the art and are exactly the kinds of project that tend to produce similar cost growth when attempted in the private sector. Studies comparing "megaprojects" in the Defense Department and the private sector have found that a universe of forty-seven nondefense projects, such as the construction of refineries, process plants, and nuclear plants, showed a greater average cost growth than did major Defense Department weapons projects in the 1960s, although the technological uncertainties were surely greater, on average, in the development of weapons systems than in these nondefense projects.[8] Studies of private sector projects involving the development of information technology systems have found that most came in considerably over budget and delivered less performance than expected; many were abandoned entirely.[9]

Nor is the evidence consistent with the suggestion that wily contractors are able to rip off a government asleep at the switch. Although the return on equity of the aerospace and defense industry exceeded that of the Standard and Poor's Industrials index during the defense boom years of the 1980s, that trend has been reversed: since 1988 the industry's return has generally been lower, and often dramatically lower, than the Standard and Poor's index. (During the 1994–98 period, aerospace and defense firms in the index averaged a 14 percent rate of return on equity, compared, for example, with 26 percent for chemical or diversified manufacturing firms and 17 percent for auto parts firms.)[10] To take one example of a publicly traded information technology corporation that reports separate results for its commercial and U.S. federal government divisions, Computer Sciences Corporation reports a return on sales in 2000 of 7.8 percent for commercial work and 6.3 percent for federal work, numbers that are in line with the observations of other large information technology firms selling into both markets.[11]

In contrast to the "asleep at the switch" accounts, the government, in fact, maintains a significant infrastructure dealing with contract administration. On the financial side, the Defense Department has an entire organization of contract auditors, the Defense Contract Audit Agency, that also works for civilian agency customers, along with contracting officers who manage day-to-day financial issues.

How technical or program people (as opposed to procurement people) get involved in contract administration varies by agency and by type of contract. For large contracted programs, including weapons systems and major government projects involving information technology, the agency normally has a full-time program office, headed by a program manager, with several layers within the organization under the program manager. For most contracts, though (and also for individual task orders under many larger contracts), a single technical or program person is in charge of the government's programmatic interface with the contractor, the so-called contracting officer's technical representative (COTR).[12] The COTR typically has contract administration responsibilities over and above other job responsibilities, and with respect to those other responsibilities many, if not most, COTRs are senior-level "doers," or at most first-line supervisors, not managers.

Despite all this, however, the fact remains that, with the exception of considerable attention to auditing for unallowable costs and violations of cost accounting standards, contract administration has traditionally been given insufficient attention in most parts of government. "Contracting officials often allocate more time to awarding contracts rather than administering existing contracts."[13]

This chapter addresses two questions: First, what needs to be done well if contract administration in particular is to become a core competency for government, as part of a larger competence in the strategic management of contracting? Second, is what needs to be done likely to constitute an attractive job to which government has some prospect of recruiting talented people?

Crucial to answering the first question is the recognition that the strategic management of contracting is mainly about management. The vast majority of skills required of a good contracting manager are the same skills required of any good manager. In fact, the most important responsibilities of those in charge of the administration of a contract or task order are not just managerial in general: they are analogous to those of a senior executive, not a first-line supervisor or middle manager. It is the job of the contractor's management to directly supervise its employees on a day-to-day basis. What a government person in charge of contract administration needs to be good at, on the other hand, is executive-type functions such as strategy and goal setting; the ability to inspire those doing the work, including contractors, with enthusiasm and public purpose; performance management; management of horizontal interfaces between the contractor and end users of the contractor's services; and management of vertical interfaces with higher levels of the organization and with the external environment. Contract administration leaders should be agenda setters for others, not simply accomplished doers themselves.[14]

Specific activities in which contract administration leaders should get involved include the following:

—setting, or helping to set, the strategic direction for what the government is seeking to accomplish through the contract. This implies a connection of senior contract administrators both to the underlying agency activity the contract serves and to the contractual effort itself, starting with the business strategy development phase. As one successful contract administrator stated, "I spend lots of time on visionary planning. That's the fun stuff."

—managing the process of interface between end user and contractor to find out what the end user's requirements are and to get them expressed in contractual documents and throughout contract performance.[15]

—making sure government people provide the contractor the help they need: interviews with end users about how they use their current computer software or time, for example, or resolution of conflicts about whether providing a certain kind of assistance is a government responsibility or should be done by the contractor.

—attending trade association or other professional meetings. As students of organizational social capital note, such meetings should be seen mostly as a way to get informal information and to nurture relationships.[16] As one contract administrator said, "The point is not what's on the agenda, the point is what takes place at breaks and lunch." Another noted that "people at these conferences talk among themselves about who's in financial trouble or who's won big commercial contracts. If I learn at one of these meetings that a company's in trouble, I can request a financial survey before I make them an award."

—signaling through one's personal involvement that an issue is important.

The most fundamental problem with the current system is that it insufficiently recognizes contract administration as in the first instance a management function. Correspondingly, too many contract administrators selected from the ranks of program or technical officials feel they have been dealt the short straw by being given contract administration duties. Kettl notes that in one of his case studies many contract administration responsibilities were placed in the hands of people who saw themselves as substantive experts and would rather have been performing their substantive work. "In an agency dominated by scientists, technical expertise, not administrative finesse, marked the fast track upward. Technicians and other scientifically trained managers thus had strong motivation to escape from the task—what one official called the 'administrative stigma'—as quickly as possible. Sometimes, [an Environmental Protection Agency] report said, 'contracts management [tended] to be dumped on poor performers' because it was not a high-prestige task."[17] As one of those I interviewed noted, "We're brought up to be doing stuff, which is actually much more fun than managing the stuff getting done."[18]

Furthermore, many of the functions COTRs currently perform are nonmanagerial and certainly nonstrategic. Contracting officer's technical representatives review contractor invoices, and the Office of Federal Procurement Policy's *Guide to Best Practices for Contract Administration* recommends that COTRs also examine time cards and sign-in sheets of contractor personnel and that they maintain spreadsheets of contractor expenses.[19] The government-wide Internet-based training course for COTRs, developed by the Federal Acquisition Institute, prescribes extensive paperwork activities, such as taking minutes of meetings with contractors and personally performing inspections or tests. The vast majority of COTRs who are not "doers" are first-line supervisors accustomed to directing the supervision of a modest number of employees rather than to the performance of executive-type managerial activities. They are therefore inclined to undertake the tasks contractor supervisors should be doing—namely, direct supervision of contractor employees in the form of extensive "technical direction." Such micromanagement also allows them to feel that they are making a solid and visible contribution to the success of the contract.

There are three things government must do if contract administration leadership is to become a core organizational competence: it must properly define and provide training for the job, split off lower-level tasks from executive-type tasks, and make an investment in performance measurement as a discipline. First, and most important, senior contract administration jobs, including that of COTR, should be positioned as management jobs with exciting challenges and stimulation similar to that of senior executive positions. Successful management requires very different skills from those required for success as an individual technician. But management provides a very real, if different, form of excitement. These jobs should not be for the unambitious—and clearly cannot be if the strategic management of contracting is to be a core competence for government. They should be sold to those who are currently doers or first-line supervisors (or for those being recruited directly for such positions from the outside), as an opportunity to experience job responsibilities normally held by people at more senior levels, and to entry-level people, as an aspiration for those on a fast track up.[20] Training for contract administration leaders should be training in management skills.

Second, to allow contract administration to focus on management, efforts should be made to split off repetitive, lower-level tasks from more complex, and engaging, executive-type functions.[21] (To some extent, such a division of labor already exists in organizations with a program management structure.) Not surprisingly, of those at a middle or senior level of contract administration, no one interviewed expressed enthusiasm about generating contract-monitoring paperwork. "I don't like all this monitoring stuff. All the paperwork, the high administrative burden." Agencies should scrub internal paperwork requirements, just as many have scrubbed requirements for contractor-generated reports, to see what might usefully be streamlined or eliminated, recognizing that paperwork reduces the attractiveness of these jobs. For contracts with tangible performance metrics, acceptable interim progress toward meeting those metrics should trigger reduced contractor reporting requirements. Organizations should consider assigning the tasks of minute taking and generation of meeting-related paperwork to junior people, who would also get an opportunity to learn about management by sitting in on such meetings. Documentation that does not need to go to higher organizational levels should be dictated in real time into a machine by a person's desk, to be filed as tapes and transcribed only if, and when, necessary.

One dilemma is how to deal with the role of the COTR in approving contractor labor-hour invoices in cost reimbursable contracts (essentially, verifying that contractor personnel worked the hours stated.)[22] On the one hand, people on the program or technical side, for whom the work is actually being done, are in a far better position to know whether contractor employees have been working than are contracting officers or after-the-fact auditors, especially if the work is being done on-site at the agency. On the other hand, this is a repetitive and unengaging task, and if, as is frequently the case, the contractor is working off-site, the COTR cannot observe directly whether contractor employees are working. This difficulty could be mitigated if contract management would become more serious about past performance evaluations that compare cost estimates with final costs, to provide contractors a disincentive against padding costs;[23] have clerical people, either in program or contracting offices, review time cards, when these are generated; and allow COTRs to be directly involved in the verification of invoices, in whatever ways they might choose. This last item should not be a requirement; but requests for increased involvement will typically be generated when COTRs see that results are falling way below expectations. This begins to make the COTR's role look more like performance measurement.

Third, a crucial part of the job of a contract administration leader will be responsibility for performance measurement and management of the contractor. This should be a key management responsibility in all organizations, but it is often difficult in a public sector context (whether for in-house or contracted work) because financial performance metrics common in the private sector do not suffice and sometimes do not even apply. Although business firms have begun to grapple with the special challenges of developing multiple performance measures, such as frequent difficulty developing quantitative measures and possible perverse effects of measurement, advancing the art and science of nonfinancial performance measurement is a special issue for government.[24] The Defense Department, representing government as a whole, should therefore take the initiative to develop the discipline of nonfinancial performance measurement just as it took the initiative in the 1960s to establish the discipline of project management to help with its unique needs in developing large weapons systems.[25]

It is not Panglossian to suggest that contract administration leadership jobs, correctly positioned, can be attractive to talented people. In many technical fields, such as engineering, that place a high value on "doing," people often hope to leave technical work for managing.[26] A survey of MIT engineering graduates ten to twenty years into their careers shows that those in general or engineering management positions were considerably more likely to perceive themselves as being successful in their careers than those who were still staff engineers.[27] Contract administration leadership jobs, properly positioned, are likely to be especially appealing to young people seeking quick opportunities to learn new things, to grow both professionally and personally, and to exercise significant responsibility; one study of people newly promoted into management positions from jobs in which they had performed successfully as "doers" found that "the first year of management was a period of considerable . . . personal growth"; they "matured as they confronted previously undiscovered truths about themselves."[28] Indeed, government may well be able to offer young people responsibilities more significant than those they would find in private sector jobs in large organizations.

The last question I wish to address here is the role that substantive expertise in areas involved in a contract plays in the successful strategic management of that contracting. Substantive skills are required for government to establish requirements for what the contractor is being asked to do; to evaluate "technical proposals" (defining how the bidder would accomplish the work), including analysis of the relative risks different approaches entail; to evaluate contractor cost estimates for cost-based contracts or for fixed-price task orders awarded without competition under larger contracts, where the government needs to judge the contractor's estimate of how many hours a job will take and what mix of labor categories is needed; to provide technical direction during contract performance for non-performance-based contracts; and to ensure compliance with specialized technical constraints, even in a performance-based contract (for example, constraints on disposal of infectious waste in a hospital that contracts out cleaning services). Included in "substantive expertise" are both what in government is often called "functional" knowledge, such as information technology or engineering skills, and what in government is often called "subject matter expertise," knowledge of the underlying government activity the contract is serving. So, for example, if the IRS is contracting for information technology services to modernize its collection of taxes, technical skills would include knowledge about available appropriate information technologies, while subject matter expertise would include knowledge about how the IRS conducts audits.

It is frequently thought that, to have these kinds of expertise at its disposal, government must maintain at least some in-house production in the areas for which it is contracting. By this argument, if government has no "doers" who have written software code, it cannot successfully manage contractors writing code. Thus, for example, Milward argues that in these kinds of situations, "producing some services is the only way to learn about the costs of production."[29] One prominent worry about the growing tendency toward contracting out is that as government loses its doers, it inevitably also loses its ability to be successful at contract management.

I disagree. In my view, government can be good at the strategic management of contracting even without a strong base of "doers" with technical skills in the areas being contracted. Unless there are independent reasons for the government to maintain its own in-house production capability (or the decision is at least a very close call), it does not make sense for government to maintain in-house production simply, or mostly, to retain skills at "doing" needed for managing contractors.

Before exploring this further, three remarks are in order. First, government typically has, and will continue to have, subject matter expertise available even when there are questions about the availability of functional expertise (for example, when government people are still running business processes being reengineered by contractors or are the customers for new weapons and can express what results they seek). Government loses subject matter expertise only when a function is completely outsourced and there are no government customers of the service (such as when garbage collection is outsourced). Second, existing procurement reform efforts have reduced government's need for functional expertise. The more government evaluates bidders on past performance, the smaller the role of a bidder's technical approach in source selection on the new job being bid. In a performance-based contract, where the government contracts for performance outcomes and leaves it to the contractor to decide how the work will be done, requirements for functional skills on the government's end, particularly after the contract is awarded, decline dramatically.

Third, one should not overestimate the number of situations in which government needs access to its own functional expertise. It is easier to recognize a good idea than to come up with one.[30] Often, technical skills are not necessary to judge the quality of significant parts of a bidder's technical proposal. Similarly, it is easier to judge whether performance metrics have been met than to know how to meet them. These three factors dramatically reduce the need for technical expertise in administering a performance-based contract.

There still remain significant situations, however, in which the government needs functional skills. How can these skills be made available for the strategic management of contracting without a pipeline of "doers" promoted into contracting management jobs? It can do so in several ways. Perhaps the most important is for government to begin to recruit people into midlevel contract management positions with several years of "doer" experience in the private sector rather than assuming that these positions must be filled from within the government. There will still be lots of entry-level "doer" jobs in information technology, even if they are not in government. Government still operates largely on a model that there are only two points of ingress into government employment, the entry level and the senior political level. This view is increasingly at odds with the expectation of young people that they will work in many organizations.[31] Government can get the technical help it needs for midlevel contracting management positions, even if it has no doers itself, by hiring people with three to five years of entry-level experience in industry; many if not most of them will stay only for a few years. Such jobs may appeal to young people who are generally job mobile, who may wish to do a few years of public service, who have young children and might prefer less travel or a more family-friendly work environment, or who might be attracted to positions with fairly significant responsibility.

Government can also hire contractors, other than those doing the work contracted for, to provide needed functional expertise. It is easy to ironize about this. In one of his case studies, Kettl makes disparaging references to agency use of contractors to help develop requirements, evaluate proposals, and monitor performance, writing that "it was as if (the agency) had decided to buy a car but did not have the capability to define what a car looked like, what it ought to do, or what it ought to cost."[32] Such wit does not render this solution less sensible. Even if government employed its own in-house technical experts—software programmers, for instance—there are so many specializations and idiosyncratic areas of expertise within a functional domain that for any specific effort, the in-house people would still be likely to lack technical skills in the specific are. Expertise as a COBOL programmer hardly qualifies a person as an expert on logistics or e-procurement software applications. So in-house expertise usually does not obviate the need for outside expertise. Indeed, in areas such as information technology, it is extremely common for private sector customers to use independent third-party information sources (such as the Gartner Group) to help them develop requirements and evaluate vendors. Government has done this for many years in a number of areas, including the development of weapons systems, even when it had far more "doers" with technical skills on staff.[33]

Although it needs to be careful about how it does this, government can make judicious use of contractors bidding on the work to provide some of the technical expertise needed for developing requirements for work to be done. Under procurement reform, it has become normal for government to have extensive early contact with prospective bidders to get their suggestions about what contract details the government should require. Some suggest that the government limit itself in a solicitation to a "statement of objectives," asking bidders to promote performance metrics and target values for such metrics.[34] Sometimes a contractor who will be, or may be, doing the work is actually in a better position than a third party to help an agency shape its requirements, because it has a greater interest in eventual success than does the third party and because it may know the agency more intimately. If the contractor has already been chosen for the work, there may be potential conflicts of interest, but such contractor-influenced shaping can occur without such risks using a limited competition in which perhaps two suppliers face off to receive the final contract.

A final word: in pointing out that government needs to be a smart buyer if contracting is to work well, Kettl appeals to government to make an "investment in smart buying."[35] The reinventing government initiative of the 1990s heeded that appeal for the front end of the procurement process—regarding establishing requirements, structuring the overall business arrangement, and selecting the right suppliers. It paid considerably less attention, however, to what happens after the contract has been awarded. The challenges faced by procurement reinventors of the 1990s were in the first instance institutional design challenges involving the proper role for rules and discretion. By contrast, the challenges of reinventing contract administration are predominantly challenges of human resources management—of people and job design. Given the growing concern with government's human capital crisis, the beginning of the new millennium represents an opportunity to address this important unfinished business.

Notes

1. Federal Procurement Data Center, *Federal Procurement Report, 2001* (General Services Administration, 2001). Information on the size of the discretionary budget (as proposed by the president) for fiscal year 2002 was provided by the Office of Management and Budget.

2. In the Department of Defense, the word *procurement* is used more narrowly to denote the selection of suppliers, with the word *acquisition* applying more broadly to all stages of the process.

3. Donald F. Kettl, *Sharing Power: Public Governance and Private Markets* (Brookings, 1993), chapter 8.

4. I use the slight neologism *strategic contracting management* to refer to all three contracting functions listed above (business strategy, source selection, and contract administration); I later use the phrase *contract administration* (often referred to these days as *contract management*) to refer more specifically to the management of a contract once it has been signed.

5. For a discussion, see my companion paper, "Remaking Federal Procurement," Working Paper 3 (Cambridge: Harvard University, John F. Kennedy School of Government, Visions of Governance in the Twenty-First Century Project, 2001).

6. To prepare this chapter, two research assistants and I conducted a series of in-person interviews with senior and midlevel government officials involved in contracting as well as program officials in information technology and space programs. Interviews were conducted at the U.S. Customs Service, the Internal Revenue Service, NASA Goddard Space Center, Hanscomb Air Force Base, the Defense Supply Center in Philadelphia, and the Offices of the Secretary of Defense and the Air Force. I would like to acknowledge the assistance of Greg Dorchak and Michael Jung in conducting the interviews.

7. Donald F. Kettl, *Government by Proxy: (Mis?)managing Federal Programs* (Washington: CQ Press, 1988); H. Brinton Milward, Keith G. Provan, and Barbara A. Else, "What Does the 'Hollow State' Look Like?" in Barry Bozeman, ed., *Public Management: The State of the Art* (San Francisco: Jossey-Bass, 1993), pp. 309–22; H. Brinton Milward, "Capacity, Control, and Performance in Interorganizational Settings," *Journal of Public Administration Research and Theory*, vol. 6 (January 1996), pp. 193–95.

8. Edward W. Merrow, Stephen W. Chapel, and Christopher Worthing, *A Review of Cost Estimation in New Technologies* (Santa Monica, Calif.: RAND Corporation, 1979), p. 73; Edward W. Merrow, *Understanding the Outcomes of Megaprojects* (Santa Monica, Calif.: RAND Corporation, 1988), pp. 32–33. To be included in the study, projects needed to take at least four years and cost at least $11 billion.

9. Bill Kern, "Relief from Out-of-Control Projects," *Contract Management*, vol. 41 (September 2001), pp. 32–35.

10. Defense Science Board, *Preserving a Healthy and Competitive U.S. Defense Industry to Ensure Our Future National Security: Final Briefing*, M-U 40607-150 (U.S. Department of Defense, 2000), pp. 1–48.

11. Author's calculations, based on Computer Sciences Corporation, *Result* (El Segundo, Calif., 2000), p. 63.

12. This official has a different title, such as the COR (contracting officer's representative) or "task manager," in various agencies or various kinds of contractual situations.

13. Office of Federal Procurement Policy, *A Guide to Best Practices for Contract Administration* (Office of Management and Budget, 1994), chapter 5.

14. On the latter distinction, see Richard N. Haass, *The Power to Persuade: How to Be Effective in Government, the Public Sector, or Any Unruly Organization* (Boston: Houghton Mifflin, 1994), chapters 3 and 5; Linda A. Hill, *Becoming a Manager* (Harvard Business School Press, 1992), p. 6.

15. To quote from one interview, "You've got to be able to bring both parties together. . . . You've got to force people to continue to raise issues, to keep communicating, to keep bringing it back to the common goal. When things go bad, the government wants to point at the contractor for screwing things up, wasting money, and the contractor comes back and says, 'You didn't define your requirements clearly. You didn't give us a focused direction.' You don't want it to get there. . . . You've got to keep reminding the government people that we've got to have the requirements, we've got to get them nailed down. The same thing with the contractors. 'If you see us not giving you what you need, you've got to tell us. You can't keep cashing our checks and moving along happily.'"

16. See, for example, Don Cohen and Laurence Prusak, *In Good Company* (Harvard Business School Press, 2001), pp. 71–72.

17. Kettl, *Sharing Power: Public Governance and Private Markets*, pp. 123–24.

18. The activities of government program managers for weapons systems or for major agency projects that establish a program management organization come closest to the kinds of executive-type functions described earlier, although special features of the management environment of the Department of Defense's weapons system program make it difficult for the program manager to get sufficiently involved in these executive functions. Program managers are typically military officers on relatively short (two- or three-year) tours of duty, a fact that makes it difficult for them to set and execute a program strategy. Weapons programs are in such competition with one another for budget funds that program managers often have an interest in presenting wildly optimistic plans at the beginning of a project and, later on, playing down problems rather than confronting them, especially given their brief tenures. The enormous hierarchy of the military services and the Office of the Secretary of Defense produces a situation in which inordinate time is spent "briefing" superiors and preparing for reviews. Until recently, the culture of program offices played relatively modest attention to cost control; and of course there are inherent problems in keeping work on new weapons systems to cost, schedule, and performance targets. See generally J. Ronald Fox, *The Defense Management Challenge: Weapons Acquisition* (Harvard Business School Press, 1988).

19. Office of Federal Procurement Policy, *A Guide to Best Practices for Contract Administration,* chapter 3.

20. Some civil servants might complain they should not be "required" to undertake executive-type responsibilities at more modest seniority levels. Others—particularly the

kind the government now must try to recruit—will welcome the opportunity for such challenges at an earlier career stage.

21. This suggestion has also been made, in somewhat different form, by Suzanne Kirchhoff of Science Applications International Corporation (SAIC) in work she is doing for the U.S. Army.

22. Only a contracting officer may actually approve the payment of an invoice.

23. Change orders would need to be taken into account.

24. Robert S. Kaplan and David P. Norton, *The Balanced Scorecard: Translating Strategy into Action* (Harvard Business School Press, 1996); Visions of Governance in the Twenty-First Century Project, Executive Session on Performance Management in the Public Sector, *Get Results from Performance Management* (Harvard University, John F. Kennedy School of Government, 2001).

25. Jack R. Meredith and Samuel J. Mantel Jr., *Project Management: A Managerial Approach* (Wiley and Sons, 2000), chapter 1.

26. Robert Zussman, *Mechanics of the Middle Class: Work and Politics among American Engineers* (University of California Press, 1985), p. 151.

27. Lotte Bailyn, *Living with Technology: Issues at Mid-Career* (MIT Press, 1980), p. 95. An alternative path that produces significant career satisfaction is a scientific research path, on which the engineer is a "doer" as well as an independent professional.

28. Hill, *Becoming a Manager,* p. 7.

29. H. Brinton Milward and Keith G. Provan, "Governing the Hollow State," *Journal of Public Administration Research and Theory,* vol. 10 (April 2000), pp. 359–80, p. 376.

30. I owe this formulation to Chip Mather, though we have developed the underlying idea independently.

31. Paul C. Light, *The New Public Service* (Brookings, 1999), pp. 137–39.

32. Kettl, *Sharing Power: Public Governance and Private Markets,* pp. 77, 86.

33. See, for example, Kettl's discussion of the government's procurement of telephone services during the l980s (ibid., pp. 76–77).

34. Chip Mather and Ann Costello, "An Innovative Approach to Performance-Based Acquisition," working paper (Washington: Acquisition Solutions, 2001).

35. Kettl, *Sharing Power: Public Governance and Private Markets,* p. 211.

PART II

Supply Side

5

GEORGES DE MENIL

Market and State Provision of Old-Age Security: An International Perspective

How best to meet changing human needs over the life cycle is a central and defining issue for any society. At the end of their lives, in old age, human beings cannot provide for themselves with their own labor. The provision of old-age security is, like the organization of exchange or the maintenance of law and order, one of society's central functions.

A society's solutions to this issue may be individualistic or collective. Human beings may provide for their old age individually, by setting aside resources from which they can draw when their years of productive labor have ended. Alternatively, they may enter into an intergenerational compact in which successive generations agree that the young will support the old; in many traditional societies, families are structured according to just such a compact. In the modern welfare state, mandatory old-age insurance schemes link all the old and all the young members of society in an impersonal, general compact. In many countries, the transfers involved generate expenditures in the state budget that exceed any other category of transfers.

I have benefited greatly from comments from Peter Diamond, John D. Donahue, Jeffrey Liebman, and Eytan Sheshinski, as well as others attending the conference sponsored by the Visions of Governance in the Twenty-First Century Project. I am grateful for the research assistance of Yosuke Tada and Christian Ponce de Leon and the help of Laura Medeiros in preparing the manuscript.

Under either regime—state or market—trust in the provision of old-age income affects social cohesion. Whether the provision is individualistic or collective, whether it is organized traditionally or passes through a market, its reliability is a central feature of the stability of any society. A community in which the young were structurally incapable of providing for their old age, and the old were regularly abandoned by the collectivity, would be unlikely to survive for long; the tensions associated with the failure to provide old-age income would undermine the community's legitimacy.

The Development of Provisions for Old-Age Security in Western Europe and the United States

Over the past two hundred years, the transformations of the rural and agricultural societies of Europe and North America into urban, nonagricultural ones disrupted and eventually put an end to traditional patterns of provision of old-age security. Many elderly men and women who were no longer capable of working lived precarious lives, on the margins of their families and on the edge of destitution.[1]

Over time, a variety of mutual aid associations evolved in response to the new needs of the urban and industrial working classes. These covered sickness, accident, death, and unemployment in addition to the risks inherent to old age. In the nineteenth century, in Europe and America, "the number of local (risk-pooling) clubs . . . is lost beyond counting. Unstable and actuarially unsound, a cross between a gambling club and a mutual assistance fraternity, they were ubiquitous throughout the domain of wage labor."[2]

These associations took many forms. In Germany, journeymen's, trade, and fraternal associations coexisted with *Hilfskassen*, a system of funds administered by local authorities that collected voluntary contributions. In France, *sociétés de secours mutuels* grew to such an extent that they were subject to regulations by the state, under Napoleon III, and received guaranteed rates of interest for the contributions that they were required to deposit in a central, state-administered fund. In Great Britain, national "friendly societies" absorbed local clubs and pooled their risks. In the United States, local clubs, lodges, and fraternal societies abounded, with no obligation of regulation or even registration.

In addition, in Great Britain and the United States, but less so on the Continent, for-profit companies emerged, selling primitive forms of insurance to working people. These were the mail-order "collecting societies"

Table 5-1. *Coverage of Mutual Associations and Industrial Insurance Policies, Great Britain, France, and the United States, ca. 1911*
Millions of persons or policies

Category	Great Britain	France	United States
Members of mutual associations	6.0	4.0	1.9
Policies of "industrial insurance" companies and collection societies	26.0[a]	n.a.	24.7
Total population	48.0	40.0	92.0

Source: Isaac Rubinow (1911) and Statistical Abstracts; Daniel Rodgers, *Atlantic Crossings: Social Politics in a Progressive Age* (Harvard University Press, 1998).
n.a. Not available.
a. In 1900 (Rodgers, *Atlantic Crossings*, p. 218).

and the "industrial insurance" companies, so called because they sold insurance policies principally to industrial workers. Aggressive, well organized, and driven by the profit motive, these companies grew more rapidly than the nonprofit mutual associations. By 1911, a massive study of social insurance in Europe, conducted by the U.S. Bureau of Labor and codirected by the American physician-turned-statistician Isaac Rubinow, found that the number of "industrial insurance" policies sold far exceeded the membership in the fraternal associations of both the United States and the United Kingdom, as table 5-1 illustrates. In the United States, the combined market share of the two largest companies in the business, Metropolitan and Prudential, was 80 percent.[3] Although they were many in number, however, neither the mutual association policies nor the commercial policies were sufficient in value to cover the major risks facing industrial and urban workers at the time.

On neither side of the Atlantic did the institutions of voluntary risk hedging insure participants against more than a fraction of the calamities the future held in store for working-class families. Sick pay and (especially in the United States) funeral costs were the most common benefits. With steeper fees, some mutual assistance associations provided the services of a contract doctor or, more rarely, survivors' insurance. Beyond this core, the covered risks diminished dramatically. Only the best organized of the skilled workers' unions provided benefits against unemployment. Except for employees of a few of the larger corporations, retirement pensions were a luxury enjoyed only by portions of the business class.[4]

It is interesting to speculate as to why these private markets did not develop further, and, in particular, why markets for retirement annuities did not develop. The large number of other policies suggests that information costs and the costs of marketing were not the problem. The difficulty may have been that few people expected to live long beyond their working years, and those who did were suspected of being bad "life" risks. Alternatively, there may have been too few assets of long maturities with which the companies could hedge the long liabilities inherent in the provision of life annuities. However, the existence in Great Britain of consoles and in France of *rentes* would seem to belie the latter explanation. The long and the short of it seems to be that the people who needed the protection did not have the money to pay for it—and in any case were considered poor risks. The problem was partly one of market failure and partly one of disparity between social needs and economic means.

The inadequacy of these markets, the needs that they left unsatisfied, called for a public response. The plight of the elderly and the fear of the working population that the same fate might await them became key aspects of "the social question," which dominated much of domestic policy in Europe in the nineteenth century. Into this breach entered what was to become the central pillar of the welfare state—state old-age and survivors' insurance.

There was nothing inevitable about the emergence of old-age and survivors' insurance. Public state response could have taken other forms—and, in several countries, it initially did. In France, the Second Empire subsidized voluntary mutual insurance schemes; Sweden, Denmark, Belgium, Italy, and Switzerland followed suit. In 1910, French progressives passed legislation instituting mandatory private mutual old-age insurance. (The system was short lived: the workers rejected the mandatory wage reductions, and the courts refused to enforce them.) Great Britain initially opted for simple, redistributive minimum old-age pensions financed out of general state revenues.

The subsequent prevalence of the social insurance model was shaped by the fact that the country that provided the first comprehensive state response to the unmet needs of the new industrial and urban working classes was Germany. The "social question" erupted in Germany simultaneously with Prussia's efforts to mold a strong federal state. The key figure in the changes that resulted was the German chancellor, Otto von Bismarck. In Bismarck's mind, the two central domestic problems of the German Empire—the danger of social democracy and the need for a stronger state—had one answer: state socialism. His analysis is worth quoting. Referring to the repressive set of Anti-Socialist Laws instituted in response to the strikes of 1873, Bismarck later wrote that

> the effect of these repressive measures can only be of a partial and temporary nature, since the evil lies deeper than these manifestations. ... I am convinced that the dreadful economic situation, as experienced by the whole community and not just certain individuals, is the main source of discontent among the workers and artisans—and it is not limited to the working classes. The governments' lack of money is also a contributory factor, in that it prevents us from paying the lower ranks of the civil service adequately, thus driving them, including even the police, the lower judiciary, and the postal and telegraphic services, into the arms of the socialists.[5]

In a further memorandum, in December 1880, specifically devoted to accident, old-age, and disability insurance, Bismarck wrote that "all those willing to insure themselves must be entitled to a state supplementary benefit. This is an idea taken from state socialism! Society as a whole must undertake to support those who own no property, and ... [thus] ... produce that conservative mentality in the great mass of have-nots, which the right to a pension brings with it."[6]

Bismarck's remarks notwithstanding, the insurance-like solution, whereby the old-age pensions he called for came to be financed with wage-based taxes, was an accident. Bismarck shared with his adviser, Adolf Wagner, an intense distrust of the insurance industry and felt that it should be nationalized. (According to Gerhard Albert Ritter, Wagner called for "organizing private insurance in accordance with public welfare.")[7] Neither Wagner nor Bismarck, however, initially intended to nationalize pension insurance.

Bismarck's original plan, formulated in 1880, was to create a tobacco monopoly, similar to that of France, and use the proceeds to pay for a system of flat, noncontributory public pensions. He reasoned that the political appeal of the pension provision would help carry the unpopular tobacco proposal in the Reichstag, and he wanted the tobacco monopoly as a future source of general revenue for the state. As it turned out, the linkage worked the other way: opposition to the tobacco monopoly defeated the pensions proposal. Faced with this setback, Bismarck eventually turned, in the Principles of 1887 legislation, to wage-based contributory financing. As modified in 1889, the system called for equal contributions by employees and employers, on a progressive scale with five brackets. Pensions were to vary with the contribution level of the employee and the number of years he or she had contributed. The system was to be administered jointly by labor and management. On top of this, the state was to pay every retiree an annual flat fifty-mark "supplementary pension." Thus was universal public old-age insurance born.

Why did the German model spread and eventually become the dominant form for public provision of old-age security? Its spread was initially limited. Austria adopted Germany's system shortly after Germany did, but Great Britain rejected it as too statist. When Herbert Asquith's Liberal government passed Great Britain's first comprehensive public pension law in 1908, it opted for a noncontributory, means-tested, flat pension, financed from general revenues. This approach focuses on redistribution to the elderly poor and leaves the greatest room for private market provision of earnings-related pensions. The private industrial insurance companies had lobbied intensively against the use of the German model for old-age pensions in Great Britain.

Adoption in other countries of either the British model or the German model was roughly balanced until the passage in the United States of the Social Security Act in 1935.[8] The act created Old-Age Insurance (OAI), Old-Age Assistance, Unemployment Insurance, and Aid to Dependent Children. Whereas many of the other institutions of the New Deal have disappeared, the Social Security program has endured and expanded and is today, both in terms of its financial implications and the breadth of its popular support, a central pillar of the welfare state in the United States.

It was not initially obvious that compulsory insurance would figure prominently in the New Deal's Social Security agenda. From a cyclical point of view, contributory insurance was not considered good economic policy in 1935. Collecting taxes to build up a reserve fund from which no benefits would be paid for a decade was the opposite of the deficit spending called for by Keynesian logic. In fact, the pressure in Congress was for immediate relief for the elderly poor, not for new taxes. It was only at Franklin D. Roosevelt's personal insistence—inspired by his conviction that government should provide "comprehensive risk insurance for everyone: universal insurance against old age, unemployment, ill health, and disability, administered simply and efficiently through the Post Office"— that the concept of contributory insurance figured at the core of the act.[9] How much this vision owed to the influence on an American progressive's mind of German social thinking and how much it was tempered by a deep suspicion of markets left to themselves, and their potential for social harm, is not clear. Certainly the experience of the Great Depression could only have reinforced a personal skepticism about markets. What is clear is that Roosevelt knew that what he was supporting was not a temporary economic expedient but, rather, a major structural change.[10]

Emergency relief for the elderly poor, through the Old-Age Assistance program, was also included in the Social Security Act of 1935. Its political appeal may have helped ensure passage, but the broad-based and contributory nature of the Old-Age Insurance program may have helped ensure the longevity of the whole program. The fact that OAI was not a targeted assistance program, and that the entire working population perceived it to be broadly beneficial, was probably an important factor in its continuing popularity and subsequent expansion. Tolerance for targeted assistance, though high in a crisis, tends to wane in normal times. A highly redistributive program might not have enjoyed the same degree of lasting political support as OAI has.[11]

Both German social insurance and OAI were initially funded systems. In Germany, the state social insurance fund invested in projects of a social nature—hospitals, public baths, public water supply, and sewage disposal. In 1913 the system's reserve fund held 3 billion marks.[12] By 1930, the devastations of war and hyperinflation had exhausted the fund. In the United States, the slippage was more rapid. Budgetary pressures were such that, by World War II, the balance in the Social Security Trust Fund had been reduced to a minimum, and OAI was operating on a pay-as-you-go basis.

In retrospect, 1935 can be seen to have been a turning point for the rest of the world as well as for the United States. The New Deal established social retirement insurance as a central feature of the welfare state. Its adoption around the world after 1945 has to be understood, at least partly, as a feature of the momentum to adopt the economic and social model of the most powerful and prosperous country of the world.

Two Paradigms

The fifty years that followed the end of World War II witnessed both expanded coverage worldwide of state Social Security systems and the growth of financial markets for private old-age insurance. Among the high-income countries, the balance between these two developments

Table 5-2. *Evolution of Pension Fund and Life Insurance Company Assets, Various Years, 1980–98*
Percent of GDP

Country and sector	1980	1990	1998[a]
United States	43.0	68.5	115.2
Life insurance companies' share	17.5	24.9	33.2
Autonomous pension funds' share	25.5	43.6	82.0
United Kingdom	47.9	97.2	176.3
Life insurance companies' share	23.3	42.1	93.3
Autonomous pension funds' share	24.6	55.1	83.0
Germany	14.1	22.0	27.4
Life insurance companies' share	11.9	18.6	24.1
Autonomous pension funds' share	2.2	3.4	3.3
France	7.6	16.0	39.0
Life insurance companies' share	7.6	16.0	38.9
Autonomous pension funds' share	n.a.	n.a.	0.1
Japan	n.a.	39.8	46.5
Life insurance companies' share	n.a.	27.5	29.5
Autonomous pension funds' share	n.a.	12.3	17.0

Source: Organization for Economic Cooperation and Development, *Institutional Investors' Statistical Yearbook, 2000* (Paris, 2000). For Japan, "National Accounts in Japan."
a. 1997 for France.

varies. The simple logic of life-cycle saving suggests that "countries with larger Social Security systems would be expected to have smaller levels of private saving."[13]

Table 5-2 illustrates the relative magnitude of pension fund and life insurance assets in the five largest countries of the Organization for Economic Cooperation and Development (OECD) at the end of the twentieth century. These markets are most developed, in absolute terms, in the United States. The growing importance of deferred benefits in labor contracts negotiated through collective bargaining is an important part of this phenomenon. Many of the pension funds included in the numbers are company or union funds. The average value of pension fund and life insurance assets per employed person in the United States was $75,334 in 1998; pension fund assets accounted, on average, for $53,650 of the total.[14]

By the third quarter of the twentieth century there were two principal paradigms for the provision of old-age security: private markets and state social insurance. Under ideal circumstances, both approaches are potentially effective; both also have failings. The original British model of targeted assistance—no longer dominant in Great Britain itself—is, by its nature, not comprehensive. It is more appropriately viewed as poverty relief, which can coexist with majority provision through either private markets or state insurance.

Two underlying economic processes are capable of producing the real flows of purchasing power that old-age security requires: One is the classical process of saving and investment, a process that entails funding. The second process involves investing in what Paul Samuelson has called the "biological rate of interest": the young agree to support the old in exchange for the assurance that they, in turn, will be supported in their old age by the next generation. In such a pay-as-you-go system, if contribution rates are fixed, the pool of benefits available for distribution to pensioners grows with the rate of growth in the number of contributors and their incomes.

Theoretically, either paradigm could be used to administer either economic process. State insurance systems can be funded, and in principle, pay-as-you-go systems could be private. One can imagine a mutual society forming on the principle that the funds received from new members will be used to provide income to old members. Such a scheme would, however, be a Ponzi scheme, and Ponzi schemes are intrinsically unstable because the incentive is always to expand as quickly as possible. The only viable Ponzi scheme is one that is compulsory and is run by a state monopoly. A state old-age insurance system is such a system. In practice, therefore, the basic choices in the provision of old-age insurance are public provision, which may be either funded or pay-as-you-go, and private provision, which must be funded.

Financial Markets as Providers of Old-Age Security

Private pension provision requires both markets for instruments of accumulation and markets for life annuities. Do such markets exist? If so, are they complete, and are they free of significant market failures? If the answer is, to a reasonable degree, yes in each case, private capital and insurance markets should be capable of providing for old-age insurance in an economically efficient manner. The answers, however, vary with the nature of existing institutions and are therefore subject to change as economic institutions evolve over time.

The insurance aspect of old-age security must be emphasized. If I am a person of working age looking to my retirement, I want to be assured of income for as long as I live. In a traditional context, I may receive this assurance because I own the family home and it is understood that my children will live in it in exchange for supporting me for the rest of my life. In a more individualistic context, this assurance cannot be efficiently replaced exclusively by stocks and bonds. The portfolio I would have to accumulate to guarantee my income for the longest possible life expectancy would be substantially larger—and would require substantially greater sacrifice of current consumption—than what would be necessary if I knew in advance, and with certainty, the date of my death. To provide efficiently for my old age, I need to accumulate savings in a retirement fund and, at some appropriate point, to begin progressively to convert those savings into a life annuity. A number of the shortcomings of market provision have to do with difficulties with the insurance markets.

Market Failures and Other Shortcomings

In the past, many problems have limited reliance on financial markets for comprehensive old-age insurance. These include limited accessibility to market information, missing instruments, market volatility, adverse selection by risk category, and myopia and moral hazard on the part of workers.

Until recently, financial markets have been inaccessible to many working people. They have historically been dominated by insiders who released little or no information about the underlying facts of the businesses involved. When such information was available, working people did not have sufficient understanding or knowledge to interpret or process it. They were easily taken advantage of and thus subject to exploitation. Early financial history is indeed replete with stories of financial swindles.

Financial history is also the history of the progressive emergence of new instruments that fill existing gaps. Long-term bonds, particularly long-term indexed bonds, have not been prevalent until recently and still do not exist in many countries. This has constituted a serious obstacle to the development of life insurance companies, which, by their nature, must seek to balance their long-term liabilities with long-term assets. Life insurance companies have traditionally relied, instead, on such physical assets as office or apartment buildings, but diversification of individual investment risk, or of business-cycle risk, was consequently difficult to achieve.

Another missing market, which some have seen as significant, is the market for selling one's own future labor. In the feudal period, peasants agreed implicitly to be indentured in exchange for protection. Absent that institution, the peasants might have been less well protected against the violence of the times.

Income from financial investments is generally more volatile than income from labor. Martin Feldstein and Jeffrey Liebman report that in the United States between 1946 and 1995, the mean real rate of return on a balanced portfolio of stocks and bonds was 6.9 percent, with a standard deviation of 12.5 percent. Both the mean and the standard deviation are high.[15] Some commentators, reflecting on this fact, have opposed total reliance on pension funds for old-age security.[16]

Several comments are in order. First, realized real returns on state pay-as-you-go systems are also volatile. In real down cycles, everything suffers, including labor income and state revenue. In the great crises of the past hundred years—the two world wars, the hyperinflations of the 1920s, and the Great Depression—markets have crashed, but public pension systems have crashed along with them. More important, the volatility of annual market returns is not the relevant factor. Retirement portfolios are held, on average, for about twenty years. The long holding period provides, intrinsically, for substantial averaging of year-to-year volatility. It is therefore the variability of the twenty-to-forty-year return that is important for the worker; and this is much lower.

Financial volatility does bring with it a new kind of lifetime risk for savers—the risk of retiring at the bottom of a business cycle and therefore of having to convert one's retirement savings into a pension annuity at a disadvantageous moment. The answer to this problem is to average, by annuitizing continuously and increasingly over one's later years. Annuitizing over such long periods, however, requires life annuity markets that are more developed than those currently in existence in many countries.

Another obstacle to the development of annuity markets has been the difficulty of establishing objective indicators of risk. If applicants cannot be allocated to different risk classes, insurance companies will tend to write fewer policies than they otherwise would, to avoid carrying more risk than their premiums warrant. They will eliminate the applicants who are the most eager for insurance, on the assumption that they are the applicants who personally expect to live the longest. This pattern will tend to stunt the growth of the industry.

A strong, recurrent argument against market provision of old-age security turns on the purported myopia of a fraction of the working population. Indigent or reckless individuals may discount the future highly and thus, if given the choice, systematically underprovide for their later years. Some form of compulsory insurance may therefore be required.

In a society that provides means-tested minimum pensions, individuals whose income is close to the level that qualifies may, in addition, undersave in order to game the system. The promise of the minimum pension creates a moral hazard in that it provides an incentive for low-income individuals to avoid saving in order to benefit from the guarantee.

Over the past hundred years, as financial markets have grown in volume and in institutional complexity, some of the problems mentioned above have diminished. Regulations—the strengthening of processes, disclosure requirements, and measures to discourage or prohibit manipulation—have made financial markets more accessible. Increasing access has, in turn, educated the broad population and made it more knowledgeable. New instruments of increasing sophistication have filled previously missing gaps. The life insurance industry has developed new products, improved its management of risk classes, and learned how to explain its products to the general public. Myopia and moral hazard, however, remain, calling by their nature for an element of compulsion in the provision of old-age security.

State Provision of Old-Age Security

An omniscient, efficient, and benevolent state could solve many of the market failure problems identified above. If the technician civil servants do their job well, the citizens need not understand how the system works. An omniscient state can legislate any payoffs that complete and efficient financial markets could provide. The absence of choice in a state system eliminates the problem of adverse selection. Finally, because citizens are compelled to participate, both myopia and gaming disappear as problems. No state, however, is omniscient, efficient, and benevolent, and state provision is itself subject to many failures. The very discretion that makes first-best policies possible also permits manipulation of all kinds.

Although the literature on state failures is less developed than that on market failures, certain categories can nonetheless be delineated. These include state-induced market volatility, electoral myopia, and state capture by special interests.

State provision may increase the volatility of the real value of pensions. Governments that are short of revenue may arbitrarily break pension promises either directly or indirectly, through the more or less deliberate use of inflation. Recent history is replete with instances in which weak governments have allowed inflation to cut the real value of benefits. Peter Diamond makes the general point that, for structural reasons, state revenues may vary proportionately more than general economic activity, and state expenditures may therefore tend to be more volatile than general economic activity.[17]

The tendency toward volatility in government spending may be exacerbated by the limited horizon of elected officials in a democracy. Populist largesse on the part of incumbent governments seeking reelection may lead to commitments to unsustainably large pensions, which require budget-cutting swings in the opposite direction by subsequent administrations.

Organized special interests frequently undermine the capacity of governments to act in the public interest. Special benefits may be bought by corrupt groups. In countries in which democratic processes are not well established, governments may secure the support of the military, for example, by giving it special treatment. The power to strike in the provision of key urban services—transportation and electricity, for example—can give certain labor associations the ability to extract restricted privileges. These tendencies are incipient in all states but may become rampant in countries in which the state is weak. In the extreme case, the result may be nightmarish public policies that are a labyrinth of special interest provisions.

Such fracture has been common in state pension provision in a number of middle-income countries in Latin America and in postcommunist Europe. In many countries in those regions, at least until a recent phase of reform, public pension systems were fragmented in a variety of special regimes—for miners, teachers, the military, and church officials—each with different retirement ages, provisions for early retirement, contribution rates, and disability and survivor benefits. In those countries, state provision, far from providing a comprehensive system of self-financing old-age security, created a patchwork of unsustainable fiefdoms, each requiring general budget subsidies.

Compulsory Insurance through Regulated Private Pension Providers

In the last quarter of the twentieth century, a third paradigm of old-age security provision emerged: mandatory insurance through regulated private pension funds. The principle is simple: Each worker is required to contribute a portion of his or her earnings to an individual retirement account in a privately managed fund, which is regulated by a state agency. The agency initially licenses enough private funds and managers—through an open process based on experience and professional merit—to ensure that they will have to compete with one another. Each worker is free to choose his or her own fund and free to change funds at regular intervals. The funds are protected against manipulation by regulations that limit investment to securities that are traded in regulated markets, prohibit borrowing, prohibit related investments and investments in controlling interest, require diversification, and require the legal separation of fund assets from the manager's assets.[18]

Upon retirement the worker is required to convert the assets accumulated in his or her account into an indexed life annuity. Provisions differ regarding the freedom to withdraw some of the assets in a lump sum and the life tables that may be used for the annuity conversion. Annuity providers are subject to additional regulations, which require them to keep adequate reserves.

Because the contribution is mandatory, the state also provides a guarantee. Provisions vary, but the one entailing the least moral hazard is a guarantee to each individual account holder that he or she will benefit, at a minimum, from an amount at retirement equal to his or her life-time contributions, indexed to inflation to the point of retirement.[19]

The model corrects many of the problems associated with private markets discussed above. Through its licensing and regulations, the public agency screens and monitors the funds for the benefit of, and in the place of, the individual beneficiaries. If the agency is truly professional, independent, and honest, the individual beneficiaries do not have to have much knowledge of financial markets for the system to be beneficial. To the extent that annuitization is compulsory, market failure through adverse selection is avoided. The compulsory nature of the contribution also compensates for any myopia, eliminates moral hazard from the existence of minimum flat pension provisions, and precludes the use of gaming strategies to take advantage of those provisions. Finally, the compulsory nature of the contributions also ensures that fund accumulations rapidly exceed the critical mass necessary to justify the creation of market instruments that previously did not exist: corporate bonds—presently absent in some developing countries—indexed long-term government bonds, and the like.

The model also corrects many of the problems associated with publicly administered old-age insurance. One of the principal advantages that its originators claim for this model is that it isolates pension provision from political interference. The logic of a defined-contribution system is that the pension cannot be cut at the moment of payment. During the accumulation phase, the accounts are the private property of the individual contributor, a fact that also protects the funds, in principle, from being raided to provide budgetary revenue. In countries lacking a strong tradition of enforcement of constitutions, these protections are not perfect; but, at the least, they provide more insulation from state-induced volatility than a pay-as-you-go system of public provision would. The same provisions protect against the boom-and-bust cycle that electoral myopia can generate and against the fragmentation that weak states captured by special interests have frequently brought about.

The model of compulsory private insurance is distinctly separate and different from the public provident fund model. In the latter, workers are required to contribute a portion of their earnings to a pooled fund, which is managed by the state and from which benefits are paid to pensioners at the discretion of the state.[20] Both systems are funded. Both involve a combination of public compulsion and private markets. The distinction between private defined-contribution accounts and a public pool providing defined-benefit payments, however, is crucial.[21]

The model of compulsory insurance with private accounts has its own failings. It depends critically on the capacity of the state to establish an independent, professional, and honest supervisory agency. The costs of administering this system are inherently higher than those of administering a public pay-as-you-go system.[22] They include several categories of cost that are simply not present in a pay-as-you-go system: the costs of managing the accumulating funds, the costs of annuitizing at retirement, the costs of accommodating switching by individuals, and marketing costs. The latter two are inherent to the competition between funds that is central to this system.

Reliance on a smoothly functioning market for annuities is an important shortcoming of mandatory private pension fund systems. In a public system, the state simply calculates the pension and pays it. In a private system, the annuities are sold by for-profit enterprises based on individual actuarial calculations. In the United States, 10–20 percent of the premium for individual fixed life annuities goes into administrative costs and profit margin for the insurance company. Without a broad and efficient annuities market, the private system cannot correct the problem of volatility owing to the timing of retirement. That requires continuous annuitization after a certain age. Moreover, if the market for indexed annuities is not well developed, private provision subjects the beneficiary to an inflation risk.[23]

Finally, the mandatory private pensions model has been criticized for not being amenable to redistributive modifications, when redistribution is desired. Supporters counter that redistributive allocations to individual accounts are simple to include in the system. In summary, the mandatory individual account model protects the pension system from many of the political risks inherent in a public system. It also avoids some of the drawbacks of purely voluntary private pension funds, though the costs of administering it are likely to be as high as those of purely voluntary private funds.

International Experience with Pension Systems Based on Mandatory Private Accounts

Chile was the first country to design and fully implement a pension system based on mandatory private accounts.[24] During the 1970s it experienced, in uniquely radical fashion, both the fragmentation and demoralization of its state pension system and an authoritarian political reaction to the chaotic conditions under which this had occurred. The military dictatorship that seized power in 1973—and remained in power for sixteen years—ruthlessly suppressed human rights. It did not, however, engage in populist economic policies. To the contrary, heeding the advice of U.S.-trained economists, it proceeded to implement a series of far-reaching market-oriented economic reforms.[25] Many of these remain a model for much of Latin America twenty years later. One of these reforms was the large-scale replacement, in 1981, of a highly regressive state Social Security system with a system of mandatory individual accounts. That system is, in fact, now known as the Chilean model.

The verdict of twenty years' experience is that the system has functioned reasonably well. Although Chile had only a rudimentary stock market and was financially underdeveloped at the time of their introduction, the pension funds realized a yearly average real rate of return of 10 percent over the following twenty years—a period that included two major recessions. The country's workers, who might otherwise have retired with diminished state pensions, are retiring now with reasonable annuities. The system has not to date been tainted with any scandal involving major fraud or embezzlement.

In addition, Chile's financial markets have experienced remarkable deepening and growth since 1981. The private pension funds were not the only factor contributing to those developments, but they were an important factor. Finally, the national rate of private savings also rose in Chile over the period. Again, many policies affected this outcome, but the introduction of the pension funds and the accompanying deepening of financial markets appear to have contributed significantly.

For a time, it looked as though such a system could be introduced only in a military dictatorship. Then, beginning with Argentina in 1994, a number of other developing countries followed suit, introducing variants of the mandatory individual account system. The earliest of these were mostly in Latin America: Peru, Columbia, Mexico, Uruguay, and Bolivia. In 1997 the adoption of this model spread to the former communist countries of central and eastern Europe. Hungary and Poland each voted in such a system in 1997; it has now been legislated in Croatia, Bulgaria, and Romania.[26] Most of the new adherents have opted for a two-track reform, featuring rationalization of the existing public system and the introduction of a new, mandatory private account system.[27] The intent, in these instances, has been to establish a new regime with both public and mandated private pension systems. The World Bank has termed these regimes "multipillar" pension systems and has supported their implementation in a number of developing countries.[28] The two systems, when they work well, provide beneficiaries with different expectations and variability of yield. An argument can be made for diversifying provision of old-age security by combining the two systems.[29]

Latin America and the European transition countries have two things in common: weak states and underdeveloped financial markets. The multipillar approach addresses both conditions. Reform of the public pillar attempts to correct the worst distortions of the state's conduct. Implementation of the private pillar can, if successful, jump-start the growth of financial markets and contribute to rendering them accessible to the needs of the working population.

Implications for the OECD

The transition countries in Latin America and Europe are also low-income countries. Is the multipillar program a program for developing countries and not for those already industrialized? What are the implications of the reform movement of the past twenty years for the OECD? There are large differences in the provision of old-age security across the countries of the OECD. Some rely almost exclusively on public pay-as-you-go systems. In others, private markets provide a substantial portion of retirement benefits.

The United Kingdom, where public provision was already relatively low twenty years ago, has taken major steps—similar in spirit, though different in important ways, to the Chilean reform—in the direction of privatization. After dramatically reducing public pension benefits, the government led by Margaret Thatcher passed legislation in 1986 allowing contributors to the State Earnings–Related Pension Schemes to opt out of a portion of their contributions and transfer them to Personal Pension Schemes, consisting of individual accounts (initially only lightly regulated).[30] The basic thrust of the reform was continued by the government of Tony Blair in legislation, passed at the end of 1999, that further reformed the earnings-related portion of the public system and created a legal framework for the provision of collective private pension arrangements, known as Stakeholder Pension Schemes. An important difference between the Thatcher-Blair reforms and the Chilean reform involves the element of choice: under the British system, the decision to opt out is left to the contributor. (In Chile, new entrants to the labor force are automatically enrolled in the mandatory private pension funds.)[31]

The OECD countries share a growing demographic imbalance between young contributors and retired pensioners. Declining birth rates and increasing life expectancy are radically undermining the sustainability of pay-as-you-go systems throughout the region. The problem is most acute in countries—such as France, Italy, and Germany—that already have high levels of public pension provision. In Germany, in which the net reproduction rate is 0.7 and the population is expected to begin to decline in absolute numbers in ten years, it is estimated that the real rate of return of the state pay-as-you-go system will be negative in the decades ahead.[32]

Some of these countries are responding by cutting back benefits and raising contributions in their public pay-as-you-go systems. This rationalization has taken a particularly sophisticated form in Sweden and Italy, both of which have introduced "notional defined-contribution" schemes (Sweden in 1994, Italy in 1995). Although these schemes may sound like a form of funding, they are, in fact, a subtle means of reducing benefits in a pay-as-you-go system.[33] The reduction comes through a change in the formulas for calculating benefits. Traditional formulas, relating benefits to some average of previous years' wages, are phased out. Under the new formulas, benefits are calculated in such a way that their present discounted value is equal to the present discounted value of all contributions during the worker's lifetime. (The state sets the discount rate equal to what it expects the growth rate of the wage fund to be.) This implies, for instance, that, as life expectancy increases, the average pension declines. It also implies that early retirement reduces pension benefits. The approach avoids contentious focus on symbolic road markers, such as "the retirement age."

In countries in which public pension benefits are already high and the demographic imbalance is particularly great, such parametric changes are not likely to be sufficient. In such countries, a move toward funding will be necessary. Pension provision will require that investment in the "biological interest rate" be supplemented with investment in capital (which can be expected to produce, on average, a significantly higher real rate of return.)[34] In 2001, the Gerhard Schroeder government in Germany passed a law creating a mandatory supplementary contribution of 4 percent of wages to private pension accounts, a revision destined to raise retirement income above what the public pension system will be able to provide. Similar movements toward the funding of pensions are likely to become necessary elsewhere. Whether the new saving is managed by the state, by private markets, or by mandatory savings procedures is, to some degree, a matter of political choice. It can only be hoped that those choices will be informed by the evidence and the considerations analyzed here.

The relevance for the OECD countries of systems of mandatory, individual retirement accounts depends on the extent of the demographic transition each faces. In severe cases, in which pay-as-you-go provision is definitely not sustainable, replacement of part of the ailing pay-as-you-go system with contributions to funds whose growth reflects the real return on capital seems inevitable. The approaches experimented with in the developing world may, at that time, inform the choices of the developing world. As the countries of the OECD face those choices, they would do well to learn from the experiences with social reform of developing countries during the last quarter of the twentieth century.

Notes

1. This section draws heavily on Gerhard Albert Ritter, *Social Welfare in Germany and Britain: Origins and Development,* trans. Kim Traynor (Learnington Spa, N.Y., 1986), and Daniel Rodgers, *Atlantic Crossings: Social Politics in a Progressive Age* (Harvard University Press, 1998).
2. Rodgers, *Atlantic Crossings: Social Politics in a Progressive Age,* p. 217.
3. Ibid., p. 262.
4. Ibid., pp. 220, 221.
5. Confidential letter of 1879, quoted in Ritter, *Social Welfare in Germany and Britain,* p. 51.
6. Quoted ibid., p. 53.
7. Ritter, *Social Welfare in Germany and Britain,* p. 60.
8. In 1929 tax-financed flat pensions were the dominant form of provision for the elderly in Great Britain, Canada, Australia, and New Zealand. Contributory systems were dominant in Germany, Austria, and, after 1928, France (Rodgers, *Atlantic Crossings: Social Politics in a Progressive Age,* pp. 226, 227, 431).
9. Ibid., p. 438.
10. In Rodgers's view, it is a misreading to perceive the passage of the Social Security Act as "a straightforward response to the economic collapse of the 1930s" (ibid., p. 429). The act was part of an ideological agenda, he argues, made possible by crisis politics but not conceived as a response to the immediate economic problems at hand.
11. Redistribution may be built in to the benefit and taxation formulas of contributory old-age insurance, but it is not intrinsic to the system in the way that it is intrinsic to a pension system based on a flat means-tested pension. In fact, in the post–World War II period the contributory systems that functioned the best and lasted the longest—among them, old-age insurance in the United States—were not very redistributive.

Roosevelt emphasized the contributory and individualized nature of the system to ensure that every worker felt that he or she had a stake in the old-age insurance plan. He viewed that sense of ownership as a bulwark against the dismantling of the program by future governments. His intent is reflected in the following anecdote, as told by Senator Patrick Moynihan: "A Social Security card was issued to each worker, with the faint suggestion that there was a savings account of some sort somewhere in the system. Franklin D. Roosevelt famously told Luther C. Gulick, a member of his committee on government organization, that while it might indeed be a bit deceptive, that account number meant that 'no damned politician' could ever take his Social Security away" (Daniel Patrick Moynihan, "A Thrift Savings Component for Social Security: Bipartisanship Beckons," Kirk O'Donnell Memorial Lecture on American Politics, Washington, April 30, 2001).

12. Ritter, *Social Welfare in Germany and Britain,* p. 126.
13. Martin Feldstein and Jeffrey Liebman, "Social Security," *Handbook of Public Economics,* vol. 4, edited by Alan Auerbach and Martin Feldstein (Amsterdam: Elsevier,

forthcoming, 2002). Feldstein and Liebman point out that the intrinsic difficulties of cross-national comparisons have made empirical verification of this proposition elusive.

14. These estimates are obtained by dividing the dollar amounts implicit in table 5-2 by the total number of employees in 1998. They are aggregate and are averaged over all employees. They do not describe the position of new retirees.

Using household survey data that relate to the beginning of the decade rather than the end of the decade, James M. Poterba, Steven F. Venti, and David A. Wise have estimated that "in 1991, the median value of the future social security benefits of retired families with heads aged 65–70 was about $100,000, the median value of housing was about $50,000, and the median value of future employer-provided pension benefits was about $16,000." The difference between the two estimates may reflect, among many things, capital appreciation during the decade, the profit margins of the pension providers, and the fact that, in a positively skewed distribution, the median may be substantially lower than the mean. See Poterba, Venti, and Wise, "Personal Retirement Saving Programs and Asset Accumulation: Reconciling the Evidence," in David A. Wise, ed., *Frontiers in the Economics of Aging* (University of Chicago Press, 1998), pp. 23–124; the quotation is from p. 23.

15. Feldstein and Liebman, "Social Security."

16. Hal R. Varian, for instance, takes an extreme position in "Economic Scene," *New York Times,* May 31, 2001, p. C2.

17. Peter Diamond, "Insulation of Pensions from Political Risk," in Salvador Valdes-Prieto, ed., *The Economics of Pensions: Principles, Policies, and International Experience* (Cambridge University Press, 1997), pp. 33–57.

18. See World Bank Policy Research Report, *Averting the Old Age Crisis* (Oxford University Press, 1994); Peter Diamond and Salvador Valdes-Prieto, "Social Security Reforms," in Barry Bosworth, Rudiger Dornbusch, and Raul Laban, eds., *The Chilean Economy: Policy Lessons and Challenges* (Brookings, 1994), pp. 257–328; and José Piñera, "Toward a World of Worker-Capitalists," monograph in the series "The Boston Conversazioni" (Boston University, The University Professors, 2001).

19. This is the individual zero-real-return minimum guarantee.

20. "The first nationally mandated provident fund was established in Malaysia in 1951. . . . Several African countries followed in the 1960s, and several Caribbean and Pacific island countries did in the 1970s and 1980s. But economic instability, inflation, and devaluation in most African and some Caribbean countries have produced large negative rates of return and widespread dissatisfaction with the performance of the funds. So, several of these countries . . . have replaced their national provident funds with defined benefit pay-as-you-go pension schemes" (World Bank Policy Research Report, *Averting the Old Age Crisis,* pp. 203–04). The Malaysian provident fund is described in Hazel Bateman and John Piggott, "Mandatory Retirement Saving: Australia and Malaysia Compared," in Salvador Valdes-Prieto, ed., *The Economics of Pensions: Principles, Policies, and International Experience* (Cambridge University Press, 1997), pp. 318–49.

21. When the state contracts out the management of the provident fund to private managers, an additional layer of insulation is created. Nonetheless, the difference between private accounts and a pooled provident fund remains central.

22. The costs of managing the accumulating funds may be roughly the same in a well-run mandatory, individual account system as in completely private occupational funds. Diamond and Valdes-Prieto conclude that this was the case for the period they studied in

Chile's mandatory, individual system. They find total administrative costs per contributor to have been $52 per year in Chile and $47 per year in the United States. However, these costs can be much lower in a well-managed, pooled provident fund because such a fund need not be concerned with the administration of individual accounts that are switching between funds. The comparable cost was $10 per contributor per year in Malaysia's pooled provident system.

Again, in Chile, in 1991, the combination of marketing costs and managers' profits (both of which are absent in a public, pay-as-you-go system) constituted one-third of the total payments to fund managers for administering the system. For all of the above, see Diamond and Valdes-Prieto, "Social Security Reforms," pp. 260, 285–97, including table 6.9.

23. In the United States, individually indexed fixed-life annuities are not common. Their absence is, however, compensated by the growing market for individual variable-life annuities, in which the payout varies with market returns. These were first introduced by the Teachers Insurance and Annuity Association College Retirement Equity Fund in 1952 (see James Poterba, "The History of Annuities in the United States," Working Paper W6001 [Cambridge, Mass.: National Bureau of Economic Research, April 1997]).

24. Chile's pension reform has been extensively analyzed, notably by Diamond and Valdes-Prieto, "Social Security Reforms." See also Oscar Godoy and Salvador Valdes-Prieto, "Democracy and Pensions in Chile: Experience with Two Systems," in Salvador Valdes-Prieto, ed., *The Economics of Pensions: Principles, Policies, and International Experience* (Cambridge University Press, 1997), pp. 58–91.

25. See Sebastian Edwards and Alejandra Cox Edwards, *Monetarism and Liberalization: The Chilean Experiment* (University of Chicago Press, 1991), and Michael Bruno, *Crisis, Stabilization, and Economic Reform: Therapy by Consensus* (Oxford University Press, 1993).

26. Michal Rutkowski, "Bringing Hope Back: Pension Reforms in Transition Economies," paper presented to the Ten Years Later conference, Center for Social and Economic Research, Warsaw, October 15–16, 1999. See also David Lindeman, Michal Rutkowski, and Oleksi Sluchynskyy, *The Evolution of Pension Systems in Eastern Europe and Central Asia: Opportunities, Constraints, Dilemmas, and Emerging Best Practices*, monograph (World Bank, August 2000); Robert Holzmann, "Starting Over in Pensions: The Challenges Facing Central and Eastern Europe," *Journal of Public Policy*, vol. 17, no. 2 (1997), pp. 195–222; and Georges de Menil, "A Comment on the Place of funded Pensions in Transition Economies," *International Tax and Public Finance*, vol. 7 (August 2000), pp. 431–44.

In Romania, national elections and a change of government in December 2000 led to indefinite postponement of the new mandatory private pension fund system. See Georges de Menil and Eytan Sheshinski, "Pension Reform in Romania: From Crisis to Reform," in Martin Feldstein and Horst Siebert, eds., *Social Security Pension Reform in Europe* (University of Chicago Press, forthcoming).

27. In addition to Chile, Bolivia and Mexico are the principal countries to have decided on a nearly complete switch, leaving only the provision of a flat minimum pension in the public system. Kazakhstan has also largely totally replaced its previous public system but with a pooled provident fund, with very different political implications.

28. The case for combining a public system (the first pillar) with a mandatory private system (the second pillar) is made in World Bank Policy Research Report, *Averting the Old*

Age Crisis (Oxford University Press, 1994). The multipillar model includes provisions for voluntary private pensions (the third pillar). A World Bank publication (*From Plan to Market*, Alan Gelb, ed.[Oxford University Press, 1996]), offers caveats, and Peter Orzag and Joseph Stiglitz ("Rethinking Pension Reform: Ten Myths about Social Security Systems," in *New Ideas About Old Age Security* [World Bank, 2001]), are critical.

29. Georges de Menil and Eytan Sheshinski analyze the logic of this diversification argument in "The Optimal Balance of Intergenerational Transfers and Funded Pensions in the Presence of Risk" (Paris, November 21, 2001).

30. A major selling scandal resulted, as many individuals were convinced by unscrupulous salespersons to switch from generous public pension entitlements to meager private accounts. The managers of such accounts subsequently were required to pay a total of £11,000 million BPS in compensation. One interesting aspect of the scandal was that the Blair government acted to correct the abuses but not to change the course (David Blake, "The United Kingdom: Examining the Switch from Low Public Pensions to High-Cost Private Pensions," in Martin Feldstein and Horst Siebert, *Social Security Pension Reform in Europe* [University of Chicago Press, forthcoming]).

31. Because it is voluntary, the new U.K. system is still subject to problems of moral hazard and adverse selection.

32. See Hans-Werner Sinn, "Pension Reform and Demographic Crisis: Why a Funded System Is Needed and Why It Is Not Needed," *International Tax and Public Finance*, vol. 7 (August 2000), pp. 431–44.

33. In Sweden, the notional defined-contribution scheme is also accompanied by a small mandatory contribution of 2 percent of wages to private accounts (Edward Palmer, "Swedish Pension Reform: How Did It Evolve and What Does It Mean for the Future?" in Martin Feldstein and Horst Siebert, eds., *Social Security Pension Reform in Europe* (University of Chicago Press, forthcoming).

34. During the transition, some contributors will have to pay twice, once to meet obligations to existing and soon-to-be pensioners and a second time to accumulate funds for themselves. On a strictly actuarial basis, these individuals do not benefit from the reform. The additional pensions they earn just compensate them for the additional taxes they have to pay (see Feldstein and Liebman, "Social Security"; and Hans-Werner Sinn, "The Crisis of Germany's Pension Insurance System and How It Can Be Resolved," in C. Sijbren and Hans-Werner Sinn, eds., *Essays in Honor of Richard Musgrave* (Munich: CES-IFO, forthcoming). If a major social and political crisis is thereby avoided, however, society as a whole gains.

6

FREDERICK SCHAUER
VIRGINIA J. WISE

Bundling, Boundary Setting, and the Privatization of Legal Information

A CENTRAL FEATURE of the rule of law is the ready availability of information about the law. When the content of the law is secret, or even if not secret is not conveniently available to those who are subject to the law and must manage their affairs in light of the law, it is difficult to maintain that there exists a system of law.[1] Indeed, without a mechanism for transmitting information about what the law is to those whom law purports to govern and control, there is perhaps no law at all.[2]

Yet despite the central position of legal information in the idea of legality, and despite the fact that law itself is intimately related to government and to the state,[3] the provision of legal information, especially in the United States, has not always been thought of as a governmental function. Spurred largely by technological changes and changes in the market structure of legal information industry, the role of private sector entities in the provision of official information about the content of the law has recently become even greater. Examining the role of private enterprises in the provision of legal information can tell us much about privatization in general; even if it could not, it is an important story in its own right just because of the importance of readily available legal information to the rule of law.

A Brief History of the Role of Private Enterprise in the Provision of American Legal Information

As with schools and colleges, which were private (or church operated) before they were public, the debate about the "privatization" of legal information—authoritative information about the official acts of legal institutions or the authoritative statements of legal institutions themselves—takes place against the background of a history that originally involved private actors more than public ones. Especially in common-law countries, in which law made by judges is central and in which a system of reported precedent lies at the center of the concept of law, providing information about the rulings and official opinions of judges was, perhaps surprisingly, not historically a governmental function.[4] In English courts until very recently, and in American courts through much of the nineteenth century, judges, including appellate judges ruling on matters of law, did not themselves write down their rulings or their opinions. Rather, the judges delivered their judgments and the opinions supporting them in the form of oral "speeches" in open court, and the recorded content of these speeches provided the precedents that were the stuff of the common law.[5]

Although one might suppose that these official pronouncements about the content of the law would have been recorded, assembled, and distributed by the state, in fact this was not the case. Rather, private entrepreneurs called reporters would routinely sit in the courtroom and transcribe by hand the arguments of the lawyers and the speeches (opinions) of the judges. Sometimes they would also have the benefit of the notes of the judges themselves. Using their own notes and the notes of the judges, the reporters would then assemble and index the transcriptions and offer them for sale as reports of judicial action.[6] Over time, some of the reporters succeeded and others failed, and eventually in most common-law countries one and only one of these private reporters came to have something akin to quasi-official status. That the reports of the opinions of the Supreme Court of the United States are still officially identified by the name of the reporter (Dallas, Cranch, Wheaton, Peters, Howard, Black, and Wallace) for cases before 1875 is a sign of the private provenance of the provision of much public legal information in most common-law countries.

Over the course of the nineteenth century, however, the distribution of official legal information came to be a task that government took upon itself. In both the federal and state systems in the United States, the publication of case reports, as well as the publication of statutes and regulations, was a function increasingly performed by government, and a public official, known as the Reporter of Decisions, was in charge of publishing the case law, usually through the same state printing and publication operation that published statutes, regulations, and various other official materials.

Because the opinions of judges were public documents in terms of their availability, and because they were in the public domain as a matter of copyright law,[7] the publication of these materials by the state did not create state exclusivity. Although one might think that governmental publication of official and governmentally generated information would have been an ideal domain for the existence of a natural state monopoly, such a prediction would ignore the fact that lawyers typically prefer to have guideposts to their legal materials rather than having to confront and manage legal materials in raw form. Because the official legal materials, especially the reported opinions of judges, are presented in a form in which one can find a case by topic rather than just by date or by court or by judge, there is a potential area of competition between the public and private sectors if private sector actors can provide guideposted legal materials that are sufficiently superior to those supplied by public authority as to justify the (ordinarily but not necessarily) higher cost of the private materials.[8]

Seizing on this opportunity, in 1870 a man named John B. West invented what has come to be called the "keynumber" system, an elaborate typology of all of American law arranged according to large divisions of law (torts, principal and agent, constitutional law, bailments, and so forth) and numerous levels of subdivision such that, for example, in 2001 one can locate freedom of speech as Constitutional Law 90(1). West identified and categorized not only every reported decision but also every paragraph of every reported decision by the keynumber of its topic and provided both paragraph-by-paragraph case summaries and indexes arranged by keynumber. The same numbering and indexing system, known as the National Reporter System, was applied by the West Publishing Company to the decisions of every state and federal jurisdiction in the United States. As a consequence, someone seeking to find "the law" on whether a beneficiary of a will who has killed the testator can still inherit according to the will[9] can first locate through the indexing system or through a West-published legal encyclopedia the keynumber under which this issue is placed and then, through a series of digests, locate every paragraph in every opinion in every decision in every jurisdiction in which the issue is discussed by a court.

This system was perceived by the consumers—largely practicing lawyers—as sufficiently superior to any other system that West's company quickly dominated the market, using its increasing revenues and increasing market power to buy up numerous other private publishers of legal materials. Some of the original names still exist—*Purdon's Pennsylvania Statutes Annotated* and *Smith-Hurd Illinois Compiled States Annotated* are but two examples—but the names are mere milestones of a system in which a very small number of private publishers, primarily but not exclusively the West Publishing Company, dominated the industry of the private publication of statutes, judicial opinions, and other forms of official legal information.

Although books of annotated and indexed official materials published by West, Bancroft-Whitney, the Lawyers Co-operative Publishing Company, and a small number of other private enterprises dominated the market from 1870 until 1980, it is important that the contours of the relevant market be carefully and accurately specified. First, with only a few exceptions the market existed parallel to the market for officially published legal information. Although West published all of the opinions of the Supreme Court of the United States in an indexed, digested, and keynumbered set of books entitled the *Supreme Court Reporter,* this set existed simultaneously with the official publication by the Government Printing Office of the *United States Reports.* Similarly, the Government Printing Office publishes all of the compiled federal laws in the *United States Code,* but West publishes the same laws in indexed, digested, keynumbered, and annotated form as the *United States Code Annotated.* Although the Commonwealth of Massachusetts publishes the decisions and opinions of the Massachusetts Supreme Judicial Court in the *Massachusetts Reports,* the same decisions and opinions are also available from West as part of a series entitled the *Northeastern Reporter,* conveniently linked through the aforementioned digesting, indexing, and finding systems to West's *Massachusetts General Laws Annotated.*

Until recently, therefore, materials published by West existed, in almost every jurisdiction, in parallel with but not to the exclusion of officially and governmentally published versions of the same materials.[10] From this perspective, the model followed in the parallel public and private publication of official legal information resembled the model of parallel primary and secondary schools, in which private schools coexist with public schools, more than the model of prisons, in which privatization, when it occurs, substitutes for rather than coexists with the governmental operation of the same institutions.

Because official legal information is technically available to everyone—even before Supreme Court opinions were available online, any citizen could walk into the office of the Clerk of the Supreme Court and obtain a copy of a decision for at most a nominal copying cost; and judicial opinions and other official materials are from the moment of issuance treated as being in the public domain and are thus not protected by copyright—the ability of West to dominate the market was largely a function of the dominance of West's indexing and annotating system compared with that of any of its actual or potential competitors. As a result, West took quite aggressive steps to preserve its position. First, it jealously protected the copyright of its annotations, its indexing and digesting system, and its pagination.[11] The actual words of the court or the legislature might be in the public domain, West was forced to concede, but West took a strikingly pro-active stance in its attempt to ensure that any copying or resale of public-domain primary materials would remain unaccompanied by any of the modifications, guideposts, descriptions, numbers, or categories that West had appended to those materials.

Second, and perhaps more famously, West took active steps to ensure that citations to West materials—including citations to the online legal research service WESTLAW—would become the standard form of citation to legal materials.[12] Attempts by the courts or important legal publications like the *Harvard Law Review* to allow other forms of citation to authority were vigorously opposed by West at every turn, for reasons that should be obvious: If the mandatory or at least generally accepted form of reference to legal materials in documents submitted to courts and articles published in major legal publications was one that required access to West materials, then the dominance of West would become entrenched, in much the same way that commonly accepted evaluation and rating systems—for example, the Scholastic Aptitude Test, for college admissions, and the Graduate Record Exam, for graduate school admissions—have become entrenched.

Third, West has for years attempted to penetrate the world of legal education to ensure that students learning how to find the law will learn how to find it through the use of West materials. It provides trainers, at no cost to law schools,[13] to educate students in the use of West materials. It provides West materials at low or no cost to law libraries in law schools. It provides access to the online WESTLAW at no charge to law students while they are in law school. Behind all of this is the view that if students are provided the incentives necessary to ensure that they associate doing legal research with doing legal research with West materials, then when they leave law school and have to buy the books or pay for the online services, they will still think first, and perhaps exclusively, of West materials.

Several other characteristics of the legal information market have reinforced the hegemony of the West Publishing Company. First, a number of states, recognizing the pervasiveness of West's materials, have ceased the official publication of their own judicial decisions. The only method of obtaining the state case law in an increasing number of states, therefore, is through the West system, just as for an increasing number of specialized parts of federal law (the "no-action" letters of the Securities and Exchange Commission are a good example) the only even plausibly convenient way to access the law is through a private compiler and publisher of legal information. If the provision of official legal information over the past century is viewed as a competition between public and private providers of the same raw information, then increasingly we see that the private provider—for reasons of service and not of price—has prevailed over the public provider.

Second, the universe of legal information has increasingly become an online universe, one in which the number of major players is only two—WESTLAW, created and operated by the West Publishing Company, and LEXIS, created and originally operated by Mead Data Central. Although LEXIS remains a major player in the legal information world, WESTLAW has by some margin the larger market share for the legal market.[14] By designing its online legal research and legal information service around its already dominant accessing and indexing system, WESTLAW was able to overcome the initial advantage obtained by LEXIS as the originator of online legal information services.

Third, the number of private providers of legal information has decreased as a consequence of numerous mergers and acquisitions. The larger publishers have acquired the smaller ones, and some smaller ones have simply gone out of business. The most important change in market structure, however, has come about as a consequence of the acquisition of the survivors by large multinational publishing conglomerates. West Publishing is now a subsidiary of the Canadian-based multinational publisher Thomson, and the Dutch companies Kluwer and Reed-Elsevier own all of the remaining legal publishers of any consequence. Most significantly, none of these companies specializes in legal information in the way in which their acquired predecessors did. One of the most noteworthy characteristics of the West Publishing Company, the Lawyers Co-operative Publishing Company, the Michie Company, Shepard's Citations, and a number of their smaller competitors was that law was, for all practical purposes, all they did.[15] Law is not, however, all that Thomson, Kluwer, and Reed-Elsevier do. They are all heavily involved in mass-market publishing, financial publishing, nonlegal academic and scientific publishing, and in many other dimensions of publishing and information collection and transmission. Accordingly, an industry previously dominated by law specialists is now dominated by multifaceted information enterprises for whom law is but one component.[16] What this change in the structure of the industry means for the provision of legal information is the subject of the hypotheses explored in the remainder of this chapter.

The Bundling of Legal Information

One consequence of developments related in the foregoing material is a change in the way legal information is now packaged, or bundled. Most significantly, the bundling of legal information to make it available to users reflects the financial incentives and internal structures of the enterprises offering the information. One possibility, of course, is that this is an interesting feature of the industrial organization of the legal information industry but has no effect on the actual patterns of use of legal information and on the actual development and nature of law itself. If the use of legal information were exclusively a demand-driven enterprise, this would most likely be true. It turns out, however, that the use of legal information, as we have documented in previous work, is significantly, albeit not exclusively, supply driven.[17] The information that lawyers and judges actually use, and thus the information that forms and informs the nature of law itself, is a function of the cost of access to that information, and as that information becomes more readily available, its use increases.[18] Consequently, to the extent to which the bundling of legal information affects the supply of such information, and affects the array of information supplied, it affects the nature of law itself.

One important dimension of this bundling is the bundling of legal with nonlegal information. Just as law-specific publishers like the "old" West Publishing Company, Lawyers Co-operative Publishing Company, the Michie Company, and Shepard's Citations had a reasonably obvious motive for bundling their products—all of which were law—together, so too do the new successors of these companies have an equally obvious motive for bundling their current products—law and much nonlaw—

together. Indeed, "bundling" may be only the term that is used for an attempt to link a firm's less demanded products to the products for which there is more demand. When this situation falls on the wrong side of U.S. antitrust law, we call it a tying arrangement, as when a hypothetical franchiser requires its franchisees to buy franchiser-supplied napkins and cleaning supplies, which provide the franchisee no advantage in either price or quality, as a condition for being able to use the franchiser's trademark, brand name, and recipes. Even when the arrangements are lawful, however, and we call it bundling and not tying, a great deal turns on the bundles that are offered: bundles are usually assembled in such a way that the bundler can encourage the purchase of products perhaps not otherwise desired by the purchaser. Legal information enterprises in earlier days might have had an interest in bundling their less desired legal information products with their more desired legal information products. But what we see now is modern legal information enterprises—which are no longer just legal information enterprises—bundling their traditionally less desired nonlegal information products with their traditionally more desired legal information products, such as the bundling of newspapers, popular magazines, and nonlegal journals with purely legal materials, for example, either in WESTLAW itself or in the linking of Lexis and Nexis.

A vivid example of the consequences of bundling can be seen from the bundling that takes place by virtue of West's division of the fifty states of the United States into seven regions, designated as Atlantic, Northeastern, Southeastern, Northwestern, Southwestern, Southern, and Pacific. Although one could buy a set of the *Massachusetts Reports* from the Commonwealth of Massachusetts, if one wanted to buy the hard-copy opinions of the Massachusetts Supreme Judicial Court from the West Publishing Company, one was compelled to purchase the *Northeastern Reports,* containing not only the decisions of the Massachusetts Supreme Judicial Court but also the decisions of the highest courts of New York, New Jersey, Connecticut, Illinois, and Ohio. Because the division into regions goes back to the earliest days of West's National Reporter System, and because states have never been reassigned from one region to another—that would require a dramatic retrospective republication of all existing reports—the arrangement of the West regional reporters is such that lawyers find themselves with especially ready access to opinions from certain states solely by virtue of the West bundling system.

That this is far from inconsequential is demonstrated by a study conducted some years ago by Gregory Caldeira and by the earliest results from a more extensive research project we have just commenced that focuses exclusively on cross-jurisdictional patterns of citation.[19] To determine whether this bundling makes a difference, we have examined the use of out-of-state cases by various courts, trying to determine whether the West bundling system has an effect on which out-of-state authorities are cited. Consider first the decisions of the state courts of California. California is in the Pacific region of the West system, as is Kansas, but Nebraska is not. Given approximately equal populations, approximately equal distance from California, approximately equal legal histories, and approximately equal legal issues, one might expect the California courts to have cited Kansas and Nebraska authority to approximately the same extent.[20] Yet this has not been the case. From 1950 to 1960, California courts cited Kansas opinions 250 times but Nebraska opinions only 156 times, and from 1960 to 1970 cited Kansas opinions 247 times and Nebraska opinions 171 times. Given that, when seen from California, Kansas and Nebraska are quite legally similar, there appears a substantial possibility that the bundling of opinions from Kansas but not from Nebraska courts within the set of law books that most California lawyers and judges own may have played a significant role.

Similar results were obtained for a number of other states. Texas is in the Southwestern region, as are Kentucky and Tennessee but not Virginia or North Carolina, the latter two being in the Southeastern region. Without this subdivision, one might have expected the Texas courts to rely as heavily on North Carolina and Virginia decisions as on those from Tennessee and Kentucky, but the results are again surprising: from 1950 to 1960 the Texas courts cited Tennessee decisions 276 times, Kentucky decisions 258 times, Virginia decisions 247 times, and North Carolina decisions 119 times; from 1960 to 1970, the figures are 262 for Kentucky, 216 for Tennessee, 209 for Virginia, and 99 for North Carolina. Rhode Island is in the Atlantic region, with Pennsylvania, but New York is in the Northeastern region. Despite New York's size and political and economic importance, Rhode Island courts from 1950 to 1960 cited New York decisions 54 times but Pennsylvania decisions 65 times and from 1960 to 1970 cited New York decisions 51 times and Pennsylvania decisions 83 times. Finally, the Massachusetts courts from 1950 to 1960 cited decisions from Illinois, within the same Northeastern region, 216 times but those for Michigan, within the Northwestern region, only 104 times, and from 1960 to 1970 they cited to Illinois authority 193 times and Michigan authority 109 times.

These preliminary results strongly suggest that bundling decisions made on the basis of economics, history, corporate organization, and dubious geography have had a significant effect on the patterns of use of legal information. These results are compatible with results we have reached earlier in examining the consequences of the changes in bundling practices for legal and nonlegal information.[21] Before the ownership changes described above took place, and before the rise of online legal research services, legal information was largely segregated from nonlegal information. Legal publishers were separate from publishers of other sorts of information, law libraries were physically distinct from general libraries and from academic libraries, and in numerous other ways the domain of legal information was cordoned off from the rest of the informational universe. It would not be a huge exaggeration to describe the universe of legal information as historically the universe of information found in books published by the West Publishing Company and located only in buildings formally designated as "law libraries."

As both the computerization of legal information and the reorganization of the legal information industry have made access to nonlegal information substantially easier, we have seen a substantial increase in the use by lawyers and judges of nonlegal information, a rise that cannot be explained by an increase in the volume of reported cases, by an increase in the use of information generally, or by an increase in the general use of secondary authority. Indeed, as to the last, it is noteworthy that the use by American appellate courts of nonlegal information—newspaper articles, journals in economics and other nonlegal academic fields, books about nonlegal subjects, articles in nonlegal periodicals, and reference books that are not focused on law—has increased at the same time that use of legal secondary material—legal treatises and articles in law journals—has decreased. If the preference for the use of secondary material is relatively fixed, and at this point this is only a hypothesis, what we appear to be seeing is an important substitution of nonlegal secondary information for legal secondary information, a substitution that has potentially profound implications for the nature of legal education, the nature of legal argument, the nature of legal practice, and the nature of law itself.[22]

The indication from both of these lines of research is not only that publisher-driven decisions about what to bundle with what matter, and not only that these bundling decisions matter to the very idea of what counts as law, but also that they are likely to be the consequence of the organization and incentives of the entity that controls the bundling process. If legal information were gathered and published only by the government, we might well expect that information to be commonly bundled with other government information, or with other government information published by the same government printing operation, and we might even expect the subbundles to track the way in which government is organized. When legal information is gathered and published by nongovernmental entities, however, it is likely to be bundled in a way that reinforces the particular product line and particular commercial motivations of the nongovernmental entity. Perhaps more important, it is unlikely that any government would bundle the official information it produces with information from other jurisdictions, including other countries. Indeed, an interesting recent study by Kurt Metzmeier documents the way in which the development of Kentucky legal information reflects Kentucky's "fierce" desire, for reasons of political identity and political status, that "the state's own case law be the sole basis for legal decision by Kentucky courts."[23] Similarly, there has traditionally been no reason for states to bundle their legal information with the legal information from other states and no reason for countries to bundle their national legal information with legal information from other countries. If the increasingly privatized nature of the legal information industry leads the major players— none of which are now American owned—to start bundling American legal information with non-American information, we might again see significant effects on perceptions of what is to count as law in the first instance.

Implications

Legal information is not just information about law. Because law is itself an information-dependent idea and institution, legal information is best seen as constituting law rather than just describing it.[24] If this is so, then the very boundaries of the law are likely to be determined by the information constituting the law, and the roles of the boundary setters and the bundlers will be especially important. When the nature of law is significantly determined by the array of enterprises in which the providers of legal information happen to be engaged, the future shape of the law may wind up being determined by previously underappreciated forces.

The same issue may of course apply to other providers of services commonly and previously provided by the state. When private schools are run by those who also provide television programming, the problems and the possibilities are obvious, as they would be if prisons were run by those who had a need for field labor. The point here, however, is simply that these bundling decisions are more pervasive than is ordinarily thought. If that is so, then the issue of nongovernmental provision of functions traditionally performed by government may be intimately tied up with, as it is in the case of legal information, the array of activities in which the nongovernmental provider is engaged.

Again, none of this is to say that the nonpublic provision of public legal information is necessarily a good or a bad thing. It is to say, however, that a transformation that on its face may have looked technical and inconsequential could have far more impact on the nature of law itself than has hitherto been understood. The question of the bundling and rebundling of legal information involves a fascinating interplay among legal, economic, technological, cultural, and sociological factors, and in this sense provides a potentially valuable laboratory in which to examine both the changing nature of law and the consequences of privatization.

Notes

1. Kafka puts it well: "K. must remember that the proceedings were not public; they could certainly, if the Court considered it necessary, become public, but the Law did not prescribe that they must be made public. Naturally, therefore, the legal records of the case . . . were inaccessible to the accused and his counsel, consequently one did not know in general, or at least did not know with any precision, what charges to meet in the first plea; accordingly it could only be by pure chance that it contained really relevant matter" (Franz Kafka, *The Trial,* translated by Willa Muir and Edwin Muir [New York: Schocken Books, 1988], p. 115, as quoted in James H. Wyman, "Freeing the Law: Case Reporter Copyright and the Universal Citation System," *Florida State University Law Review,* vol. 24 [Fall 1996], pp. 217–81, p. 217).

2. This is the claim of Lon Fuller, who maintains that there are eight necessary and largely procedural conditions for the existence of law properly so called, one of which is promulgation (Lon. L. Fuller, *The Morality of Law,* rev. ed. [Yale University Press, 1964], pp. 49–51).

3. The claim that law is necessarily related to the state and to sovereignty is most fully developed by John Austin, especially in Wilfred E. Rumble, ed., *The Province of Jurisprudence Determined* (Cambridge University Press, 1995).

4. See Erwin C. Surrency, *A History of American Law Publishing* (Boston: Little, Brown, 1990), and Robert C. Berring, "Legal Research and Legal Concepts: Where Form Molds Substance," *California Law Review,* vol. 75 (January 1987), pp. 15–27.

5. See William H. Holdsworth, "Law Reporting in the Nineteenth and Twentieth Centuries," in *Essays in Law and History* (Oxford University Press, 1946), pp. 284–317;

Norman Lindley, "The History of the Law Reports," *Law Quarterly Review*, vol. 1 (1885), pp. 1–14; P. H. Winfield, "Early Attempts at Reporting Cases," *Law Quarterly Review*, vol. 40 (1924), pp. 316–41.

6. See Robert C. Berring, "Legal Information and the Search for Cognitive Authority," *California Law Review*, vol. 88 (December 2000), pp. 1673–1708; Craig Joyce, "The Rise of the Supreme Court Reporter: An Institutional Perspective on the Marshall Court Ascendancy," *Michigan Law Review*, vol. 83 (April 1985), pp. 1291–1324; and Thomas J. Young Jr., "A Look at American Law Reporting in the Nineteenth Century," *Law Library Journal*, vol. 68 (Winter 1975), pp. 294–318.

7. See James H. Wyman, "Freeing the Law: Case Reporter Copyright and the Universal Citation System," *Florida State University Law Review*, vol. 24 (Fall 1996), pp. 217–81.

8. See Kurt X. Metzmeier, "Blazing Trails in a New Kentucky Wilderness: Early Kentucky Case Law Digests," *Law Library Journal*, vol. 93 (Winter 2001), pp. 93–104.

9. This is the famous case of *Riggs* v. *Palmer*, 22 N.E. 188 (N.Y. 1889), decided by the New York Court of Appeals and a centerpiece of both Ronald Dworkin, *Taking Rights Seriously* (London: Duckworth, 1977), and Ronald Dworkin, *Law's Empire* (Harvard University Press, 1986).

10. An interesting exception is federal case law other than that recorded in the *United States Reports*. Although the Government Printing Office and the Reporter of Decisions of the United States compile and publish this official version of the decisions of the Supreme Court of the United States, the decisions of the U.S. Courts of Appeals and the U.S. District Courts are published only as West's *Federal Reporter* and *Federal Supplement*.

11. For an intriguing manifestation of this posture, see Donna M. Bergsgaard and William H. Lindberg, "AALL Task Force on Citation Formats Report, March 1, 1995: A Dissenting View," *Law Library Journal*, vol. 87 (Summer 1995), pp. 607–23. For a sampling of reported cases, see *West Publishing Company* v. *Mead Data Central, Inc.*, 616 F. Supp. 1571 (D. Minn. 1985), *aff'd*, 799 F. 2d 1219 (8th Cir. 1986); *Oasis Publishing Co.* v. *West Publishing Co.*, 924 F. Supp. 918 (D. Minn. 1996); and *Mathew Bender and Co.* v. *West Publishing Co.*, 158 F. 3d 674 (2d Cir. 1998).

12. See Bergsgaard and Lindberg, "AALL Task Force on Citation Formats Report, March 1, 1995: A Dissenting View." See also Coleen M. Barger, "The Uncertain Status of Citation Reform: An Update for the Undecided," *Journal of Appellate Practice and Process*, vol. 1 (Winter 1999), pp. 59–99.

13. In most American law schools, training in legal research is provided either by law students, who tend to do it poorly, or by members of the law library staff, or by faculty members specializing in legal research and legal writing. Because the costs of this training are always incremental—faculty members who teach torts or constitutional law would consider the requirement to teach legal research a great burden, not a benefit—law schools that are less wealthy or more lazy are susceptible to overtures by legal publishing companies to provide training in legal research, grudgingly (or not so grudgingly) outsourcing their teaching mission to teachers whose goals are more focused on the profit-based desire to maximize post-law-school use of the materials produced by their own company than on maximizing facility with the full range of legal materials.

14. Were it not for LEXIS's advantage in the market for nonlegal information—the NEXIS news and information service remains superior to WESTLAW's nonlegal informa-

tion services in the eyes of many legal and most nonlegal users—the WESTLAW advantage would be even greater.

15. One of the most noteworthy of these smaller legal publishers was the Equity Publishing Company, a small operation in Orford, New Hampshire, whose profitability in publishing New England legal materials provided the financial platform for its owner, Meldrim Thompson, to run successfully for governor of New Hampshire.

16. A personal anecdote may be of some interest here. One of the authors of this chapter is coauthor of a textbook and anthology entitled *The Philosophy of Law*, published by the large college textbook publisher Harcourt Brace. Harcourt Brace was recently acquired by Thomson, and this acquisition required approval of the Antitrust Division of the U.S. Department of Justice. Although the Justice Department approved the acquisition, it did so on the condition that the acquisition not be a vehicle for an increase in Thomson's market share in the law market, in which, because of its ownership of West, Thomson is already the major player. As a consequence, the Justice Department conditioned its approval of Thomson's acquisition of Harcourt Brace on Harcourt Brace's divestiture of all of its law titles, including *The Philosophy of Law*.

17. Frederick Schauer and Virginia J. Wise, "Nonlegal Information and the Delegalization of Law," *Journal of Legal Studies*, vol. 29 (January 2000), pp. 495–515; Frederick Schauer and Virginia J. Wise, "Legal Positivism as Legal Information," *Cornell Law Review*, vol. 82 (July 1997), pp. 1080–110.

18. This claim is defended at great length in Schauer and Wise, "Nonlegal Information and the Delegalization of Law," and "Legal Positivism as Legal Information."

19. Gregory A. Caldeira, "The Transmission of Legal Precedent: A Study of State Supreme Courts," *American Political Science Review*, vol. 79 (March 1985), pp. 178–94.

20. Although there might be reason to suspect that courts interested in issues of securities law would look more to federal courts in New York (the Second Circuit Court and the Southern District Court of New York) than to the state courts in Wyoming, for example, we have no reason to believe that such factors affect the distinction between Kansas state courts and Nebraska state courts.

21. Schauer and Wise, "Nonlegal Information and the Delegalization of Law," and "Legal Positivism as Legal Information."

22. In her commentary on this chapter, Deborah Hurley implies that we exaggerate the effect of the use of what she calls "nonbinding" materials, but there is little empirical evidence that the universe of empirically important information is limited to that which first-year law students are trained to think of as "binding," and there is much empirical evidence to the contrary. See, for example, the various articles collected in William W. Fisher III, Morton Horwitz, and Thomas A. Reed, eds., *American Legal Realism* (Oxford University Press, 1993), and also the various political science studies reflecting the "attitudinal" model of judging, many of which are described in Frederick Schauer, "Incentives, Reputation, and the Inglorious Determinants of Judicial Behavior," *University of Cincinnati Law Review*, vol. 68 (Spring 2000), pp. 615–36. Hurley also questions whether our analysis is applicable to civil law systems, but the rise of precedent and the rise of the role of commentators in such systems suggest that the same factors at work in civil law systems are at work in common law systems, even though the two systems have historically different views about the role of codes.

23. Metzmeier, "Blazing Trails in a New Kentucky Wilderness: Early Kentucky Case Law Digests," pp. 93–94.

24. See Robert Berring, "On Not Throwing Out the Baby: Planning the Future of Legal Information," *California Law Review,* vol. 83 (March 1995), pp. 615–35; Berring, "Legal Information and the Search for Cognitive Authority"; Molly Warner Lien, "Technocentrism and the Soul of the Common-Law Lawyer," *American University Law Review,* vol. 48 (October 1998), pp. 85–134; Eugene Volokh, "Technology and the Future of Law," *Stanford Law Review,* vol. 47 (May 1995), pp. 1375–92.

PART III

Inside and Outside

7

ARCHON FUNG

Making Social Markets: Dispersed Governance and Corporate Accountability

> *There is one and only one social responsibility of business—to use its resources and engage in activities designed to increase its profits so long as it stays within the rules of the game, which is to say, engages in free and open competition, without deception or fraud. . . . Few trends could so thoroughly undermine the very foundations of our free society as the acceptance by corporate officials of a social responsibility other than to make as much money for their stockholders as possible.*
>
> MILTON FRIEDMAN, *Capitalism and Freedom*

IN WRITING THESE WORDS four decades ago, Milton Friedman posited an economic world in which considerations about business are cleanly separated from the social good. In his view, and that of many others before and after him, the social good hardly needs to be aimed at to be achieved. Wise officials can set rules of the economic game—rules of property, finance, corporate governance, and regulation—to forge an invisible hand that will harness the self-interested pursuits of businesspeople, investors, and consumers toward a social good that none of them need embrace or even recognize. Indeed, those with the arrogance to pursue their own conceptions of the social good risk usurping their responsibility as trustees of

---

I would like to thank John Donahue, Robert Lawrence, Joseph Nye, Dani Rodrik, and Monica Toft for generous and insightful comments on previous drafts of this chapter.

other peoples' resources and undermining well-tuned market institutions.[1] The adage of this perspective might be "Mind your own business, and the business of society will take care of itself."

Since the 1980s the line separating these domains of private economic interest and social responsibility has blurred as investors, consumers, and social activists have demanded that large enterprises adopt policies and practices intended to improve the environmental, labor, and other social consequences of their business activities. Patrons and financiers, in other words, are increasingly injecting their social values into the realm of economic transaction. When they do so, corporate officers must advance notions of social responsibility in order to make money for their shareholders. To the extent that consumption and investment decisions depend not only on preferences about the price, quality, or features of products or about the risk and return characteristics of securities but also on preferences concerning the labor and environmental consequences of production processes and corporate policies, social values become important components of economic markets. When markets become infused with such values, they can appropriately be called social markets. Because increasing profits requires that other social ends be advanced, the distinction that Friedman poses breaks down in social markets.

Should we, as proponents argue, look forward to this play of values in product and capital markets, the spread of the so-called triple bottom line (environmental and social as well as economic performance) as a new era in which corporations become more responsible, burdens on overextended governments grow lighter, and communities and environments benefit?[2] Should we, perhaps, be less sanguine about social markets? After all, can we really expect millions of consumers or investors, many of them ill informed and many adhering to clashing values, to make choices that induce enterprises to act in ways that yield social benefits? In aggregate, consumers might demand expensive remedies that result in unemployment or drive up the price of goods by overreacting to insignificant risks. The mass of those with social preferences might not be sufficiently large to induce any changes at all. Large corporations might deploy clever public relations strategies to claim social impact without making substantive operational improvements. Extravagant claims about the efficacy of social markets might themselves erode support for important conventional regulatory approaches and capabilities.

The severe critic, one who anticipates that the intrusion of public values into the marketplace will generate high social costs, might wish for a return to the hypothetical Friedmanesque political economy in which consumers, capitalists, and managers need only heed their private concerns and can ignore social values. For reasons described momentarily, however, the prospects for returning to such a world are dim. Rather than railing against these developments, it would be perhaps more constructive to explore how social markets might be made to realize the expectations of its proponents rather than those of its critics.

The Idea of a Well-Ordered Social Market

Imagine a world in which the environmental, labor, and other social aspects of products and processes of firms were fully transparent for everyone to see and judge.[3] Such transparency would be a step toward building a well-ordered social market in which consumers and investors could act confidently on their ethical preferences. Those with preferences about how firms treat their workers or the environment could incorporate these values by accurately selecting appropriate securities or products. Just as consumers care about price, quality, styling, and features of various products, many also have preferences, often latent, about the conditions under which these products are manufactured: What is the environmental impact of production? Under what labor conditions is the product manufactured? Swelling ranks of so-called ethical investors have preferences against firms that, for example, manufacture tobacco and firearms, have poor labor relations, or disregard the environmental consequences of their actions.

In current marketplaces these consumers and investors, and firms that might do well by catering to them, have a difficult time acting on and responding to these social preferences, because mature market institutions serve economic preferences, not social ones. Laws of property and exchange aim to allow consumers, proprietors, and investors to protect their economic interests. Over the past seventy years, financial regulators and auditing firms in the United States have developed impressive standards for disclosure that allow firms to credibly communicate their performance and prospects and investors to make informed, comparative choices. A range of associations, from the Financial Accounting Standards Board to Public Citizen, are devoted to making these economic markets work by generating standards, information, and analysis.[4] Although social activists have used economic market choices to advance their causes for at least 250 years, these strategies have become much more prominent since the 1980s.[5] Owing in part to the youth of this phenomenon, there are few corresponding institutions to facilitate the play of social values in economic markets.

Well-ordered social markets, then, require a range of public and private institutions that establish resources for education, choice, transparency, and competition with respect to the ethical and political preferences of consumers, investors, and corporate officers. Existing markets are not well ordered in this way. If they were, they would offer important advantages, but also some potentially serious costs, for regulators, firms, and the consuming and investing public.

Regulation

Some of the most obvious benefits accrue to regulators in their efforts to alter the behavior of firms. If consumers have preferences that align with broad public aims such as improving labor conditions or reducing environmental harms, then regulators gain consumers as important allies in bridling corporate behavior. Many firms are acutely more sensitive to punishments and rewards meted out in marketplaces—such as boycotts, loss of reputation, customer defection, and stock price declines—than to sanctions levied by officials. Consumer force may also be a kind of Pandora's box, however, unleashing pressures on firms that push them to become so green or to raise wages or improve workplace conditions so much that they reduce employment or raise prices. Another concern is that energy spent on creating social markets will erode political support for more traditional governmental regulation.

Firms

Faced with demands from many quarters to become more socially responsive, firms would be affected by well-ordered social markets in at least three important ways. First, those who could demonstrate good performance in areas like energy, environment, community responsibility, or labor might capture new markets of consumers and investors who were sensitive to these issues. Conversely, however, firms that performed poorly on such dimensions would become less competitive.

Second, a stable background of rules for social competition in the marketplace would help firms control risks to their reputations. Currently, high-profile firms are vulnerable to singular exposés of outrageous behavior. Prominent firms such as Nike, the Gap, Timberland, and the Body Shop have recently been subjected to damaging attacks from social activists complaining about their labor practices and armed with scandalous anecdotes.[6] Because there is little infrastructure through which such firms can credibly claim that they are, all things considered, socially responsible, it is difficult for large firms to manage this source of risk to their brands and reputations. Well-ordered social markets, by contrast, aim to establish levels of transparency sufficient for firms, investors, and consumers to make credible and comparable assessments of overall corporate social performance. Although scandals about corruption and horrible working conditions will always be shocking, the availability of judicious assessments would mitigate damage from embarrassing revelations for firms with otherwise proven records.

Third, businesses and industries that successfully respond to pressures to improve their social performance may forestall, or obviate the need for, more burdensome regulation. On the other hand, firms that excelled under social market pressures would quite likely be able to operate successfully under a more demanding regulatory environment as well. Methods that corporations develop to reach levels of social or environmental performance are also likely to be less costly and more compatible with complex, quickly changing business practices than detailed rules and constraints imposed by government regulators. Many so-called voluntary programs, such as the Chemical Manufacturers Association's Responsible Care effort, were undertaken in part as a less burdensome substitute that might preempt conventional regulatory intervention.[7] A common criticism of such programs is that they fail to generate substantial improvements.[8] Well-ordered social markets pressure such programs to show results and facilitate evaluation of their outcomes. Both the public and regulators could thereby better gauge whether, in specific instances, "voluntary" responses were indeed adequate substitutes for conventional regulatory approaches.

The Public

Consumers, investors, and the public at large constitute the main beneficiaries of well-ordered social markets. From the Friedmanesque perspective, markets are an arena in which individuals realize freedom by making choices about consumption and investment. Acting on social commitments and values is certainly as important a component of freedom as preferences oriented toward consumption or accumulation. Well-ordered social markets, therefore, enhance individual liberty and freedom by allowing consumers and investors to advance their social values in the marketplace.

From a different perspective, often thought to be in tension with the first, well-ordered social markets also extend the reach of democracy and popular sovereignty. They constitute new, potentially quite powerful, mechanisms for expressing and aggregating civic, social, and political preferences. Well-ordered social markets supplement conventional channels of political expression and popular control by creating distinctive arenas of governance in which citizens participate directly, through their market choices, in influencing the behavior of powerful economic entities often resistant to other forms of social control. Like other methods of political aggregation, however, social action in the marketplace, even a well-ordered marketplace, suffers from characteristics defects. Chief among these are inequality between citizens (wealthy consumers will have more voice than poor ones), the clash of values that may result in poor or incoherent governance (some will favor job creation, others the environment), and the risk that the machinery of aggregation will lend institutional force to abhorrent or immoral preferences ("buying American," for example, can lead to protectionism). In politics, however, the benefits of democratic rule lead us to accept these dangers and attempt to manage them as best we can rather than to reject democracy. Analogously, the dangers of incorporating social values into economic markets call for deliberate institutional design and management, not efforts to purge these values from the marketplace.

Emerging Social Markets

As with any market, well-ordered social markets depend upon interest and engagement from many fronts. Do consumers and investors act on their social values in product and capital markets, or does this social activity occur only on the irrelevant margins? Do firms have the wherewithal or willingness to respond to appeals for them to become more socially responsible? Can officials facilitate the development of social markets, or are they trapped in more conventional approaches to regulation? Recent developments on each of these fronts—consumer, investor, enterprise, and government—suggest that social markets are emerging in many sectors and regions. Because incorporation of social values into these markets has been piecemeal and haphazard, social markets exhibit many difficulties and fall short of the ideal described above.

Ethical Consumerism

Survey data and investment patterns show that consumers in developed countries increasingly care about the social consequences of their market behavior. Socially responsible investing, for example, has grown dramatically in the past decade, far outpacing the expansion of investment in general. Between 1995 and 1999 the total assets in U.S. investment funds utilizing "social screens," which exclude firms contributing to activities like tobacco and firearms manufacture or environmental degradation, grew almost tenfold, from $162 billion to $1.5 trillion.[9]

Direct surveys of consumer preferences and behavior report widespread willingness to pay premiums based on the social and ethical character of production processes. Marymount University's Center for Ethical Concerns conducted a telephone survey in 1999 on consumer attitudes about garment production.[10] Three-quarters of respondents reported that they would avoid shopping at a retailer whom they knew to sell garments made in sweatshops. Eighty-six percent said that they would pay an extra dollar on a twenty-dollar garment if they could be sure that it had not been made under sweatshop conditions. In October 1988, Harvard University's Richard Freeman conducted a survey that yielded similar results: "80 percent of respondents said that they would not buy products made under poor conditions or that they were willing to pay more if they knew the items were made under good conditions."[11] Environics International conducted a mammoth survey in 1999 of individuals in twenty-three countries on their attitudes about corporate social responsibility. Although respondents from North America and western Europe felt more strongly than those from developing nations, substantial percentages of respondents everywhere felt that large companies had responsibilities as ethical and social leaders. In North America, 51 percent of respondents reported having punished a company for being socially irresponsible in the past year, while 39 percent of northern European respondents claimed to have done so.[12]

Corporate Responses

In response to these concerns of consumers, investors, and critics, corporations of many stripes have begun to add social concerns such as community connectedness, environmental impact, and labor relations to the long list of dimensions on which they already compete for market and mind share—product diversity and quality, design, development cycle time, and logistical and supply chain management. This trend bears names such as "corporate social responsibility" and "ethical sourcing."[13]

These responses began with isolated initiatives. Since the 1980s, many corporations have developed codes of conduct according to which they issue declarations of intent or internal ethical standards. Although these codes often grapple with a variety of social concerns, they tend to focus on labor and environmental issues.[14] Comprehensive estimates are unavailable, but surveys indicate that the adoption of such codes is widespread, especially among larger firms. In one international survey of three hundred large companies, 76 percent reported having a code of conduct.[15] A U.S. Department of Labor survey of the largest apparel manufacturers and retailers reports that thirty-six out of forty-two companies had codes restricting child labor.[16] At one extreme of corporate social responsibility, the Body Shop issued a four-volume social statement in 1995 that included three in-depth audits of its environmental, social, and animal testing policies.[17]

Critics who doubt the sincerity of these corporate policies have argued that they yield few benefits for workers. Many firms, in turn, have responded by hiring independent social auditing agencies, developing partnerships with credible nongovernmental organizations, and incorporating these codes into their own internal quality management and supply chain practices. Some of these firms have also responded by incorporating labor and other social priorities directly into their internal design, management, and supplier relations protocols. Nike, for example, established a code of conduct on labor and environmental practices in 1992 and two years later began a program of external monitoring. Subcontractor compliance with the code is monitored through a program of internal self-evaluation conducted by Nike staff and factory managers and then reviewed by external accounting, health and safety, and environmental consulting firms.[18] Reebok and Adidas, Nike's main competitors, as well as companies such as Levi, Disney, the Gap, and other prominent merchandisers, have established similar programs that combine in-house assessment with audits by consulting firms. Reebok has instituted a worldwide Human Rights Production Standards factory performance assessment, and Adidas has implemented a Standards of Engagement Survey Form on Health, Safety, and Environment for all its subcontractors.

Associational Efforts

Public skepticism about the sincerity and effectiveness of these corporate efforts, even when subject to social auditing, has fueled the proliferation of independent monitoring, social certification, and social standards efforts in North America, Europe, and other regions. Typically, nongovernmental organizations lead these initiatives and develop standards for the social performance, process, inspection, or reporting of enterprises that wish to affiliate with them. As with more strictly economic certifications such as the International Organization for Standardization (ISO) series of standards, companies can then advertise their affiliations with these programs to attract more discerning customers or investors. Frequently, multiple social standards associations compete with one another within a particular sector. A well-ordered social market would offer mechanisms for assessing the relative merits of such competing efforts, comparisons that are currently difficult to make.

In wood products, for example, more than a half dozen major associational programs inculcate ecologically sound forestry practices that cater to environmentally concerned customers. One of the most prominent of these is the Forest Stewardship Council (FSC). Founded in 1993 and now supported by major environmental groups including the World Wildlife Fund, Greenpeace, and the Sierra Club, the FSC convenes regional working groups that develop contextually sensitive standards to advance the body's international principles, which include forest conservation, minimization of environmental impact, and harmonious relations with workers, indigenous peoples, and local communities. To become certified by the FSC, a forest must be submitted to third-party certification to ensure compliance with regional and international standards, which include environmental performance objectives. Products from such certified forests may bear an FSC logo.

Consumer companies that target customers who are sensitive to design and environmental quality, such as Ikea of Sweden, have been part of the FSC since its inception. However, major consumers and producers of wood products in the United States, Europe, and elsewhere have also formed working partnerships with the FSC following public campaigns by environmental activists. In 1996, for example, a major buyer's group in the United Kingdom, representing 22 percent of wood use there, adopted FSC standards.[19] Home Depot and Lowe's Home Improvement agreed to preferentially purchase FSC-certified wood in 1999 and 2000, respectively. Worldwide, the FSC and its subsidiary organizations have certified 49 million acres of forests in thirty-five countries.[20]

In the face of mounting public criticism and possible additional regulation, the American Forest and Paper Association created the Sustainable Forestry Initiative (SFI), an industry self-regulation initiative, in 1992.[21] The program seeks to develop standards and management practices to increase forest productivity while ensuring long-term sustainability, preserving biodiversity and wildlife habitat, and protecting water quality. Member companies of the trade association, which represents 80 percent of all paper and 50 percent of all wood production in the United States, are required to participate in the SFI, and fifteen companies have been expelled for failure to comply with SFI standards. As of May 2001, 93.7 million acres of forest land were enrolled in the initiative.[22]

Although it enjoys a wide range of sponsorship, the SFI has suffered criticism for being dominated by industry actors. Conversely, the Forest Stewardship Council has been perceived as controlled by environmental activists. Critics have charged that the SFI lacks independent review, that its guidelines require little performance reporting, that they do not require independent certification or auditing, and that they offer no consumer label to indicate a company's compliance with their standards. In part responding to criticisms and to the competing FSC standards, the SFI has attempted to address each of these public concerns: program managers have convened an external expert review panel, diversified the composition of its governing board, and dramatically expanded the practice of third-party certification.[23]

A similar dynamic of associational competition has emerged around labor standards in the international production of apparel. Public controversies surrounding child labor, low wages, and poor working conditions have fueled the proliferation of independent monitoring and third-party social certification programs in the United States and Europe. The major initiatives in this area all have codes of conduct informed by the International Labor Organization's core standards, though they differ substantially in procedures for monitoring, enforcement, and financing inspections.

The Fair Labor Association emerged from the Clinton administration's Apparel Industry Partnership.[24] It is one of the most advanced initiatives, but it has been criticized for being controlled by industry. SA8000, created in 1997 by the Council on Economic Priorities, an American nongovernmental organization, is patterned on the ISO family of standards. SA8000 requires corporations seeking the council's stamp of approval to hire certified auditors to evaluate their subcontractors' compliance with the code of conduct. The Ethical Trading Initiative, established by a British coalition in 1998, is also developing a monitoring system, conducting pilot studies, organizing training programs for monitors, and building coalitions in developing countries to carry out verification work. Finally, the Worker Rights Consortium, developed by United Students against Sweatshops in 1999, focuses on information forcing, verification systems, and pro-active inspections. The consortium differs from the other four models in that it explicitly does not certify company compliance with a code of conduct or standard.

Compared with the forest products programs, social market associations in apparel production are relatively immature regarding standards development, certification and monitoring capacity, and market penetration. In these sectors and others, public and market demands for social responsibility have triggered associational efforts to satisfy customers by changing corporate practice. Some of these initiatives, such as the SFI and perhaps the Fair Labor Association, are led by firms themselves. Others, such as the Forest Stewardship Council and the Workers Rights Consortium, emerged from social activism. Although each of these associative efforts has its own comparative advantages, they all face the common challenges of developing standards and management methods to solve complex social and environmental problems, balancing these ends against pressing economic imperatives, and credibly communicating their successes to consumers and the general public. The complexity of these issues, relatively low incentives to acquire information about social performance, and frequent lack of transparency in the standard setting, monitoring, and performance evaluation practices of these social market associations make it difficult for consumers and others to know whom to believe or which associational endorsements best advance particular social preferences.

Governmental Initiatives

Regulatory efforts might help ease this confusion by providing structure and standards by which to adjudicate the competing claims of these various associations. Although regulators have not been blind to the emergence and importance of social markets, their strategies have not for the most part utilized these developments. Instead, some regulatory initiatives have mimicked associational efforts by establishing public social labels or convening particular initiatives, such as the Fair Labor Association. Other regulatory approaches have created social markets out of whole cloth by imposing information disclosure requirements upon the private sector.

One characteristic regulatory social market strategy has been to create official governmental labels that qualifying products may bear. In the area of environmental performance, such "eco-labels" include Germany's Blue Angel, the European Union's EuroFlower, the Nordic Swan, and the U.S. Environmental Protection Agency's Energy Star.[25] Although there is no definitive evaluation of the success of such efforts, particular labels, such as the Energy Star program for computer peripherals, have induced socially desirable technological innovation throughout entire product categories.[26] More generally, however, there is little evidence to support or reject proponents' claims about the market or environmental impacts of such programs.[27]

Another market-oriented regulatory strategy involves compelling firms to publicly disclose information about their social and environmental performance. Such disclosure allows consumers, investors, and others to act on their social preferences by conveying or withdrawing their support from enterprises based on these disclosures. The most prominent example of such a program is the Toxics Release Inventory (TRI) in the United States, which compels all facilities meeting certain size and sectoral criteria to report the amounts of their releases of more than six hundred toxic chemicals to the Environmental Protection Agency. The agency then posts these data on the Internet, making them widely available to firm managers, reporters, activist groups, consumers, and many others. Between 1988 and 1999, reported releases of chemicals consistently tracked by the program decreased by 45 percent.[28]

This is a stunning decline in toxics emissions nationwide, but experts debate many dimensions of this success, including the veracity of reported figures, whether declines can be attributed to the information disclosure program, the sustainability of this trend in the future, the potential for public overreaction, and the relation between these toxic releases and risks posed to human health.[29] Nevertheless, the intermediate effects of information disclosure are well established. The annual publication of TRI data is an occasion for journalists at local, state, and national levels to generate reports of the worst polluters on their beats. Many managers and corporate officials have pursued toxics reduction strategies within their own organizations to avoid public embarrassment by TRI data. Firms that perform poorly in TRI rankings suffer declines in securities markets.[30]

Official social labels and information-forcing strategies illustrate that regulators have recognized the power of social market forces and the capacity of state action to construct these markets by, for example, forcing every firm within a broad category to disclose socially relevant, but potentially embarrassing, information. However, regulatory strategies have thus far failed to leverage, and may even stifle, the powerful social market developments among trade associations and within society more broadly. For example, state-sponsored eco-labels, prominent and dominant because they are official, may compete with similar, perhaps technically superior, initiatives from trade associations and nongovernmental organizations and even from different levels of government.[31] Similarly, the comprehensiveness of disclosure programs like the TRI make them attractive, but they sacrifice depth and meaning for the sake of scope. Richer information, perhaps conveying progress on dimensions like pollution prevention and real reductions in health risk, requires more concerted cooperation and the development of technical expertise of the sort that the associational efforts described above have begun to generate.

Building Social Market Institutions

These trends among consumers and investors, the responses of corporations, the creation of mediating associations, and novel regulatory strategies all highlight the possibility and potential power of social markets. Currently, however, these emerging social markets face chaos and severe limitations. Where single firms have responded to activist critics, it has been difficult for outsiders to gauge whether substantial improvements have followed. Where multiple associations offer competing social standards, it is difficult for consumers and others to adjudicate their claims and know which efforts align with their own preferences. Where there is only one such association or publicly sponsored label, there is weak pressure for innovation and risks of capture by private interests. Even absent these imperfections, the aggregation of individual social preferences in economic markets may generate harmful unintended consequences such as unemployment, barriers to trade, and reduced economic growth.

Will these problems take care of themselves as social markets mature over time? The dynamics of demands from consumer and public interest associations and responses from corporations may eventually generate the institutions, norms, and explicit agreements necessary to render the play of social values in economic markets well ordered and transparent. However, familiar problems with capital and product markets—such as the difficulty of coordinating conflicting standards, domination of large actors, and private resistance to public disclosure—often require regulatory remedy. Similarly, mitigating analogous defects in emerging social markets will come more quickly through public and private strategies that deliberatively and collectively establish institutions and ongoing management mechanisms. More specifically, well-ordered social markets require five foundations that are unlikely to develop in the absence of deliberate, cooperative, and public initiative: scope, transparency, competition, robust and open intermediaries, and resources for preference transformation.

Scope

Perhaps the greatest weakness of currently emerging social markets is their narrow scope: only a few firms in a sector or niche claim to be good social performers. Consumers and analysts focus their attention, and apply the rewards and punishments of their patronage, to just a few firms, and consequently many others—who may perform more poorly in environmental impact or in their treatment of workers—escape scrutiny. Expanding scope frequently requires affirmative regulatory action. Mandatory disclosure policies, such as the Toxics Release Inventory, illustrate one way in which regulation can help "complete" social markets. Another route, one that demands more regulatory expertise and nuance, would require vastly more firms to undergo social audits and rankings now provided by private, associational, and nongovernmental venders. Financial market regulation offers one promising model along these lines. Since its inception after the Great Depression, the Securities and Exchange Commission has honed mediated, but mandatory, disclosure requirements into a fine art by means of which the agency quite successfully leverages market forces to expand its regulatory reach.[32]

Transparency

Beyond scope, well-ordered social markets require transparency in both the processes of accumulating relevant performance information and the data itself. Just as financial markets do not function well when investors cannot reliably assess managers' contentions about their assets and market performance, so social markets require institutional arrangements by which corporations can credibly demonstrate that their environmental, labor, and social policies result in concrete gains and are not just public relations programs. The recent surge of social market activity has failed to generate such a transparent environment. Although devices such as corporate codes of conduct, social auditing services provided by major consulting and accounting firms, and independent monitoring have proliferated and become increasingly sophisticated over the past decade, these mechanisms still fail to satisfy skeptics because they are opaque and often initiated by the very firms they seek to hold accountable.

Such mechanisms are opaque for several reasons. Many firms are reluctant to disclose information that they consider to be proprietary, such as the names and locations of their suppliers' facilities. Consulting and accounting firms that conduct social audits and offer monitoring services and are anxious to maintain competitive advantages over their peers typically do not disclose either social monitoring protocols or the full results of their inspections. Even if these firms and monitoring organizations wanted to make their operations and social performance fully public, many of them would find it difficult to collect the complex array of information—not only about their own operations but also about their suppliers and partners—relevant to social performance. The opacity that results from these incentive and capacity problems not only hampers consumers and investors from advancing their social preferences in the marketplace but also prevents firms from making credible claims about their social performance.

The currently opaque situation could be made more transparent through the same public and associative measures used to extend the scope of social markets. Labor regulators could, as their counterparts in environmental regulation have, require firms and their suppliers to collect and disclose information about how they treat their workers. Acting independently or with governmental encouragement, the associations and consultancies that currently perform social audits and monitoring might forge cooperative frameworks that would make their efforts comparable and publicly accessible. Standards and agreements that require certification and monitoring efforts to be transparent to outsiders and verifiable by skeptics would underwrite the ability of firms to compete with one another on social dimensions and dramatically increase order in these social markets.

Comparability into Competitiveness

Even with comprehensive scope and greater transparency, however, social markets might nevertheless be uncompetitive because current assessments do not facilitate the comparison of firms against one another. Many programs, such as the eco-labeling programs, offer only black-and-white assessments of social performance. It is difficult to tell, for example, how firms certified under the Forest Stewardship Council label compare with one another because it is a binary distinction: firms are designated simply as good or bad, not better or worse than others. Many labor-rights monitoring efforts, in which investors or nongovernmental organizations engage in bilateral dialogues with corporations, generate high-quality information on workplace practices and improvements, but there are few standards and mechanisms for comparing the social performance of firms that engage in such partnerships with one another or with companies that pursue other social performance strategies.

Given scope and transparency, two additional measures would gradually enhance the competitiveness of social markets by facilitating the ability of consumers, investors, and others to make differentiated judgments regarding firm social performance. First, public and private assessment programs that now issue binary determinations—such as proposed "no-sweat" labels or certification programs—about whether firms pass social muster should also provide disaggregated evaluations through ordinal rankings or categorical grades.[33] Second, nongovernmental organizations that form partnerships with large firms to improve aspects of their social performance should seek to develop common (and public) principles and standards against which they can benchmark both the success of their own efforts and the performance of corporations with whom they engage.

Intermediary Associations

Those who advance their social preferences through consumption and investment decisions lie at one end of social markets. At the other are the firms that capture their attention and patronage by, for example, improving their treatment of workers or the environmental impact of their products. Appropriate regulatory action can increase the integrity of social markets by extending their scope, transparency, and competitiveness from above.

Well-ordered social markets also depend, however, on a variegated host of intermediary associations that operate beneath state regulation and between those who advance social preferences in the marketplace and those who attempt to satisfy those preferences. Industry and nongovernmental associations, for example, have already begun to play a crucial role in establishing feasible yet demanding social and environmental standards. Owing to the technical complexity and conflict of interest involved, associations of firms, monitors, and advocacy organizations will be essential to serious efforts to make firm social performance and monitoring results more transparent and comparable. Another critical role for intermediary organizations in social markets is to translate complex data and signals from firms and monitoring organizations into forms that consumers, investors, and the general public can understand and use. It is patently unrealistic to expect substantial proportions of consumers or investors to understand voluminous reports and adjudicate between claims and counterclaims of firms and advocacy organizations. They are far more likely to take their cues from organizations they trust to provide reliable summaries and judgments. Just as intermediaries such as financial analysts, consumer groups, and professional auditors provide crucial interpretations that make ordinary economic markets work, so social markets will depend upon sophisticated, often competing, digestive intermediaries.

Every association acting in social markets will naturally attempt to advance its own interests and viewpoint. Industry associations and initiatives may de-emphasize the severity of violations, and consumer watchdog and social activist organizations may stress failures and, as they have in the past, use scandals and exposés to disparage and defame corporations. Social markets rely, currently and for the foreseeable future, upon such associations not only to interpret and disseminate social performance information but also to be the agents of transparency, developing standards and monitoring products and workplace practices. Powerful associations and organizations may therefore distort the operation of social markets in particular industries if they manage to capture, or unduly influence, standard setting and monitoring practices.

Would social markets be better off without these intermediate associations? Despite the possibility of capture and informational distortion, social markets are likely to operate more effectively when they deliberately incorporate the efforts of private and nongovernmental organizations for two reasons. First, perfecting methods of effectively gathering social performance information, and standards by which to accurately assess that information, is a dauntingly complex challenge that, for many industries and issue areas, exceeds the competence of governmental regulators and so will require the capacities and expertise of these associations. Second, many such associations are already deeply engaged and interested in social market activities, and they cannot be easily disentangled. Therefore, it seems more promising to constructively integrate these intermediary associations into social markets rather than to attempt to exclude them. Public rules intended to compel transparency and ensure openness of entry would reduce the danger that corporate or activist associations would be able to unfairly control standard setting or monitoring in an issue area or industrial sector.

Preference Articulation and Transformation

Perhaps much more than familiar economic markets, well-ordered social markets depend on the capacity of market actors to transform their initial preferences in the course of acquiring new knowledge and encountering challenging arguments. Untutored consumer or investor preferences may have market consequences that fail to advance the deeper values that ground those preferences. It is thus possible for individuals to have mistaken preferences. These mistakes occur when people form preferences and make decisions based on limited information, such that they later realize, upon receipt of fuller information, that they do not want what they initially thought they wanted.

To take just one example, consider the case of child labor. Many consumers from wealthy developed countries enter social markets with a preference against child labor and shun firms that employ children in developing countries. Many economists and local organizations in those countries, however, contend that simply prohibiting child labor often has the unintended consequence of forcing children into more punishing forms of work or of pushing their families below subsistence levels. More effective interventions involve providing educational opportunities for these children and providing subsidies to their families to reduce their dependence upon children's incomes.[34] Effective social markets in the case of child labor therefore require sophisticated consumers (as well as investors and intermediary organizations) willing to entertain such arguments and appropriately transform their preferences in light of them.

The play of unschooled social preferences in the marketplace may similarly aggregate to generate harmful effects in other contexts. For example, overestimation of small risks may lead to product price increases, demands for environmental improvement may lead to unemployment or capital flight, and preferences for unrealistic working conditions may drive sorely needed investment from developing areas or improve the quality of some jobs but diminish their number.[35] In these and other such circumstances, the preferences of individuals must be transformed for social markets to advance broadly shared values and even to properly balance values when they conflict. Whether or not the infrastructure of social markets or the interest groups and associations that utilize them will possess the resources and capacities to achieve such preference transformation will certainly vary across issues and markets.

The Limitations of Social Markets

The efficacy and thus desirability of creating well-ordered social markets, as with any regulatory instrument or approach, varies according to the content and strength of consumer and investor preferences, industrial structure, and a host of other factors. Consider three factors that favor or limit social markets: the depth of public sentiment, the susceptibility of regulatory targets to consumer and investor pressure, and the advantages and liabilities of social market strategies compared with regulatory tools that rely primarily on governmental capacities and authority. Although the effectiveness of any particular social market will depend on a host of particular contextual details, these three considerations offer preliminary guidance concerning the general conditions under which this approach will be promising.

Public Sentiment

Because the impacts of this mechanism depend upon concerned consumers and investors, public efforts to create and perfect social markets should focus on issues and sectors in which public concern runs deep. One major source of public concern stems from the self-interest of individual consumers. Tar-level labeling of cigarettes, nutritional labeling of food products, and public dissemination of water quality data, for example, all allow individual consumers to better advance their own preferences for health and safety in the marketplace. Social activism that raises public awareness of issues and causes has been another other major source of public sentiment. The contemporary environmental movement in the North Atlantic industrialized democracies is more than three decades old. This movement built the foundations for nascent social markets that have emerged around many environmental concerns, including pollution prevention and forest management. Over the past decade, concerns about the conditions of workers in developing countries has increased among consumers and investors in industrialized countries. There too, elements of social markets have developed out of demands from consumers and activists and private sector responses to them.

Regulatory and nongovernmental efforts to create, expand, and order social markets should concentrate on issue areas in which public sentiment runs deep from individual self-interest, issue awareness, or other sources. The social market regulatory strategy attempts to leverage social and economic trends for regulatory purposes and so should focus on areas in which those currents are strong and favorable. Environmental and labor regulation—international but also domestic—are promising examples of such issue areas, as are concerns around nutrition, health care, and food safety.

Firm Vulnerability

Although favorable public sentiment is necessary for effective social market regulation, it is far from sufficient. This regulatory approach is likely to be effective only with firms who are susceptible to pressure from consumers and investors. Brand- and reputation-sensitive firms in the high-end apparel and footwear industries—such as the Gap, Nike, and Reebok—lie at the most vulnerable end of this spectrum. Because of their prominence and exposure, these firms have been among the primary targets and first movers in the emerging social markets around international labor practices. Sectors with poor public images—such as the tobacco and chemical industries—are also susceptible to social market forces. At the other end of the spectrum, formal and informal sector operations in developing countries that produce exclusively for internal markets are almost completely insulated from the influence of social markets, however poor their labor practices may be. The vast majority of firms—including suppliers of large firms, mass-market companies whose customers care about price to the exclusion of social considerations, and commodity producers—lie in the middle range of this spectrum of public vulnerability.

At first glance, firms in this middle range may seem well insulated from social market forces. Their products often lack discernable branding. Many of these firms are anonymous to all but industry insiders. Firms whose primary customers are other businesses may be able to deny obligations to cater to the social scruples of their associates. Conversely, the prominent firms that do business with them may deny knowledge of or control over the practices or social consequences of their suppliers. Recent experiences such as those discussed above show how social market pressures can reach deeply into this middle range of firms. Corporations that attempt to demonstrate their social responsibility have quickly learned that consumers and critics demand that they improve not only their own operations and products but also those of their suppliers, and so on down the supply chain. Firms, such as Home Depot and Lowe's Home Improvement, that sell commodity products like wood to broad consumer markets have responded to demands from consumers and nongovernmental organizations that they source their products from environmentally responsible providers. Even Wal-Mart, the world's largest retailer, thought of as competing primarily on price rather than social or environmental hedonics, has not escaped these pressures. Although many remain critical of the company, it has worked with social responsibility organizations such as the Interfaith Council on Corporate Responsibility to improve its operations.

Because experiences like these are quite young and underdeveloped, no one knows how far social market forces might reach into the middle range of less prominent and elite firms if this instrument were pursued as deliberate public policy and regulatory action. As a matter of policy choice, officials should seek to extend social market mechanisms such as transparency and comparability in industries whose firms are vulnerable to such pressures but not yet fully subject to them. Where firms are not vulnerable, regulators should emphasize other instruments.

Comparative Regulatory Advantage

As a regulatory mechanism, social markets are distinctive in two respects. First, they harness social forces—especially the purchasing power of consumers and investors but also the monitoring and inspection capabilities of firms and nongovernmental bodies—to regulatory ends and so do not rely primarily on official powers and sanctions. This difference favors social markets when state capacities are relatively weak with respect to some goal. In many regulatory arenas, however, official powers will be adequate to the task at hand, and so relying upon potentially fickle social forces will be unnecessary. Second, whereas many official regulations specify a minimum standard, or floor, to be met, private actors will respond variably in social markets, with wide differences in social performance.[36] Sometimes—for example, with minimum wage and maximum hours laws—the public priority is to assure that all actors comply with a minimum standard. By contrast, in other areas—pollution prevention and occupational health and safety, for example—desirable minimum standards and the methods to reach them are difficult to specify with precision. In such instances variable performance and method may be desirable because it can allow firms to generate innovations that later improve social performance overall, to match methods to particular circumstances, and to adapt to changing competitive or technical conditions.

These two features of social markets, then, constitute their comparative advantage over a variety of more familiar regulatory mechanisms. Specifically, given the necessary conditions of public sentiment and firm vulnerability noted above, social market mechanisms offer a comparatively attractive approach when government capacity to regulate is weak (for example, the problem of too few inspectors for too many sites) and variation in social performance or approaches to generating social performance is desirable and more urgent than the need for firms to reach specific minimum standards. Figure 7-1 illustrates the likelihood of successful implementation of social market mechanisms along these two dimensions.

The capacity of regulators in various issue areas is depicted along the horizontal axis, with weak governmental capacity on the left and strong state capacity indicated at the right. For example, laws governing wages and hours worked among large employers in the United States (lower right-hand quadrant) are relatively easy for regulators to enforce, owing in large measure to well-established tax and documentation procedures. By contrast, these laws are routinely violated by apparel manufacturers and subcontractors who operate in small, informal, and fly-by-night shops (lower left-hand quadrant). The vertical axis plots issue areas according to the level of performance desired: at the bottom of the vertical axis, minimum standards, or "floors," are particularly important; at the top are issues in which performance above a given floor is also a priority.

On one account, the importance of wage and hours laws is to establish minimum standards of acceptable labor contracts. Workers and employers should be able to agree to a broad range of actual wages and hours for any particular worker, as long these minimums are respected. Similarly, the prohibition of forced labor is a clear minimum standard about which there is broad international consensus. Because the prime regulatory goal is to reach these floors rather than to secure gains above them, minimum wage and maximum hours laws fall in the bottom part of the figure. For many

Figure 7-1. *Where Social Markets Make Sense: A Schema*

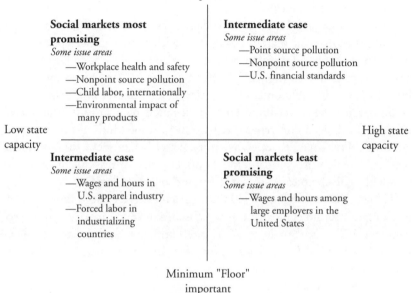

other regulatory issues, such as reducing point source pollution, the public interest extends beyond minimum standards to the continuous reduction of toxics use and emission. More controversially, the issue of international child labor is also placed in the top, "variable outcome" region. Although most agree that the elimination of child labor is a desirable long-term goal, concrete programs to reach that goal must grapple with a host of unintended consequences and complex program designs. Because there are many ways to work toward the eventual elimination of child labor, none of them obviously best, variations in approach and intermediate outcomes are desirable.

The upper left-hand quadrant is the region in which social market approaches seem most promising because they press for variable outcomes, where such outcomes are desirable, and enlist social forces to bolster insufficient governmental capacities. We have already discussed emerging social markets in some of these issue areas—such as labor and environment. For issues that lie in the lower right-hand quadrant, social market approaches are not particularly promising: governmental reach is sufficient to the task, and there is little regulatory interest in pressing for variable improvements above minimum standards.

For issue areas in the two intermediate cases it is more difficult to gauge the promise of social markets compared with that of other approaches. Both state-centric and social market mechanisms have been used to control point source pollution (upper right-hand quadrant), for which state capacity is high but variable outcomes are desirable. Chapter 8 in this volume demonstrates that state-imposed market-based mechanisms (not social markets) have been effective for reduction in some kinds of point source pollution. The Toxics Release Inventory, which establishes a kind of social market in which firms must publicly disclose their emissions of some six hundred toxic chemicals, also targets point source pollution.

The other intermediate region is characterized by the importance of reaching minimum standards but the absence of state capacity and will to compel private actors to do so. Some international labor standards, such as the prohibitions on forced labor and violent infringements on freedom of association (lower left-hand quadrant), fit this category. Issues in this region of the schema spark the deepest disagreements about the appropriateness of social market instruments. When a clear minimum acceptable level of behavior is at stake—for instance, with respect to minimum wages, bars on forced labor, or bans on the use of highly toxic substances—a public standard often assumes the gravity of a basic right or criminal prohibition. Opponents might object that social market mechanisms, even those intended to advance social aims, are incompatible with such basic standards because they implicitly endorse the behavior of those whose performance falls below the minimum. Can it be appropriate to build institutions that measure the extent to which various firms contract with suppliers that enslave workers so that consumers and investors can support firms that use fewer slaves than others? State action to eliminate such practices would certainly be preferable, but sometimes states are unable, or unwilling, to enforce such bans—this region of the figure is defined by precisely this governmental weakness.

Whether public or nongovernmental power should be used to expand and improve social markets under such circumstances rests on case-by-case practical judgments that elude generalization: How quickly might social markets improve the behavior of firms to the point at which they comply with social minimum standards? Would strengthening conventional regulatory instruments result in more rapid compliance? Would efforts to expand social markets erode support for conventional regulation?

On this last question, critics of social markets frequently assert, without offering supportive evidence, that advances in social market mechanisms entail retrenchment of conventional regulation and weakening of state power. It seems equally probable, however, that social markets would work to spread public concern about issues such as forced labor and that this concern would build support for traditional regulation as public sentiment spilled over from the economic and social realms to the political one. Only further experience will reveal whether the dynamics of social markets and more familiar state-centered regulation turn out to be competitive or mutually reinforcing, and these dynamics in turn surely depend on the details of how those markets are constructed.

Conclusion

From the perspective of organizing economic markets and social regulation, the project of creating social markets now lies on a cusp. We can look back to a perhaps imagined time when social values did not enter into investment, consumption, and corporate management decisions. Given the degree to which individual moral and social preferences have already penetrated marketplaces, it seems impossible to recapture that separation between economic and social motives. Nevertheless, the chaos in emergent social markets—the difficulty consumers have in distinguishing firms that act on their values from those that just talk, the converse inability of firms to make credible social commitments, and the clash of conflicting or uninformed social preferences—makes many long for just such a divorce.

The effort to deploy public and private energies toward improving social markets seems more promising than trying to scrap them. Making social markets "well ordered" would mean extending their scope, increasing transparency and competitiveness, and providing resources that allow market actors to articulate and even transform their preferences. For any given social market, these reforms are daunting. By way of analogy, social markets today are perhaps as underdeveloped as U.S. financial markets were before the Great Depression. Reforming those markets—making them transparent, credible, and competitive—required diligent and clever public and private efforts over many decades. Similar progress in the institutionalization of well-ordered social markets could yield large advances for the technology of regulation, individual freedom in the marketplace, corporate social accountability, and effective public standards for the environment, human rights, and labor.

Notes

1. Martin Wolf, "Sleep-Walking with the Enemy: Corporate Social Responsibility Distorts the Market by Deflecting Business from Its Primary Role of Profit Generation," *Financial Times,* May 16, 2001.

2. Michael Hopkins, *The Planetary Bargain: Corporate Social Responsibility Comes of Age* (St. Martin's Press, 1999); John Elkington, *Cannibals with Forks: The Triple Bottom Line of Twenty-First-Century Business* (Stony Creek, Conn.: New Society Publishers, 1998).

3. Dani Rodrik has called this situation one in which the "full hedonics" of products and firms are known (personal conversation with author, July 23, 2001).

4. For a discussion of the general role of associations in fulfilling this information function, see Mark E. Warren, *Democracy and Association* (Princeton University Press, 2001), pp. 71–82.

5. Eric Becker and Patrick McVeigh, "Social Funds in the United States: Their History, Performance, and Social Impacts," in Archon Fung, Tessa Hebb, and Joel Rogers, eds., *Working Capital: The Power of Labor's Pensions* (Cornell University Press, 2001), pp. 44–66.

6. Archon Fung, Dara O'Rourke, and Charles Sabel, "Stepping Up Labor Standards," *Boston Review,* vol. 26 (February–March 2001), pp. 4–10.

7. Joseph Rees, "Development of Communitarian Regulation in the Chemical Industry" (manuscript, 1999; in possession of author).

8. Andrew King and Michael Lenox, "Industry Self-regulation without Sanctions: The Chemical Industry's Responsible Care Program," *Academy of Management Journal,* vol. 43 (August 2000), pp. 698–717.

9. Social Investment Forum, *1999 Report on Responsible Investment Trends in the United States* (November 4, 1999) (www.socialinvest.org/areas/research/trends/1999-Trends.htm [February 26, 2002]).

10. International Communications Research and Marymount University Center for Ethical Concerns, *The Consumer and Sweatshops,* research report prepared by International Communication Research for Marymount University Center for Ethical Concerns (Arlington, Va., November 1999). The Center for Ethical Concerns conducted similar surveys in 1995 and 1996, with similar results. Approximately one thousand people responded, and the data were weighted to reflect demographic characteristics of U.S. adults aged eighteen and over. The authors report a margin of error at the 95 percent confidence level of +/–3 percent (www.marymount.edu/news/garmentstudy [May 2001]).

11. Richard B. Freeman, "What Role for Labor Standards in the Global Economy" (November 12, 1998) (www.nber.org/~freeman/Papers%20on%20RBF%20website/un-stan.pdf [February 27, 2002]).

12. Environics International (with the Prince of Wales Business Leaders Forum, PricewaterhouseCoopers, BP Amoco, and Bell Canada), "The Millennium Poll on Corporate Social Responsibility" (November 1999) (www.environics.net/eil/millennium [February 2001]).

13. Raj Thamotheram, ed., *Visions of Ethical Sourcing* (London: Financial Times–Prentice Hall, 2000).

14. Kathryn Gordon and Maiko Miyake, "Deciphering Corporate Codes of Conduct: A Review of Their Contents," Working Papers on International Investment 1999/2 (Geneva: Organization for Economic Cooperation and Development, March 2000).

15. Ronald Bernebeim, *Corporate Ethics* (New York: Conference Board, 1991).

16. U.S. Department of Labor, *The Apparel Industry and Codes of Conduct: A Solution to the International Child Labor Problem?* (1996).

17. Hopkins, *The Planetary Bargain: Corporate Social Responsibility Comes of Age*, pp. 72–79.

18. Elkington, *Cannibals with Forks: The Triple Bottom Line of Twenty-First-Century Business*, pp. 219–44.

19. Jason McNichol, "Contesting Governance in the Global Marketplace: A Sociological Assessment of British Efforts to Build New Markets for NGO-Certified Sustainable Wood Products" (manuscript, 1999) (in possession of the author).

20. World Wildlife Fund, *The Forest Industry in the Twenty-First Century* (Washington, 2001).

21. Joseph Rees, "Regulation by Association in the U.S. Forest Products Industry," paper presented at the annual meeting of the Law and Society Association, Aspen, Colorado, June 1998.

22. Sustainable Forestry Initiative, *SFI Program Sixth Annual Progress Report* (Washington, 2001).

23. In 1998 fewer than 2 percent of SFI-member forest lands had undergone third-party certification. By 2000 that figure had risen to 41 percent, and managers project that by the end of 2001, 85 percent of SFI forestland, or 80 million acres, will have been certified (ibid., p. 14).

24. For a more detailed discussion of these and other monitoring programs in the apparel industry, see Dara O'Rourke, "Sweatshops 101: Monitoring Apparel Production around the World," *Dollars and Sense*, no. 237 (September–October 2001), pp. 14–18.

25. Ralph Piotrowski and Stefan Kratz, "Eco-Labelling in the Globalised Economy," *International Politics and Society Online* (April 1999) (www.fes.de/ipg/ipg4_99/artpiotr.htm [February 27, 2002]; see also Organization for Economic Cooperation and Development (OECD), *Eco-Labelling: Actual Effects of Selected Programs*, OECD/GD(97)105 (Geneva, 1997).

26. Bruce Paxton, "Converging and Separating Mechanisms in Voluntary Labeling Programs," paper presented at the Workshop on Voluntary, Collaborative, and Information-Based Policies: Lessons and Next Steps for Environmental and Energy Policy in the United States and Europe, Harvard University, John F. Kennedy School of Government, May 10–11, 2001.

27. See OECD, *Eco-Labelling: Actual Effects of Selected Programs*.

28. Environmental Protection Agency, *Toxics Release Inventory 1999 Data Release* (April 11, 2001).

29. Archon Fung and Dara O'Rourke, "Reinventing Environmental Regulation from the Grassroots Up: Explaining and Expanding the Success of the Toxics Release Inventory," *Environmental Management,* vol. 25 (February 2000), pp. 115–27; Bradley Karkkainen, "Information as Environmental Regulation: TRI and Performance Benchmarking, Precursor to a New Paradigm?" *Georgetown Law Journal,* vol. 89 (January 2001), pp. 257–370.

30. James T. Hamilton, "Pollution As News: Media and Stock Market Reactions to the Toxics Release Inventory Data," *Journal of Environmental Economics and Management,* vol. 28 (January 1995), pp. 98–113.

31. Thus conflicts between national and European Union labeling criteria have caused controversy in the EuroFlower labeling program (Piotrowski and Kratz, "Eco-Labelling in the Globalised Economy").

32. Joel Seligman, *The Transformation of Wall Street: A History of the Securities and Exchange Commission and Modern Corporate Finance* (Boston: Houghton Mifflin, 1982).

33. The Program for Pollution Control, Evaluation, and Rating (PROPER) in Indonesia, for example, ranks industrial facilities according to their water-pollution performance along five color grades: black, red, blue, green, and gold (Shakeb Afsah, Allen Blackman, and Damayanti Ratunanda, "How Do Public Disclosure Pollution Control Programs Work? Evidence from Indonesia," Discussion Paper 00-44 [Washington: World Resources Institute, 2000]).

34. Kaushik Basu, "Child Labor: Cause, Consequence, and Cure, with Remarks on International Labor Standards," *Journal of Economic Literature,* vol. 37 (September 1999), pp. 1083–119.

35. See Cass Sunstein, "Consequences?" in Charles Sabel, Archon Fung, and Bradley Karkkainen, *Beyond Backyard Environmentalism* (Boston: Beacon Press, 2000), pp. 94–100.

36. I thank Robert Lawrence for emphasizing this aspect of social markets.

8

ROBERT N. STAVINS

Lessons from the American Experiment with Market-Based Environmental Policies

IT IS NOW A BIT MORE than a decade since Senators Timothy Wirth and John Heinz launched Project 88, a bipartisan effort to apply market-based approaches to environmental and resource problems. In a series of reports, Project 88 put forward a set of innovative ways in which public policies could work through the market, rather than against it, to stimulate cost-effective environmental protection.[1] In the intervening years, as more and more market-based environmental policy instruments have been proposed and implemented, the concept of harnessing market forces to protect the environment has evolved from political anathema to political correctness. It is now time to reflect on our experiences and search for lessons

---

This chapter draws extensively on Robert N. Stavins, "Market-Based Environmental Policies," in P. R. Portney and Robert N. Stavins, eds., *Public Policies for Environmental Protection* (Washington: Resources for the Future, 2000), and Robert N. Stavins, "Experience with Market-Based Environmental Policy Instruments," in Karl-Göran Mäler and Jeffrey Vincent, eds., *Handbook of Environmental Economics* (Amsterdam: Elsevier Science, 2001). Sheila Cavanagh provided valuable research assistance, and helpful comments on a previous version of the manuscript were provided by Jeffrey Frankel, John Donahue, Sanjeev Khagram, and other participants in the 2001 Bretton Woods Conference. The author alone is responsible for any errors.

from this set of experiments with economic incentive approaches to public policy.

Environmental policies typically combine the identification of a goal with some means to achieve that goal. Although these two components are often linked within the political process, I focus in this chapter exclusively on the second component, the means—the "instruments"—of environmental policy. Market-based instruments are regulations that encourage behavior through market signals rather than through explicit directives regarding pollution control levels or methods. These policy instruments, such as tradable permits or pollution charges, can reasonably be described as harnessing market forces, because if they are well designed and implemented, they encourage firms or individuals to undertake pollution control efforts that are in their own interests and that collectively meet policy goals.[2]

By way of contrast, conventional approaches to regulating the environment are often referred to as command-and-control regulations because they allow relatively little flexibility in the means of achieving goals. Such regulations tend to force firms to take on similar shares of the pollution control burden, regardless of the cost. Command-and-control regulations do this by setting uniform standards for firms, the most prevalent of which are technology- and performance-based standards. Technology-based standards specify the method, and sometimes the actual equipment, that firms must use to comply with a particular regulation. A performance standard sets a uniform control target for firms while allowing some latitude in deciding how this target will be met.

Holding all firms to the same target can be expensive and, in some circumstances, counterproductive. Although standards may effectively limit emissions of pollutants, they typically exact relatively high costs in the process by forcing some firms to resort to unduly expensive means of controlling pollution. Because the costs of controlling emissions may vary greatly across firms, and even across sources within the same firm, the appropriate technology in one situation may not be appropriate (cost-effective) in another. Thus, control costs can vary enormously owing to a firm's production design, physical configuration, the age of its assets, and other factors. One survey of eight empirical studies of air pollution control found that the ratio of actual aggregate costs of the conventional command-and-control approach to the aggregate costs of least-cost benchmarks ranged from 1.07 for sulfate emissions in the Los Angeles area to 22.00 for hydrocarbon emissions at all domestic DuPont plants.[3]

Furthermore, command-and-control regulations tend to freeze the development of technologies that might otherwise result in greater levels of control. Little or no financial incentive exists for businesses to exceed their control targets, and both technology-based and performance-based standards discourage adoption of new technologies. A business that adopts a new technology may be "rewarded" by being held to a higher standard of performance and not given the opportunity to benefit financially from its investment, except to the extent that its competitors have even more difficulty reaching the new standard.

In theory, if properly designed and implemented, market-based instruments allow any desired level of pollution cleanup to be realized at the lowest overall cost to society by providing incentives for the greatest reductions in pollution by those firms that can achieve these reductions most cheaply.[4] Rather than equalizing pollution levels among firms (as with uniform emission standards), market-based instruments equalize the incremental amount that firms spend to reduce pollution—their marginal cost.[5] Command-and-control approaches could—in theory—achieve this cost-effective solution, but to do so would require that different standards be set for each pollution source and, consequently, that policymakers obtain detailed information about the compliance costs each firm faces. Such information is simply not available to government. Market-based instruments, on the other hand, provide for a cost-effective allocation of the pollution control burden among sources without requiring the government to have this information. In contrast with command-and-control regulations, market-based instruments have the potential to provide powerful incentives for companies to adopt cheaper and better pollution control technologies: with market-based instruments, particularly emission taxes, it always pays firms to clean up a bit more if a sufficiently low-cost method (technology or process) of doing so can be identified and adopted.[6]

Highlights of Experience

Experiments and experiences in the United States with market-based environmental policy instruments have been both numerous and diverse. It is convenient to consider them within four major categories: pollution charges, tradable permits, reductions in market friction, and reductions in government subsidies.

Charge Systems

Pollution charge systems assess a fee or tax on the amount of pollution that a firm or source generates.[7] Consequently, it is worthwhile for the firm to reduce emissions to the point at which its marginal abatement cost is equal to the tax rate. One challenge with charge systems is identifying the appropriate tax rate. Ideally, it should be set equal to the marginal benefits of cleanup at the efficient level of cleanup, but policymakers are more likely to think in terms of a desired level of cleanup, and they do not know beforehand how firms will respond to a given level of taxation.

The conventional wisdom is that this approach to environmental protection has been ignored in the United States, but this perception is not correct. If one defines charge systems broadly, a significant number of applications can be identified. The closest that any U.S. charge system comes to operating as a true Pigovian tax may be the unit-charge approach to financing municipal solid waste collection, whereby households and businesses are charged the incremental costs of collection and disposal.[8] So-called pay-as-you-throw policies, whereby users pay in proportion to the volume of their waste, are now used in well over one thousand jurisdictions. The collective experience provides evidence that unit charges have been successful in reducing the volume of household waste generated.[9]

Another important set of charge systems implemented in the United States has been deposit-refund systems, whereby consumers pay a surcharge when purchasing potentially polluting products and receive a refund when they return the product to an approved center for recycling or disposal. A number of states have implemented this approach through "bottle bills" to control litter from beverage containers and to reduce the flow of solid waste to landfills, and the concept has also been applied to lead-acid batteries.[10]

In addition, there has been considerable use of environmental user charges in the United States, through which specific environmentally related services are funded. Examples include insurance premium taxes, such as the excise tax on specified hazardous chemicals used to fund partially the cleanup of hazardous waste sites through the Superfund program. Another set of environmental charges are sales taxes on motor fuels, ozone-depleting chemicals, agricultural inputs, and "gas-guzzling" motor vehicles. Finally, tax differentiation has become part of a considerable number of federal and state attempts to encourage the use of renewable energy sources.

Tradable Permits

Tradable permits can achieve the same cost-minimizing allocation of the control burden as a charge system while avoiding the problem of uncertain response by firms.[11] Under a tradable permit system, an allowable overall level of pollution is established and allocated among firms in the form of permits.[12] Firms that keep their emission levels below the allotted level may sell their surplus permits to other firms or use them to offset excess emissions in other parts of their operations.

Applications have included the U.S. Environmental Protection Agency's (EPA) emissions trading program, the leaded gasoline phasedown, water quality permit trading, chlorofluorocarbon (CFC) allowance trading, the sulfur dioxide (SO_2) allowance trading system for acid rain control, the RECLAIM emissions reduction program in the Los Angeles metropolitan region, and tradable development rights for land use.[13] At least two of these programs merit particular attention.

The lead allowance trading program, developed in the 1980s, allowed gasoline refiners greater flexibility in meeting emission standards at a time when the acceptable lead content of gasoline had been reduced to 10 percent of its previous level. The program was successful in meeting its environmental targets, and the EPA estimated cost savings of about $250 million per year.[14] Furthermore, the program provided measurable incentives for the diffusion of cost-saving technology.[15]

Arguably, the most important application made of a market-based instrument for environmental protection has been the SO_2 allowance trading program for acid rain control, established under the 1990 amendments to the Clean Air Act and intended to reduce emissions by 10 million tons below 1980 levels. A robust market of bilateral SO_2 permit trading has emerged, resulting in cost savings on the order of $1 billion annually over the costs under some command-and-control regulatory alternatives.[16] Trading levels were low in the early years of the program but increased significantly over time.[17]

Market Friction Reduction

Reduction in market friction can also serve as a policy instrument for environmental protection. Three types of such policies stand out: First, in a number of cases markets have been created for inputs or outputs associated with environmental quality. Examples include measures implemented over the past fifteen years that facilitate the voluntary exchange of water rights and thus promote more efficient allocation and use of scarce supplies. Second, liability rules have frequently been designed to encourage firms to consider the potential environmental damages of their decisions. One important example is the Comprehensive Environmental Response, Compensation, and Liability Act of 1980, which establishes liability for companies that are found responsible for hazardous waste contamination.

Third, because well-functioning markets depend, in part, on the existence of well-informed producers and consumers, information programs can help foster market-oriented solutions to environmental problems.[18] These programs have been of two types. Product-labeling requirements have been implemented to improve the information set available to consumers. There has been relatively little analysis of the efficacy of such programs, but limited evidence suggests that energy-efficiency product labeling has had significant impacts on efficiency improvements, essentially by making consumers and therefore producers more sensitive to changes in energy prices.[19]

Another set of information programs involves reporting requirements. The U.S. Toxics Release Inventory, which has been expanded significantly during the past decade, requires firms to make available to the public information on the use, storage, and release of specific hazardous chemicals. Such information reporting may increase public awareness of firms' actions, and consequent public scrutiny may encourage firms to alter their behavior, although the evidence to date is mixed.[20]

Government Subsidy Reduction

Reduction in government subsidies is the fourth and final category of market-based instruments. Subsidies are the mirror image of taxes and, at least in theory, can provide incentives to address environmental problems.[21] In practice, however, many subsidies promote economically inefficient and environmentally unsound practices. Unfortunately, assessing the magnitude, let alone the effects, of these subsidies is difficult. For example, owing to concerns about global climate change, increased attention has been given to federal subsidies that promote the use of fossil fuels. One EPA study indicates that eliminating these subsidies would have a significant effect on reducing carbon dioxide (CO_2) emissions, but a substantial share of these subsidies were enacted during previous "oil crises" to encourage the development of domestic energy sources and reduce reliance on imported petroleum.[22]

Normative Lessons

Although there has been considerable experience in the United States with market-based instruments for environmental protection, this relatively new set of policy approaches has not come close to replacing conventional command-and-control approaches. Furthermore, even when and where these approaches have been used in their purest form and with some success, they have not always performed as anticipated. It is therefore timely to ask what lessons can be learned from our experiences.

Normative Lessons for Design and Implementation

The performance to date of market-based instruments for environmental protection provides compelling evidence for environmentalists and others that these approaches can achieve major cost savings while accomplishing their environmental objectives. The performance of these systems also offers lessons about the importance of flexibility, simplicity, the role of monitoring and enforcement, and the ability of the private sector to make markets of this sort work.

In regard to flexibility, it is important that market-based instruments should be designed to allow for a broad set of compliance alternatives, in terms of both timing and technological options. For example, allowing flexible timing and intertemporal trading of permits—that is, banking allowances for future use—played an important role in the SO_2 allowance trading program's performance, much as it had in the U.S. lead rights trading program a decade earlier.[23] One of the most significant benefits of using market-based instruments is simply that technology standards are thereby avoided. Less flexible systems would not have led to the technological change that may have been induced by market-based instruments nor to the induced process innovations that have resulted.[24]

In regard to simplicity, transparent formulas—whether for permit allocation or tax computation—are difficult to contest or manipulate. Rules should be clearly defined up front, without ambiguity. For example, requiring prior government approval of individual trades may increase uncertainty and transaction costs, thereby discouraging trading; these negative effects should be balanced against any anticipated benefits owing to the requirement of prior government approval. Such requirements hampered the EPA's Emissions Trading Program in the 1970s, and the absence of such requirements was an important factor in the success of lead trading.[25] In the case of SO_2 trading, the absence of requirements for prior approval reduced uncertainty for utilities and administrative costs for government and contributed to low transactions costs.[26]

Although some problematic program design elements reflect miscalculations of market reactions, others were known to be problematic at the time the programs were enacted but nevertheless were incorporated into programs to ensure adoption by the political process. One striking example is the "20 percent rule" under the EPA's Emission Trading Program. This rule, adopted at the insistence of the environmental community, stipulates that each time a permit is traded, the amount of pollution authorized thereunder must be reduced by 20 percent. Because permits that are not traded retain their full quantity value, this regulation discourages permit trading and thereby increases regulatory costs.[27]

Experience also argues for using absolute baselines, not relative ones, as the point of departure for credit programs. The problem is that without a specified baseline, reductions must be credited relative to an unobservable hypothetical—that is, the level of toxics the source would have emitted in the absence of the regulation. A combined system—one in which a cap-and-trade program is combined with voluntary "opt-in provisions"—creates the possibility for "paper trades," whereby a regulated source is credited for an emissions reduction (by an unregulated source) that would have taken place in any event.[28] The result is a decrease in aggregate costs among regulated sources, but this is partly a function of an unintentional increase in the total emissions cap. As was experienced with the EPA's Emissions Trading Program, relative baselines create significant transaction costs by essentially requiring prior approval of trades as the authority investigates the claimed counterfactual from which reductions are calculated and credits generated.[29]

Experiences with market-based instruments also provide a powerful reminder of the importance of monitoring and enforcement. These instruments, whether price or quantity based, do not eliminate the need for such activities, although they may change their character. In the many programs reviewed in this chapter in which monitoring or enforcement (or both) have been deficient, the results have been ineffective policies. One counterexample is provided by the SO_2 allowance trading program in the United States, which includes (costly) continuous emissions monitoring of all sources. On the enforcement side, the stiff penalties mandated by the Clean Air Act Amendments of 1990 (much greater than the marginal cost of abatement) have provided sufficient incentives to induce the high degree of compliance that has been achieved.[30]

In nearly every case of implemented cap-and-trade programs, permits have been allocated without charge to participants. The same characteristic that makes such allocation attractive in positive political economic terms—the conveyance of scarcity rents to the private sector—makes allocation without charge problematic in normative efficiency terms.[31] It has been estimated that the costs of SO_2 allowance trading would be 25 percent lower if permits were auctioned rather than allocated without charge, because revenues could then be used to finance reductions in preexisting distortionary taxes.[32] Furthermore, in the presence of some forms of transaction costs, the posttrading equilibrium—and hence aggregate abatement costs—are sensitive to the initial permit allocation.[33] For both reasons, a successful attempt to establish a politically viable program through a specific initial permit allocation can result in a program that is significantly more costly than anticipated.

Improvements in instrument design will not solve all problems. One potentially important cause of the mixed performance of implemented market-based instruments is that many firms are simply not well equipped to make the decisions necessary to fully utilize these instruments. Because market-based instruments have been used on a limited basis only, and firms are not certain that these instruments will be a lasting component on the regulatory landscape, most companies have chosen not to reorganize their internal structures to fully exploit the cost savings these instruments offer. Rather, most firms continue to have organizations that are experienced in minimizing the costs of complying with command-and-control regulations, not in making the strategic decisions allowed by market-based instruments.[34]

The environmental, health, and safety departments in private firms have focused primarily on problem avoidance and risk management rather than on the creation of opportunities made possible by market-based instruments. This focus has developed because of the strict rules imposed by command-and-control regulation, in response to which companies have built skills and developed processes that comply with regulations but do not help them benefit competitively from environmental decisions.[35] Absent significant changes in structure and personnel, the full potential of market-based instruments will not be realized.

Normative Lessons for Analysis

When assessing market-based environmental programs, economists need to employ some measure by which the gains of moving from conventional standards to an economic incentive scheme can be estimated. When comparing policies with the same anticipated environmental outcomes, aggregate cost savings may be the best yardstick for measuring the success of individual instruments. The challenge for analysts is to make fair comparisons among policy instruments, either idealized versions of both market-based systems and likely alternatives or realistic versions of both.[36]

It is not enough to analyze static cost savings. For example, the savings owing to banking allowances should also be modeled (unless this is not permitted in practice). It can also be important to allow for the effects of alternative instruments on technology innovation and diffusion, especially when programs impose significant costs over long time horizons.[37] More generally, it is important to consider the effects of the preexisting regulatory environment. For example, the level of preexisting factor taxes can affect the total costs of regulation, as indicated above.[38]

Normative Lessons for Identifying New Applications

Market-based policy instruments are considered today for nearly every environmental problem that is raised, ranging from endangered species preservation to what may be the greatest of environmental problems, the greenhouse effect and global climate change.[39] Experiences with market-based instruments offer some guidance as to the conditions under which such approaches are likely to work well and those under which they may face greater difficulties.

First, where the cost of abating pollution differs widely among sources, a market-based system is likely to have greater gains, relative to conventional command-and-control regulations.[40] For example, it was clear early on that heterogeneity with respect to SO_2 abatement cost was great because of differences in the ages of plants and their proximity to sources of low-sulfur coal. Where abatement costs are more uniform across sources, however, the political costs of enacting an allowance trading approach are less likely to be justifiable.

Second, the greater the degree of mixing of pollutants in the receiving airshed or watershed, the more attractive will a market-based system be relative to a conventional uniform standard. This is because taxes or tradable permits, for example, can lead to localized "hot spots" with relatively high levels of ambient pollution. This is a significant distributional issue, and it can also become an efficiency issue if damages are nonlinearly related to pollutant concentrations. In cases in which this is a reasonable concern, the problem can be addressed, in theory, through the use of "ambient permits" or through charge systems that are keyed to changes in ambient conditions at specified locations.[41] Despite the extensive theoretical literature on such ambient systems going back to David Montgomery, however, they have never been implemented, with the partial exception of a two-zone trading system under Los Angeles's RECLAIM program.[42]

Third, the efficiency of price-based (tax) systems compared with quantity-based (tradable permit) systems depends on the pattern of costs and benefits. If uncertainty about marginal abatement costs is significant, and if marginal abatement costs are quite flat and marginal benefits of abatement fall relatively quickly, then a quantity instrument will be more efficient than a price instrument.[43] Furthermore, when there is also uncertainty about marginal benefits and marginal benefits are positively correlated with marginal costs (which, it turns out, is not uncommon), then there is an additional argument in favor of the relative efficiency of quantity instruments.[44] On the other hand, the regulation of stock pollutants will often favor price instruments when the optimal stock level rises over time.[45] It should also be recognized that despite the theoretical efficiency advantages of hybrid systems—nonlinear taxes, or quotas combined with taxes—in the presence of uncertainty, virtually no such hybrid systems have been adopted.[46]

Fourth, the long-term cost-effectiveness of taxes versus tradable permit systems is affected by their relative responsiveness to change. This arises in at least three dimensions: In the presence of rapid rates of economic growth, a fixed tax leads to an increase in aggregate emissions, whereas with a fixed supply of permits there is no change in aggregate emissions (though there is an increase in permit prices). In the context of general price inflation, a unit (but not an ad valorem) tax decreases in real terms, and so emissions levels increase, whereas with a permit system, there is no change in aggregate emissions. In the presence of exogenous technological change in pollution abatement, a tax system leads to an increase in control levels— that is, a decrease in aggregate emissions—whereas a permit system maintains emissions, with a fall in permit prices.[47]

Fifth, tradable permits will work best when transaction costs are low, and experience suggests that properly designed private markets will tend to render transaction costs minimal. Sixth, a potential advantage of tradable permit systems in which allocation is without charge, relative to other policy instruments, is associated with the incentive thereby provided for pollution sources to identify themselves and report their emissions (in order to claim their permits).

Seventh, it is important to keep in mind that in the absence of decreasing marginal transactions costs (essentially volume discounts), the equilibrium allocation and hence aggregate abatement costs of a tradable permit system are independent of initial allocations.[48] Hence an important attribute of a tradable permit system is that the allocation decision can be left to politicians, with limited normative concerns about the potential effects of the chosen allocation on overall cost-effectiveness. In other words, cost-effectiveness or efficiency can be achieved while distributional equity is simultaneously addressed with the same policy instrument. This is one of the reasons an international tradable permit mechanism is particularly attractive in the context of concerns about global climate change. Allocation mechanisms can be developed that address legitimate equity concerns of developing countries, and thus increase the political base for support, without jeopardizing the overall cost-effectiveness of the system.[49]

Eighth and finally, considerations of political feasibility point to the wisdom (more likely, the success) of proposing market-based instruments when they can be used to facilitate a cost-effective aggregate emissions reduction (as in the case of the SO_2 allowance trading program in 1990) as opposed to a cost-effective reallocation of the status quo burden. Policy instruments that appear impeccable from the vantage point of research institutions, but consistently prove infeasible in real-world political institutions, can hardly be considered "optimal."

Positive Political Economy Lessons

The increasing use of market-based instruments for environmental protection raises a number of political economy questions: First, why was there so little use of market-based instruments in the United States, relative to command-and-control instruments, over the thirty-year period of major environmental regulation that began in 1970, despite the apparent advantages these instruments offer? Second, when market-based instruments have been adopted, why has there been such great reliance on tradable permits allocated without charge, despite the availability of a much broader set of incentive-based instruments? Third, why has the political attention given to market-based environmental policy instruments increased dramatically in recent years? To address these questions, it is useful to consider the demand for environmental policy instruments by individuals, firms, and interest groups and their supply by the legislature and regulatory agencies.[50]

The Dominance of Command-and-Control Instruments

Command-and-control instruments have dominated because all of the main parties involved—affected firms, environmental advocacy groups, organized labor, legislators, and bureaucrats—have had reasons to favor them. On the regulatory demand side, affected firms and their trade associations have tended to prefer command-and-control instruments because standards can improve a firm's competitive position while frequently costing a firm less than pollution taxes or (auctioned) tradable permits. Command-and-control standards are inevitably set up with extensive input from existing industry and trade associations, which frequently obtain more stringent requirements for new sources and other advantages for existing firms. In contrast, auctioned permits and pollution taxes require firms to pay not only abatement costs to reduce pollution to some prescribed level but also regulatory costs associated with emissions beyond that level, in the form either of permit purchases or tax payments. Because market-based instruments focus on the quantity of pollution, not on who generates it or the methods used to reduce it, these instruments can make the lobbying role of trade associations less important.

For a long time, most environmental advocacy groups were actively hostile toward market-based instruments. One reason was philosophical: environmentalists frequently perceived pollution taxes and tradable permits as licenses to pollute. Although such ethical objections to the use of market-based environmental strategies have greatly diminished, they have not disappeared completely.[51] A second concern was that damages from pollution—to human health and ecological well-being—were difficult or impossible to quantify and monetize and thus could not be summed up in a marginal damage function or captured by a Pigovian tax rate.[52] Third, environmental organizations have opposed market-based schemes out of a fear that permit levels and tax rates, once implemented, would be more difficult to tighten over time than command-and-control standards. If permits are given the status of property rights, then any subsequent attempt by government to reduce pollution levels further could meet with demands for compensation.[53] Similarly, increasing pollution tax rates may be unlikely because raising tax rates is always politically difficult. A related strategic issue is the concern that moving to tax-based environmental regulation would shift authority from environment committees in the Congress, frequently dominated by pro-environment legislators, to tax-writing committees, which are generally more conservative.[54] Finally, environmental organizations have objected to decentralized instruments on the grounds that even if emission taxes or tradable permits reduce overall levels of emissions, they can—in theory—lead to localized "hot spots" with relatively high levels of ambient pollution.

Organized labor has also been active in some environmental policy debates. In the case of restrictions on air pollution, organized labor has taken the side of the United Mine Workers, whose members are heavily concentrated in eastern mines that produce high-sulfur coal and had therefore opposed pollution control measures that would increase incentives for using low-sulfur coal from the largely nonunion (and less labor-intensive) mines in Wyoming's and Montana's Powder River Basin. Thus, in the 1977 debates over amendments to the Clean Air Act, organized labor fought to include a command-and-control standard that effectively required scrubbing, thereby seeking to discourage switching to cleaner western coal.[55] Similarly, the United Mine Workers opposed the SO_2 allowance trading system in 1990 because of a fear that it would encourage a shift to western low-sulfur coal.

Turning to the supply side of environmental regulation, legislators have found command-and-control standards attractive for a number of reasons. First, many legislators and their staffs are trained in law, which predisposes them to favor legalistic regulatory approaches. Second, standards tend to help hide the costs of pollution control, whereas market-based instruments generally impose those costs more directly.[56] Compare, for example, the tone of public debates associated with proposed increases in gasoline taxes with those regarding commensurate increases in the stringency of the Corporate Average Fuel Economy standards for new cars.

Third, standards offer greater opportunities for symbolic politics because strict standards—strong statements of support for environmental protection—can readily be combined with less visible exemptions or with lax enforcement measures. Congress has frequently prescribed administrative rules and procedures to protect intended beneficiaries of legislation by constraining the scope of executive intervention.[57] Such stacking of the deck is more likely to be successful in the context of command-and-control legislation because market-based instruments leave the allocation of costs and benefits up to the market, treating polluters identically. Of course, the underlying reason symbolic politics works is that voters have limited information, and so respond to gestures while remaining relatively unaware of details.

Fourth, if politicians are risk averse, they will prefer instruments that involve more certain effects.[58] The flexibility inherent in market-based instruments creates uncertainty about distributional impacts and local levels of environmental quality. Typically, legislators in a representative democracy are more concerned with the geographic distribution of costs and benefits than with comparisons of total benefits and costs. Hence aggregate cost-effectiveness—the major advantage of market-based instruments—is likely to play a less significant role in the legislative calculus than whether a politician is getting a good deal for his or her constituents.[59]

Finally, legislators are wary of enacting programs that are likely to be undermined by bureaucrats in their implementation; and bureaucrats are less likely to undermine legislative decisions if their own preferences over policy instruments are accommodated. Bureaucratic preferences—at least in the past—have not been supportive of market-based instruments, on several grounds: bureaucrats were familiar with command-and-control approaches; market-based instruments do not require the same kinds of technical expertise that agencies have developed under command-and-control regulation; and market-based instruments can imply a scaled-down role for the agency by shifting decisionmaking from the bureaucracy to the private sector. In other words, government bureaucrats—like their counterparts in environmental advocacy groups and trade associations—might be expected to oppose market-based instruments to prevent their expertise from becoming obsolete, that is, to preserve their human capital.[60]

The Focus on Tradable Permits Allocated without Charge

Economic theory suggests that the choice between tradable permits and pollution taxes should be based upon case-specific factors, but when market-based instruments have been adopted in the United States they have nearly always taken the form of tradable permits rather than emission taxes. Moreover, the initial allocation of such permits has always been through initial distribution without charge rather than through auctions, despite the apparent economic superiority of the latter mechanism in terms of economic efficiency.[61]

Again, many actors in the system have reason to favor tradable permits allocated without charge over other market-based instruments. On the regulatory demand side, existing firms favor tradable permits allocated without charge because they convey rents to them. Moreover, like stringent command-and-control standards for new sources but unlike auctioned permits or taxes, permits allocated without charge give rise to entry barriers because new entrants must purchase permits from existing holders. Thus the rents conveyed to the private sector by tradable permits allocated without charge are, in effect, sustainable.

Environmental advocacy groups have generally supported command-and-control approaches, but given the choice between tradable permits and emission taxes these groups strongly prefer the former. Environmental advocates have a strong incentive to avoid policy instruments that make the costs of environmental protection highly visible to consumers and voters, and taxes make those costs more explicit than permits. Moreover, permit schemes specify the quantity of pollution reduction that will be achieved, in contrast with the indirect effect of pollution taxes. Overall, some environmental groups have come to endorse the tradable permits approach because it promises the cost savings of pollution taxes without the drawbacks that environmentalists associate with environmental tax instruments.

Because no money is exchanged at the time of the initial permit allocation, the costs imposed on industry are less visible and less burdensome. Thus tradable permits allocated without charge are easier for legislators to supply than taxes or auctioned permits. Permits allocated without charge also offer a much greater degree of political control over the distributional effects of regulation, facilitating the formation of majority coalitions. Paul Joskow and Richard Schmalensee, in their examination of the political process of allocating SO_2 allowances in the 1990 amendments, have found that allocating permits on the basis of prior emissions can produce fairly clear winners and losers among firms and states.[62] An auction allows no such political maneuvering.

Increased Attention to Market-Based Instruments

Given the historical lack of receptiveness by the political process to market-based approaches to environmental protection, why has there been a recent rise in the use of these approaches? It would be gratifying to believe that increased understanding of market-based instruments played a large part in fostering their increased political acceptance, but how important has this really been? My colleague Steven Kelman, in his 1981 survey of congressional staff members, finds that support and opposition to market-based environmental policy instruments was based largely on ideological grounds: Republicans who supported the concept of economic incentive approaches said they did so because "the free market works" or because "less government intervention" is desirable, but they had no real awareness or understanding of the economic arguments for market-based programs. Similarly, Democratic opposition was largely based upon ideological factors, with little or no apparent understanding of the real advantages or disadvantages of the various instruments.[63] What would happen if we were to replicate Kelman's survey today? My refutable hypothesis is that we would find increased support from Republicans and greatly increased support from Democrats but insufficient improvements in understanding to explain these changes.[64] So what else has mattered?

First, one factor has surely been the increase in pollution control costs, which have led to greater demand for cost-effective instruments. By the late 1980s even political liberals and environmentalists were beginning to question whether conventional regulations could produce further gains in environmental quality. During the previous twenty years, pollution abatement costs had continually increased as stricter standards moved the private sector up the marginal abatement-cost function. By 1990 pollution control costs in the United States had reached $125 billion annually, nearly a 300 percent increase in real terms from 1972 levels.[65]

Second, strong and vocal support from some segments of the environmental community became an important factor in the late 1980s.[66] By supporting tradable permits for acid rain control, the Environmental Defense Fund seized a market niche in the environmental movement and successfully distinguished itself from other groups.[67] Third, the SO_2 allowance trading program, the leaded gasoline phasedown, and the CFC phaseout were all designed to reduce emissions, not simply to reallocate them cost-effectively among sources. Market-based instruments are most likely to be politically acceptable when proposed to achieve environmental improvements that would not otherwise be feasible (politically or economically).

Fourth, deliberations regarding the SO_2 allowance system, the lead system, and CFC trading differed from previous attempts by economists to influence environmental policy in an important way: the separation of ends from means—that is, the separation of consideration of goals and targets from the policy instruments used to achieve those targets. By accepting—implicitly or otherwise—the politically identified (and potentially inefficient) goal, the ten-million-ton reduction of SO_2 emissions, for example, economists were able to focus successfully on the importance of adopting a cost-effective means of achieving that goal. The risk, of course, was that they might be designing a fast train to the wrong station.

Fifth, until the SO_2 allowance trading program of 1990, acid rain was an unregulated problem; and the same can be said for leaded gasoline and CFCs. Hence there were no existing constituencies—in the private sector, the environmental advocacy community, or the government—for the status quo approach, because there was no status quo approach. We should be more optimistic about introducing market-based instruments for "new" problems, such as global climate change, than about the prospects for such approaches applied to existing, highly regulated problems, such as abandoned hazardous waste sites.

Sixth, by the late 1980s there had already been a perceptible shift of the political center toward a more favorable view of using markets to solve social problems. The administration of George H. W. Bush, which proposed the SO_2 allowance trading program and then championed it through an initially resistant Democratic Congress, could be characterized (at least in its first two years) as "moderate Republican," and phrases such as "fiscally responsible environmental protection" and "harnessing market forces to protect the environment" do have the sound of quintessential moderate Republican issues.[68] Beyond this, however, support for market-oriented solutions to various social problems had been increasing across the political spectrum for the previous fifteen years, as was made clear by deliberations on deregulation of the airline, telecommunications, trucking, railroad, and banking industries. Indeed, by the mid-1990s the concept (or at least the phrase) "market-based environmental policy" had evolved from being politically problematic to politically attractive. Seventh, and finally, the adoption of the SO_2 allowance trading program for acid rain control—like any major innovation in public policy—can partly be attributed to a healthy dose of chance that placed specific persons in key positions, in this case at the White House, the Environmental Protection Agency, the Congress, and environmental organizations.[69]

Conclusions

Economists first proposed the use of corrective taxes to internalize environmental (and other) externalities some eighty years ago. It was only a little more than a decade ago, however, that the portfolio of potential economic incentive instruments was expanded to include quantity-based mechanisms—tradable permits—and these incentive-based approaches to environmental protection began to emerge as prominent features of the policy landscape.

Given that most experience with market-based instruments has been generated quite recently, one should be cautious about drawing conclusions from these experiences. Important questions remain. For example, relatively little is known empirically about the impact of these instruments on technological change. Much more empirical research is also needed on how the preexisting regulatory environment affects performance, including costs. Moreover, the great successes with tradable permits have involved air pollution: acid rain, leaded gasoline, and chlorofluorocarbons. Experience (and success) with water pollution is much more limited, and in other areas there has been no experience at all. Even for air pollution problems, the differences between SO_2 and acid rain, on the one hand, and the combustion of fossil fuels and global climate change, on the other, suggest that a rush to judgment regarding global climate policy instruments is unwarranted.

There are sound reasons why the political world has been slow to embrace the use of market-based instruments for environmental protection, including the ways economists have packaged and promoted their ideas in the past, a failure to separate means (cost-effective instruments) from ends (efficiency), and a tendency to treat environmental problems as little more than externalities calling for corrective taxes. Much of the resistance is also attributable, of course, to the very nature of the political process and the incentives it provides to both politicians and interest groups to favor command-and-control methods over market-based approaches.

Despite this history, market-based instruments have moved to center stage, and policy debates are no longer characterized as licenses to pollute or dismissed as completely impractical. Market-based instruments are considered seriously for each and every environmental problem that is tackled, ranging from endangered species preservation to regional smog to global climate change. Market-based instruments—and, in particular, tradable permit systems—will enjoy increasing acceptance in the years ahead.

No particular form of government intervention, no individual policy instrument—whether market-based or conventional—is appropriate to all environmental problems. Which instrument is best in any given situation depends upon a variety of characteristics of the environmental problem and the social, political, and economic context in which it is being regulated. There is clearly no policy panacea. Indeed, the real challenge for bureaucrats, elected officials, and other participants in the environmental policy process comes in analyzing and then selecting the best instrument for each situation that arises.

Notes

1. R. N. Stavins, ed., *Project 88: Harnessing Market Forces to Protect Our Environment—Initiatives for the New President*, a public policy study sponsored by Senator Timothy E. Wirth, Colorado, and Senator John Heinz, Pennsylvania (Washington, December 1988); R. N. Stavins, ed., *Project 88, Round II: Incentives for Action—Designing Market-Based Environmental Strategies*, a public policy study sponsored by Senator Timothy E. Wirth, Colorado, and Senator John Heinz, Pennsylvania (Washington, May 1991).

2. See Organization for Economic Cooperation and Development, *Economic Instruments for Environmental Protection, 1989* (Paris, 1989); Organization for Economic Cooperation and Development, *Environmental Policy: How to Apply Economic Instruments, 1991* (Paris, 1991); Organization for Economic Cooperation and Development, *Applying Market-Based Instruments to Environmental Policies in China and OECD Countries* (Paris, 1998); Stavins, *Project 88: Harnessing Market Forces to Protect Our Environment—Initiatives for the New President*; Stavins, *Project 88, Round II: Incentives for Action—Designing Market-Based Environmental Strategies;* U.S. Environmental Protection Agency, *Economic Incentives: Options for Environmental Protection*, Document P-2001 (1991); U.S. Environmental Protection Agency, *The United States Experience with Economic Incentives to Control Environmental Pollution*, EPA-230-R-92-001 (1992); U.S. Environmental Protection Agency, *The United States Experience with Economic Incentives for Protecting the Environment*, EPA-240-R-01-001 (2001). Another strain of literature—known as free market environmentalism—focuses on the role of private property rights in achieving environmental protection (Terry Anderson and Donald Leal, *Free Market Environmentalism* [Boulder: Westview Press, 1991]).

3. Tom Tietenberg, *Emissions Trading: An Exercise in Reforming Pollution Policy* (Washington: Resources for the Future, 1985). One should not make too much of these numbers, given that actual command-and-control instruments are being compared with theoretical benchmarks of cost-effectiveness—that is, what a perfectly functioning market-based instrument would achieve in theory. A fair comparison among policy instruments would involve either idealized versions of both market-based systems and likely alternatives or realistic versions of both (R. W. Hahn and R. N. Stavins, "Economic Incentives for Environmental Protection: Integrating Theory and Practice," *American Economic Review*, vol. 82 (May 1992), pp. 464–68.

4. This chapter focuses on market-based policy instruments in the environmental realm, chiefly those instruments that reduce concentrations of pollution, as opposed to those that operate in the natural resources realm. This means, for example, that tradable development rights, wetlands mitigation banking, and tradable permit systems used to govern the allocation of fishing rights are not reviewed. The distinction between environmental and nat-

ural resource policies is somewhat arbitrary. Some policy instruments that are seen to bridge the environmental and natural resource realm, such as the removal of barriers to water markets, are considered.

5. David Montgomery, "Markets in Licenses and Efficient Pollution Control Programs," *Journal of Economic Theory*, vol. 5 (1972), pp. 395–418; W. J. Baumol and W. E. Oates, *The Theory of Environmental Policy*, 2d ed. (Cambridge University Press, 1988); Tietenberg, *Emissions Trading: An Exercise in Reforming Pollution Policy*.

6. P. B. Downing and L. J. White, "Innovation in Pollution Control," *Journal of Environmental Economics and Management*, vol. 13, no. 1 (1986), pp. 18–27; D. A. Malueg, "Emission Credit Trading and the Incentive to Adopt New Pollution Abatement Technology," *Journal of Environmental Economics and Management*, vol. 16, no. 1 (1989), pp. 52–57; S. R. Milliman and Raymond Prince, "Firm Incentives to Promote Technological Change in Pollution Control," *Journal of Environmental Economics and Management*, vol. 17, no. 2 (1989), pp. 247–65; A. B. Jaffe and R. N. Stavins, "Dynamic Incentives of Environmental Regulation: The Effects of Alternative Policy Instruments on Technology Diffusion," *Journal of Environmental Economics and Management*, vol. 29, no. 3 (1995), pp. S43–S63; and Chulho Jung, Kerry Krutilla, and Roy Boyd, "Incentives for Advanced Pollution Abatement Technology at the Industry Level: An Evaluation of Policy Alternatives," *Journal of Environmental Economics and Management*, vol. 30, no. 1 (1996), pp. 95–111.

7. A. C. Pigou, *The Economics of Welfare* (London: Macmillan, 1920).

8. A Pigovian tax is a charge levied per unit of pollution equal to the marginal damages of pollution at the optimum.

9. See J. M. McFarland, "Economics of Solid Waste Management," in Sanitary Engineering Research Laboratory, *Comprehensive Studies of Solid Waste Management, Final Report*, Report 72-3:41-106 (Berkeley: University of California, College of Engineering and School of Public Health, March 1972); K. L. Wertz, "Economic Factors Influencing Households' Production of Refuse," *Journal of Environmental Economics and Management*, vol. 2, no. 2 (1976), pp. 263–72; B. J. Stevens, "Scale, Market Structure, and the Cost of Refuse Collection," *Review of Economics and Statistics*, vol. 40, no. 3 (1978), pp. 438–48; Fritz Efaw and William N. Lanen, "Impact of User Charges on Management of Household Solid Waste," report prepared for the U.S. Environmental Protection Agency under contract 68-3-2634 (Princeton, N.J.: Mathtech, 1979); L. A. Skumatz, "Volume-Based Rates in Solid Waste: Seattle's Experience," report prepared for the Seattle Solid Waste Utility (Seattle: Skumatz Economic Research Associates, 1990); Lester Lave and Howard Gruenspecht, "Increasing the Efficiency and Effectiveness of Environmental Decisions: Benefit-Cost Analysis and Effluent Fees," *Journal of Air and Waste Management*, vol. 41, no. 5 (1991), pp. 680–90; M. L. Miranda, J. W. Everett, D. Blume, and B. A. Roy Jr., "Market-Based Incentives and Residential Municipal Solid Waste," *Journal of Policy Analysis and Management*, vol. 13, no. 4 (1994), pp. 681–98; Don Fullerton and T. C. Kinnaman, "Household Responses to Pricing Garbage by the Bag," *American Economic Review*, vol. 86, no. 4 (1996), pp. 971–84; and Robert Repetto, Roger Dower, Robin Jenkins, and Jacqueline Geoghegan, *Green Fees: How a Tax Shift Can Work for the Environment and the Economy* (Washington: World Resources Institute, 1992).

10. Peter Bohm, *Deposit-Refund Systems: Theory and Applications to Environmental, Conservation, and Consumer Policy* (Johns Hopkins University Press, for Resources for the

Future, 1981); Peter Menell, "Beyond the Throwaway Society: An Incentive Approach to Regulating Municipal Solid Waste," *Ecology Law Quarterly,* vol. 17, no. 4 (1990), pp. 655–739.

11. Ronald Coase, "The Problem of Social Cost," *Journal of Law and Economics,* vol. 3, no. 1 (1960), pp. 1–44; T. D. Crocker, "The Structuring of Atmospheric Pollution Control Systems," in Harold Wolozin, ed., *The Economics of Air Pollution* (W. W. Norton, 1966), pp. 61–86; J. H. Dales, *Pollution, Property, and Prices* (University Press of Toronto, 1968); Montgomery, "Markets in Licenses and Efficient Pollution Control Programs." Thirty years ago, Crocker and Dales independently developed the idea of using transferable discharge permits to allocate the burden of pollution control among sources. Montgomery provided the first rigorous proof that such a system could provide a cost-effective policy instrument. A sizable literature has followed, much of it stemming from R. W. Hahn and Roger Noll, "Designing a Market for Tradeable Permits," in W. A. Magat, ed., *Reform of Environmental Regulation* (Cambridge, Mass.: Ballinger Publishing, 1982), pp. 119–46. Early surveys were provided by Tom Tietenberg, "Transferable Discharge Permits and the Control of Stationary Source Air Pollution: A Survey and Synthesis," *Land Economics,* vol. 56 (1980), pp. 391–416, and Tom Tietenberg, *Emissions Trading: An Exercise in Reforming Pollution Policy.* Much of the literature may be traced to Coase's treatment of negotiated solutions to externality problems.

12. Allocation can be without charge or through sale, including by auction. The program described above is a cap-and-trade program, but some programs operate as credit programs, whereby permits or credits are assigned only when a source reduces emissions below the level required by source-specific limits.

13. In addition, the Energy Policy and Conservation Act of 1975 established Corporate Average Fuel Economy standards for automobiles and light trucks, requiring manufacturers to meet minimum sales-weighted average fuel efficiency standards for their fleets sold in the United States. A penalty is charged per car sold per unit of average fuel efficiency below the standard. The program operates like an intrafirm tradable permit system, in that manufacturers can undertake efficiency improvements wherever they are cheapest within their fleets. For reviews of the program's costs relative to "equivalent" gasoline taxes, see R. W. Crandall, H. K. Gruenspecht, T. E. Keeler, and L. B. Lave, *Regulating the Automobile* (Brookings, 1986), and P. K. Goldberg, "The Effects of the Corporate Average Fuel Efficiency Standards," working paper (Princeton, N.J.: Princeton University, Department of Economics, 1997), mimeographed. Light trucks, which are defined by the federal government to include sport utility vehicles, face weaker Corporate Average Fuel Economy standards.

14. U.S. Environmental Protection Agency, Office of Policy Analysis, *Costs and Benefits of Reducing Lead in Gasoline: Final Regulatory Impact Analysis* (1985).

15. Suzi Kerr and R. G. Newell, "Policy-Induced Technology Adoption: Evidence from the U.S. Lead Phasedown," draft manuscript (Washington: Resources for the Future, 2000).

16. Curtis Carlson, Dallas Burtraw, Maureen Cropper, and Karen Palmer, "Sulfur Dioxide Control by Electric Utilities: What Are the Gains from Trade?" Discussion Paper 98-44-REV (Washington: Resources for the Future, 2000).

17. Dallas Burtraw, "The SO_2 Emissions Trading Program: Cost Savings without Allowance Trades," *Contemporary Economic Policy,* vol. 14, no. 2 (1996), pp. 79–94; Richard Schmalensee, P. L. Joskow, A. D. Ellerman, J. P. Montero, and E. M. Bailey, "An

Interim Evaluation of Sulfur Dioxide Emissions Trading," *Journal of Economic Perspectives*, vol. 12, no. 3 (1998), pp. 53–68; R. N. Stavins, "What Have We Learned from the Grand Policy Experiment: Lessons from SO_2 Allowance Trading," *Journal of Economic Perspectives*, vol. 12, no. 3 (1998), pp. 69–88; Dallas Burtraw and E. Mansur, "The Environmental Effects of SO_2 Trading and Banking," *Environmental Science and Technology*, vol. 33, no. 20 (1999), pp. 3489–94; A. D. Ellerman, P. L. Joskow, Richard Schmalensee, J. P. Montero, and E. M. Bailey, *Markets for Clean Air: The U.S. Acid Rain Program* (Cambridge University Press, 2000).

18. For a comprehensive review of information programs and their apparent efficacy, see Tom Tietenberg, "Information Strategies for Pollution Control," paper presented at the Eighth Annual Conference of the European Association of Environmental and Resource Economists, Tilburg, The Netherlands, June 26–28, 1997. The International Organization for Standardization's (ISO) benchmark, ISO 14001, provides standards for environmental management systems. To obtain certification, firms must commit to environmental performance targets. More than eight thousand plants worldwide obtained certification through 1999. David Wheeler, *Greening Industry: New Roles for Communities, Markets, and Governments*, World Bank Report (Oxford University Press, 2000).

19. R. G. Newell, A. B. Jaffe, and R. N. Stavins, "The Induced Innovation Hypothesis and Energy-Saving Technological Change," *Quarterly Journal of Economics*, vol. 114, no. 3 (1999), pp. 941–75.

20. *Toxic Chemicals: EPA's Toxics Release Inventory Is Useful but Could Be Improved* (U.S. General Accounting Office, 1992); James T. Hamilton, "Pollution as News: Media and Stock Market Reactions to the Toxics Release Inventory Data," *Journal of Environmental Economics and Management*, vol. 28, no. 1 (1995), pp. 98–113; Linda T. M. Bui and C. J. Mayer, "Public Disclosure of Private Information as a Means of Regulation: Evidence from the Toxics Release Inventory in Massachusetts" (Boston, 1997), mimeographed; Shameek Konar and M. A. Cohen, "Information as Regulation: The Effect of Community Right-to-Know Laws on Toxic Emissions," *Journal of Environmental Economics and Management*, vol. 32, no. 1 (1997), pp. 109–24; A. Ananathanarayanan, "Is There a Green Link? A Panel Data Value Event Study of the Relationship Between Capital Markets and Toxic Releases," working paper (New Brunswick, N.J.: Rutgers University, Department of Economics, 1998); and James T. Hamilton and W. Kip Viscusi, *Calculating Risks? The Spatial and Political Dimensions of Hazardous Waste Policy* (MIT Press, 1999).

21. Although subsidies can advance environmental quality (see, for example, Jaffe and Stavins, "Dynamic Incentives of Environmental Regulation: The Effects of Alternative Policy Instruments on Technology Diffusion"), it is also true that subsidies, in general, have important and well-known disadvantages relative to taxes (Baumol and Oates, *The Theory of Environmental Policy*); hence, I do not consider them as a distinct category of market-based instruments in this chapter.

22. Michael Shelby, Robert Shackleton, Malcolm Shealy, and Alexander Cristofaro, *The Climate Change Implications of Eliminating U.S. Energy (and Related) Subsidies* (U.S. Environmental Protection Agency, 1997).

23. A. D. Ellerman, Richard Schmalensee, P. L. Joskow, J. P. Montero, and E. M. Bailey, *Emissions Trading under the U.S. Acid Rain Program: Evaluation of Compliance Costs and Allowance Market Performance* (MIT Center for Energy and Environmental Policy Research, 1997); Suzi Kerr and David Maré, "Efficient Regulation through Tradeable

Permit Markets: The United States Lead Phasedown," Working Paper 96-06 (College Park: University of Maryland, Department of Agricultural and Resource Economics, January 1997).

24. Burtraw, "The SO$_2$ Emissions Trading Program: Cost Savings without Allowance Trades"; A. D. Ellerman and J. P. Montero, "The Declining Trend in Sulfur Dioxide Emissions: Implications for Allowance Prices," *Journal of Environmental Economics and Management*, vol. 36, no. 1 (1998), pp. 26–45; Douglas Bohi and Dallas Burtraw, "SO$_2$ Allowance Trading: How Do Expectations and Experience Measure Up?" *Electricity Journal*, vol. 10, no. 7 (1977), pp. 67–75; N. O. Keohane, "Essays in the Economics of Environmental Policy," Ph.D. dissertation, Harvard University, 2001; Joseph Doucet and Todd Strauss, "On the Bundling of Coal and Sulphur Dioxide Emissions Allowances," *Energy Policy*, vol. 22, no. 9 (1994), pp. 764–70.

25. R. W. Hahn and G. L. Hester, "Marketable Permits: Lessons for Theory and Practice," *Ecology Law Quarterly*, vol. 16, no. 2 (1989), pp. 361–406.

26. Renee Rico, "The U.S. Allowance Trading System for Sulfur Dioxide: An Update of Market Experience," *Environmental and Resource Economics*, vol. 5, no. 2 (1995), pp. 115–29.

27. R. W. Hahn, "Regulatory Constraints on Environmental Markets," *Journal of Public Economics*, vol. 42, no. 2 (1990), pp. 149–75.

28. J. P. Montero, "Voluntary Compliance with Market-Based Environmental Policy: Evidence from the U.S. Acid Rain Program," *Journal of Political Economy*, vol. 107, no. 5 (1999), pp. 998–1033.

29. Albert Nichols, J. Farr, and Gordon Hester, "Trading and the Timing of Emissions: Evidence from the Ozone Transport Region" (Cambridge, Mass.: National Economic Research Associates, 1996).

30. R. N. Stavins, "What Have We Learned from the Grand Policy Experiment: Lessons from SO$_2$ Allowance Trading."

31. Don Fullerton and Gilbert Metcalf, "Environmental Controls, Scarcity Rents, and Pre-Existing Distortions," Working Paper 6091 (Cambridge, Mass.: National Bureau of Economic Research, July 1997).

32. Lawrence Goulder, Ian Parry, and Dallas Burtraw, "Revenue-Raising versus Other Approaches to Environmental Protection: The Critical Significance of Pre-Existing Tax Distortions," *RAND Journal of Economics*, vol. 28 (Winter 1997), pp. 708–831.

33. R. N. Stavins, "Transaction Costs and Tradable Permits," *Journal of Environmental Economics and Management*, vol. 29, no. 2 (1995), pp. 133–48.

34. For some interesting exceptions, see J. B. Hockenstein, R. N. Stavins, and B. W. Whitehead, "Creating the Next Generation of Market-Based Environmental Tools," *Environment*, vol. 39, no. 4 (1977), pp. 12–20, 30–33.

35. F. L. Reinhardt, *Down to Earth: Applying Business Principles to Environmental Management* (Harvard Business School Press, 2000).

36. Hahn and Stavins, "Economic Incentives for Environmental Protection: Integrating Theory and Practice."

37. Milliman and Prince, "Firm Incentives to Promote Technological Change in Pollution Control"; Jaffe and Stavins, "Dynamic Incentives of Environmental Regulation: The Effects of Alternative Policy Instruments on Technology Diffusion"; Doucet and Strauss, "On the Bundling of Coal and Sulphur Dioxide Emissions Allowances"; Newell,

Jaffe, and Stavins, "The Induced Innovation Hypothesis and Energy-Saving Technological Change."

38. Goulder, Parry, and Burtraw, "Revenue-Raising versus Other Approaches to Environmental Protection: The Critical Significance of Pre-Existing Tax Distortions."

39. See, for example, J. B. Goldstein, "The Prospects for Using Market Incentives to Conserve Biological Diversity," *Environmental Law,* vol. 21 (1991), pp. 985–1014; and M. J. Bean, "Shelter from the Storm: Endangered Species and Landowners Alike Deserve a Safe Harbor," *New Democrat* (March–April 1997), pp. 20–21, on species protection. See, for example, Brian Fisher, Scott Barrett, Peter Bohm, Masahiro Kuroda, James Mubazi, Anwar Shah, and R. N. Stavins, "Policy Instruments to Combat Climate Change," in J. P. Bruce, Hoesung Lee, and E. F. Haites, eds., *Climate Change 1995: Economic and Social Dimensions of Climate Change* (Cambridge University Press, 1996), pp. 397–439; R. W. Hahn and R. N. Stavins, "Trading in Greenhouse Permits: A Critical Examination of Design and Implementation Issues," in Henry Lee, ed., *Shaping National Responses to Climate Change: A Post-Rio Policy Guide* (Cambridge, Mass.: Island Press, 1995), pp. 177–217; Richard Schmalensee, *Greenhouse Policy Architecture and Institutions,* paper prepared for National Bureau of Economic Research conference, Economics and Policy Issues in Global Warming: An Assessment of the Intergovernmental Panel Report, Snowmass, Colorado, July 23–24, 1996; and R. N. Stavins, "Policy Instruments for Climate Change: How Can National Governments Address a Global Problem?" *University of Chicago Legal Forum* (1997), pp. 293–329, on applications to global climate change. More broadly, see R. E. Ayres, "Expanding the Use of Environmental Trading Programs into New Areas of Environmental Regulation," *Pace Environmental Law Review,* vol. 18, no. 1 (2000), pp. 87–118.

40. R. G. Newell and R. N. Stavins, "Abatement Cost Heterogeneity and Potential Gains from Market-Based Instruments," Working Paper RWP00-006 (Cambridge, Mass.: Harvard University, John F. Kennedy School of Government, December 2001).

41. R. L. Revesz, "Federalism and Interstate Environmental Externalities," *University of Pennsylvania Law Review,* vol. 144 (1996), p. 2341.

42. Montgomery, "Markets in Licenses and Efficient Pollution Control Programs."

43. Martin L. Weitzman, "Prices versus Quantities," *Review of Economic Studies,* vol. 41 (1974), pp. 477–91.

44. R. N. Stavins, "Correlated Uncertainty and Policy Instrument Choice," *Journal of Environmental Economics and Management,* vol. 30, no. 2 (1996), pp. 218–32.

45. Richard G. Newell and William A. Pizer, "Regulating Stock Externalities under Uncertainty," Discussion Paper 98-02 (Washington: Resources for the Future, 2000).

46. M. J. Roberts and A. M. Spence, "Effluent Charges and Licenses under Uncertainty," *Journal of Public Economics,* vol. 5, nos. 3–4 (1976), pp. 193–208.; L. Kaplow and S. Shavell, "On the Superiority of Corrective Taxes to Quantity Regulation," Working Paper 6251 (Cambridge, Mass.: National Bureau of Economic Research, November 1997). In addition to the efficiency advantages of nonlinear taxes, they also have the attribute of reducing the total (although not the marginal) tax burden of the regulated sector, relative to an ordinary linear tax, which is potentially important in a political economy context.

47. R. N. Stavins and B. W. Whitehead, "Pollution Charges for Environmental Protection: A Policy Link between Energy and Environment," *Annual Review of Energy and the Environment,* vol. 17 (1992), pp. 187–210.

48. R. N. Stavins, "Transaction Costs and Tradable Permits," *Journal of Environmental Economics and Management*, vol. 29, no. 2 (1995), pp. 133–48.

49. See, for example, the proposal for "growth targets" by J. A. Frankel, *Greenhouse Gas Emissions*, Policy Brief 52 (Brookings, June 1999).

50. This "political market" framework was developed by N. O. Keohane, R. L. Revesz, and R. N. Stavins, "The Choice of Regulatory Instruments in Environmental Policy," *Harvard Environmental Law Review*, vol. 22, no. 2 (1998), pp. 313–67; these sections of the chapter draw upon that work and also upon R. W. Hahn and R. N. Stavins, "Incentive-Based Environmental Regulation: A New Era from an Old Idea?" *Ecology Law Quarterly*, vol. 18, no. 1 (1991), pp. 1–42; and Stavins, "What Have We Learned from the Grand Policy Experiment: Lessons from SO_2 Allowance Trading."

51. M. J. Sandel, "It's Immoral to Buy the Right to Pollute," *New York Times*, December 15, 1997, p. A29.

52. Steven Kelman, *What Price Incentives? Economists and the Environment* (Boston: Auburn House, 1981).

53. This concern was alleviated in the SO2 provisions of the 1990 amendments to the Clean Air Act by an explicit statutory provision that permits do not represent property rights.

54. Kelman, *What Price Incentives? Economists and the Environment*. These strategic arguments refer, for the most part, to pollution taxes, not to market-based instruments in general. Indeed, as I discuss later, one reason some environmental groups have come to endorse the tradable permits approach is that it promises the cost savings of taxes without the drawbacks that environmentalists associate with tax instruments.

55. B. A. Ackerman and W. T. Hassler, *Clean Coal, Dirty Air* (Yale University Press, 1981).

56. M. D. McCubbins and T. Sullivan, "Constituency Influences on Legislative Policy Choice," *Quality and Quantity*, vol. 18 (1984), pp. 299–319.

57. M. D. McCubbins, R. G. Noll, and B. R. Weingast, "Administrative Procedures as Instruments of Political Control," *Journal of Law, Economics, and Organization*, vol. 3 (1987), pp. 243–77.

58. "Legislators are likely to behave as if they are risk averse, even if they are personally risk neutral, if their constituents punish unpredictable policy choices or their reelection probability is nearly unity" (M. D. McCubbins, R. G. Noll, and B. R. Weingast, "Structure and Process, Politics and Policy: Administrative Arrangements and the Political Control of Agencies," *Virginia Law Review*, vol. 75 [1989], pp. 431–82).

59. K. A. Shepsle and B. R. Weingast, "Political Solutions to Market Problems," *American Political Science Review*, vol. 78 (1984), pp. 417–34.

60. This same incentive subsequently led EPA staff involved in the acid rain program to become strong proponents of trading for other air pollution problems.

61. See Fullerton and Metcalf, "Environmental Controls, Scarcity Rents, and Pre-Existing Distortions"; Goulder, Parry, and Burtraw, "Revenue-Raising versus Other Approaches to Environmental Protection: The Critical Significance of Pre-Existing Tax Distortions"; Stavins, "Transaction Costs and Tradable Permits." The EPA does have an annual auction of SO_2 allowances, but this represents less than 2 percent of the total allocation (E. M. Bailey, "Allowance Trading Activity and State Regulatory Rulings: Evidence from the U.S. Acid Rain Program," MIT-CEEPR 96-002 WP (Massachusetts Institute of

Technology, Center for Energy and Environmental Policy Research, 1996). Although the EPA auctions may have helped in establishing the market for SO_2 allowances, they are a trivial part of the overall program (P. L. Joskow, Richard Schmalensee, and E. M. Bailey, "Auction Design and the Market for Sulfur Dioxide Emissions," *American Economic Review*, vol. 88 (September 1998), pp. 669–85.

62. P. L. Joskow and Richard Schmalensee, "The Political Economy of Market-Based Environmental Policy: The U.S. Acid Rain Program," *Journal of Law and Economics*, vol. 41, no. 1 (1998), pp. 35–84.

63. Kelman, *What Price Incentives? Economists and the Environment*.

64. There has, however, been some increased understanding of market-based approaches among policymakers. This has partly been the result of increased understanding by their staffs, a function—to some degree—of the economics training that is now common in law schools and of the proliferation of schools of public policy (Hahn and Stavins, "Incentive-Based Environmental Regulation: A New Era from an Old Idea?").

65. U.S. Environmental Protection Agency, *Environmental Investments: The Cost of a Clean Environment*, report of the administrator to Congress (1990); A. B. Jaffe, S. R. Peterson, P. R. Portney, and R. N. Stavins, "Environmental Regulation and the Competitiveness of U.S. Manufacturing: What Does the Evidence Tells Us?" *Journal of Economic Literature*, vol. 33, no. 1 (1995), pp. 132–63.

66. The environmental advocacy community is by no means unanimous in its support for market-based instruments, however; see, for example, D. A. Seligman, *Air Pollution Emissions Trading: Opportunity or Scam? A Guide for Activists* (San Francisco: Sierra Club, 1994).

67. When the memberships (and financial resources) of other environmental advocacy groups subsequently declined with the election of the environmentally friendly Clinton-Gore administration, the Environmental Defense Fund continued to prosper and grow (R. C. Lowry, "The Political Economy of Environmental Citizen Groups," Ph.D. dissertation, Harvard University, 1993).

68. The Reagan administration enthusiastically embraced a market-oriented ideology but demonstrated little interest in employing actual market-based policies in the environmental area. From the Bush administration through the Clinton administration, interest and activity regarding market-based instruments—particularly tradable permit systems—continued to increase, although the pace of activity in terms of newly implemented programs declined during the Clinton years, when a considerable part of the related focus was on global climate policy (see R. W. Hahn and R. N. Stavins, "National Environmental Policy during the Clinton Years," paper prepared for the Center for Business and Government conference, Economic Policy during the 1990s, Harvard University, John F. Kennedy School of Government, Center for Business and Government, June 28, 2001).

69. Within the White House, among the most active and influential enthusiasts of market-based environmental instruments were Counsel Boyden Gray and his deputy, John Schmitz, Domestic Policy Adviser Roger Porter, Council of Economic Advisers member Richard Schmalensee, Council of Economic Advisers senior staff economist Robert Hahn, and Office of Management and Budget associate director Robert Grady. At the EPA, Administrator William Reilly—a "card-carrying environmentalist"—enjoyed valuable credibility with environmental advocacy groups, and Deputy Administrator Henry Habicht was a key early supporter of market-based instruments. In the Congress, Senators Timothy

Wirth and John Heinz provided high-profile, bipartisan support for the SO_2 allowance trading system and, more broadly, for a wide variety of market-based instruments for various environmental problems through their Project 88 (Stavins, *Project 88: Harnessing Market Forces to Protect Our Environment—Initiatives for the New President*). Finally, in the environmental community, the Environmental Defense Fund's executive director Fred Krupp, senior economist Daniel Dudek, and staff attorney Joseph Goffman worked closely with the White House to develop the initial allowance trading proposal.

9

CARY COGLIANESE
DAVID LAZER

Management-Based Regulatory Strategies

A LL REGULATORY STRATEGIES seek to encourage private firms to manage their affairs in ways that reduce social harms. Government authorities have traditionally used regulatory strategies that command firms either to use specified technologies or processes that governmental decisionmakers believe will achieve social goals (technology-based regulation) or to achieve specified levels of socially desirable outputs or performance, allowing them flexibility in deciding what technologies or processes to use to achieve that performance (performance-based regulation). This chapter develops a theoretical framework with which to understand yet another regulatory strategy, which we label "management-based regulation," whereby the regulator seeks to embed within the management practices of the firm a consciousness of public goals. What is distinctive about management-based regulation is that it commands firms to engage in the planning and decisionmaking required to identify both technologies and performance targets needed to achieve socially desired goals.[1]

The authors gratefully acknowledge support from the Ash Fund for Research on Democratic Governance at Harvard's John F. Kennedy School of Government and research assistance from Alice Andre-Clark. We are grateful for the comments we received on early drafts of this chapter, as well as for helpful written comments from John Donahue, Jane Fountain, Howard Kunreuther, Jerry Mechling, and Richard Reibstein.

The potential advantage of management-based regulation is that it shifts the discretion as to how a regulation is applied in a particular setting to the actor with the most knowledge of that setting—the regulated party. The potential disadvantage of management-based regulation is exactly the agency concern that resulted in the need for regulation in the first place: regulated entities need to be regulated because otherwise they will not achieve public goals. The critical issue with management-based regulation is to identify the circumstances under which regulators can evaluate whether regulated entities have properly internalized public goals into their management processes.

Management-based regulatory strategies are beginning to emerge in a variety of regulatory areas, including food safety, occupational health, and environmental protection. In some cases these approaches can help overcome some of the well-known limitations associated with more conventional approaches to regulation. In other cases they may be the only feasible alternatives for addressing public regulatory goals.

The Advantages of Management-Based Regulation

Regulation can be used to correct failures or deficiencies in the market—for example, where monopolies exist, where information is scarce, or where externalities or commons problems exist.[2] Although regulation has been effective in correcting certain market failures, traditional regulatory strategies also suffer from their own kinds of failures. Traditional regulation often consists of technology-based strategies requiring that firms adopt specific technologies or methods designed to promote social goals such as environmental quality, worker safety, or consumer protection. Yet uniform technology-based standards are sometimes too stringent in areas where the costs of regulation exceed the benefits or too lax in areas where the benefits of regulation would outweigh the costs.[3] Regulation that imposes requirements for specific technologies may also inhibit innovation in new, and potentially more cost-effective, technologies. Technology-based regulation also provides little incentive for firms to go beyond compliance and achieve further improvements in regulatory goals.

An alternative to technology-based regulation is performance-based regulation, according to which government specifies the desired outcome but gives firms flexibility in meeting those outcomes. Such an approach avoids locking in a technological fix and allows firms to innovate and search for less costly means of achieving the desired outcome. Cost-effectiveness can be enhanced by allowing firms to average their performance across time, facilities, products, and firms. A special kind of performance-based regulation utilizes market-based instruments, such as tradable permits or emissions taxes.[4] Market-based instruments seek to make use of market dynamics to overcome the limitations of both technology-based and static performance-based regulation.[5] They either create internal costs through taxes to match the external costs of production or create a market in rights to engage in socially costly behavior (such as pollution). These methods give firms the flexibility to achieve higher levels of performance in those processes or facilities where it is cheaper to do so, making the achievement of regulatory goals even more cost-effective. They also can provide firms with incentives to innovate and go beyond what current technologies can do.

The main limitation of performance-based regulation, including the use of market-based instruments, lies in the difficulty of implementing it in many areas of social concern. Market-based approaches have proved to be politically difficult to create and probably will be still more difficult to expand into new areas.[6] Hence, in the area of environmental regulation, emissions trading regimes have proved useful for achieving cost-effective reductions in nontoxic pollutants, such as sulfur dioxide emissions, but it would be challenging, and ethically problematic, to create a market in workers' injuries. More significant for our purposes, it is simply difficult or costly to accurately measure many of the harmful activities that the government is trying to control and administratively difficult to create a functioning market in all these harms. This is a fundamental limitation of performance-based regulation in general. Governmental authorities simply lack the resources to measure and monitor all the potentially harmful activities of all economic firms.[7]

Management-based regulation, the approach of concern to us here, is an alternative to both technology-based and performance-based regulation. In management-based governance, firms are required to produce plans that comply with general criteria outlining how to achieve the public goals in question. These plans may be subject to approval by regulators and sometimes are even developed with their assistance. They generally require firms to produce documentation of subsequent compliance; and third-party auditors or periodic audits by regulators can be used to certify compliance.[8]

Management-based regulatory strategies hold a number of potential advantages over traditional regulation. Like performance-based regulation, they locate regulatory decisionmaking at the level at which the most information about processes and potential control methods is available. Thus the behaviors that firms adopt under a management-based approach have the potential to be less costly and more effective than those initiated under cruder, government-imposed technology standards.[9] Moreover, by placing the locus of standard-setting authority at the firm level, it can be expected that there will be a greater "buy-in" from firm management, a circumstance that should lead to greater compliance with the standards and could eliminate certain barriers to "beyond-compliance" behavior.[10] It is well recognized that government enforcement resources are inadequate to ensure thorough oversight of regulated firms. Hence much compliance with government regulation is, in a sense, already voluntary compliance, because in many cases the probability of detection of a violation is low.[11] Privatized regulation may be able to overcome this limitation somewhat both by enlisting the assistance of private, third-party certifiers and through the potential buy-in effect that comes from firms' creating their own standards. Firms are likely to see their own standards as more reasonable and legitimate and thus to be less resistant to compliance.[12]

Finally, by giving firms flexibility to create their own regulatory approaches, management-based approaches can promote innovation and social learning. The International Organization for Standardization's set of standards governing environmental management systems, for example, requires that firms deliver continual improvement, anticipating that these firms will have an incentive to seek out innovative solutions that achieve greater cost-effectiveness in meeting regulatory goals. The potential for diverse approaches to achieving regulatory goals will allow for experimentation, which in turn can lead to solutions that those who set government standards perhaps would never have even considered.

Conditions for Effective Management-Based Regulation

We recognize that the case we have just made for management-based regulation accentuates only the positive potential for this approach. The preceding discussion is intended, of course, only to suggest the viability of the strategy as one possible option within the government's regulatory toolbox. None of these approaches is without disadvantages, though. By placing the locus of decisionmaking within the firm, for example, management-based approaches by themselves may not provide sufficient incentives for firms to incur costly changes that might be needed to achieve social goals. As Ian

Ayres and John Braithwaite note, even if firms "are more capable, they are not necessarily more willing to regulate effectively."[13] When appropriate technologies intended to achieve social goals are easily knowable to the government, or when government can easily define and measure desired performance, it is likely that technology-based or performance-based approaches will remain superior to management-based regulation. The challenge is to clarify the conditions under which management-based regulation is an appropriate choice for governmental decisionmakers.

We begin with a simple model of private behavior. Private production occurs when a private actor makes some plans, processes inputs, and produces some set of outputs. Actors anticipate and learn what processes produce what outputs, thereby generating feedback used in the planning stage. Those outputs may include both private goods (salable products or services) and social goods and bads (positive and negative externalities). Social goods are those goods in which the public has some interest. These include the traditional notion of public goods (for example, a clean environment) as well as other cases of "market failure" (for example, worker safety). The first working assumption we make in this chapter is that private actors maximize private gain and will thus potentially underproduce social goods. The question then is this: How should the government intervene to increase the production of social goods? One key part of the answer must lie in the stage of production at which government intervenes: planning, process, or outputs.

The different regulatory approaches we have discussed may be categorized according to the stage at which they intervene. Technology-based regulatory strategies intervene in the process stage, specifying technologies to be used or steps to be followed. Performance-based approaches, including market-based strategies, intervene at the output stage. Management-based approaches, in contrast, intervene at the planning and processing stages. Under what circumstances should the government use which approach? In particular, under what circumstances is a management-based approach effective?

Just as there are no market failures in a world in which the market faces no transaction costs,[14] there are no government failures where government faces no transaction costs. In such a perfect word, when technology-based regulation were used, the government could craft the ultimately nuanced regulation, whereby each technological requirement is delicately balanced as to the benefits and burdens imposed on society and regulatory change is appropriately elastic in the face of new technological developments. When performance-based tools were used, government could precisely determine the social costs of particular outputs and impose the appropriate tax (or industry-wide quota for a trading system), and business will effortlessly adjust internal processes to internalize these costs. When management-based tools were used, government could easily evaluate the planning and subsequent implementation of controls on the production of social goods and bads by private actors.

Of course, we live in a world in which both government and market face substantial transaction costs, inevitably resulting in government and market failure. What, then, is the ideal regulatory instrument? The answer must lie, in part, with the locus of the transaction costs in government and market. Our second working assumption is that the transaction costs for market actors to understand the linkages between process and outputs is at least as good as, and usually better than, those for government actors—that is, we assume that a market actor can more easily determine the ideal output of social goods than the government.

This assumption, by itself, does not determine the choice of instrument, because market actors do not have the motivation to incur transaction costs to achieve social goods nor to reveal their superior knowledge of the relation between process and outputs.[15] The key question then becomes Where do the relative competencies of the state lie? How good is the state at determining outputs, understanding the processing of inputs, and identifying the linkages between process and output and between input and output?

Consider, then, two dimensions along which the competence of government can be tracked (figure 9-1). The first dimension is the government's ability to evaluate the social outputs of a private party. By "evaluating social output" we mean the tangible measurement of outputs and evaluation of their social impact. In the environmental area, for example, this would mean that the government is able to measure emissions and evaluate the health impact of those emissions.[16] We assume that when ease of measuring social output is high, the government can cheaply measure and evaluate social outputs. The second dimension is the homogeneity of regulated parties. We treat homogeneity as encompassing both location and time. A sector is considered to be homogeneous if at a given point in time most industry actors have similar operations and if over time the technology used by industry actors is stable. If the population of regulated parties is highly homogeneous, the institution of one-size-fits-all technological standards become more practical, because everyone is the "same size."

Figure 9-1. *Framework for Selecting Regulatory Strategies*

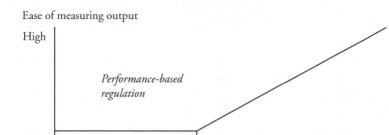

In our assessment, performance-based regulation, including that which employs marketlike incentives, dominates the alternatives in circumstances in which it is easy to measure output. Furthermore, as heterogeneity of regulated sectors increases, and it becomes more difficult to regulate process or technology, performance-based regulation may be desirable even when measuring output becomes relatively more difficult or costly. In such cases, the role of the government should be to provide incentives to private parties to produce the desired outputs. Such "incentive-compatible" or "market-based" policies would include creating a tax or subsidy proportional to the output of social bad or good or determining quotas and allowing trading of social bads among private firms to occur. Alternatively, if such incentive-compatible policies are impossible, performance standards would still be most appropriate, as they allow firms flexibility in choosing the lowest-cost approaches to achieve the desired performance levels.

Under these circumstances, in short, there is a clear division of labor between government and private actors. The government determines the social value of the outputs of private parties and structures incentives of the private parties accordingly. The private parties then engineer their processes consistent with these incentives.

However, it often is not possible to accurately measure critical outputs. In food safety, for example, sensory inspection (the "poke-and-sniff" model) does not detect many important contaminants, and it is impractical to sample a sufficient quantity of a shipment of food to measure contamination in an accurate and timely way. Under circumstances in which the regulated sector is homogeneous and measuring outputs is impractical (lower right-hand quadrant of figure 9-1), it should be possible to cheaply produce a technological standard based on "best practices."

The most difficult regulatory scenario is that in which it is costly, if not impossible, to measure social outputs—making performance-based regulation impractical—and heterogeneity is high—making technological regulation impractical. In such cases there may be a general understanding of how to achieve social objectives, but the appropriate response in particular situations depends on contextual factors. Under these circumstances, we would argue, there is a theoretical justification for management-based regulation, whereby the government lays out criteria for planning, as well as general parameters for process, and certifies (and enforces) private behavior consistent with these processes. That is, as one moves from the lower right-hand quadrant to the lower left-hand quadrant in figure 9-1, the informational advantage of firms grows, as does the potential social benefit to granting firms greater flexibility in deciding how to achieve the regulator's goals.

The Enforcement of Management-Based Strategies

Private firms' informational advantage is a necessary but not sufficient condition for the successful application of management-based regulation. To be successful, management-based regulatory strategies must overcome principal-agent problems so that firms better take into account the public's interests in their behavior. The principal-agent challenge is complicated by the fact that government must seek to influence behavior that, consistent with our assumption, it does not well understand or cannot easily measure. In distinguishing between conventional forms of regulation and management-based regulation, it is useful to envision the social good produced by regulation as a function of a set of technologies and processes in place at regulated firms and a set of situational factors at those locations. Thus,

$$S = f(r_1, r_2, \ldots, r_n; s_1, s_2, \ldots, s_m),$$

where S is the social good produced by a regulation, $r_1, r_2, \ldots, r_n$ are technological requirements that the regulator might impose, and $s_1, s_2, \ldots, s_m$ are situational factors that vary from one situation to another (location, particular products, the type of production process in place, and so forth).

Choosing a set of technological requirements will be relatively easy if the technological requirements, r, and the situational factors, s, are independent of each other. Essentially, the regulator can choose the optimal value one dimension at a time, disregarding for the time being the other dimension. The regulator's challenge becomes exponentially more difficult, however, as the technological requirements interact with situational factors and, consequently, an effective set of values of r for one set of s is dysfunctional for another set of s.

By decentralizing the decisionmaking through management-based regulation, the regulatory process essentially eliminates the need to calculate the effects of these interactions, because for every regulated site (where the decisions are made), the value of s is given, and the social good "merely" has to be optimized along the various dimensions of r. The regulator will then need to calculate the social good resulting from the particular choices a firm has made with respect to r (and perhaps that neighborhood of r) rather than all of the permutations of r and s.

Of course, regulated sites will not optimize for the social good along these dimensions voluntarily—otherwise there would not be a need for regulation. Government must back up any regulation with enforcement. Yet given our assumption that the regulator cannot a priori produce an effective technology-based regulation (owing to sector heterogeneity) and cannot a priori select a clear performance measure of the social good (owing to the difficulty of measuring output), how can the regulator, ex post, judge whether the planning and process implemented under a management-based strategy achieves public goals?

We focus first on the enforcement challenges at the planning stage. The planning stage may be viewed as the investment made by the firm to search the "r space" for the maximum amount of social good. Management-based regulation at the planning stage requires the firm to analyze the impact its production process has on social goals, to evaluate alternative interventions to achieve those social goals, and to create a system of continuous feedback as to the achievement of those social goals. For example, a management-based approach to environmental regulation might require firms to evaluate the amounts of particular emissions, to select among alternative approaches to controlling those emissions, and to set up a system of continuous feedback to evaluate whether emissions reduction standards are being met.

Such an informational search will quite likely be expensive for firms. The enforcement question is this: To what extent can the regulator evaluate whether the firm has conducted such a search correctly and effectively? The firm's investment in the human and physical capital required to do the necessary planning is the easiest to evaluate. Are there employees with the necessary training? Is the monitoring equipment necessary for data collection present? The more difficult challenge for the government is evaluation of the data, data analysis, and conclusions drawn from that analysis. First, data may be falsified so that firms can circumvent the requirement to make costly modifications to the production process. Hence it is critical to establish ramifications for falsifying data and perhaps to establish whistleblowing procedures. Second, in the absence of clear guidelines or benchmarks, firms will usually need to take a large leap from gathering raw data to drawing conclusions about what processes and technologies should be implemented. As a result, in the absence of vigorous enforcement, firms may have a tendency to hide knowledge from the government and to adopt plans that are less than optimal.

Assuming that the planning has been done properly, government's next enforcement challenge centers on the implementation of the plan. Under certain circumstances, enforcement will not be necessary to secure implementation. For example, for some firms most of the costs of compliance with management-based regulation will accrue at the planning stage. If the plan adopted by the firm is also in the firm's private interest (for example, if it reduces both private and social costs through reduction of waste), then the firm can be expected to implement, or voluntarily "self-enforce," its plan. The likelihood of this outcome depends on the extent to which public and private interests are correlated in carrying out the firms' plan—a linkage that is far from clear in many cases.[17]

If it is not in the interest of the firm to follow through on its own plan, then the government's role is to monitor and enforce a firm's violations of its own plan. As with the enforcement of planning, some dimensions of implementation will be easier to monitor than others. Investments in physical and human capital will be easiest to monitor. Thus, it will be easy to see whether refrigerators required by a plan for the safe processing of food have been installed or whether workers with particular training are employed. The record keeping required by a firm's plans will be easy to monitor but not to validate.[18] More difficult to monitor will be the deployment of resources. For example, a food-processing plant may have refrigerators on-site, but is food placed in those refrigerators in a timely fashion? Food safety plans could also call for the deployment of certain time-sensitive sanitation practices, but does the firm actually deploy its personnel when it says it will?

To be effective, management-based regulation will need to lay out parameters for acceptable plans and resulting processes to facilitate effective monitoring and oversight.[19] For example, it may be virtually impossible to process certain foods safely without monitoring the temperature at which the food is stored. A plan that did not incorporate that feature would necessarily be unacceptable. Wherever feasible, government will need to establish parameters that are important for any effective private response and are easy to enforce. Yet such parameters will still permit an enormous variety of processes and allow for continued innovation to achieve regulatory goals more cost-effectively.

A central challenge for systems of management-based regulation will be to identify the appropriate degree of precision in the parameters government establishes for firms' internal management.[20] On the one hand, it may be tempting for government to make its parameters for management plans highly specific, in which case management-based regulation will effectively become a form of technology-based regulation, with all its attendant problems. On the other hand, if the parameters government selects are highly general, effective monitoring of firms by enforcers may prove to be extremely difficult, especially in the absence of sound performance measures.

Management-Based Regulation of Food Safety

Given these challenges, can government effectively use management-based regulation? Food safety is a key regulatory arena in which management-based strategies have emerged in recent years. It is a classic case of asymmetric information as the basis for government intervention. It is difficult, if not impossible, for consumers to identify contamination of food at the time of purchase. Furthermore, food-borne illness is not always recognized as such.[21] Even when the nature of the illness is correctly identified, the consumer may not be able to determine which food caused it, and even if the food is identified, it is possible (particularly in the case of meat purchased uncooked) that the consumer will not be able to determine from which of the several distributors the product originated. It can be difficult for consumers to establish that the contamination was caused by the manufacturer's or distributor's actions rather than by their own improper storage or preparation.[22] As a result, firms are unlikely to internalize all of the costs of lapses in food safety procedures without some government intervention. In all, the Centers for Disease Control (CDC) estimates that five thousand deaths each year and 76 million illnesses can be traced to food.[23]

The regulatory regime around food safety in the United States dates to the public outrage over the slaughterhouse conditions described in Upton Sinclair's *The Jungle*.[24] In response, Congress passed both the Federal Meat Inspection Act, giving the U.S. Department of Agriculture (USDA) jurisdiction over the processing of most meat and poultry products, and the Pure Food and Drugs Act, which charges the Food and Drug Administration (FDA) with oversight of most other food products (including seafood).[25] The Federal Meat Inspection Act requires continuous inspection of meat production plants by USDA personnel. The inspectors must conduct a visual inspection of each slaughtered animal and must maintain a "continuous inspection" presence in meat-processing plants, overseeing the inspection process and verifying sanitary conditions in the plant each day.[26] The FDA also inspects plants under its jurisdiction, but it relies to a greater degree on manufacturers' good faith in protecting food safety—even high-risk plants are typically inspected less than once a year.[27]

In response to the challenges posed by microbial risks, in particular, regulators developed a new regulatory approach that requires processors to develop a Hazards Analysis and Critical Control Points (HACCP—pronounced "Hassip") plan. Management-based regulation of food processing is appropriate because the heterogeneity of the sector and the difficulty in measuring output render traditional approaches to regulation problematic.

Ease of Output Measurement

The traditional poke-and-sniff model of sensory inspection of contaminated meat is ineffective at detecting microscopic contamination. The obvious alternative is to take samples from the final product of the handling process and test them at a laboratory. One of the key drawbacks to microbiological testing, however, is that it takes some time to achieve results, so that, particularly in the case of perishable items, the product often must be shipped out before lab results are received.[28] Moreover, some contaminants vary greatly in concentration even within the same lot, and the representativeness of a sample also depends on the firm's consistency in its production processes.[29]

However, the most significant reason that monitoring by federal agencies is insufficient is the sheer number of sources of hard-to-detect risk. When it attempts to monitor visually for hazards, the inspecting agency might easily focus attention on one set of production activities while missing a substantial risk posed by another.[30] Even with substantially greater inspection resources, government agencies would be hard pressed to identify and test for all of the invisible risks that foods might face. Firms themselves are likely to know more about the unique risks of their products and processes and are probably in a better position to judge where and when microbial threats are liable to result from their processes.[31]

Heterogeneity

The food-processing industry is also extremely heterogeneous. As the FDA notes in a recent rule implementing a HACCP plan in the area of juice safety, "Even when producing comparable products, no two processors use the same source of incoming materials or the same processing technique, or manufacture in identical facilities."[32] The USDA exercises some jurisdiction over producers of products ranging from milk to meat-topped pizza to uncooked ground beef to processed egg products.[33] Within each category, firms may employ many different combinations of processes to create the finished product. Inevitably, many firms will have, but the USDA will lack, an everyday knowledge of how a particular step in the process could go wrong and the likely effects of a change in technologies on the cost and speed of the production line. Firms know something about the vulnerabilities of their personnel and equipment, and they may understand their own processes at a level of detail that allows them to foresee risks that an agency inspector would easily miss.[34]

A Management-Based Regulatory Instrument

The Hazards Analysis and Critical Control Points protocol is an attempt to deal with the heterogeneity and difficulty of performance measurement in the food-processing industry. It sets forth a number of mandates that require firms to evaluate, monitor, and control potential dangers in the food-handling process. The United Nations Food and Agriculture Organization's Codex Alimentarius Commission has identified seven principles that constitute the HACCP system, and these have been incorporated into U.S. federal regulations defining the firm's obligation to produce a HACCP plan.[35] The seven principles are as follows: performance of a rigorous hazards analysis of risks at every stage of production; identification of critical control points (CCPs)—points in the production process at which hazards identified at the first step can be managed; establishment of critical limits for each CCP at which the point must be controlled in order to eliminate the hazard; creation of a system to monitor CCPs; corrective actions when firms exceed a critical limit for a given CCP; continuous validation of the selection of CCPs and critical limits; and documentation of implementation of the HACCP plan.[36]

Notably, although HACCP regulations offer a great deal of flexibility to firms, regulators do lay out particular constraints with respect to the control of specific hazards. For example, because the presence of histamines in tropical fish is a potential danger, an acceptable HACCP plan with respect to tropical fish must incorporate monitoring of histamines somewhere in the firms' process.

Enforcement Challenges

The critical question regarding the HACCP protocol is whether it can overcome the enforcement challenges that arise when firms lack incentives to invest in safety measures absent government intervention. In the food safety area, new regulations grant inspectors access to essentially all records related to the HACCP, including the firm's choice of CCPs, its plans of action to ensure that safety is maintained at each CCP, and the records indicating whether the CCP has exceeded the critical limit.[37] Furthermore, regulators may evaluate the processes that it actually observes. Are regulators competent to evaluate the quality of HACCP plans? Clearly, regulators can judge whether plans meet the broad constraints they lay out (for example, the presence of histamines in tropical fish), but it is less clear how well regulators can evaluate whether firms "optimize" within those constraints.

At the implementation stage, the FDA, in particular, relies heavily on the paperwork trail that the HACCP plan should generate. The FDA inspects each fish processor once a year, examining its plan, its records, and the actual process associated with a single product line (usually one of the high-risk product lines). What this inspection process does not reveal is the effectiveness of the HACCP plans regarding noninspected product lines. It also does not directly reveal whether a firm carries out its plan in the various contingencies specified in the plan that do not occur while the inspector is watching. Instead, inspectors must rely on the firm's records of what has occurred.

This leads to the question of whether firms maintain accurate records of their actions in those instances in which damaging information may lead to the imposition of penalties.[38] One critic warns that under the HACCP protocol, firms have little reason not to falsify records, particularly in the absence of whistle-blower protections or other incentives encouraging knowledgeable persons to verify what goes on in the production line.[39] Even if firms are not outright untruthful, they would probably do themselves little good by including in the plan any hazards that inspectors are unlikely to spot on their own, particularly if these cannot be resolved cheaply. The HACCP system is designed to incorporate a firm's specialized expertise in its product and processes into the safety plan, and yet the very instances in which a firm's expertise would help it to identify hidden hazards may be the ones in which the firm has the least incentive to do so.[40]

Two factors counterbalance this predicament: First, inspectors have access to all HAACP plan records, which can assist them in conducting more effective inspections. Second, monitoring capital investments consistent with the HACCP plan will be easier than monitoring day-to-day behavior. Inspectors from the FDA, in particular, often approach a firm with little knowledge of its operations, because of the infrequency of FDA oversight. Under the HACCP protocol, inspectors are able to review the firm's records regarding its choice of CCPs, the results of monitoring, and corrective actions taken.[41] With this history, they can get a clearer picture of where they are likely to find unresolved health risks than would be possible if they had to make that judgment based on a quick observation of the firm's work processes.[42] Inspectors from the USDA, who are likely to be more familiar with a plant's operations, may also be better able to allocate their time effectively when it is not occupied by the mandated visual inspection tasks. In addition, getting firms to identify many safety hazards in advance has the potential to reduce enforcement costs.[43] A recall of adulterated food and participation in court proceedings to appeal such a decision are more costly ways to use regulatory resources. If firms are able to catch a problem further back in the pipeline, the savings can be used for cheaper forms of oversight.

A critical issue, then, with respect to the decisions of regulated firms is at what stage in production the costs of compliance lie—planning, capital expenses, or day-to-day behavior; the last is the most difficult for the regulator to monitor. Approximately one-third of the costs associated with HACCP plans are "routine" and thus difficult to monitor.[44] The critical issue with respect to compliance is that the routine activities may be necessary to get most of the advantages of the HACCP plan—for example, the use of thermometers to gauge whether fish are being kept at the right temperature means little if nothing is done when it is found that they are not. The critical question is whether, having invested in the training and the equipment, it pays to follow through with the plan absent the likelihood of enforcement? If the answer is affirmative, then the FDA model of enforcement has some hope of being effective. If not, a far more regular inspection schedule, as with the USDA program, will be necessary. In fact, many other countries that have implemented the HACCP protocol for seafood inspection conduct far more regular inspections than the United States. The Canadian program includes quarterly inspections and requires documentation of the analysis underlying the HACCP plan a firm develops as well as preapproval of the plan by the regulator. The U.S. system is designed for a regulator with far less capacity to monitor and inspect firms—with no pre-approval required, because the FDA would be unable to process the plans; no required hazard analysis, because the inspector would not have the time to examine the product; and only annual inspections of firms. Finally, the United States mandates that some employees of each firm undergo certified HACCP training—a requirement that is cheap to monitor but is causally more distant from the objective of preventing food poisoning than evaluating the process a firm has implemented.[45]

Assessment of Success

Mandatory HACCP programs were implemented in the United States only in 1997 and 1998, and the available data on their success is limited and mixed. Since implementation of its HACCP program, the USDA has found dramatic reductions in the presence of salmonella in the meat it inspects. In large plants, for example, the incidence of salmonella bacteria in broilers dropped from 20 to 10.3 percent, in swine from 8.7 to 4.4 percent, in ground beef from 7.5 to 5.8 percent, and in ground turkey from 49.9 to 34.6 percent.[46]

The FDA has not tracked the incidence of pathogens as the USDA has. It does, however, survey industry practice with respect to sanitation, and there have been some large improvements in practice. For example, the FDA has found that whereas in 1992 only 45 percent of manufacturers of cooked ready-to-eat foods maintained adequately clean food contact surfaces, that number jumped to 74 percent in 1997 and to 90 percent in 1999.[47] These achievements are counterbalanced by a recent report from the U.S. General Accounting Office (GAO) that is harshly critical of the FDA program.[48] The GAO report expresses concerns about the scope of coverage and compliance with the HACCP rules.

The ultimate metric for evaluating the success of HACCP is the incidence of food-borne illness. The year-to-year variations are too large to allow conclusive interpretation of CDC data, but it is difficult to discern dramatic declines from 1996 to 2000. The incidence of salmonellosis, for example, was 17 percent less in 2000 than in 1996—a nontrivial decline, though not as large as the declines reported by USDA. However, this decline has not been a result of a year-to-year monotonic decrease, so it may just be a downward blip. The incidence of infection with the dangerous *Escherichia coli* bacterium was actually higher in 2000 (2.9 per 100,000 people) than in 1996 (2.7 per 100,000 people).[49]

The U.S. experience with the HACCP protocol provides some indication that a management-based approach can be a viable regulatory strategy, as is suggested by the USDA's finding of a lower incidence of salmonellosis. Other evidence, however, suggests that the impact of the HACCP program, at least as it is currently implemented in the United States, has been less than ideal. The critical reviews of the program suggest that the design of a management-based regulatory regime matters just as the design of technology-based and performance-based regimes matters. It may well be that management-based systems will prove to be more sensitive to the way firms are monitored and requirements are enforced, and more frequent inspections by government or independent third-party auditors may well be critical to the HACCP program's success.

Of course, the HACCP approach need not be perfect to justify adoption of its management-based approach to food safety. Rather, it simply needs to be better than the alternatives. As the foregoing example demonstrates, it is difficult to develop standard technologies when food-processing facilities are so heterogeneous and when contamination can occur from practices that have no technological fix. It has also been difficult to apply realistic and effective performance measures. To many observers, the traditional poke-and-sniff approach to monitoring meat and poultry products hardly seems an optimal regulatory strategy. The test for management-based regulation will be whether it can provide some improvement over alternative regulatory practices.

Conclusion

The application of HACCP regulation in the area of food safety illustrates the potential, as well as some of the pitfalls, of management-based regulation. As indicated at the outset of this chapter, interest in management-based approaches is growing in a number of policy areas, including environmental and worker health and safety regulation. The U.S. Occupational Safety and Health Administration (OSHA) and the U.S. Environmental Protection Agency have established management-based regulations designed to reduce accidents in firms that process hazardous chemicals. In addition, OSHA has been developing a rule—yet to be proposed—on the management of firms' safety and health programs. In addition, management planning was part of the OSHA ergonomics rule recently withdrawn by congressional action. Similarly, environmental regulators have taken considerable interest in encouraging firms to implement environmental management systems, such as those that meet international standards set by the International Organization for Standardization, ISO 14000.

It is becoming evident that management-based regulation increasingly competes in the regulatory toolbox with technology-based and performance-based regulation. We have argued that management-based regulation will probably be preferable to its alternatives in those situations in which it is difficult for government to measure performance and the target industry or sector is made up of heterogeneous firms facing heterogeneous conditions. Characterized this way, management-based regulation appears to be a strategy that can be applied to some of the most intractable regulatory problems. Problems such as worker fatigue, chemical accidents, ergonomic injuries, and contamination of food are problems for which government often lacks clear performance measures (short of the dire consequences regulators seek to prevent in the first place). These are also problems for which government is often unable to prescribe standard technological fixes. Problems of this sort require fine-grained analysis of local circumstances that is too costly, if not undesirable for other reasons, for government to provide.

Yet as can also be seen from the HACCP case, the implementation of a set of management processes does not necessarily equate with motivation to achieve socially optimal results. Firms that lack the motivation or incentive to use the planning process to achieve social benefits may go through the motions or game the system. Management-based approaches still require a governmental enforcement presence to ensure that firms conduct the necessary planning and implement their plans effectively. This enforcement challenge may be greater because the same conditions that make it difficult for government to impose technological and performance standards may also make it difficult for government to determine what "good management" is.

The key question for decisionmakers appears to be whether firms can be sufficiently motivated to use management and planning to achieve greater social benefits than would arise from the use of alternative, command-and-control regulatory strategies. A management plan or system is a tool firms can use to reduce contamination, accidents, pollution, or other social bads. How well individual firms use these systems, however, will in all likelihood depend on the firm's incentive structure, and this incentive structure can be affected by a number of factors, including the frequency of system monitoring by governmental or nongovernmental auditors, the presence of performance measures and liability for system failures, the extent to which firms perceive a collective self-interest in preventing system failure, and the probability that firms will confront future, more costly technology-based or performance-based standards if they do not effectively deploy required management strategies. If management-based regulation is to live up to the potential outlined for it in the opening part of this chapter, government will need to create policies that align firms' incentives so that they take seriously the idea of managing to reduce social harm. Yet even if these incentives cannot be fully aligned, and management-based regulation proves to be only an imperfect strategy, it may well be useful to remember that the alternatives to management-based regulation have imperfections of their own.

Notes

1. Neil Gunningham and Peter Grabosky also distinguish among three types of regulation in a way that generally tracks the typology we employ here. They use the phrase "design or specification standards" to refer to what we call technology-based regulation and "process-based standards" to refer to management-based regulation (Neil Gunningham and Peter Grabosky, with Darren Sinclair, *Smart Regulation: Designing Environmental Policy* (Oxford University Press, 1994).

2. For extended discussions of the rationales for regulation, see W. Kip Viscusi, John M. Vernon, and Joseph E. Harrington, *Economics of Regulation and Antitrust* (MIT Press,

2000); Neil Komesar, *Imperfect Alternatives: Choosing Institutions in Law, Economics, and Public Policy* (University of Chicago Press, 1994); Cass Sunstein, *After the Rights Revolution* (Harvard University Press, 1989).

3. See, for example, Robert W. Hahn, ed., *Risks, Costs, and Lives Saved: Getting Better Results from Regulation* (Oxford University Press,1996).

4. There is a large literature on market-based regulatory instruments; see, for example, Robert N. Stavins, "What Can We Learn from the Grand Policy Experiment? Lessons from SO_2 Allowance Trading," *Journal of Economic Perspectives,* vol. 12, no. 3 (1998), pp. 69–88; Tom Tietenberg, "Economic Instruments for Environmental Regulation," *Oxford Review of Economic Policy,* vol. 6, no. 1 (1990), pp. 17–33; Robert Hahn and Gordon Hester, "Marketable Permits: Lessons for Theory and Practice," *Ecology Law Quarterly,* vol. 16, no. 2 (1989), pp. 361–406.

5. See, for example, chapter 7 in this volume.

6. For a political economy analysis of market-based regulation, see Nathaniel Keohane, Richard Revesz, and Robert Stavins, "The Choice of Regulatory Instruments in Environmental Policy," *Harvard Environmental Law Review,* vol. 22, no. 2 (1998), pp. 313–67.

7. See Ian Ayres and John Braithwaite, *Responsive Regulation: Transcending the Deregulation Debate* (Oxford University Press, 1992), p. 103.

8. What we refer to as management-based regulation is similar to what Ayres and Braithwaite call "enforced self-regulation" (ibid., 102–8). Joe Rees, *Reforming the Workplace: A Study of Self-Regulation in Occupational Safety* (University of Pennsylvania Press, 1988), in a still earlier study, uses the term "mandated self-regulation" (p. 9) to describe approaches to occupational safety and health regulation that bear some affinities with management-based regulation. Because a good management system within a firm will surely generate internal rules and procedures to be followed, much of the literature on enforced self-regulation is certainly relevant to an analysis of management-based regulation. However, under the concept of enforced self-regulation as Ayres and Braithwaite (*Responsive Regulation: Transcending the Deregulation Debate,* p. 131) describe it, companies develop their own rules, which the government ratifies and then enforces as it would any law. In this way, their particular approach seems to be a method for case-by-case decisionmaking, a system of regulatory covenants or contracts rather than one based on requirements that firms develop plans and management systems. Under management-based regulation, firms need not necessarily have their management plans approved in advance by government and need not necessarily take on the equivalent force of law. For those familiar with recent experiments in environmental regulation, enforced self-regulation seems to more closely resemble the model used by the U.S. Environmental Protection Agency in Project XL, through which the agency has negotiated individual regulatory agreements and site-specific rulemakings with certain firms (see Eric W. Orts and Kurt Deketelaere, *Environmental Contracts: Comparative Approaches to Regulatory Innovation in the United States and Europe* (Boston: Kluwer Law International, 2001). What we mean by management-based regulation is more closely analogous to the environmental impact assessment requirements imposed on government agencies under the National Environmental Policy Act (see Serge Taylor, *Making Bureaucracy Think: The Environmental Impact Statement Strategy of Administrative Reform* [Stanford University Press, 1984]).

9. See Ayres and Braithwaite, *Responsive Regulation: Transcending the Deregulation Debate*, pp. 110–11.

10. Ibid., p. 113. See also Cary Coglianese and Jennifer Nash, *Regulating from the Inside: Can Environmental Management Systems Achieve Policy Goals?* (Washington: Resources for the Future, 2001), chapters 10–11.

11. Enforcement, it should be noted, is almost always "incomplete" (Kip Viscusi and Richard Zeckhauser, "Optimal Standards with Incomplete Enforcement," *Public Policy*, vol. 27 [Fall 1979], pp. 437–56).

12. Paul Kleindorfer, "Understanding Individuals' Environmental Decisions: A Decision Science Approach," in Ken Sexton, Alfred A. Marcus, K. William Easter, and Timothy B. Burkhardt, eds., *Better Environmental Decisions: Strategies for Governments, Businesses, and Communities* (Washington: Island Press, 1999), pp. 37–56.

13. Ayres and Braithwaite, *Responsive Regulation: Transcending the Deregulation Debate*, p. 106.

14. Ronald Coase, "The Problem of Social Cost," *Journal of Law and Economics*, vol. 3 (October 1960), pp. 1–44.

15. Note that there may be a collective interest in regulation, because a bad outcome for one party (with respect to product safety, for example) affects the whole industry. There may therefore be a private collective interest in government intervention (or, alternatively, industry certification and self-regulation).

16. This incorporates cases in which the regulator can accurately project social outputs based on internal processing of inputs. For example, in the case of carbon dioxide (CO_2) emissions, it is possible to project how much CO_2 will be emitted based on particular inputs. It is therefore not necessary to have CO_2 detectors to measure CO_2 emissions—it is necessary only to measure particular inputs.

17. See, for example, Michael E. Porter and Claas van der Linde, "Toward a New Conception of the Environment-Competitiveness Relationship," *Journal of Economic Perspectives*, vol. 9, no. 4 (1995), pp. 97–118; Karen Palmer, Wallace E. Oates, and Paul R. Portney, "Tightening Environmental Standards: The Benefit-Cost or the No-Cost Paradigm?" *Journal of Economic Perspectives*, vol. 9, no. 4 (1995), pp. 119–32.

18. The development of new and cheaper monitoring technologies may reduce these enforcement problems.

19. The enforcers could well be independent private auditors rather than government officials (Howard Kunreuther, Patrick McNulty, and Yong Kang, "Third Party Inspection as an Alternative to Command and Control Regulation," in Eric Orts and Kurt Deketelaere, eds., *Environmental Contracts: Comparative Approaches to Regulatory Innovation in the United States and Europe* (Boston: Kluwer Law International, 2001]), pp. 389–408. In such cases, government would need standards or performance measures that are appropriately specified for government oversight of the private overseers.

20. The problem of regulatory specificity goes well beyond the domain of management-based regulation; see, for example, Eugene Bardach and Robert Kagan, *Going by the Book: The Problem of Regulatory Unreasonableness* (Temple University Press, 1982); and Colin Diver, "The Optimal Precision of Administrative Rules," *Yale Law Journal*, vol. 93 (1983), pp. 65–109. For a provocative argument hypothesizing that regulations reach a specificity equilibrium over time, with regulatory systems created at the extremes of generality or

specificity tending to converge toward one another, see Frederick Schauer, "The Convergence of Rules and Standards," Working Paper RPP-2001-07 (Cambridge, Mass.: Center for Business and Government, Regulatory Policy Program, 2001).

21. For example, the Centers for Disease Control and Prevention estimates that salmonellosis alone accounts for more than $1 billion a year in lost wages and medical costs (Centers for Disease Control, "Foodborne Illness: Technical Information" [www.cdc.gov/ncidod/dbmd/diseaseinfo/foodborneinfections_t.htm (January 28, 2002)]), though only one case in thirty-eight is actually diagnosed and reported to public health authorities (Centers for Disease Control, "Foodborne Illness: General Information" [www.cdc.gov/ncidod/dbmd/diseaseinfo/foodborneinfections_g.htm#howdiagnosed (January 28, 2002)]).

22. See Sharlene W. Lassiter, "From Hoof to Hamburger: The Fiction of a Safe Meat Supply," *Willamette Law Review,* vol. 33 (1977), pp. 411, 417–18, 435.

23. Centers for Disease Control, "Preliminary FoodNet Data on the Incidence of Foodborne Illnesses: Selected Sites, United States," *Morbidity and Mortality Weekly Report* (April 6, 2001), pp. 241–46.

24. See James A. Albert, "A History of Attempts by the Department of Agriculture to Reduce Federal Inspection of Poultry Processing Plants: A Return to the Jungle," *Louisiana Law Review,* vol. 51 (1991), pp. 1183, 1184–89; U.S. Department of Agriculture, "Pathogen Reduction: Hazard Analysis and Critical Control Point (HACCP) Systems," *Federal Register* 60, no. 23 (February 3, 1995), pp. 6774, 6775–76.

25. *Federal Meat Inspection Act of 1906,* chapter 3915, 34 Stat. 1260 (codified at 21 U.S.C. 601–95); *Federal Food and Drugs Act of 1906,* P.L. 59-384, 34 Stat. 768 (codified at 21 U.S.C. 301–97).

26. See 21 U.S.C. 601–24 for a description of the inspection requirements of the Federal Meat Inspection Act.

27. See Michael R. Taylor, "Preparing America's Food Safety System for the Twenty-First Century: Who Is Responsible for What When It Comes to Meeting the Food Safety Challenges of the Consumer-Driven Global Economy?" *Food and Drug Law Journal,* vol. 52, no. 13 (1997), pp. 13–30, especially pp. 15–18, contrasting the USDA and FDA food safety paradigms. A continuing obstacle to coherent food safety strategy is the fragmented nature of its overseers. About twelve federal agencies (and numerous state and local entities) are involved in food safety regulation. This means that change such as the adoption of a HACCP program tends to be piecemeal and that similar products may face very different patterns of oversight. For example, frozen pepperoni pizza makers, regulated by the USDA, receive daily inspections, whereas FDA-regulated frozen cheese pizza makers can expect an inspection about once every ten years (ibid., p. 18; Caroline Smith DeWaal, "Food Safety Inspections: A Call for Rational Reorganization," *Food and Drug Law Journal,* vol. 54, no. 3 [1999], pp. 453–58).

28. National Academy of Sciences, *An Evaluation of the Role of Microbiological Criteria for Foods and Food Ingredients* (Washington: National Academy Press, 1985). This, at least, was the case in 1985. It is possible that testing proceeds more quickly now.

29. Ibid., pp. 132–44.

30. Ibid., pp. 48–49.

31. Chryssa V. Deliganis, "Death by Apple Juice: The Problem of Foodborne Illness, the Regulatory Response, and Further Suggestions for Reform," *Food and Drug Law Journal,* vol. 53, no. 4 (1998), pp. 681, 709–10.

32. *Federal Register* 66, no. 13 (January 19, 2001), pp. 6138–202, p. 6141.

33. See Taylor, *Making Bureaucracy Think: The Environmental Impact Statement Strategy of Administrative Reform,* pp. 18–20, for a discussion of how food safety oversight is allocated. The FDA, too, has broad jurisdiction, overseeing most nonmeat food items (see p. 15).

34. As a National Academy of Sciences report advocating the dissemination of HACCP explains, "From a regulatory standpoint, a complete familiarity with and understanding of processes and product flows would greatly aid agency assessment of the effectiveness of a food firm's programs designed to assure product safety and quality. [HACCP] would do much to obviate need for an investigator to know everything about the intricacies of a firm's processing systems" (National Academy of Sciences, *An Evaluation of the Role of Microbiological Criteria for Foods and Food Ingredients,* pp. 311–12).

35. Codex Alimentarius Commission, "Guidelines for the Application of the Hazard Analysis Critical Control Point System," CAC/GL, 18-1993, in *Codex Alimentarius,* vol. 1B, *General Requirements (Food Hygiene),* pp. 21–30 (Rome: World Health Organization, Food and Agriculture Organization).

36. *Code of Federal Regulations* 9, sec. 417.3, 2001. See *Code of Federal Regulations* 21, sec. 123.9, 2001, for FDA requirements, which are less specific and appear somewhat more limited.

37. *Code of Federal Regulations* 9, sec. 417.6; *Code of Federal Regulations* 21, sec. 123.10, 2001. It is not altogether clear whether agencies have legal authority to grant themselves such broad access; see Stephen H. McNamara, "A Legal Assessment of FDA's New HACCP Regulations," *Food and Drug Law Journal,* vol. 52, no. 1 (1997), pp. 39–45.

38. Note that the FDA has tried to reassure firms that it will not automatically declare food adulterated simply because of a small deficiency in the HACCP but rather will tailor its response to the seriousness of the problem. Even if the FDA's response to some adverse information is measured, firms must be concerned about the possibility that citizens alleging food-borne illness in a lawsuit will gain access to the information during discovery (McNamara, "A Legal Assessment of FDA's New HACCP Regulations").

39. Lassiter, "From Hoof to Hamburger: The Fiction of a Safe Meat Supply," pp. 444–56.

40. That said, the food industry does have some interest in maintaining a good reputation. Industry experts might therefore be useful to the FDA in identifying appropriate CCPs and monitoring procedures for particular products. The National Academy of Sciences report suggests that industry groups might play a role in creating processing guidelines, providing technical input, and developing HACCP training programs (National Academy of Sciences, *An Evaluation of the Role of Microbiological Criteria for Foods and Food Ingredients,* pp. 309–10).

41. Taylor, *Making Bureaucracy Think: The Environmental Impact Statement Strategy of Administrative Reform,* pp. 21–23.

42. National Academy of Sciences, *An Evaluation of the Role of Microbiological Criteria for Foods and Food Ingredients,* p. 311.

43. U.S. Department of Agriculture, "Pathogen Reduction: Hazard Analysis and Critical Control Point (HACCP) Systems."

44. According to the National Seafood Industry HACCP Implementation Survey Report (2000), for the average respondent, $14,346 out of $41,346 of annual compliance

costs were routine (U.S. Food and Drug Administration, *Evaluation of the Seafood HACCP Program for 1998–1999,* December 8, 2000).

45. *Federal Oversight of Seafood Does Not Sufficiently Protect Consumers,* GAO-01-204 (U.S. General Accounting Office, January 2001), p. 43.

46. U.S. Department of Agriculture, *Progress Report on Salmonella Testing of Raw Meat and Poultry Products* (2000).

47. Ibid.

48. *Federal Oversight of Seafood Does Not Sufficiently Protect Consumers.*

49. Centers for Disease Control, "Preliminary FoodNet Data on Incidence of Foodborne Illnesses: Selected Sites, United States." Note that the number of sites in the FoodNet program expanded in 2000, but for comparability the data reported here include only the original five sites.

PART IV

Upside and Downside

10

ELAINE CIULLA KAMARCK

The End of Government as We Know It

ONE OF THE RESULTS of the September 11, 2001, terrorist attacks on America was that government made a comeback. For thirty years Americans' opinions of government, especially the government in Washington, had been getting progressively worse. Favorable opinions about government began to creep back up in the late 1990s as the economy soared and the treasury balance went from deficit to surplus. Nothing did as much for the image of government, however, as the horror of September 11, the patriotism it inspired, and the heroism of the government workers who came to the rescue.[1]

None of this should be surprising. War is a central task of the government, and it has a way of pulling nations together around their government—except, that is, when it is pulling them apart, as did the war in Vietnam. This resurgence in trust in government may or may not be short lived. Alongside the thirty-year decline in trust in government was a dissatisfaction with a particular kind of government—bureaucratic government. Bureaucratic government is perceived as a composite of large, ponderous, lumbering organizations staffed by insensitive people whose mission in life seems to be to drive citizens crazy. Americans may feel better about government in general, but the dissatisfaction with bureaucratic government runs deep. For example, the post–September 11 emergency legislation to increase aviation security stalled over whether or not security personnel at airports should be civil servants—thus creating a new and very large federal bureaucracy—or contract employees paid by the federal government. At a time when legislation was moving almost as fast as American missiles, the question of bureaucracy and the desire to avoid it intruded and stalled the legislation.

For quite some time now, government organizations have looked obsolete to some and downright counterproductive to others. Bureaucracy itself—expensive, inflexible, unfriendly—has become the enemy, above and beyond the public purposes to which it has been dedicated. Citizens who used to argue about the ends of government now find themselves more or less universally dissatisfied with the means of government.

In the last decades of the twentieth century, American political leaders—adept, as are all political leaders, at putting their ears to the ground—identified and articulated these feelings. For Ronald Reagan, "government does not solve problems, it is the problem." Across the Atlantic, Margaret Thatcher took on the sacrosanct British bureaucracy, calling them "protagonists of the failed Keynesian-Beveridgite consensus who had brought Great Britain low."[2] Dissatisfaction with bureaucracy turned out to be a bipartisan obsession. Democrat Bill Clinton, running on a campaign of reinventing government, readily admitted that most people thought the government could "screw up a two-car funeral." In the mid-1990s the title of a best-selling book on government regulation, *The Death of Common Sense,* handily captured what so many Americans thought had happened to their government.[3]

By the last decade of the twentieth century the revolt against bureaucracy was in full swing, though confused politicians who thought they had won a great ideological battle began to see that their victory was fleeting at best. In Great Britain, Thatcher took the country through a wrenching era of privatization only to realize, toward the end of her term, that she really could not privatize the whole darn thing after all. For all of Ronald Reagan's rhetoric to the contrary, he actually increased the size of government and did little in the way of fundamental reform. Under George H. W. Bush, the government began to experiment with "total quality management" and other favorites of the corporate world, but for the most part the federal government remained largely immune from the productivity revolution occurring in the private sector during these years.

To the dismay of some on the left, the power of antibureaucracy sentiment was such that it transcended political ideology. President Bill Clinton had his vice president, Al Gore, preside over one of the longest reform initiatives in American history, but the energy generated by the reinventing government initiative was not sufficient to save the Clinton administration's 1994 health-care plan. That plan reminded people of the big old bureaucratic government that had fallen into such disfavor, and though this was, in some ways, a bum rap, it was sufficient to cause the plan to fail.

On the other hand, to the dismay of those on the right who felt that their day had come, the victories of the antibureaucratic revolt were meager at best. Newt Gingrich found that his conservative revolution, for all its drama, and his sense of mandate could end neither the welfare state nor the regulatory state.

The revolt against bureaucracy has been global. Nowhere were the hopes and failures of this revolt more evident than in the fall of communism. In its Soviet manifestation, the combination of bureaucracy with totalitarianism proved a humanitarian disaster. However, those who hoped that once the old state had been dismantled the free market would make everything right were dismayed to find that free markets without governments resembled something on the order of the Wild West. In the developing world, the first step—getting the "dead hand" of government off the market—meant extensive privatization. The developing world soon discovered, however, that free markets in the absence of "government capacity" were no better than planned economies at producing widespread prosperity.[4]

Against this backdrop it is not surprising that government the world over has been shrinking.[5] No one seems to be a fan of government any more—especially "big" government. Even left-of-center governments are abandoning government as they search for a "third way." Sometimes the abandonment is so precipitous and so at odds with political rhetoric as to be almost laughable. In Brazil, Governor Jose Orricirio dos Santos of the left-wing Workers' Party ran for office in Mato Grosso do Sul promising to govern for the workers and to give big pay raises to teachers, health workers, and the police. He also ran in opposition to Brazil's "fiscal adjustment" program. Once in office, however, Orricirio dos Santos cut the number of political appointees in state government in half, shut down state firms that were not making a profit, and raised the out-of-pocket contributions state workers had to make to their pensions. What was the reason for the sudden conversion? Brazil's new fiscal responsibility law banned the federal government from bailing out debt-ridden states and cities as it had done in the past. In a variation on Bill Clinton's famous State of the Union line, the candidate of the Workers' Party was quoted as saying, "The era of the big spending state is over."[6]

In Guyana, the Marxist government elected in 1992 under Chedi Jagan began a privatization program. In four years the country had divested fourteen of its forty state-owned enterprises and introduced private management in some other large industries.[7] In Cuba, a 1993 decree allowed for limited private enterprise, and in 1995 the Foreign Investment Law provided for greater security and assurances to foreign investors. As the privatization of Cuba creeps along, Fidel Castro continues to condemn the world's financial order and rail against privatization.[8] The largest remaining communist country in the world, China, recently signaled that it too would be withdrawing from state ownership of industries. Following a report that two-thirds of the state-run firms had cooked the books and reported billions of dollars in fake profits, Zhu Rongji promised to shut down enterprises that consistently operated at a loss and sell off others.[9] Several months later the Communist Party of China made a historic decision to allow businessmen to become members of the party.

If free market first-world countries, developing countries, and avowedly communist countries are all moving away from government, what comes next? These trends seem to herald the end of government—and in a sense, they do. Until the attack on the World Trade Center it was hard to imagine that any politician would propose the creation of a new bureaucracy or the rapid expansion of government control over the economy. Even in the aftermath of that attack, discussion of new government organizations is strictly limited to the realm of security. In my experience in government in the Clinton administration, policy options that involved new bureaucratic offices were routinely rejected (if not hooted down) in internal policy meetings of Democrats. The first Democratic administration in twelve years created exactly one new office—the Corporation for National Service—and made sure it was a public corporation. Not only were bureaucratic policy proposals continually rejected, but speechwriters were called upon to extol the virtues of new proposals by emphasizing that they were "market oriented" and did not involve the creation of any new bureaucracies.

Although "government" in its bureaucratic manifestation may be fading away, the continuing need for government—disappointing for many conservatives and reaffirming for many liberals—remains. This has led people to talk about how "governance" is replacing "government" as the modus operandi of democratic societies.[10] Governance is a broader term, encompassing not just the state but all sorts of organizations—public, private, semipublic, and even religious—that somehow contribute to the pursuit of the public interest. The evolution of the bureaucratic state has led many scholars to note that "governance without government is becoming the dominant pattern of management for advanced industrial democracies."[11]

Even "governance" theory, however, presupposes the existence of the state. What will the postbureaucratic state of the twenty-first century look like? Will it work in all areas of policy? Will it work in some better than in others? Will it serve democratic ideals better than the bureaucratic state of the twentieth century? These topics are just beginning to be explored, and an understanding of them requires, first, an outline of this new state—the sequel, if you will, to government as we know it.

New Forms of Government

Three new governmental forms seem to be replacing the bureaucratic state—entrepreneurial government, networked government, and market government. The term *entrepreneurial government* was coined by David Osborne in his best-selling 1992 book, *Reinventing Government,* and the concept is the substance of many of the government reform movements currently in vogue around the world.[12] Stripped to its essence, entrepreneurial government is bureaucratic government without all the things that have made bureaucratic government so irritating to the citizens of information age economies. Entrepreneurial government is government that is run as much as possible like a private sector business. The literature and practice of entrepreneurial government is replete with praise for competition, flexibility, employee empowerment, and customer service, causing some to refer to this as market government.[13] These governments have shed the civil service, and they have shed centralized procurement. They have adopted performance goals, they use bonuses to reward their workers, and they place a premium on service to the citizen and on productivity. In New Zealand, one of the most radically reformed governments in the world, cabinet ministers "purchase" government outputs from what used to be the bureaucracy, which must "compete" with other public or private organizations to do the work of the government.[14] Entrepreneurial governments go out of their way to hide the fact that they are government organizations, and for that reason they are the last, best hope of the traditional public sector.

On a continuum of governance moving away from traditional bureaucracy, entrepreneurial government is the first step and networked government is the second. The term *networked government* has been used in a variety of ways by a number of authors attempting to think about the future of government.[15] In networked government the formal state is but one actor in an informal network of organizations. Networked government comes in two forms—the domestic and the international. In domestic policy, the organizational efforts in the network involve some form of activity that the state wants done—getting welfare mothers to work, doing research on weapons—that would not necessarily happen by itself in the free market. The state is often the primary funder of the network, but after that its role is much diminished. The autonomous nature of the organizations in the network means that they can choose to do their work more or less as they want and employ whom they want. They are presumably, therefore, more efficient.

Compared with bureaucratic government, networked government has another outstanding advantage: it can discover creative and innovative solutions to complex problems in a way that traditional, rule-bound, one-size-fits-all government cannot. Because pieces of government networks can often deliver creative solutions to difficult human problems, it is the last, best hope of those who want to see government pursue solutions to social problems.

In the international arena, networked government appears to be the emerging adaptive alternative to the unrealistic notion of world government. John Peterson and Laurence O'Toole discuss the operations of the European Union in terms of an effective (if sometimes slow) network.[16] Anne Marie Slaughter has described the existence of networks that form below the national level and apart from the traditional diplomatic level.[17] To the extent that these networks operate independently to harmonize policy, they are creating the "governance" that is needed for the global economy. Indeed, the fast pace of government reform movements around the world and the commonality of language and concepts being used by governments in very different countries is further evidence of the ways in which networks are forming to solve the global governance problem.[18]

In both entrepreneurial government and networked government, the traditional state has a role. In the first instance, the behaviors and norms of entrepreneurial government make it almost unrecognizable to those who are dismayed by traditional bureaucracy. In the second instance, the role of government is much diminished. In its domestic version, networked government usually retains the power of the purse but often little more. In the international version, states seek to harmonize policy as equal players (although the hegemony of the United States often distorts the power relationships—to the dismay of other players).

The appeal of the third and final new mode of government—market government—is that it barely involves traditional bureaucratic government at all. In that respect it is the model furthest away from government as we know it. This model does, however, presuppose a society based on the rule of law and a government able to enforce the law. Market government occurs when the government uses its power to create a marketplace to fulfill a public purpose.[19] Other than having in place some form of enforcement mechanism for those who try to cheat the system, market government operates with almost no government as we know it—and that fact explains its current attraction and popularity. The essence of market government is to use government power to place costs on things that contribute—positively or negatively—to the public good. Historically, the government has created markets to encourage productive behavior and to deter or correct for nonproductive behaviors.

The classic American example of market government is the much admired G.I. Bill. Through the bill, enacted after World War II to encourage college education, the U.S. government gave tuition vouchers to the returning soldiers. It could have gone in another direction (as it did with veterans' health) and build a system of "G.I. universities"; instead, it expanded the marketplace of higher education. In more recent years state governments have created markets for the millions of beer bottles and soda cans that used to be tossed on American highways. The federal government created a market for pollution when it passed a bill providing for permit trading in SO_2 (sulfur dioxide) emissions from industrial plants.

How should these emerging forms of government be evaluated? In all three instances their advantages should be weighed against their disadvantages. The advantages of these new governmental forms are their capacity for innovation and flexibility, their potential for saving public money, their ability to adapt to changing needs and situations, and thus their potential to be more acceptable to the citizens to whom they are accountable.

The disadvantages are that often these systems are diffuse and lack transparency and thus accountability. Most of the thoughtful writers on this topic concentrate their criticisms on the accountability mechanisms inherent in these new forms. B. Guy Peters writes that public administration "is also a statement of basic values about matters such as probity, accountability, and responsibility, values about which the present alternatives and the market model, in particular, have little to say."[20] Transparency is even more important to public sector organizations than to those in the private sector. When transparency declines the potential for abuse increases. In the new systems it is harder to see exactly where public money is being spent and on what.

Accountability in traditional bureaucratic systems depended on "input controls." As disenchantment with the bureaucratic form grew, input controls became a singularly unsatisfactory and ineffective way to justify the spending of taxpayer money. Emphasis thus switched to trying to measure "outcomes," but the measurement of outcomes is also fraught with problems that range from the theoretical to the operational. Nevertheless, at the heart of postbureaucratic government is a change in the way democratic accountability is understood and applied.

Although many of the models described in this chapter have existed for years, the use of nonbureaucratic organizational forms as means of implementing public policy has been largely unconscious and organic. One of my purposes here is to articulate these models in such a way that they crystallize into distinct options for policymakers. The capacity of these new forms of government to answer public needs while continuing to shrink the size of the state will make experimentation with them irresistible for politicians in the future. For this reason it is important to identify these emerging forms, figure out their pros and cons, and apply them to those areas in which the advantages outweigh the disadvantages.

The Triumph of Markets and the Revolt against the Bureaucratic State

The 1995 book *The Death of Common Sense* begins with an apocryphal story about Mother Teresa and the New York City building bureaucracy.[21] Mother Teresa comes to New York and tries to turn two abandoned buildings into a shelter for homeless men. She gets the buildings for nothing and sets aside money to reconstruct them. Then she encounters the New York City building authorities. After a year and a half of truly Kafkaesque bureaucratic obstacles, Mother Teresa gives up. The Missionaries of Charity leave the city, and the homeless shelter is never built. Lesson: even the patience of a saint can be exhausted by late-twentieth-century bureaucracy.

"The death of common sense" is a good way of describing the feeling most Americans had about government at the end of the twentieth century. The disillusionment had been going on more or less for three decades. The

American assault on government can be traced to the presidency of Ronald Reagan. A master storyteller, Reagan had an anecdote for everything—welfare mothers driving Cadillacs, out-of-control regulators terrorizing innocent businessmen and -women. He proclaimed that he had come to Washington to "drain the swamp."[22] What apparently started with Reagan did not stop with him, however. American culture picked up the antibureaucratic wave. The NBC Nightly News began airing a segment called "The Fleecing of America," which contained, more often than not, stories of government malfeasance or just plain ineptness. Late-night comedians could barely get through a routine without some reference to governmental idiocy. Even the election of Bill Clinton in 1992 was inspired, at least in part, by his assertion that government was broken and needed to be fixed or "reinvented." It is no accident that the first Democrat since Franklin Roosevelt to be elected for a second term declared, in his 1996 State of the Union speech, that "the era of big government is over."[23]

The public assault on the American state was part of a solid three-decade-long decline in Americans' trust in government.[24] No simple solution emerged to this erosion of trust. It persisted in the face of changing economic fortunes, it persisted in the face of real governmental accomplishments, and it persisted in the face of changes in political parties and policies.[25] By overwhelming margins Americans attributed the lack of trust in government to the belief that the government itself was full of "waste, fraud, and abuse."[26] By the time Bill Clinton became president, the political class, left and right alike, assumed that government itself was to be avoided. Something about government—its form, its behavior—just stuck in the American craw—regardless of its professed purposes.

The depth and breadth of antigovernment sentiment in the United States at the end of the twentieth century was initially another example of American exceptionalism. In Europe, whose nations were home to much larger welfare states, even the right-of-center parties were traditionally more friendly than many Americans in the Democratic Party to the large state structures that had developed in the twentieth century. Margaret Thatcher changed that for Great Britain, however, and the effects were felt first throughout the Commonwealth countries and eventually around the world.

In 1979, Thatcher campaigned for election as prime minister of the Conservative Party in Great Britain by arguing that top-down centralized systems in nonauthoritarian regimes shared many of the problems those kinds of systems encountered in authoritarian countries. One year before

Reagan and ten years before the formal fall of communism, Thatcher launched a broadside against the bureaucratic state, referring to it as the "greedy and parasitic public sector." As conservatives, Reagan and Thatcher had disagreements with the expressed purposes of modern government. But they also had disagreements with the means by which the state accomplished those purposes.[27]

Taken together, these campaigns, and the governments that followed them, ushered in an era of intense dissatisfaction with government bureaucracy. Among other things, the supposedly neutral civil service became a political issue. This came as an enormous shock to many civil servants, most of whom viewed themselves as neutral administrators of the law.[28] After all, the great accomplishment of the Progressive reforms at the start of the twentieth century was the separation of government administration from politics. Classic public administration theory, dating back to the days of Woodrow Wilson and Frank Goodnow, relied on the "policy-administration dichotomy."[29] According to this theory, governmental decisions were to be implemented by a "value-free administrative specialist whose major contribution to the system was his impersonal, expert objectivity."[30] By midcentury this theory was undergoing substantial revisions; the apparatus of government itself had never been a central political issue.[31] Suddenly, the system in which thousands of civil servants worked was fodder for the political fight

The bureaucracy itself had become the enemy—above and beyond the public purposes to which it was dedicated. Donald Savoie describes the politics of the 1980s as follows: "The rhetoric of politicians, particularly at election time, is often adversarial, but it also speaks to some of their fundamental values and basic beliefs. Thatcher, Reagan, and [Canadian prime minister Brian] Mulroney often took full flight when speaking about the public service. They all regarded it as part of the problem, and no one tried to attenuate their obvious dislike for the institution, even in public speeches."[32]

In the United States and in Great Britain, the revolt against bureaucracy was staged in ideological terms and was led, in both instances, by strong, charismatic right-wing leaders. In many other parts of the world a similar but less dramatic change in attitudes was taking place. In many countries, public opinion polls indicated a decreased respect for institutional authority, a phenomenon that is often associated with a rise in "postmodern" values.[33]

Yet no gradual changes in public opinion are more important in explaining the move away from bureaucracy in Europe than the various requirements imposed on states to become part of the European Union. Written in 1991 and ratified in 1993, the Maastricht Treaty set out the framework for the European Union and put it on the path toward the creation of a single currency. For the purpose of this chapter, the most important provision of that treaty is found in Article 104c, which begins with the simple sentence, "Member states shall avoid excessive governmental deficits." That one sentence, and the fact that real economic sanctions were associated with a country's failure to achieve deficit reduction, contributed as much to the death of the bureaucratic state in Europe, with its proud tradition of democratic socialism, as did the campaigns of Ronald Reagan and Margaret Thatcher in America and Great Britain. The prohibition against excessive governmental deficits started countries with legendary huge and inefficient bureaucracies, such as Italy, down the road toward smaller, more efficient states.[34]

Meanwhile in the rest of the world, the revolt against the bureaucratic state took place in two stages. The first involved getting the state out of state-owned businesses. The decade of the 1980s saw extensive privatization of state-owned enterprises all over the world, but particularly in Latin America. As more and more countries privatized and concentrated on getting their macroeconomic policies straightened out, attention turned to the state itself. The Thatcher model was repeated over and over again. Once the state had gotten out of controlling large portions of the market, reformers realized that there still remained a need for an effective functioning state, and they set out to reform the bureaucracy.

In Great Britain, the need to focus on reform of the bureaucracy was a movement generated internally in the latter years of the Thatcher government and continued in the government led by Prime Minister John Major. In the United States, the movement to reform the bureaucracy was a Democratic continuation of the Reagan revolution. In the developing world, however, the impetus for reform of the state came, more often than not, from the development institutions on which those countries relied when they got into economic trouble. Thus in the developing world, the second stage of the revolt against bureaucracy involved the re-creation of the state along lines that would help, not hinder, the newly created market economies. Starting in the 1990s, the development banks turned their attention and their funding to "governance issues." The World Bank, the

International Monetary Fund, the Inter-American Development Bank, and the Organization for Economic Cooperation and Development all developed extensive programs offering aid and financial resources to countries interested in developing "state capacity."[35]

The development advice the lenders offered (often linked to their funding) did not seek directly to re-create the bureaucracies of the twentieth century. Instead, it was generally couched in the language of the new public management and reinventing government movements that were popular in first-world countries. All protestations about respecting the traditions and cultures of individual countries to the contrary, the development advice offered to industrializing nations echoed the new antibureaucratic themes being pushed by reformers in the developed countries. Much of the advice recorded in David Osborne's *Reinventing Government* seems to have been aimed at the rest of the world; the World Bank, for example, in its 1997 *World Development Report*, defines development of state capacity thus: "[State capacity] means subjecting state institutions to greater competition, to increase their efficiency. It means increasing the performance of state institutions, improving pay and incentives. And it means making the state more responsive to people's needs, bringing government closer to the people through broader participation and decentralization."[36]

Conservative politics, the fiscal demands on the states of the European Union, the demands of the large international lending institutions—all of these are important in explaining the near-term factors in the revolt against bureaucracy. In the larger scheme of things, however, perhaps nothing is as important as the fall of communism, the one major alternative paradigm to free markets. The natural result was a global celebration of the virtues of the free market; and fairly or unfairly, when the virtues of free markets in the private sector were applied to organizations in the public sector, bureaucracy failed.

The revolt against bureaucracy in the public sector was enhanced by the ideological triumph of market models in the private sector, but real changes in the private sector were also taking their toll on traditional bureaucracy. Most important, new information technology was changing the private sector so quickly that the experience of citizens in the private and the public sectors was increasingly divergent. Take, for instance, personal banking. In the 1950s, it required a trip to the bank during the day (bankers' hours), where the customer had to stand in line. If the bank was a monopoly (as many were), the teller may or may not have been pleasant to the customer. Customization of products was rare. In other words, an experience at a private sector institution was not likely to be different in duration, convenience, or quality from the experience of getting a driver's license or a passport.

Beginning in the 1980s, however, the private sector rushed to use new information technology tools. These created a new and more profound ability to be "customer friendly." Convenience—banking at automated teller machines, shopping on the telephone or on the Internet—and customization in the private sector stood in sharp contrast to the rigid and inconvenient one-size-fits-all mode of the public sector. To citizens accustomed to the new customer service efforts of the 1980s, the public sector looked hopelessly obsolete and unresponsive.

At the same time that information technology was remaking the customer side of business, it was also remaking the organizational side of business. Businesses cut product cycle times at dizzying rates. They also began to cut middle management, back-office operations, and hierarchical forms of organization. The revolt against bureaucracy in the business world was celebrated in the titles of business books. Tom Peters, the famous pop management guru, titled a book from this era *You Can't Shrink Your Way to Greatness: The Circle of Innovation*. The founder of Visa wrote a book titled *Birth of the Chaordic Age*, celebrating institutions that blended characteristics of order and chaos.[37]

As the information age economy began to replace the industrial age economy, the failures of bureaucracy seemed more and more apparent. In a 1995 book, *What Comes Next*, Jim Pinkerton traces the evolution of the American bureaucracy. He refers to it as the BOS (bureaucratic operating system), noting that "no software is trouble-free; over time it accumulates bugs." He then outlines five bugs in the bureaucratic operating system:

—Parkinsonism, after Parkinson's law: "Work expands to fill the time available for its completion."

—Peterism, after the Peter Principle: "In a hierarchy, every employee tends to rise to the level of incompetence."

—Oligarchism, after the "iron law of oligarchy": "Someone has to be in charge."

—Olsonism, after Mancur Olson's insight that the accretion of special interests buries economic growth.

—Information Infarction, from the economist Friedrich Hayek: "Bureaucratic decision making must fail because it cannot know all relevant information."[38]

What Comes Next is rich with examples of bureaucratic failure. Having had a close-up look at the bureaucracy while working for Presidents Ronald

Reagan and George H. W. Bush, Pinkerton decided that the bugs in its operating system were fatal.

The demise of bureaucracy, however, was not simply the province of conservative writers. At about the same time, Morley Winograd and Dudley Buffa, both Democrats, wrote *Taking Control: Politics in the Information Age,* in which they link the downfall of the bureaucratic state and the politics that supported it to the emergence of a new information-based economy.[39] The book attempts to explain a phenomenon that began to occur in American politics in the late 1980s and 1990s—the apparent blurring of ideological lines. According to Winograd, the emergence of "knowledge workers" confuses the political divisions of the industrial age. Economic conservatives are cultural liberals, and their votes are thus all over the lot. Central to the political beliefs of these workers is the fact that they are employed in organizations very different from those of their predecessors—organizations that are, at least on the surface, everything that government bureaucracies are not.

By the end of the twentieth century, intellectuals, politicians, the public, and international organizations were all searching for something to replace the bureaucratic state of the industrial age. Just what that new form would be, however, was a bit unclear. Several assumptions underlay the various attempts at reform; these assumptions will be tested over time as governments the world over evolve into more modern forms. First is the assumption that the problems of monopoly, lack of innovation, insufficient responsiveness, and inefficiency that plague both the private and the public sector can be overcome or at least mitigated in the public sector (as they are in the private sector) by the injection of greater competition. Second is the assumption that there are no major differences between management in the public and in the private sector. Third is the assumption that the public interest can be articulated and measured and that this measurement will create a "market proxy" for the public sector—thus allowing the public sector a new, and stronger, form of accountability. These operating assumptions can be seen in the three emerging models of this new postbureaucratic state.

Entrepreneurial Government

One of the most significant aspects of David Osborne's book is the simple fact that, in 1992, a book about government reform became a best-seller in the United States and was translated and reprinted extensively throughout the world. For a population steeped in cynicism and reporting record-low levels of trust in government, the popularity of a book titled *Reinventing Government* was testament to the desire for change. It was also testament to the fact that the desire for reform was centered not on the ends of government, as had been the case in prior periods in modern history, but on the means by which government implemented its policy.

Osborne, a journalist, not a public administration theorist, simply observed what was happening with governments and hit upon some characteristics that appeared to apply to successful government. It is interesting to note that before writing *Reinventing Government,* Osborne wrote a book called *Laboratories of Democracy,* which featured elected officials who were successful innovators at the state government level.[40] Not surprisingly, many of these—Bill Clinton in Arkansas, Bruce Babbitt in Arizona, and Richard Reilly in South Carolina—had managed to be activist Democratic governors in conservative Republican states. What was the secret of their success? They were innovators in the very means of government. For them, innovation was essential to their survival as proponents of government in intensely antigovernment environments and to their ability to carry out traditional, activist Democratic policies.

Successful government, according to Osborne, is catalytic—it does not row, it steers. It is community owned; it empowers its employees; it uses competition to increase results; it is mission driven, results driven, and customer driven. Successful government is "entrepreneurial"—a term so infrequently linked with government that it is almost an oxymoron. Successful government is anticipatory, decentralized, and market oriented. In other words, successful government draws from the entrepreneurial spirit to revitalize itself and in so doing takes on concepts that were previously the sole province of the private sector.

In the context of this chapter, it is important to remember that entrepreneurial government is still government. However, it is government shorn of its public sector trappings, especially the rigid rules regarding budget, personnel, and procurement—rules that impose restrictions on government managers that are unusual, if not unheard of, in the private sector. The underlying assumption behind entrepreneurial government is that with respect to management, there are few significant differences between the public and the private sector. A second but equally important assumption behind entrepreneurial government is that the goals of public sector organizations can be clearly articulated and measured.

This second assumption is vitally important to the success of entrepreneurial government because it allows government organizations freedom from the central control agencies that so dominate public sector life. These agencies were invented as accountability mechanisms, and they made it possible to identify and track the spending of every single bit of government money. But this kind of accountability came with a price. In practice, civil service personnel agencies often made it impossible for line managers to hire the best people and fire the worst; centralized procurement agencies often made it impossible for line managers to buy what they needed at good prices; and central budget agencies often made it impossible to move funds from one category to another to get the job done.

Entrepreneurial government began in Great Britain in 1982, in New Zealand in 1984, and in American statehouses in the 1980s. In Great Britain, the establishment, under Minister Michael Heseltine, of the Efficiency Unit began the process of bringing private market accountability for results to the civil service. The eventual report of this unit argued that "to solve the management problem, the government would [first] have to separate service-delivery and compliance functions from the policy-focused departments that housed them—to separate steering from rowing. Second, it would have to give service-delivery and compliance agencies much more flexibility and autonomy. And third, it would have to hold those agencies accountable for results, through performance contracts."[41]

The British government put these theories into action with the publication of *Improving Management in Government: The Next Steps,* written under the leadership of Sir Robin Ibbs. Out of this report came the creation of Next Step agencies, or Executive Agencies. These agencies were to be public sector agencies without public sector trappings. Next Step agencies would be run by chief executive officers hired from within or without the civil service on a performance contract basis and with the potential for large bonuses. The agencies would have more control over their budget, personnel, and other management systems. The new agency heads would negotiate a "framework" agreement between the agency and the relevant cabinet minister. Perhaps most important, the heads of these agencies could be fired for not living up to their performance agreements.

By 1997, 130 British agencies had been set up under the Next Step framework, accounting for about 75 percent of the British civil service.[42] Now that the Next Step agencies are more than a decade old they can boast of a considerable record of accomplishments: improvements in the processing of passport applications, savings in "running costs" (administrative costs) in the National Health Service Pensions Agency, improvements in waiting times in the National Health Service, and reductions in per unit costs at the Patent Office.[43]

As Great Britain was remaking its large government bureaucracies into entrepreneurial governments, New Zealand was undergoing an even more dramatic revolution. Unlike other government reform movements, the New Zealand experience is unique for its boldness, its continuity across political parties, and its intellectual coherence. (It is no wonder that government reform seems to have outstripped lamb as the most popular New Zealand export.) In the mid-1980s, New Zealand faced an economic and political meltdown of striking proportions. As the new Labour government took over in 1987, it published a postelection briefing paper described as the "manifesto" of the new public management.[44]

Like the Thatcher reforms, the New Zealand reforms injected the language of competition, incentives, and performance into public administration. In absolute terms these reforms were remarkable—even more so against the quasi-socialist record of previous governments. They called for getting the government out of those activities that could be more effectively carried out by nongovernmental bodies. They recommended a clear separation of the responsibilities of ministers and departmental heads, giving the traditional civil service both more autonomy and more responsibility for results than ever before. Perhaps the most revolutionary aspect of all was the directive that everything that was publicly funded—even policy advice—was to be made "contestable and subject to competitive tendering."[45] In so doing New Zealand broke the public monopoly of government on governance. While officials in the United States were still asking, "What is a core governmental function?" New Zealand had already decided, "Essentially, nothing."

Entrepreneurial government started at the national level in Great Britain and New Zealand, but in the United States entrepreneurial government started at the state and local levels. Unlike the federal government, the statehouses could not print their own money. Forced to live within their means and buffeted by tax revolts on the one hand and continued demands for services on the other, mayors and governors had no choice but to try and do more with less—even if it meant stepping on some toes. When Mayor Ed Rendell took over the troubled city of Philadelphia in the late 1980s, he quickly recognized the Hobson's choice he faced: he could raise taxes, thereby pushing even more of the tax base to the suburbs, or he could cut services, thereby pushing even more of the tax base to the suburbs. As a

Democratic mayor, he had to take on the status quo, including the powerful public sector unions, and reinvent government. The Republican mayor of Indianapolis, Steve Goldsmith, got national attention when he put twenty-seven city services out to bid. The governor of Minnesota set out to dismantle the state government's central control mechanisms and to reconstruct them in ways that would add to, not detract from, agency missions.[46]

For American state and local officials and for British and New Zealand national officials in the 1980s, entrepreneurial government was the only way out of an impossible governing situation. What began as an adaptation to budget crises evolved into a more or less coherent philosophy variously known as the "new public management" or the "reinventing government" initiative.

As this new way of implementing policy became more widespread, many scholars expressed fears about where it was going—chief among those being the fear that somehow this new philosophy would undercut the rule of law.[47] However, as many a practitioner of entrepreneurial government knows, though the law itself is often flexible, the administrative application of the law, over time, can introduce a degree of rigidity into the implementation of a program that seriously impedes its original mission. Mark Considine and Jenny Lewis set out to explore the behavior of civil servants on the frontlines of these reforms. Somewhat to their surprise, they found that, with respect to the importance of rules in their work, civil servants in newer, "reformed" organizations did not differ much from other civil servants. "It . . . is possible that rules are always so much a part of even the most flexible public programs that they do no more than define the parameters of action and fail to define actual work strategies."[48]

Entrepreneurial government is still government, albeit a government that attempts to rid itself of the self-inflicted wounds of the bureaucratic culture. It is fundamentally a lot less threatening to traditional government, however, than the other two models on offer.

Networked Government

As these new forms of government take shape, they do so amid a vibrant and ongoing argument about what, exactly, is a "core governmental function." In the future, entrepreneurial government will be the chosen method of implementing government policy in those areas in which it is determined that a government organization, populated by public employees, is the best way to go about the government's business. Making that determination will not be so easy, however, as is evident in the case of the second new governmental form—networked government.

In recent years the term *network,* when applied to government, has come to have at least three separate meanings. Sometimes *networked government* is used to refer to policy networks or the constellation of organizations, public, private, and semipublic, that influence a policy world. This use of the term is not new and is similar to what an earlier generation of political scientists might have called "the iron triangle" of bureaucrats, congressional staff, and interest groups.[49]

Networked government has also been used to describe emerging relations between states. As the economy has become global, the need for global governance measures has increased. International bureaucracy has proved even less attractive to states than domestic bureaucracy, however. "World government" is a nonstarter with all but the most sanguine futurists. Instead, as Anne Marie Slaughter and others have documented, the response to the need for international governance has been the development of relations between subunits of national governments through which law and administrative processes are harmonized—thus allowing for governance in the place of actual government.[50] John Peterson and Laurence O'Toole use the term to refer to the complex, mutually adaptive behavior of subunits of states in the European Union, a process that, though often slow and opaque, also solves an important supranational governance problem.[51]

The term *networked government* has come to be used in yet a third way, and that is in those instances in which the government chooses to implement policy by creating, through its power to contract and to fund, a network of nongovernmental organizations. The diminished role of traditional bureaucracy in networked government has led H. Brinton Milward and Keith G. Provan to dub these forms of government the "hollow state": "The hollow state refers to any joint production situation where a governmental agency relies on others (firms, nonprofits, or other government agencies) to jointly deliver public services."[52]

Milward and Provan note that in spite of the prevalence of networked government, we know relatively little about how to manage networks.[53] In fact, it is only in the past ten years that the term has been used with any regularity in reference to implementation of policy. One possible explanation is that the emergence of networked government has been largely an unconscious choice on the part of policymakers, who have sought to create networks out of a desire to avoid traditional bureaucracies. Hence networks, like entrepreneurial government, have become popular implementation choices for what they are not rather than for what they are.

In networked government the bureaucracy is replaced by a wide variety of other kinds of institutions, almost all of which have better reputations (and sometimes better performance records) than government itself. In networked government, the government stops trying to do anything itself; instead, it funds other organizations who do the actual work that the government wants done. The variety of organizations that have been part of networked government is immense and growing. Churches, research labs, nonprofit organizations, for-profit organizations, universities—all have been called upon to perform the work of the government. Although some look at the emergence of this form as a "hollowing out" of the state, it pays to remember that the sum total of all this activity by different kinds of organizations is still something that the state wants done and for which it is willing to pay. Despite the view of some who persist in seeing networks as a weakening of the state, networked government can also be looked at as a different way of implementing the goals of the state.

Networked government holds two major attractions: it is not bureaucratic, and it has the potential to be flexible and to innovate—characteristics that traditional bureaucracies do not seem to have. In fact, networked government has been used in the past in those cases in which the government valued innovation so much that it was willing to give up a certain degree of control. The famous military-industrial complex is the example of networked government of the longest standing. The offensive and defensive capacity of the U.S. military is much more than the total of its actual military assets. Faced with the need for massive mobilization at the beginning of World War II, President Franklin Roosevelt did not socialize the industrial might of the United States. Instead, he used the government's financial and other powers to create a network of participants in the war effort. As Americans discovered during World War II, the military might of the United States rested as much on its ability to produce weaponry (a private sector function) for itself and all its allies as on the ability of its soldiers, seamen, and airmen to fight.

As we moved from World War II to the cold war, the model remained the same. Seeking ever better weapons against the Soviet Union, the United States engaged countless corporations, universities, and private laboratories along with its own internal research laboratories in the development of sophisticated weaponry. In the kind of controlled experiment that rarely happens in the real world, the Soviet Union, a totalitarian state, kept its weapons research within the all-encompassing bureaucracy of the communist state. By 1989 the experiment was over. When the Soviet empire fell, we learned, among other things, that its technological and military capacity had fallen way behind that of the United States. Networked government had won, bureaucratic government had lost.

As bureaucratic government has failed in one policy area after another, policymakers have adopted networked government solutions in its place. In 1996 the landmark welfare reform bill ended more than fifty years of a welfare system that had been almost universally regarded as a failure. The old welfare system was characterized by its bureaucratic attention to detail, its insistence that applicants meet all the rules, and its incentives to fill out the paperwork properly. It was a closed system, run by the bureaucratic imperative and impervious to the needs of welfare recipients.

In its place the new law sought to introduce a work-based system. Part of that transformation was to give states an unprecedented amount of freedom to create welfare-to-work networks. These networks could consist of nonprofit organizations (a traditional piece of the social service network), for-profit organizations, and religious organizations. In a dramatic abdication of control, the federal government as much as admitted that the state bureaucracies that had traditionally done this sort of work had failed and that the work of getting welfare recipients to work should be given to any organization that felt it could do it.

When the government creates a network, the private sector is quick to respond. Take, for example, Lockheed-Martin, a giant American corporation that almost single-handedly exemplifies the military-industrial complex. Imagine how surprised people were when, in 1996, Lockheed-Martin IMS (a subdivision of the company) announced that it was going into the welfare-to-work businesses. Lockheed-Martin was simply using its years of experience in government contracting to get into the latest and one of the biggest government sectors ever—the delivery of social services. For the anticorporate do-gooders of the old left, this was a jarring development indeed. One of Lockheed's competitors for this business, Maximus, tells potential investors that social services administration is a potential $21 billion market. The owner of America Works, one of the oldest for-profit welfare-to-work companies in existence, urges local governments to set tough standards for their contracts, knowing that it will then have a greater advantage over its competitors.

Networked government is not necessarily cheap and, frankly, not necessarily efficient, but it has two chief virtues. The first, of course, is that it does not look like government. The second is that it permits a variety of experimentation and produces innovation—it allows a thousand flowers to bloom. That is why networked government tends to appear in those areas in which one solution cannot be expected to solve the problem. There is no one solution to moving people from welfare to work or off drugs, encouraging children to learn, or educating youth and adults in how to avoid contracting AIDS.

Although networked government is a familiar form in the world of social services, the diversity inherent in a network is likely to make networked government a staple of law enforcement and the fight against terrorism. Even before the tragedy at the World Trade Center, it was clear to many that the bureaucracy was a major impediment in the fight against crime and terrorism. Pieces of the terrorism puzzle crossed an enormous number of agencies—the Immigration and Naturalization Service, the Central Intelligence Agency, the Federal Bureau of Investigation, and U.S. Customs, to name but a few. Each of these agencies came of age in a time in which the danger the world over was fairly neatly divided between internal threats and external threats. The amorphous nature of terrorism, organized international crime, and new crimes such as cyberterrorism means that the closed worlds of the intelligence agencies and the law enforcement agencies will have to change.

Tipped off to an attack, or in the aftermath of an attack, cooperation tends to be ideal. However, as has been seen in the case of the World Trade Center bombings, finding the suspects quickly is no substitute for having prevented the attack in the first place. The answer is not to combine all these different agencies into one giant agency. That would decrease, not increase, the diversity of information. The answer is, rather, to tie them into a network in which each player reinforces the other in order to yield results needed before an attack, not after.

In spite of the advantages that the diversity of networked government presents, the fact that policymakers have used it as a sort of default mode of implementation for difficult "sticky" public policy problems means that little attention has been paid to what makes for successful networked government. Kenneth Meier and Laurence O'Toole, in their study of school superintendents in Texas, have found that those who were conscious of the other environmental factors impacting education had better results than those who were not.[54] In their work on mental health networks, Milward and Provan note that though resources matter, effective principal-agent relationships and stability are also important to the effectiveness of the network.[55]

However, the soft underbelly of networked government is the near 100 percent probability that, over time, some actor in some part of the network will screw up, by stealing money, or wasting money, or simply proving to be ineffective. On the other hand, overzealousness against waste, fraud, and abuse on the part of actors in the network can recreate all the pathologies and rigidities of traditional bureaucratic governments that networked government is otherwise able to avoid. Bruce Reed, the architect of the Clinton administration's welfare reform bill, understood this problem. In a recent interview he remarked that "under the new arrangement the country has to accept a greater level of risk, and states have to accept responsibility, and they get more ability to experiment." When asked why the country seemed so ready to delegate the entire system and accept more risk, he replied, "there was greater willingness to take that risk because the old system was so encumbered by dumb federal rules."[56]

The reason networked government looks "hollow" to many who observe it is that few people in government really understand how to manage networks. Often networks have been created to solve the most difficult governmental problems, such as creating a weapons system that does what no other weapons system before it has done or figuring out how to end a cycle of welfare dependence that has gone on for more than three decades through economic booms as well as economic busts. In addition to the difficulty of the public problems, many government managers find themselves managing networks despite the fact that their experience, their training, and their expectations have been in managing traditional or sometimes entrepreneurial bureaucracies. The management of networks is a topic that goes well beyond the scope of this chapter; suffice it to say that creating learning communities within the network and establishing accountability without stifling innovation are two of the most serious management problems.

Market Government

Entrepreneurial government and networked government are different from traditional bureaucratic government, yet they both involve a significant amount of government. In entrepreneurial government the public's work is done by people who work for the government; in networked government the public's work is paid for by the government even though it is performed by people who do not work for the government. In the third emerging model of government—market government—the work of government involves no public employees and no public money. In market government, the government uses its power to create a market that fulfills a public purpose. It takes account of what economists call "externalities."[57]

Market government is something quite distinctive, however. If entrepreneurial government is government dressed up to look like the private sector and networked government is government that hides behind the façade of much more popular organizations, market government is so well disguised that most people are not even aware that it is government in operation. Because of this it is probably the model farthest away from traditional bureaucratic government.

Those who are old enough to remember Lady Bird Johnson, the wife of President Lyndon Johnson, will probably remember that she waged a battle to clean up America's highways, which, in the 1960s, were in serious danger of being buried in beer cans and soda bottles. The solution to this problem came from government. Instead of creating the Bureau of Clean Highways and hiring workers to pick up bottles, however, government did something unusual—it created a market. By passing laws that required deposits on bottles and soda cans, government created an economic incentive to keep people from throwing bottles out of their cars. For the hardcore litterbugs who persisted in throwing bottles away, the laws created an economic incentive for other people to pick them up.

Similarly, in the 1991 Clean Air Act, Congress decided to put a price on sulfur dioxide emissions from industrial plants. Sulfur dioxide (SO_2) is the primary contaminant in acid rain. Essentially, the government determined how much sulfur dioxide the environment could handle and then developed a trading system that would allow clean plants to "sell" emissions permits and dirty plants to "buy" emissions permits. Most analysts feel this system has worked. In the past thirty years, emissions trading (and other improvements) has caused a near 50 percent drop in the amount of SO_2 in the air.[58] The "price" of SO_2 emissions was high enough to encourage plants to get new equipment for cleaner air but low enough that companies could determine their own timetables and choose the technologies they would use.

In retrospect, market government applied to an environmental problem has been a big success. Only recently, however, has this approach become politically acceptable. Professor Rob Stavins, one of the early advocates of this approach in the environmental field, recalls how, just a decade ago, environmentalists chafed at the notion that pollution could be bought and sold. Their reaction, and that of their colleagues in the government at the Environmental Protection Agency, was nothing short of horror. The use of a market to control pollution was considered to be somehow immoral. That attitude, reports Stavins, has changed dramatically in recent years. The most ardent environmentalists will admit to the attractiveness of market government, and people now seek to apply market government in places where it may well not work.[59] In the recent effort to deregulate the electricity market in the state of California, so much went wrong that energy executive Barbara Kates Garnik has referred to it as "the perfect storm."[60]

Market government has also shaped the education reform debate, through proposals to substitute a voucher system for the current state-funded education system. The voucher movement argues that the government can create a market in education by attaching education money to each student rather than to public schools. This reform movement argues that government should use tax cuts and universal tuition tax credits to turn over education purchasing power to individuals. This would create a vibrant education marketplace, offering consumers a range of services and products that the current system does not.

A vibrant market already exists in education at the college level: parents save, borrow, and do without in order to send children to élite, expensive, private institutions. In recent years, as unhappiness with the public education system from kindergarten to twelfth grade has grown, an education market of a sort has emerged even without government subsidies. Edison schools, Bright Horizons, Nobel Learning Communities (these began as child care providers and expanded business to include elementary and secondary education), and others have created a new class of educators, who have been called "edupreneurs." The advantages of creating a market in education are many: variety in curriculum, innovation in instructional methods, higher academic standards, weeding out of substandard schools, introduction of new technologies into the classroom, and investments in research, to name a few.

A well-functioning market is, of course, a marvel to behold. In our lifetimes it has given the vast majority of Americans color television, microwaves, and video cassette recorders. Who knows what it will bring in the next century? The key word here, however, is "well-functioning." For those who are attempting to design markets for public good instead of private good, the problems are immense. First are the pricing problems: Too high a price on bottles would clearly have wrecked much of the beverage industry and caused a serious outcry from the public. (To this day the beer industry remains opposed to bottle bills wherever they have not yet taken root.) Too low a price on bottles would not have solved the public problem at all. Similarly, if the number of pollution permits were so high that they cost very little to buy, they would fail to create incentives for plants to clean up their manufacturing processes. On the other hand, if the number of permits were too low, the price would be so high that older plants would have gone out of business.

Second are problems in understanding the range of the market. A major failure in the California energy debacle was the deregulation of the wholesale market without deregulation of the retail market. False expectations (that energy prices would continue to go down) and unavoidable political pressures (to reassure voters that the changes would not cost them more money) ended up creating a crisis. It is not surprising that California is retreating from its experiment with markets in the electricity field.

Third, using market government to achieve a public good presupposes a certain amount of honesty in the economic system and a certain level of honesty, as well as effectiveness, in law enforcement. Although market government when applied to environmental problems has proved a success in the United States, it is not surprising that American talk about creating "market mechanisms" to implement the Kyoto Accords falls on skeptical ears in other countries. Market government works where the rule of law is well established and where law enforcement is sufficiently effective to deter cheating. This is simply not the case in much of the world.

Fourth, a well-functioning market depends on universal access to high-quality information. There has been substantial opposition to school voucher plans from teachers' unions and other members of the education community. But parents and others with no professional stake in the status quo have been almost as reluctant to embrace the market approach to education. Lurking behind the failure of so many voucher plans is the suspicion that somehow someone will be exploited. Buying a second-grade education is simply not as easy as buying a bread-making machine. There are many sources of information about different bread-making machines, and most Americans know how to find them and understand them. Sources of information about one school's second grade versus another's are hard to come by and difficult to interpret. Good markets require good information, and in spite of the recent trend toward assessment of schools according to standardized testing scores, good information is simply not so easy to come by for most parents.

Problems aside, however, market government is a powerful alternative to bureaucratic government precisely because it allows an unlimited number of individual adaptations to achieve the overall public good. In entrepreneurial government, one entity—the government—pursues the public good. In networked government, one entity—the government—chooses a set number of organizations to pursue the public good. In contrast, market government allows every individual (as in the case of bottles) or every company (as in the case of sulfur dioxide emissions) to pursue the public good as he, she, or it sees fit. It is, therefore, perfectly suited to America, where citizens glorify individual choice and chafe at any system that constrains their freedom.

Evaluating New Forms: Trading Off Accountability and Innovation

For the complex array of reasons laid out at the beginning of this chapter, decisionmakers are likely to remain interested in a wide array of alternatives to the traditional bureaucratic state. If we are conscious about what is happening to government we can manage the transition to a twenty-first-century government. If we are not, we can proceed to waste a great deal of money and fail a great many people. That is why we need to recognize the emerging modes of postbureaucratic government and evaluate their contribution to core democratic values such as transparency and accountability. After all, entrepreneurial government can be as costly and as wasteful as the old government it is trying to dress up; and networked government, if it is not managed correctly and if the political will to hold organizations accountable is lacking, can devolve into thousands of contracting horror stories and millions of wasted dollars. Market government can be manipulated and become the source of many unintended consequences if the market is not properly designed and enforced.

Innovation

In addition to the traditional values of transparency and accountability, the rapid pace of change in the twenty-first century means that leaders have a new objective for government organizations—innovation. For Presidents Theodore Roosevelt and Franklin Roosevelt, innovation was the creation of new bureaucratic entities. For twenty-first-century political leaders, the capacity for innovation is clearly the most important advantage of postbureaucratic entities.

There is an inherent conflict between traditional transparency and accountability, on the one hand, and innovation, on the other. In matching policy problems to appropriate implementation models, decisionmakers of the future will have to ascertain the degree to which they are willing to sacrifice one for the other. Table 10-1 illustrates some of the tradeoffs.

Entrepreneurial government increases the odds of innovation because it frees government employees from the rule-driven processes that have so often either stood in the way of innovation or served as excuses for the failure of government officials to innovate. Impediments to hiring and firing under traditional civil service laws and the rule-bound structures that have governed everything from budgeting to procurement have not made it easy for traditional bureaucracies to innovate. Whether or not entrepreneurial government can overcome this legacy is questionable. For even as government reformers around the world adopt the language of "new public management" or "reinventing government," reformed structures will remain vulnerable to the pathologies of bureaucratic government. When the Clinton administration promulgated the idea of PBOs (performance-based organizations), the Office of Management and Budget insisted on creating a "template" into which each PBO had to fit. The very idea of a standard template went against the grain of the reform and caused some civil servants to conclude that the PBO idea, while attractive, was not genuine.

To the extent that entrepreneurial government involves importing commonsense private sector techniques to public sector organizations, it will most likely continue to thrive in those areas in which innovation needs to happen within the confines of a government organization. For instance, there are good reasons why the issuance of a document as important to national identity as a passport should not be contracted out to hundreds of private sector passport providers; and it is absurd to think that a market in passports could be anything but illegal. There is no good reason, however, why passport offices should not be open at convenient hours, and there is no reason why people who wait till the last minute to get their passports renewed should not pay a higher fee for expedited service. Somehow the "intrinsically governmental" nature of granting a passport means that it must be kept in government. Thus entrepreneurial government is appropriate for those things that we feel need to remain under the domain of the state and for those functions that demand a degree of uniformity.

Networked government is turned to in those areas in which innovation is most valued and most needed, which is why the networked form has emerged as the leading model in social services and in research and development. It is the form most suited to solving public problems that are difficult and defy a standard solution. The attractiveness of networked government is in the very diversity of the organizations that can be involved in attempting to accomplish a certain public goal. However, the capacity for innovation depends, to a certain extent, on the ability of those in the network to share best practices and on the capacity of the center of the network (usually a public official) to reward and punish actors in the network. Thus far, anecdotal evidence suggests that government managers of networks are not particularly effective in either the former or the latter. Political influence or simple inertia in the continuation of nonperforming contracts is an all-too-common story and one that undercuts the potential effectiveness of this mode of government.

Market government has, perhaps, the most capacity for innovation because it allows for individual responses on the part of all the actors in the system. Even networked government, through the contracting process, requires some degree of control and standardization. Market government does, however, allow for individual responses to the government's desire to clean up the highways or to reduce SO_2 emissions. Market government is an intriguing option for policymakers in those situations in which information is plentiful and a "price" can be determined for the public good in question.

Transparency

For obvious reasons, transparency is even more important in public sector organizations than it is in private sector organizations. Legislative bodies, elected officials, the press, and the citizens all expect to be able to access an accounting of how their dollars are being spent. Traditional bureaucratic organizations have very high degrees of transparency. The average public sector budget details every dollar spent—down to the costs of phones and desks. The emphasis on transparency in the traditional bureaucracy is, of course, highly correlated to the central control mechanisms that are also famous for their ability to stifle innovation.

Table 10-1. *Characteristics of Four Forms of Government*

Characteristic	Traditional bureaucracy	Entrepreneurial government	Networked government	Market government
Capacity for innovation	Low	Medium	High, depending on degree of competition	High, but limited by the difficulty of "pricing" public goods
Transparency	High, to the extent that every dollar is accounted for and every process apparent	High, although the decrease in central control mechanisms may lead to some lower transparency	Medium to low, depending on the ability of the center of the network to track and report activity	High, but limited by the need for simple measures
Accountability	High, but limited to accountability for process, not outcomes	High, assuming that performance measures replace central control mechanisms	Medium, depending on the nature of the contracting process and the quality of the outcome measures	Medium to high, but limited by the need for simple measures and the quality of enforcement

Entrepreneurial government, in theory at least, offers full transparency without the extensive control mechanisms of traditional bureaucracy. It remains to be seen, however, whether oversight bodies will allow for real organizational flexibility. As much as bureaucrats complain about the constraints of traditional government, they have not been overly bold when given the freedom to create their own systems. For instance, in spite of the passage of two major procurement reform bills in the 1990s, bills that allowed for much greater agency flexibility in the federal government's buying practices, many agencies held on to the old-fashioned rules and procedures long after the law itself had been changed.

Transparency poses a real problem for networked government. To maximize innovation a vibrant network has to have many parts—and yet the more parts there are the harder it is to know exactly what each one is doing. Rarely does the center, the governmental organization, have the capacity to know what is going on in all parts of the network all of the time. The conundrum is that attempts to monitor the network may result in the reimposition of bureaucratic constraints—and end up stifling variety and innovation in the network. In addition, it is clear that managing a network is different from managing a hierarchical bureaucracy. Today's government officials were trained to run hierarchical bureaucracies and are perplexed or ineffectual or both when they suddenly find themselves managing a network.

Market government is perhaps the most transparent of the three new modes of government: if a market is operating effectively, there are usually clear-cut measures by which success can be judged. Is there less sulfur dioxide in the air? Are there fewer bottles on the streets? The limits of market government are clear, however, when it is applied to something like elementary and secondary education, where the measures of success are varied, contentious, and a lot murkier than the number of beer bottles in the median strips.

Accountability

Transparency is, of course, directly related to accountability. It is difficult for citizens to hold government accountable if they cannot even see what government is doing. For citizens, accountability has traditionally meant electoral accountability; for public administrators, it has traditionally meant compliance with legal and budgetary rules. But the emergence of twenty-first-century government requires a rethinking of democratic accountability.

As Robert D. Behn points out, traditional government created accountability around notions of "finances and fairness. . . . But citizens also care about their public agencies' performance." Eugene Bardach and Cara Lesser argue that traditional accountability systems do a good job of creating accountability for functions but do not perform very well when it comes to "motivating performance, encouraging wise priorities, and facilitating continuous improvement." Dealing with the difficult issue of accountability in the international arena, Joseph S. Nye and Robert O. Keohane have noted that "electoral accountability is insufficient within modern democracies because many tasks are delegated to non-elected agents, from bureaucratic agencies to courts."[61]

Accountability in postbureaucratic government organizations will revolve around performance measures. Where those measures are easy to establish and can accurately capture the public mission performance accountability can replace older accountability systems. This is perhaps most clear in networked government, where accountability is only as good as the performance measures set in the contracts that create the network. So far, many governments are not good at setting these measures. Peter Cove, the president of America Works, the first for-profit welfare-to-work corporation, has complained that state and local governments with whom he contracts are still writing outcome measures based on process—how many people sign up, how many people attend class, and so on. Cove believes that his organization can really deliver long-term job stability for former welfare recipients and that it would be to his competitive advantage (and to the long-term advantage of the communities involved) if contracting success were judged on the basis of job placement, longevity in the job, and prospects for advancement.[62]

Accountability in both networked government and entrepreneurial government will depend on the measures themselves. The concept of the "balanced scorecard" pioneered by a business school professor for the corporate world has migrated to the public sector—with good reason.[63] If private sector outcomes are more complex than simply profits, imagine how complex outcomes are in the public sector. Private welfare-to-work contractors tell the story of one local government that deemed its contractors' efforts to be successful if they got a welfare recipient into a job for one day. Clearly, a more nuanced and complex measure is needed to meet the public good. The difficulty in defining that measure is a major impediment to accountability in networked government.

Government by market can be accountable if the market is properly constructed and there is an effective enforcement mechanism. Market government is limited in its use, however, by the sheer complexity of measuring public outcomes. The difficulty that proponents of school vouchers have run into over the years reflects the difficulty of pricing, measurement, and enforcement in the elementary and secondary education market. Most voucher plans offer students less than the full cost of education—in part because they also have to keep the existing public school system open. Therefore, the price is almost always too low to create a substantial market. In addition, the public school system does more than educate; it contributes to democracy by teaching citizenship and tolerance for diversity—values that are not easily measured or priced. Finally, over the past four decades enormous protection against discrimination has been built into the public school system. The suspicion lingers that antidiscrimination laws cannot be effectively enforced in a school system that is, in effect, privatized.

In spite of these problems, however, it is possible to construct accountability mechanisms for the postbureaucratic state that allow it to develop into more than an ad hoc alternative to traditional bureaucracy. Part of the transition from one mode of government implementation to another will involve the clear articulation of performance goals and standards. Another equally important part of this transition will be the training and nurturing of government employees comfortable in the postbureaucratic world—a topic for another time. In the meantime, the clear identification of alternatives to bureaucracy and an honest evaluation of where they are or are not appropriate will move us toward the generally shared goal of better governance.

Notes

1. Susan Page, "Suddenly, 'Era of Big Government Is Not Over': Federal Role Expands in Response to Crises," *USA Today*, October 1, 2001, p. 2.

2. Donald J. Savoie, *Thatcher, Reagan, and Mulroney: In Search of a New Bureaucracy* (University of Pittsburgh Press, 1994), pp. 92, 90.

3. Philip K. Howard, *The Death of Common Sense: How Law Is Suffocating America* (Random House, 1995).

4. See Merilee Grindle, "Ready or Not: The Developing World and Globalization," in Joseph S. Nye Jr. and John D. Donahue, eds., *Governance in a Globalizing World* (Brookings, 2000), pp. 182–83.

5. See Salvatore Schiavo-Campo, Giulio de Tommaso, and Amitabha Mukherjee, "An International Statistical Survey of Government Employment and Wages," report prepared by the Public Sector Management and Information Technology team, Technical Department for Europe, Central Asia, Middle East, and North Africa (World Bank, 2001). While admitting the methodological difficulties of comparing size of government across the globe, the authors conclude, nevertheless, that "a large contraction in both central government employment (relative to population) and the relative wage bill is evident in all regions, with the relative size of central government shrinking by about one-third when measured by employment and one-fourth when measured by the wage bill" (p. 9).

6. "Fiscal Prudence Goes Local," *Economist,* March 10, 2001, p. 35.

7. R. L. Bernall and W. Leslie, "Privatization in the English-Speaking Caribbean: An Assessment," working paper (Washington: Center for Strategic and International Studies, 1999). (Thanks to my student Anita Chellaraj for pointing this out to me.)

8. See, for instance, Castro's quotes regarding privatization in a BBC broadcast aired on December 17, 2000. (Thanks to my student Marissa W. Jones for pointing this out to me.)

9. "China's Confident Bow," *Economist,* March 10, 2001, p. 37.

10. See Robert O. Keohane and Joseph S. Nye Jr., introduction to Joseph S. Nye Jr. and John D. Donahue, eds., *Governance in a Globalizing World* (Brookings, 2000), pp. 1–41.

11. See, for instance, B. Guy Peters and John Pierre, "Governance without Government? Rethinking Public Administration," *Journal of Public Administration Research and Theory,* vol. 8 (April 1998), pp. 223–43, p. 223.

12. David Osborne and Ted Gaebler, *Reinventing Government: How the Entrepreneurial Spirit Is Transforming the Public Sector from Schoolhouse to Statehouse, City Hall to the Pentagon* (Reading, Mass.: Addison-Wesley, 1992).

13. See, for instance, B. Guy Peters, *The Future of Governing: Four Emerging Models* (University Press of Kansas, 1996). As various scholars have attempted to categorize what is going on in the postbureaucratic state, they have used a variety of terms. For instance, what I describe here as entrepreneurial government, others have described as "market-type bureaucracies" (see Mark Considine and Jenny M. Lewis, "Governance at Ground Level: The Frontline Bureaucrat in the Age of Markets and Networks," *Public Administration Review,* vol. 59 (November–December 1999), pp. 467–81.

14. See Tim Irwin, "An Analysis of New Zealand's New System of Public Sector Management," in *Public Management in Government: Contemporary Illustrations,* Occasional Paper 9 (Paris: Organization for Economic Cooperation and Development, 1996), pp. 7–32.

15. See, for example, Peters and Pierre, "Governance without Government? Rethinking Public Administration."

16. John Peterson and Laurence O'Toole, "Networks and Governance in Europe and America: Grasping the Normative Nettle," paper prepared for the Visions of Governance in the Twenty-First Century Project's Conference on Federalism, Harvard University, John F. Kennedy School of Government, April 19–21, 1999.

17. Anne Marie Slaughter, "The Real New World Order," *Foreign Affairs,* vol. 76 (September–October 1997), pp. 183–98.

18. See Elaine Ciulla Kamarck, "Globalization and Public Administration Reform," in Joseph S. Nye Jr. and John D. Donahue, eds., *Governance in a Globalizing World* (Brookings, 2000), pp. 229–52.

19. Other scholars (such as Peters, *The Future of Governing: Four Emerging Models*) have used the term *market government*. However, their description of market government is closer to what I have described under the term *entrepreneurial government*.

20. Peters, *The Future of Governing: Four Emerging Models*, p. 132.

21. Howard, *The Death of Common Sense: How Law Is Suffocating America*.

22. Savoie, *Thatcher, Reagan, and Mulroney: In Search of a New Bureaucracy*, p. 92.

23. President William Jefferson Clinton, State of the Union Address, January 23, 1996, *Public Papers of the Presidents of the United States*.

24. See Gary Orren, "Fall from Grace: The Public's Loss of Faith in Government," in Joseph S. Nye Jr., Zelikow, and King, eds., *Why People Don't Trust Government* (Harvard University Press, 1997), pp. 77–107.

25. See Nye, Zelikow, and King, *Why People Don't Trust Government*; in particular, see Robert Z. Lawrence, "Is It Really the Economy, Stupid?" (pp. 111–33) on the absence of a clear relation between economic performance and declining trust; and Derek Bok, "Measuring the Performance of Government" (pp. 55–77), for a discussion of government accomplishment in the face of declining trust.

26. See Robert J. Blendon, John M. Benson, Richard Morin, Drew E. Altman, Mollyann Brodie, Mario Brossad, and Matt James, "Changing Attitudes in America," in Nye, Zelikow, and King, *Why People Don't Trust Government*, pp. 205–17, p. 210.

27. See Savoie, *Thatcher, Reagan, and Mulroney: In Search of a New Bureaucracy*, for an excellent account of these campaigns and the attack they launched on the bureaucracy; Thatcher quoted on p. 90.

28. Ibid., chapter 4.

29. See, for instance, Woodrow Wilson, "The Study of Public Administration," *Political Science Quarterly*, vol. 1 (1887), pp. 197–222; and Frank Goodnow, *Politics and Administration* (New York: Macmillan, 1900).

30. Louis C. Gawthrop, *Bureaucratic Behavior in the Executive Branch* (Free Press and Macmillan, 1969), p. 16.

31. For instance, various public administration scholars have struggled with how to align the goals of elected officials with the goals of bureaucratic administrators; see, for instance, Gawthrop, *Bureaucratic Behavior in the Executive Branch*; and Herbert Simon, Donald W. Smithburg, and Victor A. Thompson, *Public Administration* (A. A. Knopf, 1950).

32. Savoie, *Thatcher, Reagan, and Mulroney: In Search of a New Bureaucracy*, p. 90.

33. See, for instance, Ronald Inglehart, "Postmaterialist Values and the Erosion of Institutional Authority," in Nye, Zelikow, and King, *Why Americans Don't Trust Government*, pp. 217–37; Pippa Norris, *Critical Citizens: Global Support for Democratic Governance* (Oxford University Press, 1999).

34. It is no accident that in 1993 Minister Franco Bassinini started Italy upon an ambitious program to downsize and restructure its bureaucracy. One of the accomplishments of the government in which Bassinini was a minister was the smooth integration of Italy into the European Monetary Union.

35. See, for example, Michael Pinto-Duschinsky, "The Rise of Political Aid," in Larry Diamond, Marc F. Plattner, Yun-han Chu, and Hung-amo Tien, *Consolidating Third Wave Democracies: Regional Challenges* (Johns Hopkins University Press, 1997), pp. 295–325.

36. World Bank, *The State in a Changing World: World Bank Development Report 1997* (Washington, 1997), p. 3

37. Tom Peters, *You Can't Shrink Your Way to Greatness: The Circle of Innovation* (A. A. Knopf, 1997); Dee Hock, *Birth of the Chaordic Age* (San Francisco: Berrett-Koehler Publishers, 1999).

38. James P. Pinkerton, *What Comes Next: The End of Big Government and the New Paradigm Ahead* (Hyperion, 1995), pp. 62, 62–67.

39. Morley Winograd and Dudley Buffa, *Taking Control: Politics in the Information Age* (Henry Holt, 1996).

40. David Osborne, *Laboratories of Democracy* (Harvard Business School Press, 1988).

41. David Osborne and Peter Plastrick, *Banishing Bureaucracy: The Five Strategies for Reinventing Government* (Reading, Mass.: Addison-Wesley, 1997), p. 25.

42. See the statement of J. Christopher Mihm, acting associate director of the General Accounting Office, Federal Management and Workforce Issues, in *Performance-Based Organizations: Lessons from the British Next Steps Initiative*, GAO/T-GGD-97-151 (U.S. General Accounting Office, July 8, 1997).

43. Ibid., p. 6.

44. Jonathan Boston, John Martin, June Pallot, and Pat Walsh, *Public Management: The New Zealand Model* (Auckland, New Zealand: Oxford University Press, 1996).

45. Ibid., p. 5.

46. For the full story of the Minnesota reforms, see Michael Barzelay, *Breaking through Bureaucracy* (University of California Press, 1992).

47. See, for instance, Linda de Leon and Robert B. Denhardt, "The Political Theory of Reinvention," *Public Administration Review*, vol. 60 (March–April 2000), pp. 89–98, in which the authors comment that "the 'shadow' side of the entrepreneur is characterized by a narrow focus, an unwillingness to follow rules and stay within bounds" (p. 92).

48. Considine and Lewis, "Governance at Ground Level: The Frontline Bureaucrat in the Age of Markets and Networks," p. 475.

49. See, for instance, Paul Sabatier and Hank Jenkins-Smith, eds., *Policy Change and Learning: An Advocacy Coalition Approach* (Boulder, Colo.: Westview, 1993).

50. "The Real New World Order," *Foreign Affairs*, vol. 76 (September–October 1997), pp. 183–98.

51. Peterson and O'Toole, "Networks and Governance in Europe and America: Grasping the Normative Nettle."

52. H. Brinton Milward and Keith G. Provan, "Governing the Hollow State," *Journal of Public Administration Research and Theory*, vol. 10 (April 2000), pp. 359–80, p. 360.

53. Ibid., p. 360.

54. Kenneth J. Meier and Laurence J. O'Toole Jr., "Managerial Strategies and Behavior in Networks: A Model with Evidence from U.S. Public Education," *Journal of Public Administration Research and Theory*, vol. 11 (July 2001), pp. 271–93.

55. Milward and Provan, "Governing the Hollow State."

56. Bruce Reed, telephone interview with the author, September 27, 2001.

57. I use the term *market government* differently from the way other scholars have. Most public administration scholars, when they talk about markets and government, are usually talking about what I have previously referred to as entrepreneurial government or networked government.

58. See Robert N. Stavins, "What Can We Learn from the Grand Policy Experiment? Lessons from SO_2 Allowance Trading," *Journal of Economic Perspectives,* vol. 12 (Summer 1998), pp. 69–88.

59. Robert Stavins, personal interview with the author, September 20, 2001, Cambridge, Massachusetts.

60. Barbara Kates Garnik, personal interview with the author, April 20, 1999, Cambridge, Massachusetts.

61. Robert D. Behn, *Rethinking Democratic Accountability* (Brookings, 2001), p. 216; Eugene Bardach and Cara Lesser, "Accountability in Human Services Collaboratives: For What? and To Whom?" *Journal of Public Administration Research and Theory,* vol. 6 (April 1996), pp. 197–212, p. 203; Robert O. Keohane and Joseph S. Nye Jr., "Democracy, Accountability, and Global Governance," working paper (Cambridge, Mass.: Harvard University, John F. Kennedy School of Government, June 27, 2001).

62. Peter Cove, lecture to Elaine Kamarck's class on innovation in government, Harvard University, John F. Kennedy School of Government, April 22, 1999.

63. See Robert Kaplan and D. P. Norton, *The Balanced Scorecard: Translating Strategy into Action* (Harvard Business School Press, 1996).

11

JOHN D. DONAHUE

The Problem of Public Jobs

INTERNATIONAL BUSINESS MACHINES (IBM) ushered in the age of the ubiquitous personal computer in the early 1980s. Two decades later, IBM stopped making desktop PCs. But it continued to design and sell desktops with the IBM nameplate while delegating the actual production to a company called Sanmina-SCI. One of several low-profile "contract electronic manufacturers," Sanmina specialized in cranking out high volumes of electronic goods for sale by a range of name-brand companies. Such outsourcing deals cut costs by 15 to 20 percent, according to a leading electronics analyst, and promised to reshape the industry.[1]

Similar stories are commonplace in the turn-of-the-century business press. In much of America's private sector the boundaries of the firm have shifted and blurred. An exotic bestiary of institutional hybrids and new organizational breeds—networks, alliances, "virtual corporations"—has evolved over recent decades. Outsourcing firms, employment brokers, permanent temps, and footloose free agents have matured into major features

---

I am indebted to participants in the Visions of Governance in the Twenty-First Century Project (and particularly to Steven Goldsmith, John White, and Richard Zeckhauser) for many helpful critiques and suggestions offered in response to drafts of this chapter. My thanks also go to my resourceful research associate, Steven Minicucci, and to the Innovations in American Government Program, which provided financial support for his assistance.

on the industrial landscape. Defining and embracing core competencies (and delegating the rest) reigns as something approaching business orthodoxy, for reasons that include but go well beyond cost reduction. What once seemed the private sector norm—a cleanly defined corporation with a fair degree of stability and integration and a high degree of distinction between inside and outside—increasingly appears antique.[2]

Does the public sector simply follow suit? A prominent government reform theme, in the United States and elsewhere, centers on shifting the balance away from hierarchies and toward markets as the core model for getting the public's work done. Improvements in information technology and increasingly sophisticated contracting techniques loosen some of the constraints on indirect production. At the state and local levels, both routine functions, such as waste management and road maintenance, and more sensitive tasks, such as corrections and social services, are delegated to private suppliers.[3] The Federal Activities Reform Act of 1998 requires agencies to comb through their operations and identify functions amenable to outsourcing.[4] About half of all federal positions are on that list, and the George W. Bush administration has declared the goal of opening half of those to competition from private suppliers.[5]

The notion of transforming government from a bundle of capacities for performing work directly into a deft choreographer of market-based arrangements by which outside agents create public value figures centrally in discussions about the future of governance.[6] Repositioning professional pedagogy to accommodate such a metamorphosis is a major strategic issue for American schools of public policy and administration. Some scholars of public management take it as a given that this transformation is already accomplished or inevitable and concern themselves with fine-tuning the response.[7]

This chapter briefly engages two broad questions about the transformation to a market-driven, heavily outsourced American government: First, is it happening? Second, should it happen? The first question is trickier than it may seem, though it turns out to be at least roughly resolvable. The second inspires (at least in this author) a quite uncomfortable degree of ambivalence.

Is Outsourcing Shrinking the Public Work Force?

The rhetoric of privatization opponents and enthusiasts alike suggests that conventional public service is being swept away by a tidal wave of outsourcing. Gerald McEntee, head of the American Federation of State, County, and Municipal Employees, warns of a "coordinated campaign to privatize government at every level [that] far exceeds anything we've seen in the past."[8] At the other end of the ideological spectrum, the Reason Foundation declares triumphantly that "privatization moves ahead in breadth and depth" and is "thriving in the United States."[9] Both organizations, like others on both the left and the right, regularly issue publications packed with examples (which are, respectively, denounced or celebrated) of services once provided by public workers being shifted to private suppliers.

One might infer, from the volume and tenor of talk about market-driven government, that American public employment (at least as we know it) has been withering away. Is it?[10] Whether public jobs are many or few and whether outsourcing is driving a significant decline in conventional public service turn out to be rather complicated questions.[11]

The Public Work Force Headcount

As of 1999—the most recent year for which complete Census Bureau data are available—there were roughly 20 million government workers.[12] Around 2.8 million of these were civilians working for the federal government, of which the largest group (876,000) consisted of postal workers and the second-largest (713,000) of civilians involved in national defense and international affairs. The federal government also employed about 1.4 million uniformed military personnel. The states, in the aggregate, employed somewhat more people than the federal government: 4.8 million overall, of which about 2 million were involved in higher education. The local government work force, at 10.6 million, exceeded federal and state workforces combined. More than half of these (5.6 million) worked in elementary and secondary education. The remaining 5 million local government workers were scattered across a score of categories, with no category except police services claiming more than half a million.

Figure 11-1 plots the number of government workers (on a full-time equivalent basis) from 1948 to 1999. Public employment roughly tripled over that half century, but by no means smoothly—sharp surges in net hiring (in the early 1950s, the late 1960s, and the late 1980s) alternated with plateaus of little growth, and the public payroll has been essentially steady since around 1990. Total government employment climbed from about 6.5 percent of the population in the early 1960s to around 8 percent by the late 1960s, and it has stayed fairly close to that level ever since. From 1975

Figure 11-1. *Full-Time Equivalent Government Work Force, 1948–99*

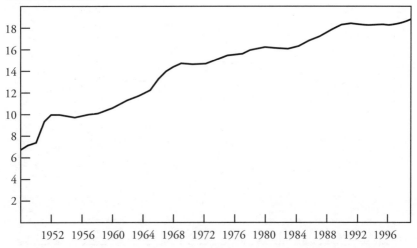

Source: U.S. Department of Commerce, Bureau of Economic Analysis, *National Income and Product Account Tables,* tables 6.5B and 6.5C, revisions as of August 2000 (for pre-1995 data) and August 2001 (for post-1995 data), online version at www.bea.doc.gov/bea/dn/nipaweb/Index.asp (September 2001 and February 2002).

through 1999, the public work force never accounted for less than 7.7 percent or more than 8.2 percent of the population, with no strong trend discernible in the quarter century's data.[13]

Public Jobs as a Share of Total Employment

The headcount of public workers and the government work force as a percentage of population are mainstays of rhetoric but not very interesting analytically. A more germane point of reference is total employment. Figure 11-2 tracks public jobs as a share of employment in the entire American economy, with both categories measured on a full-time equivalent basis. By 1999, public employment's share of the total was down by roughly a quarter from the peak it had reached in the years just before and just after 1970. This is consistent with downward pressure on the public work force caused by increasing reliance on market means for accomplishing governmental tasks. A closer look suggests a more complicated story, however. The broader work force grew at an annual pace of 2 to nearly

Figure 11-2. *Public Sector Work Force as Share of Total U.S. Full-Time Equivalent Work Force, 1948–99*

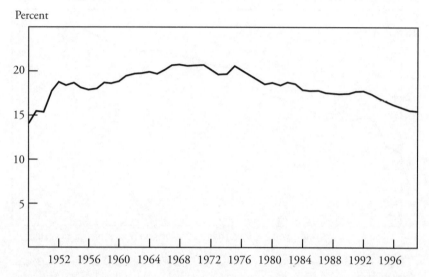

Source: See figure 11-1.

3 percent from 1994 through 1999 (after erratic or anemic growth or actual declines for most of the prior two decades), driving down the government share of the total work force for reasons having little to do with outsourcing. The public sector share of employment was lower in 1999 than in the 1970s but about the same as it had been in the middle of the century. More than half of the decline from the peak occurred before the mid-1980s, when the debate over market-based government first gained much prominence.[14]

Disaggregating the major categories of government work provides some additional perspective, at the price of what turns out to be inevitable complexity. Public workers' share of American employment wound up about the same at century's end as it had been fifty years earlier. Its composition, however, changed strikingly. In figure 11-3 the public work force is divided into four exhaustive groups: the armed services, other federal workers (including, for present purposes, postal workers), state and local workers involved in education, and all other state and local workers. In 1948 these four groups were roughly the same size, each claiming about three or four

Figure 11-3. *Government Share of Full-Time Equivalent Employment, by Major Category, 1948–99*

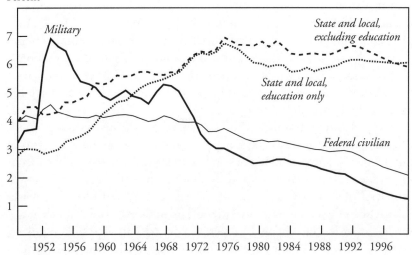

Source: See figure 11-1.

percent of employment. Over the next half century, military employment spiked and then dwindled (for well-known reasons); the share of other federal employment shrank, while state and local employment, both education related and otherwise, surged as a share of the work force. There is a story to be told here, but it is not—at least not in any obvious way—centered on rampant outsourcing.[15] Figure 11-3 does underscore a significant point: decisions about delegating public tasks to private agents at the state and local level will have a far greater impact on the big picture of American public employment than will decisions about changes at the federal level, where the headcount stakes are simply smaller.

The Government Work Force Scaled to Public Spending

Although the public sector's share of America's gross domestic product (GDP) has varied rather less than one might infer from strident arguments about the size of government, it has waxed and waned with changes in economic climate and political fashion. The combined budgets of government at all levels climbed from roughly one-quarter of GDP in the early 1960s to something over 30 percent in the mid-1970s, staying at or near that level from 1980 through 1995 and then declining somewhat for the last half of the 1990s. One intuitively appealing gauge of the scale of public employment is the relation between government employment's share of the work force and government spending's share of the economy. If this ratio goes down, government is accomplishing its mission with fewer employees, with one possible cause (among others) being more aggressive reliance on indirect production.

Along with any number of subtle objections to this approach is one obvious problem: federal transfer programs have soared as a fraction of public spending in recent decades. While the overall share of public spending in the GDP has changed only modestly in recent decades, the growth of federal transfer payments, mostly Social Security and Medicare, masks the decline of governmental activities of the sort that involve much actual service provision (as opposed to mere check writing). Ten billion dollars' worth of transfer programs does not imply the same demand for personnel as ten billion dollars' worth of teaching, policing, or mine inspecting. In 1962, Social Security and Medicare payments accounted for 2.5 percent of GDP and 10 percent of total public expenditures. In 1999, they claimed 6.5 percent of GDP and more than 23 percent of government spending.[16] These programs do not run themselves, to be sure; the Social Security Administration has about sixty-three thousand employees, and the Centers for Medicare and Medicaid Services (formerly the Health Care Financing Administration) has around five thousand. However, the disproportion between budget dollars and manpower for these functions means that their growing share of public spending risks distorting trends in the relation between government's mission and its work force.

Figure 11-4 illustrates the trend in public employment relative to the public sector share of GDP from 1962 to 1999 in two ways. The solid line compares the work force–to–GDP ratio of the public sector to that of the private sector. (A value of 100 percent means government's headcount is exactly proportional to the role of public spending in the economy; a lower value means the government's share of the work force trails its share of GDP.) The dotted line removes Social Security and Medicare spending and (less precisely) the associated headcount from the picture.[17] This figure shows that the public sector's work force–to–GDP ratio has fallen relative to that of the private sector. In the mid-1960s the government had only a

Figure 11-4. *Relationship of Full-Time Equivalent Employment to GDP, Public Sector to Private Sector, 1962–99*

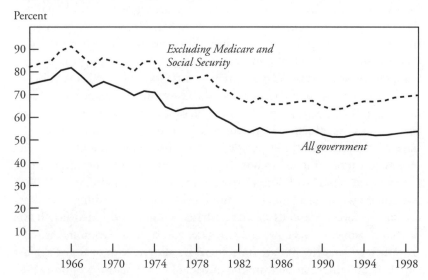

Source: Government employment data from U.S. Office of Management and Budget, *Budget of the United States Government, Fiscal Year 2001,* Historical Table 17.5. Gross domestic product and public spending data from *Budget of the United States Government, Fiscal Year 2001,* Historical Table 15.3. Private sector employment data from U.S. Department of Commerce, *National Income and Product Account Tables,* tables 6.5B and 6.5C.

Note: The data points represent the relationship between the public sector's work force–to-GDP ratio and the private sector's work force–to-GDP ratio in the given year. At 50 percent, for example, government has half as many workers (relative to its share of GDP) as the private sector.

slightly smaller work force (scaled to its share of the economy) than the private sector. In the late 1990s the ratio was a little over 50 percent for all government and a little under 70 percent for government excluding the big transfer programs. This is consistent with many scenarios, including shifts toward less labor-intensive public activities, unevenly rising productivity, and growing transfers other than Social Security and Medicare. It is also consistent with a tilt toward indirect production. The timing, however, is not quite right for the market-based governance story: most of the decline had already happened by the time privatization emerged as a buzzword, and the trend in the 1990s has been mildly upward, especially for the series excluding Social Security and Medicare.

Estimating Outsourcing from National Accounting Data

Instead of relying on fuzzy inferences from demographic and budgetary data, why not get a precise fix on the phenomenon by simply comparing trends in spending on direct versus indirect government production?[18] This seems eminently sensible. Unfortunately (and, perhaps, surprisingly), no comprehensive database on outsourcing exists. Two statistical enterprises of the U.S. Department of Commerce—the Government Finances data series of the Census Bureau and the National Income and Product Accounts prepared by the Commerce Department's Bureau of Economic Analysis—have sufficiently sweeping perspectives on how government spends its money to capture the big trends. Neither set of statistics, however, is collected or processed with an eye to accounting for outsourcing, and both have their own special blind spots and quirks that make it difficult to draw a focus on levels or trends in market-based public service delivery. It has proved possible, however, to disaggregate, adjust, and recombine existing Commerce Department data (in some cases alloyed with or tested against supplemental information from the Bureau of Labor Statistics or other official data sources) to assemble reasonably sturdy gauges of government's reliance on outside suppliers of services.[19]

Although the details are tedious, the basic approach starts by defining and measuring a baseline aggregate of annual public sector activities.[20] This means taking out of conventional budget aggregates those spending items that are not attributable to the current year (for example, debt service and the construction of long-lived assets) or that are not really "activities" amenable to outsourcing (for example, Social Security payments and transfers to other levels of government).[21] The estimate of outsourced services involves subtracting all spending on goods and all spending on compensation for public workers (defined to include benefits as well as direct payroll).

Along with many minor methodological challenges is one major one: Should Medicare and Medicaid be counted as transfers (and excluded from operations, along with Social Security and the like) or as government activities akin to the many social service programs included in operations? A case can be made for either definition, and the difference matters—especially for tracking trends, as these programs claim a growing share of public spending over time. For this reason the outsourcing estimates are presented both ways, counting Medicare and Medicaid as part of the base of public sector activities and leaving them out. Because these health programs rely on privately delivered services, the outsourcing gauge is considerably higher when they are included. Because Medicare and Medicaid are not really at the center of the debate—we have pretty well settled on using private doctors and hospitals, rather than public health agencies, as the main providers of health care—the more meaningful gauge in figures 11-4, 11-5, and 11-6 are the dotted lines.

Figure 11-5 presents these estimates of outsourced public services as shares of current operations for the national and subnational levels of government, from 1959 through 2000.[22] If the big health programs are included, outsourcing has surged from around 15 percent of state and local activities to more than a third and from around 20 percent of federal activities to more than half. Much of the gain happened in the last twenty years of the century, an observation that is consistent with a widespread strategic shift toward privatization. But that period also coincided with galloping growth in Medicare and Medicaid, which traditionally operate mostly by paying private providers. So the series that exclude the big health programs are probably better indicators of the progress of market-based delivery of government services.

Shift the focus to the dotted lines. The fraction of budgets spent on outside services at the state and local levels (excluding Medicaid) stayed fairly flat until the early 1980s. It then climbed toward a late-1980s plateau of around 20 percent before ascending more steeply to 25 percent in 1999. At the federal level, a similar, though shallower, growth pattern in non-Medicare outsourcing occurred during the 1980s, with a small increase and then a small decline in the 1990s. (Indeed, the 1990s saw a sustained increase in defense outsourcing and a significant drop in the outside share of nondefense operations.)[23]

Changes in the relative scale of the two levels of government complicate the picture of changes in direct versus delegated service delivery. The federal government's propensity to outsource is higher but since 1997 has been either stagnant or falling; the propensity for state and local governments to outsource is lower but has been rising over the past forty years. State and local operations have always outweighed federal operations in overall government spending, but the state and local edge has grown in recent decades.

Figure 11-6 combines federal, state, and local government and focuses exclusively on spending for services. This is probably the most useful single gauge of the balance between public employment and outside services, capturing shifts in the scale, shape, and responsibilities of American government as well as the propensity to rely on private agents to get the work

Figure 11-5. *Outsourced Services as Share of All Current Government Operations, 1959–2000*

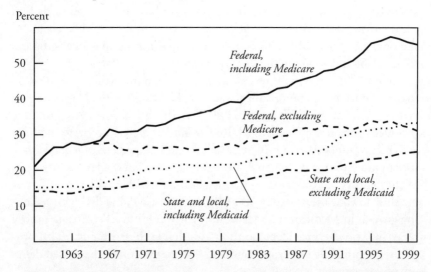

Source: The percentages in figures 11-5 and 11-6 are estimates based primarily on National Income and Product Account data as of August 2001, provided by the Commerce Department on CD-ROM, including tables 3.7, 3.9, 3.12, and 3.19. The estimates are cross-checked with data from the Census Bureau's Census of Governments and also incorporate data from Bureau of Labor Statistics, "Employer Costs for Employee Compensation," bulletin 2526 (March 2000). For more detail on the estimation method, please contact the author.

done. The broader measure including Medicare and Medicaid has risen significantly, mostly in the 1980s; but this reflects the swelling share of these quasi-transfer programs in broadly defined public operations. Excluding them from the definition of public services, the share provided by outside suppliers rose from a recent nadir of 23 percent in the late 1970s to 29 percent in the late 1980s and to more than 30 percent in the late 1990s. This cannot be dismissed as *no* change; the privately provided share grew by more than a third (from 23 to nearly 31 percent) from trough to peak. Yet neither is it entirely convincing to describe this as a revolution in governance. At century's end as at midcentury, roughly two-thirds of the government's work was still being done by public employees.

Thus the answer to the first question—Is market-based government leading to a major erosion of the public sector work force?—is, no, not really, at least not yet. There has clearly been *some* effect. We need not systematically suspect the accuracy of the voluminous case literature. But we can question

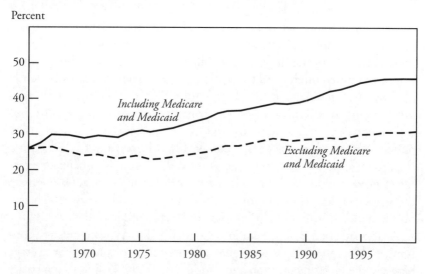

Figure 11-6. *Outsourced Services as Share of All Current Government Services, 1965–2000*

Source: See figure 11-5.

whether that record is representative of what has been happening in the structure of American public service delivery. Aside from the general human tendency to overgeneralize from anecdotes, the widespread perception of a transformative shift toward market-driven governance is quite likely shaped by the incentives of both advocates and adversaries to exaggerate the impact to date. A greater readiness to rely on private delivery almost surely has had a smaller influence on the size of the public work force than have shifts in the size and composition of government's mission, productivity growth, and simple austerity.[24] Far from cutting to the heart of public employment, privatization seems to have been (at least so far) nibbling around its edges. So at the start of the century, market-based governance is not a fait accompli to be accommodated. It is a choice to be weighed.

Are Public Jobs Special?

It is conceivable that the pattern suggested by the data in the previous section—a real but modest effect on the size of the public work force—represents an equilibrium: Those functions suited to market-driven delivery have already been outsourced, and any remaining changes will be marginal. Space limits preclude much discussion here of the criteria that make a public task more or less suitable to private delivery—an issue I have engaged in in some detail elsewhere.[25] If additional reliance on private agents to accomplish public tasks turns out to be a bad idea according to criteria other than the impact on public workers, the rest of this chapter will be of limited interest. But suppose there *are* major functions currently performed by government employees for which the evidence and arguments point to real advantages (in terms of cost reduction, quality improvements, greater flexibility, and tightened managerial focus) in exposing public work to the rigors of the market. If public sector jobs differ in no important respect from private sector jobs, this would be a negligible factor in privatization decisions, whatever portfolio of values are brought to the issue. But government work is different—in subtle ways, which will not be explored here, but also in some quite straightforward ways.

As a broad class, government jobs pay well.[26] This is by no means a constant; public sector wages were generally above the private sector average between the Great Depression and World War II, then fell to rough parity (for the federal government) or below (for state and local government) by 1949.[27] As figure 11-7 shows, average pay in government at all levels outpaced private sector pay starting in the 1970s, and even after a recent downturn still runs somewhat above the nongovernmental benchmark.

Figure 11-7, based on National Income and Product Accounts numbers, presents the data at an extremely high level of aggregation and also misses most benefits. Somewhat more complete and fine-grained data are available from the Bureau of Labor Statistics' National Compensation Survey, which records hourly compensation for many categories of workers, both in the private sector and in state and local government. Figure 11-8, based on the most recent (1998) National Compensation Survey data, shows that compensation levels for state and local government workers run higher than for those for private industry workers not just at the median and at the first decile level but at the ninth decile level as well. In other words, both near the low end and near the high end, state and local workers earn more than private workers. This general pattern holds for both broad categories, like white-collar and blue-collar workers, and for many narrower categories, including janitors, bus drivers, auto mechanics, and secondary school teachers. It is only for those working in a few especially high-paying occupations—such as lawyers, physicians, and computer analysts—that this pattern is reversed. More recent data are available from the Employ-

Figure 11-7. *Average Wage or Salary per Full-Time Equivalent Employee in Public Sector Relative to Private Sector, 1948–1998*

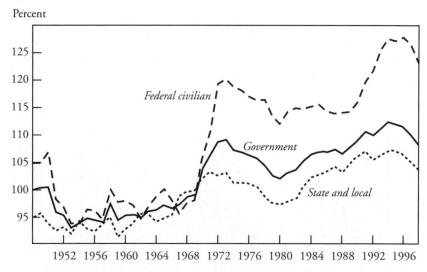

Source: Calculated from data in U.S. Department of Commerce, Bureau of Economic Analysis, *National Income and Product Account Tables,* tables 6.6B and 6.6C, revisions as of August 2000 (for pre-1995 data) and August 2001 (for post-1995 data), online version at www.bea.doc.gov/bea/dn/nipaweb/Index.asp (September 2001 and February 2002).

ment Cost Index, a larger but somewhat less detailed survey of total employment costs. The comparison for March 2000, summarized in figure 11-9, also shows compensation in state and local government running higher than in private industry for every major category except executive and managerial workers.[28]

No analogous data on total compensation are available for the federal sector. The Office of Personnel Management publishes detailed information on wages and salaries paid to federal employees, however, which can be paired with Census Bureau data to gain some sense of comparative pay levels. Figure 11-10 shows the distribution of federal pay levels relative to economy-wide pay levels (including the federal workers, but as a small share of the total) at intervals of $10,000 of annual individual earnings. Except at the very highest level—annual earnings exceeding $100,000—the federal distribution is skewed dramatically to the right.

A related distinction of public employment is well known, though its magnitude is often underestimated: the public work force is far more

Figure 11-8. *Hourly Compensation for Full-Time Workers in Private Sector and State and Local Government, 1998*

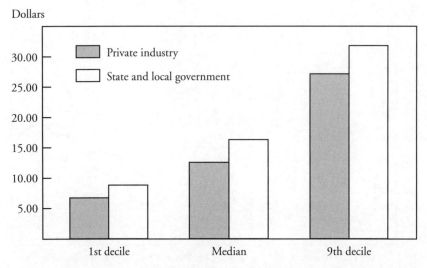

Source: U.S. Department of Labor, Bureau of Labor Statistics, *National Compensation Survey: Occupational Wages in the United States 1998* (September 2000), summary 01-04, supplementary tables 2.2 and 3.2.

unionized than the private work force. As labor organization has shriveled in the private sector it has thrived within government. As figure 11-11 illustrates, a government worker is more than four times as likely as a private sector worker to be a union member. The most heavily organized segment of the private sector (transportation and communications) is much less unionized than the least heavily organized segment of the public sector (state government).[29]

Is There a Public Sector Premium?

Considerable caution is required here. Workers in metropolitan areas earn more than rural workers, and employees of consulting firms outearn employees of fast-food restaurants. It does not follow that there is a big-city premium, or a consulting-firm premium, because differences in both the work to be done and the workers who do it may fully justify the discrep-

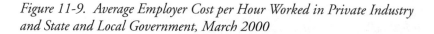

Figure 11-9. Average Employer Cost per Hour Worked in Private Industry and State and Local Government, March 2000

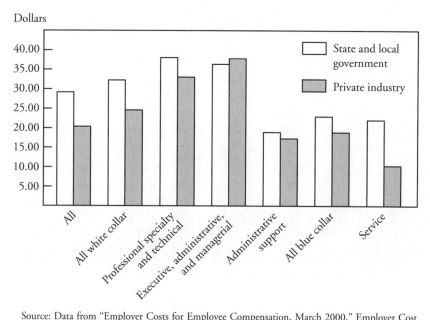

Source: Data from "Employer Costs for Employee Compensation, March 2000," Employer Cost Index release, June 29, 2000 (ftp:146.142.4.23/pub/news.release/ecec.txt [June 2001]), tables 3,4,6, and 10.

ancies. Similarly, government jobs are disproportionately administrative, professional, technical, or otherwise skill-intensive. Government workers tend to be better educated, more experienced, and more concentrated in urban areas than their private sector counterparts. So simple compensation comparisons do not tell us much. The search for government pay premiums (or discounts) requires deeper exploration, and the depths are inescapably murky.

In a perfectly efficient labor market, workers will be sorted across potential jobs so that each is paid just enough to induce him or her to do the work. Each will be adequately, but not excessively, compensated for the productivity of his or her contribution of training, experience, talent, and effort. There will be no systematic premiums (or "rents," in the economists' jargon) over this walk-away compensation package. Some workers, to be sure, will be earning more than the bare minimum to keep them on

Figure 11-10. Pay Distribution for Full-Time Workers in Federal Government and Economy-wide, 1999–2000

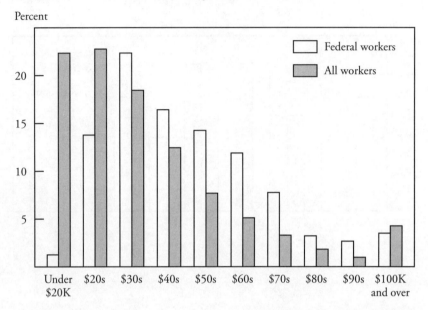

Source: Government pay data from U.S. Office of Personnel Management, "Pay Structure of the Federal Civil Service as of March 31, 2000" (Washington, November 2000), table 10. Economy-wide pay data from U.S. Department of Commerce, Bureau of the Census, *Current Population Survey, March Supplement,* Personal Income Table 10, online version at ferret.bls.census.gov/macro/03200/perinc/new10.001.htm (June 2001).

the job, because of their affinity or aptitude for a particular kind of occupation. These rents will be individual and idiosyncratic, however, rather than applying to whole classes of jobs or workers.[30]

Perfectly efficient labor markets, of course, are rare anywhere, but there are plenty of reasons to expect them to be rarer still in government. The public sector broadly lacks the characteristics on the demand side of the labor market—profit-motivated aversion to excess costs, full discretion in hiring, firing, and wage setting, and the concentrated efficiency incentives of private ownership—that would generate the textbook ideal of just-adequate compensation. So it would not be surprising for government to be more prone than business to pay more, or to pay less, than the minimum needed to recruit and retain adequately qualified workers.

Figure 11-11. Union Membership as Percentage of All Workers in the Public and Private Sectors, 2000

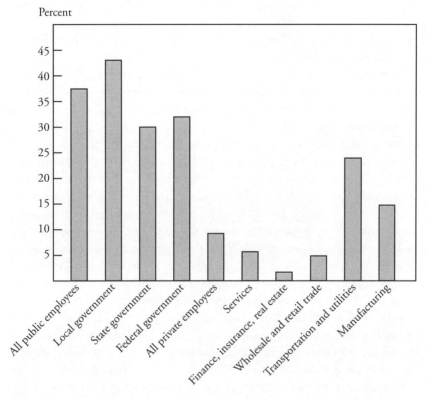

Source: U.S. Department of Labor, Bureau of Labor Statistics, "Union Members Summary," Economic News Release U3DL 02-28 (January 10, 2002), table 3.
Note: Numbers are percentages of each category of workers that are members of labor unions.

To know whether this actually occurs, we need to determine whether public sector pay differentials still show up once the effect of factors that quite properly shape relative pay are taken into account. Relevant factors may pertain to the nature of the work (skill requirements, geographic location, level of responsibility, risk of layoff or dismemberment, whether the job is tedious or gratifying, high-status or degrading) or to the nature of the workers (education and training, gender and ethnicity, years of experience, insight, capacity for teamwork, initiative, and so on). Once all such germane features have been controlled for in a statistically satisfying way, any remaining differential in compensation can be called a public sector premium or penalty. The hitch, of course, is that some of these complicating factors are measured routinely and well, some episodically and imperfectly, and some are highly resistant to measurement of any sort. Empiricists do what they can with the data they have, and the literature is illuminating but well short of conclusive.

Among the most frequently cited efforts in this area is a 1991 study of public-private wage differentials by Lawrence Katz and Alan Krueger.[31] The authors exploit a large data set drawn from the Current Population Survey to estimate relative wage levels in the private sector, the federal government, and state and local government, controlling for gender, race, education levels, years of experience, full-time versus part-time status, and urban versus nonurban locale. Their results point to a difference between more- and less-educated workers in the relative rewards of government work (see table 11-1). In 1988, white full-time workers in metropolitan areas with college degrees earned a small premium if they worked for the federal government but (especially men) suffered a much larger discount if they worked in state and local government. Workers with only a high school education, conversely, systematically fared better in government than they would have in the private sector, with a particularly large premium for female federal workers. (This benchmark Katz and Krueger study is a decade old and appears not to have been replicated recently. It seems likely that the public pay advantage for less educated workers may have narrowed somewhat as the 1990s boom solidified low-end earnings, while public sector discounts for the most educated may have grown as top rewards ratcheted up in the private sector.)

James Poterba and Kim Rueben have analyzed pay differentials between the private sector and state and local government, using an approach similar to Katz and Krueger's and a partly overlapping time period. Controlling for years of school, years of experience, location (that is, inside or outside a metropolitan area), marital status, and race, they find that the public sector advantage for less educated workers increased in the 1980s and early 1990s, while earnings for more educated workers grew more slowly than in the private sector.[32] Poterba and Rueben cite suggestive evidence that the growing public sector pay advantage at the lower end of the skills distribution is driven mostly by the eroding prospects of less educated workers in the private sector, not by improving public sector pay for such workers.[33]

Table 11-1. *Estimated Difference in Government Employee Wages Relative to Public Sector, 1988, by Level of Education Completed and Gender*
Percent

Education and gender	Federal government	State and local government
College graduates		
Men	+5	−18
Women	+2	−4
High school graduates		
Men	+16	+4
Women	+28	+10

Source: Author's calculations, data from Lawrence Katz and Alan Krueger, "Changes in the Structure of Wages in the Public and Private Sectors," *Research in Labor Economics*, vol. 12 (1991), table 1, p. 145.

Note: The estimates are for white, full-time workers with five years' work experience, living in metropolitan areas. The focus on relatively new workers is meant to better reflect recent labor market trends.

As they differentiate among categories of work and workers, Poterba and Rueben illustrate the complicated picture of comparative pay. They find that state and local government paid a premium in the early 1990s to men working as bus drivers, orderlies, cleaners, and teachers and to women working as practical nurses, receptionists, orderlies, cleaners, and (especially) primary and secondary school teachers. They find a public sector pay shortfall in the same period for men working as physicians and as truck drivers (a relatively unionized part of the private sector) and for women working as registered nurses (as opposed to licensed practical nurses) and as postsecondary teachers (as opposed to teachers of kindergarten through twelfth grade). Whereas men at all educational levels earned more in the private sector than in state and local government in 1979 (controlling for worker characteristics), by 1991 less educated men earned a modest premium in government. College-educated men working in government, conversely, earned 8 percent less than they would have in private industry, and men with postgraduate degrees earned 10 percent less. For women working in government in 1991 there was rough parity or a modest premium at all education levels, and the difference between public and private pay did not diverge sharply from what it had been twelve years earlier. There was some evidence, though, that the public sector pay edge was rising for less educated women and falling for those with more education.[34]

Claudia Goldin and Robert Margo have documented the "great compression" of American compensation that narrowed pay differentials in the 1940s and 1950s.[35] Earnings gaps shrank, both across groups (between blacks and whites, men and women, more educated and less educated workers) and within groups (a tighter pay distribution for college-educated white males with ten years of work experience, for example). The public sector shared in this midcentury tightening of the earnings distribution as both market forces and legislative changes constrained pay at the top end and propped it up at the bottom. In the 1970s this process began to reverse itself in the private economy. For a complex set of reasons—including rising trade and immigration, changing technology, shifts in labor laws and institutions, and, perhaps, a weakening of cultural scruples against disparate rewards—the earning power of less skilled workers (particularly males) crumbled in the private sector, while the prospects of better educated workers soared.

This "great *de*compression" of the past generation or so has mostly missed government. The basic story told by the pay differential literature is that America's public sector has proved largely impervious to the changes that roiled labor markets in roughly the final quarter of the past century. State and local government workers at the ninth decile earned 3.58 times as much as those at the first decile in 1998. For the private sector, the ratio was 4.03. The difference between business and government in this measure of near-the-top and near-the-bottom wage dispersion in 1998—around 13 percent—is roughly the same as the growth in the ratio of ninth- to first-decile earnings for all male workers from 1983 to 1998.[36] In short, the pattern of government pay—already less skewed toward the top than the market-driven template of the business world would suggest—flattened further in relative terms as private sector disparities intensified in the 1980s and 1990s. Two leading analysts of economic inequality suggest that the limited dispersion of pay within the modest (but not trivial) fraction of the work force employed by government has "served to dampen the overall rise in aggregate wage inequality."[37]

The pay differential literature sampled here, though revealing, is inconclusive for three broad reasons. The first is methodological uncertainty. There is room for honest disagreement about how to control for factors that blur the picture of relative pay. One study suggests that the apparent federal premium found by some authors is exaggerated by the statistical methods employed and shrinks sharply with alternative models.[38] Another claims that proper adjustment for the characteristics of occupations and workers reveals a trivial premium for state workers (in 1989) and a much larger discount for local workers.[39]

The second reason concerns limitations on data. The primary measurement instruments in this area (such as the Current Population Survey and the Employment Cost Index) are large-scale and frequent but capture only relatively coarse information. Unmeasured characteristics that surely matter in comparing relative pay, whether those of the workers (differences in native ability, energy, or diligence) or those of the work (differences in safety, tedium, status, or difficulty that gross occupational categories mask) can confound even artful analysis.

The third factor, related to the second, is that workers presumably *react* to differential pay, introducing troublesome selection bias into efforts to estimate differentials. If college-educated men, as a class, are badly paid in state and local government, the college-educated men who are nonetheless willing to work in state and local government may be less productive than average—in ways that alternative employers notice but surveys do not— and hence not underpaid at all. If less educated women fare especially well in the federal government, the women who get federal jobs may possess aptitudes that belie their limited formal schooling. Indeed, in principle workers should sort themselves out in response to premiums and discounts until nobody can do any better by switching sectors. The resulting pattern of employment may be inefficient, but any apparent government premium or discount would be illusory, the artifact of imperfect measurement.[40]

Despite murkiness about the magnitude and pattern of differences between compensation in business and government, several plausible hypotheses emerge (even if they remain something short of proven) from the evidence and arguments summarized here. First, it is highly probable that once the ambiguities discussed above were settled it would turn out that some public workers fare better than they would in the private sector, while others would fare worse. Some circumstantial evidence can be very strong, as Henry David Thoreau observed. The trout in the milk here include government's notorious difficulty in retaining top talent, the avidity with which many public jobs are sought,[41] and the grim resolve with which public workers' unions defend government work.[42]

Second, premiums are more common than discounts and go primarily to less skilled workers. At the high end, to be sure, private sector compensation vastly outpaces government pay; but the high end is a small sliver of the American work force. Median personal income in 1999 for full-time, year-round workers age twenty-five and older was less than $35,000, and only around 5 percent earned as much as $100,000. Just over one-quarter of adult workers held a four-year college degree. Fewer than 9 percent had advanced degrees of any kind—mostly masters' degrees, disproportionately in education—and barely 1.5 percent held the professional degrees that confer the greatest earning power.[43] The fact that those who debate relative public and private compensation tend to occupy high-end occupations may explain the prevalence of confusion about low-paying government work. Although public service may be financially unattractive to élites, it is quite the opposite for many workers who lack the high-level skills that the private economy increasingly rewards and demands.[44]

Third, a major shift toward market-driven service delivery would tend to worsen income inequality. If workers with high earning power have already fled government (or accommodated themselves to lower earnings in exchange for other rewards) while workers with leaner private sector prospects cling to public jobs, market-based government is likely to widen economic disparities economy wide. This is not a foregone conclusion. Only if there are rents at stake can the form of public service delivery have much of an impact on income distribution.[45] It is conceivable that workers have already sorted themselves out in response to pay differentials so that few have much to gain or lose if public service delivery becomes more exposed to the market's rigors and rewards. It is also possible that less affluent Americans would turn out to gain more from enhanced government efficiency than they would lose from tauter public labor markets.[46] But the most credible interpretation is that public employment offers a haven, for a sizable fraction of America's 20 million government workers, from a labor climate that has grown harsh for workers without advanced skills.

Suppose we were persuaded (once we invoked the criteria sidestepped here) that there is indeed a considerable range of government operations that could be improved through a heightened reliance on market principles and private providers. Suppose, further, that more detailed analysis were to confirm that one consequence (along with lower costs or improved performance) would be an erosion of the public sector enclave sheltered from twenty-first-century labor markets. Government would pay the most able workers enough to tempt them away from the soaring rewards talent can command in the private sector. At the other end of the scale, government would pay less able workers no more than they can earn in their best private sector alternative. (This could occur either by outsourcing public functions or by aligning public compensation more tightly with private sector pay scales.) Plunging deeper into the hypothetical, suppose we were confident that we could identify and seize the promising opportunities for market-driven government and avoid the traps and blind alleys.

Should we do it? The orthodox economic response is automatic and admirably coherent: Of *course*. Government's purpose is to provide collectively valuable goods and services, not to prop up individuals' paychecks. The guiding principle of a capitalist economy is that people endure competition in their roles as suppliers and are compensated with a rich menu of low-cost options in their roles as consumers. Restricting to government workers tasks that could be done more cheaply by private agents, or warping public pay distributions to limit disparities, flagrantly violates that principle. Even if we endorse the goal of curbing inequality, reserving functions for a rent-rich public work force is a cumbersome and morally arbitrary way of narrowing income differentials. It may be logically consistent to revise our basic capitalist bargain and say that the interests of producers should trump those of consumers and that government should do a great many things so that there will be a large number of good government jobs. That experiment has been run elsewhere on the planet, however, and few were persuaded by the results.

To declare that those people who happen to be currently employed by the government have rights to good, secure jobs that other workers lack, alternatively, is less radical but ethically random beyond defense, the indictment continues. Public workers' superior compensation is at best accidental and at worst organized embezzlement. So start by driving public employment practices into line with private labor markets. Then if direct government production turns out to be the most efficient and accountable way to handle postal services, or welfare-to-work counseling, or primary and secondary education, fine. If not, then turn to the private sector—and if public employment drops from 15 percent of the total to 10 percent, or 5 percent, or zero, so be it.

It is not possible to frame a similarly crisp and confident countercase, at least not without invoking theories that are badly dated, broadly discredited, and (even for socialism) heterodox.[47] To depart from the principle that government should strive for maximum productive efficiency is admittedly to invite confusion and mischief. On the other hand, I am not quite comfortable with the notion of ignoring the interests of public workers, and the idea of public employment, in decisions about how to accomplish collective tasks. The indignation of Public Choice economists at rent-seeking by parasitic public workers needs to be considered in context with the likely scale of any pay premiums; the bulge in the governmental pay distribution centers on a range of modestly middle-class incomes.[48] Public sector labor policies are one of the few mechanisms by which citizens' collectively expressed values (and not just their purchasing decisions) can influence economic outcomes.[49] Many of the past century's more laudable achievements in labor policy—including, notably, equal treatment for women and minorities—were pioneered by the public sector.

The demographic pattern of public employment, and particularly the huge overrepresentation of military veterans in federal service, hints that public sector premiums may not be quite so ethically random.[50] And even if public employment is a sadly clumsy weapon for combating economic inequality, the list of good alternatives is a short one.[51] Most broadly, public workplaces retain some features of the mid-twentieth-century American economy—status for workers that is not strictly scaled to their market leverage, effective labor organization to reinforce that respect, and a certain squeamishness about vast disparities in rewards—whose loss outside government has arguably coarsened our culture.

Yet these objections fall short of summing to a principle that no market-based reforms should be considered if they would hurt public workers. Is there some intermediate position between treating public workers' stakes as dispositive in decisions about market-driven government and ignoring those stakes altogether? Mapping the middle ground is likely to be an extensive undertaking only hinted at here. Whether it warrants the effort will depend on how long the list of otherwise-attractive restructuring candidates becomes.[52] Here I merely underscore the likelihood that we will confront at least some significant instances in which the institution of public employment and the interests of public workers will be at odds with considerations of efficient performance in decisions about how to accomplish public tasks. I offer three observations that may render the debate over market-driven government and the problem of public jobs marginally more productive.

The first observation is essentially analytical. We should be disciplined about differentiating the efficiency effects and the distributional effects of specific proposals for changing governmental operations. Cost savings can be the result of productivity advantages—a more rational scale of operations, management structures and strategies better suited to the task, a superior technical approach, and so on—or of driving a harder bargain with employees. Both of these effects occur. The two sources of savings—

real efficiency gains and losses to employees—are often commingled in the same restructuring, and both show up as simply "lower costs." The distinction is real enough in an economic sense, but it disappears in the accounting.

It is worth disentangling the two in the analysis of specific proposals and distinguishing between them in public presentations of the policy choice. Savings owing to a dismantling of relatively generous public employment practices essentially shift resources from citizens as producers to citizens as consumers. This is different from doing more with less. Virtually everyone favors the latter effect. Many favor the former as well; others oppose it. An informed public deliberation over the virtues and drawbacks of market-based government, however, requires that citizens be able to tell them apart. At present, both sides in the debate tend to see advantages in obscuring the difference, making it difficult for citizens to deal honestly with the stakes of the choice.

The second observation is operational. The best candidates for market-based reforms may be those that promise large efficiency advantages relative to the labor disruption they impose.[53] Whatever judgment one reaches about the validity of public workers' stakes, it is wise to minimize the losses inflicted on current government employees. This is true whether one believes public workers' stakes to be legitimate and those losses lamentable or whether one would simply like to economize on the political effort required to engineer efficiency gains. In practice, this implies a relative bias toward market-based approaches in newly launched services (where there are few existing interests to disrupt), or in areas in which private sector conditions of employment are not markedly inferior to those in government, or those in which the public work force is already shrinking through attrition or retirement.

The third observation is considerably broader. The more turbulent aspects of the debate over market-driven government reflect a submerged debate about labor policy. What makes outsourcing and related reforms particularly contentious in the United States is the widening gap between conditions of employment in the public and private sectors. We are awkwardly cramming a conversation about relative compensation, job security, and labor rights into a conversation about how government should select and compensate its personnel and what tasks it should delegate to outside organizations.

The American labor movement is reinforcing its stronghold in the public sector as its private sector presence dwindles and employment practices tilt toward laissez-faire. Government workers constituted nearly 44 percent of union membership in 2000, and an entirely plausible extension of recent trends would make government the employer of a majority of organized workers in the not-too-distant future.[54] As a matter of organizing tactics, this focus on the public sector makes eminent sense from labor's perspective. But on the strategic level it threatens disaster. The conscious and conspicuous defense of employment conditions for the delivery of tax-funded services that are superior to what the market offers most taxpayers promises to deepen hostility both toward government and toward the labor movement.

We will ultimately have to confront the disconnect between the conditions of employment prevailing in government and business. Some will prefer to level down toward the private sector model, dismantling governmental labor protections and creating more room for both risk and reward in the public sector. Others will prefer to level up toward the governmental model, updating and restoring bulwarks of labor rights that have eroded over recent decades. But so long as labor policy remains the tacit subtext of the debate, it will be hard to think clearly, or to talk honestly, about market-based government.

Notes

1. Robertson Stephens analyst Keith Dunne, quoted in Jed Graham, "Manufacturer Sanmina Proves to Be an Asset for Cost-Cutting IBM As $5 Billion PC Pact Inked; Outsourcing Trend Solid," *Investors' Business Daily,* January 9, 2002.

2. An example of the relevant popular literature is Daniel H. Pink, *Free Agent Nation* (New York: Warner Books, 2001); and of the scholarly literature is Katherine G. Abraham and Susan K. Taylor, "Firms' Use of Outside Contractors: Theory and Evidence," *Journal of Labor Economics,* vol. 14 (July 1996), pp. 394–424.

3. A casual scan of a random week's news yielded stories of outsourced child welfare services in Milwaukee, hospital management in Washington, D.C., highway maintenance in Oklahoma, and an open-ended list of state functions in Florida (Richard Foster, "Private Agencies to Handle Child Welfare," *Milwaukee Journal Sentinel,* May 31, 2001; "Health Care in Critical Condition," editorial, *Washington Post,* June 3, 2001; David Wasson and Mike Salinero, "Privatization Fears Spread," *Tampa Tribune,* May 29, 2001; and Bill May, "ODOT Meeting to Address Maintenance Privatization," *Oklahoma City Journal Record,* June 5, 2001. The American Federation of Government Employees charges that since the mid-1990s the number of civil servants at the Pentagon has dropped by nearly a third, while the number of contract workers has tripled to significantly outnumber the public workforce (American Federation of Government Employees, "New Report Shows Extraordinary Growth in DOD Contractor Workforce," press release, March 27, 2001).

4. *Federal Activities Reform Act of 1998*, P.L. 105-270.

5. Ellen Nakashima, "Bush Opens 40,000 Federal Workers' Jobs to Competition—Goal: Put 425,000 Positions Up for Grabs to Contractors," *Washington Post*, June 8, 2001.

6. This is particularly true for the Visions of Governance in the Twenty-First Century Project, the Harvard research program from which this book emerged.

7. See, for example, Lester M. Salamon, *The New Governance and the Tools of Public Action: A Handbook* (Oxford University Press, 2002); and Donald F. Kettl, *The Global Public Management Revolution* (Brookings, 2000). A somewhat more skeptical perspective can be found in B. Guy Peters, *The Future of Governing: Four Emerging Models* (University Press of Kansas, 1996).

8. Gerald McEntee, "Prison Privatization: Don't Be a Prisoner to Empty Promises" (www.afscme.org/private/index.html [February 27, 2002]).

9. Reason Public Policy Institute, introduction to *Privatization 2000* (Washington: Reason Foundation, 2000), p. 1.

10. The literature on this point is remarkably sparse and inconsistent. Just on the local level, for example, two studies using the same data series (a periodic survey by the International City/County Management Association) and overlapping time periods (1982 to 1992 for one, 1982 to 1997 for the other) draw different conclusions about the growth of outsourcing. The study ending in 1992 (J. D. Greene, "How Much Privatization? A Research Note Examining the Use of Privatization by Cities in 1982 and 1992," *Policy Studies Journal*, vol. 24 [Winter 1996]) finds a significant increase in privatization. The one ending in 1997 (Mildred Warner and Amir Hefetz, "Privatization and the Market Structuring Role of Local Government," paper presented at the Economic Policy Institute conference, Washington, January 11, 2001) finds that outsourced services crept up from 22 to 24 percent of all services over the fifteen-year period.

11. It is also unclear what effect market-based government should be expected to have on the size of the public work force. If changes in delivery models boost efficiency to a sufficient degree and with sufficient clarity that citizens demand (and are willing to pay for) more public goods and services, headcount could increase overall, even if it declines relative to the scale of the state. I am indebted to Richard Zeckhauser for pointing out this demand effect.

12. Different definitions yield somewhat different totals for the public work force. By some measures the 1999 total was rather less than 20 million; by others, more than 21 million. All data in the following sentence are from the tables in U.S. Bureau of the Census, Governments Division, "Federal, State, and Local Governments Public Employment and Payroll Data" (www.census.gov/govs/www/apes.html [February 21, 2001]).

13. U.S. Office of Management and Budget, *Budget of the U.S. Government, Fiscal Year 2001*, Historical Table 17.5 (www.access.gpo.gov/usbudget/fy2001/hist.html#h17 [February 27, 2001]).

14. It is worth noting, for a sense of perspective, that the relative scale of public employment was lower in the United States than in all but thirteen of the sixty-four countries for which the United Nations International Labour Organization (ILO) gathered data in the 1990s. The ratio of the government work force to the private work force during the 1990s fell in nearly all the countries the ILO surveyed—the member nations of the Organization for Economic Cooperation and Development, developing nations, and transition economies (Messaoud Hammaouya, "Statistics on Public-Sector Employment: Methods,

Structures, and Trends," Working Paper 144 (Geneva: International Labour Organization, Bureau of Statistics, 1999), tables 1 and 4, figures 16, 17, and 18.

15. Some of this story is told in John D. Donahue, *Disunited States* (Basic Books, 1997).

16. Office of Management and Budget, *Budget of the U.S. Government, Fiscal Year 2001,* Historical Table 15.5.

17. Adjusting the spending figures is simple. These transfer programs, which are reported separately by the Office of Management and Budget, are simply subtracted from the public spending totals. Adjusting headcount is trickier. The Office of Management and Budget's figures combine Social Security Administration and Health Care Financing Administration employees with all other workers in the Department of Health and Human Services as well as the Department of Education (which used to be part of the predecessor agency, the Department of Health, Education, and Welfare). Workers administering Social Security and Medicare comprise less than half of the Health and Human Services and Education Departments total, so this crude adjustment makes the ratio of public workers to public work look a little lower than it really is. Because this approach does not adjust for other transfer program spending and personnel (notably, Medicaid), it should be taken as highly approximate.

18. Paul Light, *The True Size of Government* (Brookings, 2000), has attempted a comparable estimation method, though it is at once more ambitious and more methodologically delicate and covers only the federal government.

19. This effort involved preliminary research by this author followed by well over a month of painstaking work by research associate Steven Minicucci.

20. The starting point for this baseline is "current operations" in the Government Finances series, or "government consumption" in the National Income and Product Accounts data. While the two data series are not strictly independent, they are substantially different. The basic calculation described here was carried out for selected years in two ways, one starting with the Census data, the other with the Bureau of Labor Statistics data. The two methods yielded extremely similar results, giving some reason for confidence that this approach, while coarse, is basically sound.

21. Depreciation of fixed capital is also excluded, which would be a major error for some purposes but is not directly relevant to this particular measurement question.

22. The figures for 2000 rely on more preliminary data and a higher degree of estimation than those for earlier years.

23. The share of Department of Defense spending going to nonemployee services, which had been around one-quarter from the late 1950s to the mid-1980s, surged to more than one-third in 1999, whereas the corresponding share of nondefense spending other than Medicare dropped during the late 1990s, reaching its lowest level since the early 1960s. This is at least roughly consistent with Paul Light's finding that the Department of Defense accounted for nearly 85 percent of federal positions assessed for potential outsourcing under A-76 process between 1988 and 1997 (*The True Size of Government,* table 5-1, p. 149).

24. I recognize that this may itself be included in a broad definition of "privatization."

25. John D. Donahue, *The Privatization Decision* (Basic Books, 1989).

26. As will be addressed shortly, this is owing partly to the nature of the work, partly to the characteristics of the workers, and partly (and least simply) to the distinctive dynamics of public sector labor markets.

27. Robert A. Margo and T. Aldrich Finegan, "Changes in the Distribution of Wages, 1940–1950: The Public versus the Private Sector," Working Paper W5389 (Cambridge, Mass.: National Bureau of Economic Research, December 1995), pp. 4–8. These figures, like figure 11-7 in this chapter, simply compare average wages or salaries and do not take into account differences in work or workers across sectors.

28. Benefits form a significantly higher share of employment costs in the public sector than in the private sector, making these total compensation comparisons far more relevant than wage and salary comparisons.

29. Recent statistical work by David Card supports the notion that labor organization is a factor in relatively low wage inequality in the public sector (David Card, "The Effect of Unions on Wage Inequality in the U.S. Labor Market," *Industrial and Labor Relations Review*, vol. 54 [January 2001]).

30. Some analysts suggest the right wage is generally one at a level above the walk-away point, but for present purposes we can bypass the "efficiency wage" literature catalyzed by Alan Krueger and Lawrence Summers in "Efficiency Wages and the Inter-Industry Wage Structure," *Econometrica*, vol. 56, no. 2 (1988).

31. Lawrence Katz and Alan Krueger, "Changes in the Structure of Wages in the Public and Private Sectors," *Research in Labor Economics*, vol. 12 (1991).

32. James M. Poterba and Kim S. Rueben, "The Distribution of Public Sector Wage Premia: New Evidence Using Quantile Regression Methods," Working Paper W4734 (Cambridge, Mass.: National Bureau for Economic Research, May 1994).

33. Ibid., pp. 23–24.

34. Ibid., table 7, p. 33; table 6, p. 32.

35. Claudia Goldin and Robert Margo, "The Great Compression: The Wage Structure in the United States at Mid-Century," *Quarterly Journal of Economics*, vol. 107 (February 1992).

36. The 1998 comparisons are from the Bureau of Labor Statistics National Compensation Survey and cover only earnings from work. The comparison between 1983 and 1998 is based on data from the March Current Population Survey Supplement and includes all money income, so it is only roughly comparable (Current Population Survey, "Supplemental Income Inequality Tables," table IE-2, "Measures of Individual Earnings Inequality for Full-Time, Year-Round Workers by Sex: 1967 to 2000" [www.census.gov/hhes/income/histinc/ie2.html (June 20, 2001)]).

37. Margo and Finegan, "Changes in the Distribution of Wages, 1940–1950: The Public versus the Private Sector," p. 3.

38. Brent R. Moulton, "A Reexamination of the Federal-Private Wage Differential in the United States," *Journal of Labor Economics*, vol. 8, no. 2 (1990).

39. Dale Belman and John Heywood, "The Truth about Public Employees: Underpaid or Overpaid?" Briefing Paper (Washington: Economic Policy Institute, 1993).

40. The adjustment could take place in many ways, of course. Government employers could select from applicant queues through a range of legitimate or questionable criteria; public jobs could become unpleasant enough that workers were just compensated by the higher pay; and so on. Dale Belman and John S. Heywood explore the possibility that relatively high-paying states employ an overqualified workforce ("State and Local Government Wage Differentials: An Intrastate Analysis," *Journal of Labor Research*, vol. 16 [Spring 1995], pp. 196–98).

41. A casual search on Amazon.com yielded at least eight books promising applicants an edge in landing a job with the Postal Service, with nothing comparable for FedEx. For the record, all eight appear to sell more briskly than most books written by academics, including myself.

42. The American Federation of Government Employees—the largest federal union, representing about six hundred thousand workers—has mounted a campaign entitled "Stop Wasting America's Money through Privatization" (known, of course, as SWAMP) (www.afge.org/SWAMP/index.htm [February 21, 2001]). This and other unions deploy both legal and political tactics in an aggressive struggle against federal outsourcing. At the state and local level, the 2000 convention of the American Federation of State, County, and Municipal Employees highlighted a resolution "to redouble our commitment to fighting privatization on all fronts" (American Federation of State, County, and Municipal Employees, "Resolution 86," presented at the union's International Convention, Philadelphia, June 26–30, 2000. The battle by the teachers' unions to block private school vouchers has been waged with formidable resolution and remarkable success.

43. The earning and education figures in these two sentences are based on Current Population Survey, Annual Demographic Survey, March Supplement 2000, "Selected Characteristics of People 15 Years and Over by Total Money Income in 1999, Work Experience in 1999, Race, Hispanic Origin, and Sex," table PINC-01 (ferret.bls.census.gov/macro/032000/perinc/new01_001.htm [June 20, 2001]).

44. The American Federation of State, County, and Municipal Employees Resolution 86 cited above declares that turning to outside suppliers for public service delivery "is often simply an attempt to operate in a low-wage, non-union environment" ("The AFSCME Privatization Campaign," p. 1). This is substantially (though not universally) true. James Buchanan, the Nobel-laureate dean of the Public Choice school, charges that "self-seeking bureaucrats" attempt to shape government operations in ways that serve their interests but diverge from the interests of the rest of the public ("Why Does Government Grow," in Thomas Borcherding, ed., *Budgets and Bureaucrats* [Duke University Press, 1977], p. 11). Other contributions to this theme include Don Bellante and James Long, "The Political Economy of the Rent-Seeking Society: The Case of Public Employees and Their Unions," *Journal of Labor Research,* vol. 2 (Spring 1981). There is truth in this as well. Public workers do endeavor to maintain public spending and to ensure that public services are provided by government workers. Their motives are not limited to self-interest, though they surely include it.

45. It is not clear that rents derived from public employment systematically flow toward less favored workers. At the federal level, where budgets are funded largely by progressive income taxes, the net effect is probably somewhat redistributive. The tax structure in most states, however, tilts fiscal burdens toward taxpayers who are not notably more affluent than the average state employee. The local picture is even more complex: The property taxes that dominate local government finances tend to be progressive within a jurisdiction (though not across localities), yet the biggest category of local employment is relatively well-paid education work. Without a detailed sense of how discounts and premiums are distributed across public jobs, it is impossible to specify the net distributive effect.

46. The most plausible story here is that improved efficiency, thanks to market-driven methods, would boost the willingness of better-off citizens to accept higher government spending. However, see chapter 13 in this volume for a cautionary note on this score.

47. My grasp of socialist theory is shaky, but I am not aware of any major variant that casts government employees as the vanguard.

48. This is not the case in some developing economies, and the themes of this chapter may not be exportable.

49. See, however, chapter 7 in this volume for an example of work on expanding market-based mechanisms for giving force to individuals' values.

50. The federal government payroll includes three times the number of veterans as the overall economy's proportion of veterans—the result of explicit hiring preferences. African Americans also disproportionately hold federal jobs, though women are slightly and Hispanic Americans substantially underrepresented (Office of Personnel Management, Federal Civilian Workforce Statistics, "Demographic Profile of the Federal Workforce as of September 30, 2000," table 1.1; private sector comparisons from Current Population Survey data).

51. The Earned Income Tax Credit is certainly more efficient (though of limited reach), and minimum wages prop up low-end incomes (though at some economic cost); improving education and training is a philosophically more satisfying (but long-term and uncertain) approach.

52. My guess is that the list will prove reasonably extensive.

53. The trend to outsource management while keeping rank-and-file workers on the public payroll is consistent with this.

54. U.S. Department of Labor, Bureau of Labor Statistics, *Labor Force Statistics from the Current Population Survey*, table 3, "Union Affiliation of Employed Wage and Salary Workers by Occupation and Industry" (stats.bls.gov/news.release/union2.toc.htm [June 20, 2001]).

12

MARK H. MOORE

Privatizing Public Management

Public enthusiasm for the ideas of privatization and marketization has had a profound impact on the way America thinks about the proper scope of government. By the *scope* of government, I mean the set of purposes that citizens have asked the government to assume responsibility for achieving. Those who embrace the ideas of privatization and marketization often say, for example, that government should interfere as little as possible with the natural workings of a private economy, or they say that government should stick to its "core competencies" and resist being dragged into areas in which it cannot perform well. These are claims about the proper reach of government in society.

The ideas of privatization and marketization have also had an important impact, however, on how Americans think about the means government relies upon to achieve its mandated ends as well as the ends themselves. For example, governments are urged to take advantage of market-like mechanisms to help them achieve their objectives; to take maximum advantage of private enterprise in the pursuit of public goals; and to run public organizations in more business-like ways.

The current popularity for the business model of government signals another important belief about privatization and marketization: the idea that management ideas from the private sector can make an important contribution to the way that public bureaucracies are managed. Government organizations, for example, are now expected to focus on "customer service" and to develop measurable "bottom lines" to enhance their accountability to citizens and motivate their efforts on improving performance. It is also thought that government would become more efficient if it made less and bought more—that is, if government contracted its work out to efficient private sector enterprises rather than continuing to rely on rigid, inefficient government bureaucracies.[1] These three notions—customer service, the bottom line, and contracting out—are at the heart of the privatization model of public management.

Improving Customer Service

Of all the ideas about the model of private sector management in government, the one that has probably had the broadest and most subtle impact has been the notion that government as a whole could best be conceptualized as a large "service enterprise" that lives or dies on the quality of service it provides to its customers. Just as the private sector had to learn that it could not take customer loyalty for granted, so the government has to give up the arrogance that goes along with bureaucratic power and work harder to ensure that citizens' encounters with their government are convenient and satisfying. Just as the private sector had to learn to be highly responsive to changing and heterogeneous customer demands, so the public sector needs to abandon its rigid, autocratic bureaucracy in favor of a corps of flexible civil servants who want nothing more than to be of help to citizens who contact them for assistance. This idea is considered so self-evidently meritorious that the administrations of both Bill Clinton and George W. Bush have based their management agendas on the concept of customer service.

There is much to commend this particular idea. Anyone who has had a government window snapped shut in her face, or has waited in a long line to be told that he lacked the appropriate documentation for some privilege he sought, can immediately understand the virtue of better treatment. To the extent that the focus on customer service has caused government organizations to make themselves more respectful and more conveniently accessible, all Americans can be grateful for the result. Yet the idea that the individual citizens with whom government interacts should be treated as customers has some deeply problematic aspects. To understand the problem, it is important to look closely at the idea of "customer" in the private sector and see how it carries over into the world of the public sector.

Customers in the Private Sector

The idea of a "customer" in a market has at least three important connotations. The first is that a customer has a particular location in the "value chain" that constitutes the productive processes of an enterprise. Customers are encountered in individual transactions at the business end of the organization, where the rubber meets the road, so to speak. They are the ones who get the specific product or service that the organization supplies.[2]

The second is that the customer is also the person who pays for the product or service and, in so doing, provides the financial wherewithal for the organization to carry on. At the outset, of course, before an organization is actually producing products and services, it secures resources through capital financing. That capital financing, however, will only last for a while. In the end, financial sustainability and organizational survival depend on actual customers who are willing to pay for the product or service being offered and at prices and in quantities that will more than cover the costs of producing the products and services.

The third and least commonly acknowledged but perhaps most important idea about a customer in the private sector is that it is the customer's satisfaction that provides the ultimate justification for the private firm's existence. It is tempting for someone who has been operating in the public sector, coping with problems such as the relief of hunger or the care of the handicapped, to look at the products and services produced by the private sector with a certain disdain. What, they might ask, is the value of producing such useless things as lemon-scented furniture polish or hula hoops when there are so many other urgent problems in the world? Compared with the importance of the products and services the public sector provides, where is the value in such trivial products?

Yet private sector managers have a pretty convincing answer to this question. They simply note that such things are presumed to be valuable because individual customers are willing to take hard-earned money out of their pockets and plunk it down on the counter to buy them. In doing so, customers are giving fairly incontrovertible evidence that they value these products and services and, furthermore, that they value them at a price in excess of the cost of production. To the extent that society as a whole thinks it is socially valuable to organize itself to satisfy individual consumer desires, then, one can say that a certain kind of public value is being created by the production of lemon-scented furniture polish and hula hoops. It is this kind of reasoning that provides the social justification for the spread of markets and that makes the enhancement of customer satisfaction an important normative as well as instrumental goal of private sector organizations.

Customers in the Public Sector

These three ideas associated with the idea of "customer" in the private sector point to quite different actors when the "customer" is transferred to the public sector, and there is no actor who combines all three qualities. In the first sense, as the individuals who receive the product or service an organization is producing, it is clear who the customers of government are: in a school system, it is the student (or perhaps the parents); in the health-care system, the patient; in the employment training sector, the unemployed worker hoping to learn skills; in the welfare sector, the unsupported mother seeking financial help in caring for herself and her children. These people all resemble customers in the private sector in that they receive the products or services delivered by public sector enterprises. They also, for the most part, seem both to benefit from and to like the service they receive.

As the individuals who occupy the position at the tail end of the production process, and appear as beneficiaries, however, the "customers" of government may lack some other important characteristics of customers in the private sector. Most important, perhaps, these individuals typically do not pay the full cost of the product or service they receive. (If they did, the enterprise would not have to be publicly supported in any way.) Typically, the public as a whole is subsidizing the cost of these services with tax dollars.[3]

If it is the public as a whole, rather than those who directly receive government services, that pays for the delivery of those services, then an important question arises as to whose satisfaction constitutes the normative justification for the enterprise. One can argue, of course, that the point of a government enterprise is to make its clients happy—to make sure that students like school, that patients feel well cared for in hospitals, that the jobless find their training programs inspiring and helpful, that welfare recipients feel that they are treated with dignity and compassion. It is quite possible that the public that is paying for the service would agree with this idea; given the opportunity, they might write into the mission statement of the organization that their aim includes the important goal of making its clients happy in addition to any other goals it might have. In this case, the potential tension between the ambitions of the collective and the satisfaction of the individual clients would be resolved decisively in favor of satisfying the clients.

The public often has other goals, however, in addition to satisfying clients. For example, in schools, society has the goal of educating children, not just pleasing them. It wants the children to learn to read and write, whether or not the children or their parents share this goal. Similarly, in health-care settings, the quality of the care is not judged simply by whether the rooms are comfortable and the staff treats the patients politely (the service shell that could be wrapped around low-quality medical care to make it feel good to the patients); quality care is also judged in terms of whether it achieves the socially (and individually) desired result of restoring health. Given the importance of the second goal, the public may quite appropriately deliver high-quality medical service stripped of its attractive wrapper of customer service. In the context of job training and welfare programs, it is also true that society has ambitions for these clients that differ to some degree from merely satisfying their desires. We want the poorly skilled to learn trades and get jobs, not just to enjoy themselves; and we want welfare recipients to find ways to reduce their dependency on the state.

Indeed, the fact that society has interests in such programs beyond the satisfaction of the clients is clear in the ways in which such programs are evaluated. If the clients of government programs had the same normative importance in the public sector that customers have in the private sector, government programs could be evaluated simply by asking the clients whether they valued the services they had received. If they said yes, and claimed that they would have been willing to pay at least as much as the cost of providing the service to them, then the program could be presumed valuable. That is not generally how government evaluates social programs, however. Instead, government tries to determine whether the program achieved the outcomes that society had in mind when it launched the program. Did children learn to read and write? Did patients' health improve? Have the unemployed found jobs? Have welfare recipients been able to care for their children and gain economic independence? If these social goals (in technical language, social, rather than individual, "utility functions") are achieved at a reasonable cost, the program is considered to have been socially valuable, and if the social goals are not met, the program is deemed a failure—regardless of client satisfaction.

This is not to say that client satisfaction is unimportant or entirely irrelevant. As noted above, authorization of a particular program might have included the mandate that the program should satisfy its clients. Indeed, the appropriateness of requiring government to pay attention to some aspects of individual citizen satisfaction has long been recognized and is the basis for granting the individual certain constitutional rights. These continue to have significant force in shaping the kind of services government provides in the domains of education, mental health, juvenile corrections, and so on. To the extent that such goals are present in the authorization for a government program, either as expressed aspiration for the program or as constitutional rights, the collective has enshrined concern for the welfare of individual clients as an important goal of a policy or program.

Even if the goal of satisfying clients (or protecting their rights) is not written into the policy instructions that guide public managers, however, government might still be interested in producing client satisfaction as a means to social ends rather than an end in itself. That is, in organizing a school, or a hospital, or a training program, or a welfare program to achieve social goals other than client satisfaction, the collective, or the managers who act in their name, might decide that the social goals can only, or can best, be achieved if the program is operated in ways that made the clients happy. They could decide, for example, that it is important to students' learning that they like school, not merely endure it. They could decide that it is consistent with the aim of helping welfare recipients to get off the dole to treat them with dignity and respect. Thus client satisfaction can be viewed as an important way of efficiently and effectively accomplishing the socially desired result.

Whether the collective views client satisfaction as an end or a means, however, what is important here is that the collective gets to decide on how it will value individual client satisfaction in its collectively financed enterprises. The collective's preferences count because it is the choice of the collective to tax and regulate themselves to produce the desired social result that established the public program. That choice may have given more or less standing to the satisfaction of individual clients as an object of public value.

The Delivery of Obligations

Government is not only in the business of providing services to clients. It is also in the business of imposing obligations on individual citizens. This is most obvious in law enforcement organizations. Do people serving time in prison or arrested for a crime think of themselves as receiving a service? Would society as a whole think that the point of corrections departments and police departments is to make their clients happy?

Similar issues arise in regulatory agencies designed to keep the air and water clean or the workplace safe. Here, too, the clients of the organizations are typically firms that may receive some technical advice from the government in learning how to reduce the pollution or workplace hazards created by their production practices but also often find themselves faced with obligations to change those practices. These issues arise in tax-collecting agencies, as well. Taxpayers may receive the help of the organization in understanding exactly what they owe in taxes, but ultimately they face obligations to pay up on pain of civil and criminal sanctions if they fail to comply.

Authority As an Asset

What is interesting about these situations is not only that clients are receiving obligations from the government, rather than services, but also that the government is deploying a particular asset, one that private sector firms typically cannot deploy: in these cases, the government is using its authority, rather than its money, to accomplish social purposes. To many, it seems odd to think of authority as an asset for the government. For one thing, legitimate authority lacks a physical form. We can see the effects of authority when it is exercised—we note when the tax collector has cashed our check, we are clear about the moment when the policeman demands that we drive more slowly or stand still to answer questions, we can see the regulatory inspector shut down a polluting firm. However, we cannot see and count the stock of authority that the state has at its disposal; we can only see the flow of authority as it is used.

Similarly, it is not clear that authority can be used up and consumed like other assets. The legitimacy of the state's authority can wear thin with use. Indeed, it might wear out particularly quickly with frequent abuses of authority. It is likely that as the state's legitimacy ebbs, it may have to use more physical coercion to achieve the same compliance with its rules that it once got when it enjoyed greater legitimacy. This suggests that authority can, in some important sense, get used up. The effective authority of the state can also increase with the use of it. Indeed, that is the whole idea of deterrence: that the authority of the state can be used in ways that magnify its effect. In these respects, authority is unlike other kinds of physical or economic assets.

Finally, authority is not usually thought of as achieving a result nor as justifiable based on its utility in producing a particular result. In the common conception, the use of authority should be guided by ideas of justice: of what individuals owe to one another and of what the state can expect and demand of individual citizens as a matter of principle. Authority is not to be dragged out any time it is useful. There has to be some idea that it is right to use authority, that the person who feels the obligation can understand the reason for it, as well as understanding its usefulness.

These important observations tend to undermine any simple claim that it would be possible to think of authority as an asset of government. Yet it is also important to recognize that authority is, in fact, an important asset to government in at least two significant senses. First, authority can be used interchangeably with money to achieve some desired social results. If an important goal of government is to provide for the common defense, for example, then the collective can achieve that result in either of two ways: it can raise money and offer to pay people to serve in the military, or it can institute a draft. The first method uses state money to accomplish the goal; the second uses state authority. If it wants to clean up the air and water, it can do so by offering to pay polluting firms for the costs of cleaning up or by compelling the firms to stop dumping pollutants in the air and water through the use of regulation. Again, it can use either money or authority to accomplish the job it has been assigned to do.

Authority might also be similar to money in the sense that society is as interested in economizing on its use as it is in economizing on the use of tax dollars. Generally speaking, public enterprises depend on both money and authority to achieve their purposes. Both are taken from private individuals to achieve public purposes. The money is taken from private consumption, the authority is taken from private liberty. Because liberty is highly valued in our society, it is reasonable to suppose that citizens would prefer that the least possible authority be used in accomplishing a particular purpose, on the premise that it is better to induce people to contribute to public purposes than to force them to do so. When force becomes necessary, we might want it to be used legitimately and appropriately.

The use of force differs from the use of public money in important ways, however, not the least of which is the normative framework used to evaluate it. In judging the use of public funds, we are usually primarily interested in how efficiently and effectively the funds have been used. This is a concern with the use of authority, as well. But in an evaluation of the use of authority, the focus often is on how justly or fairly, rather than how efficiently, the authority was used. We want to be sure that individuals were treated justly, that they "got what they deserved," and that their rights were protected. In short, the use of authority to accomplish goals invokes important concerns about equity and fairness as well as efficiency and effectiveness.

Most of the money that government uses to accomplish collectively defined purposes is raised through taxes—that is, through the use of collectively owned authority. If it is true that the money government uses to accomplish its purposes relies on authority, then it seems reasonable to suppose that some of the special concerns that attach to the use of authority would also attach to the use of government tax dollars. Like authority itself, money raised through the use of authority has to be spent not only economically but also fairly. This follows as a natural consequence of viewing authority as a collectively owned asset that can be used only for the benefit of all and of recognizing that government money is raised through the use of authority. Government cannot spend money for efficiency reasons alone; it must spend it fairly to produce certain kinds of equity as well.

Insofar as government is concerned about producing equity in the pursuit of substantive objectives as well as the substantive objectives themselves, then what it means to be a customer of government is again transformed. Equity brings in some notion of individual entitlement or desert as well as a notion of socially recognized need or individual ability to pay as characteristics that guide the flow of governmental activity to particular individuals. To the extent that government programs are designed to produce equity—that is, to give to individuals what the collective has entitled them to receive rather than what they need, want, or are willing to pay for—collectively defined goals, once again, trump individual desires. Here, however, the social goals include justice and fairness (as it has been collectively defined) rather than simply the efficient production of goods and services or the achievement of desired social outcomes.

In sum, the idea of a customer translates rather badly into the world of public sector production and management. Those whom government agencies meet as individual clients at the tail end of their production processes do not pay for the service. Nor does their satisfaction constitute the important justification of the enterprise. The welfare of the clients can be counted as important and socially valuable if the collective has so stated or if it turns out to be an effective means of achieving desired social results. One cannot assume at the outset, however, that the point of the exercise is to satisfy the clients.

Furthermore, both in circumstances in which society is providing services to clients and those in which they are bringing obligations to bear, public sector enterprises must be able to show that they operate fairly as well as efficiently and effectively. This follows from the fact that government authority is nearly always being used in some way when the government takes action on behalf of collectively defined ambitions, and, as a normative principle in a democratic society, government authority has to be used fairly as well as economically and effectively. Because fairness is not simply a property of the subjective experience of the client but is also a socially defined quality both in individual transactions and in the aggregate operations of a public sector entity, the overall social value produced by a public organization departs even further from individual valuations of what the organization produces. Government enterprises are in the business of achieving collectively defined goals with the least and fairest possible uses of the money and authority of the state. They are not in the business of satisfying customers.

Defining the Public Sector's Bottom Line

A second important managerial idea brought to the public sector from the world of private sector management is that government managers should create a functional equivalent to the private sector's famed "bottom line." The basic assumptions are that this will help public sector agencies become more accountable to their citizen-owners; force them to think carefully and concretely about what they really mean to accomplish; and improve performance in the organization's operations. As with the idea of "customer service," the idea that government agencies should create bottom lines for themselves is considered so self-evidently sensible that legislatures throughout the country have passed legislation mandating the development of "performance measurement systems" that can reveal the value produced by public organizations as reliably as private sector financial measures reveal the value they have been able to produce.

Again, there is much to recommend this idea—more, I think, than the idea that government should focus on customer service. Indeed, I count myself one of the most ardent supporters of the notion that government should make major efforts to improve the measurement of its performance. Developing and relying on such measures is, in my opinion, probably the single most important thing that can be done to improve the performance of public sector organizations.

Yet, once again, we must be careful in transporting an important private sector idea into the public sector environment. The difficulties in translating the concept of a "customer" both signals and helps us to understand the ways in which it is necessary to reconstruct the simple idea of business's "bottom line" in a useful form in the public sector. To see why this is so, it is necessary to understand what the "bottom line" is in the private sector and why it has the power it seems to have in producing improved performance in private sector organizations.

The Bottom Line in the Private Sector

The "bottom line" in the private sector is a financial measure. Specifically, it measures the relationship between the revenues a firm earns by selling its products and services to willing customers, on one hand, and the costs of producing those products and services, on the other. If revenues exceed costs, we say that the enterprise is profitable.

The fact that a firm is profitable means a lot. As a practical matter, it means that its investors can be paid and its managers and employees can anticipate continued employment. The fact that a private firm makes a profit also means, however, that it is plausible to assume that the firm has created value. This follows from accepting two important ideas: first, that the customers' valuations of the organization's outputs were recorded with some precision through their voluntary choice to buy them at a particular price; second, that the real social costs of producing the goods and services were accurately reflected in the prices that the firm had to pay for the materials, labor, and capital it used to create the products and services. If consumers valued the product at more than the cost of producing it, then arguably value has been created by the firm's operations.

The financial bottom line is a relatively clear and objective way of summarizing and assessing the net value that a firm produces. Because it is so clear and so objective, simple reporting of the facts tends to end arguments about whether the firm has been successful. Consequently, instead of arguing endlessly about what constitutes good performance, the firm can focus its attention on producing results. That makes the firm much more disciplined and focused.

For the bottom line to carry behavioral power, the information on which it is based must be relatively inexpensive for a firm to gather and must come in quickly and continuously. A private sector firm can understand its costs simply by keeping track of its expenditures. (This is routine cost accounting.) It can understand the value it produces simply by keeping track of its revenues. (This is routine financial management.) The firm does not have to spend time and effort going outside the boundaries of the organization to find out how the customer actually used the product and whether it really did improve the customer's quality of life in some way. Nor does it have to wait to see what effect the product or service has had on the customer. All the relevant information about value is present as the cash crosses the counter.

Private sector firms get a huge amount of information about their performance from their financial management systems. They know their costs. They know their revenues. They can interpret their revenues as a reliable expression of the value of their output. They can directly compare revenues to costs, and they can do so for a wide variety of products they produce. In all these ways, the bottom line is truly a powerful idea in the private sector. It would be terrific if the public sector could have something comparable.

A Bottom Line for the Public Sector

As in the case of "customer service," however, the idea of a bottom line has to make a somewhat tortuous journey as is crosses from the private to the public sector. The identification of the economic and financial costs of producing governmental output remains pretty much intact as it crosses from the private to the public sector. In principle, it should be no more difficult for public sector managers to discover their costs than for private sector managers. After all, government managers pay prices for factors of production just as private firms do. Those costs register in expenses the organization makes. All they need do to understand their costs is to apply the elementary principles of cost accounting.

The problem arises, however, when government managers try to capture the information contained in the second part of the bottom line—namely, the "revenue" number. Government agencies have financial revenues, of course. They need money to buy the materials, pay the salaries, and maintain the buildings in which they carry out their operations. Some of these revenues might even be earned by charging clients fees for particular products and services. For the most part, however, the financial revenues used by government agencies do not come from the sale of products and services to willing customers. They come instead from taxes imposed on the general population to support a collectively decided purpose.

This fact has three important consequences for public managers. First, it changes our ideas about who determines the value of the output of the public agency. If customers are not spending their money to buy government's products and services, then how is the value of those products and services to be determined? The answer is that it is the collective, acting through the (admittedly clumsy) machinery of representative government, that is assigning value to public sector output. It is the purposes set out in policy mandates and organizational missions, authorized and approved by legislatures and refined in executive branch policymaking—not the clients—that define the value produced by public sector organizations.

Second, if the public sector is earning its revenues not by selling products and services to customers but instead by achieving social purposes and goals that have been established by a collective process, then the metric used to define the value produced by the organization must change. The financial revenue measure does not serve the purpose, because this figure no longer has the meaning it has in the private sector. The financial revenue measure for government is a statement about the amount of money the collective has authorized to be spent on behalf of a particular purpose; it is not a record of the value that customers place on the output of the organization. The accurate measure of performance has to be, instead, some kind of social impact analysis that allows the collective to determine whether and to what extent the organization has succeeded in achieving the goals the collective has set for it. That analysis will typically be carried out by observing the effects a government program or policy has had on some objective social conditions: for example, whether drug use has been reduced, whether welfare clients have made the transition to work, whether an epidemic has been avoided through the use of immunization, and the like.[4]

Third, without revenues generated by the purchases of willing customers as a handy summary of the (gross) value produced by the organization, government managers will need more than a financial accounting system to measure the net value of their output. In fact, when they look at their financial statements and learn whether they have operated within budgeted revenues, they know nothing about the value of what it is they have produced. They know only whether they have stayed within the financial bounds of what the legislature was prepared to spend on a particular venture—whatever the results, and the value of those results, might be.

The fact that financial revenues do not measure the value of governmental output in the public sector is critical for the management of government agencies. Consider what an automobile manufacturer in the private sector would do if he could have all the cost information he wanted but knew nothing about the revenues he had earned from the sale of cars. It should be obvious that he would be in a lot of trouble. He would probably try to work his way out of trouble by doing many of the things that government managers try to do. He would conduct surveys to determine how much his customers liked the cars they bought. He would ask different kinds of engineers to set standards for what constituted a "good car" and see how closely his cars matched those standards. He might even try to find out how his cars were being used and whether they were improving the quality of individual and social life. The point is this: he would face serious challenges in determining the value of the cars he produced if he were denied information about how much customers had paid for his product.

As a practical matter we have only a few limited methods to use to gauge the value of public sector output. In the past, we have relied principally on such techniques as program evaluation, cost-effectiveness analysis, and benefit-cost analysis.[5] The difficulties have been sufficient to dash the hopes of many who thought that these techniques could fully compensate for the lack of a bottom line in government management. These techniques themselves have lacked the objectivity and simplicity of the bottom line.

There is a further problem, however. The techniques of policy and program evaluation have as their underlying unit of analysis a policy or a program. The private sector's financial balance sheet, in contrast, has as its underlying unit of analysis an organization. One might imagine that this is not a great problem—that one could easily construct some kind of crosswalk that would transform policy or program numbers to organizational numbers. This turns out to be not quite true, however. Many public policies, for example, rely on contributions from many different organizations. Similarly, many organizations consist of bundles of policies and programs that are spread across organizational subunits. Moreover, many of the policies and programs within an organization depend on contributions from other public organizations to achieve the desired results.

The most difficult problem, however, is probably that government organizations are more than the sum of the policies and programs in whose implementation they have a role. Certainly no one in the private sector would think that a private sector organization is simply the sum of its current product lines. A private sector organization has been constructed to develop synergies among its product lines. It has developed a brand and a reputation within particular markets that transcend particular products. It has information and strategic planning systems that allow it to search for and find higher-value uses of the organization's assets. It is this whole package that is valued in the market, not just the performance of the organization in its current product lines.

Consequently, the value of a public sector organization might not lie simply in the summation of the value of the policies and programs for which it is responsible or to which it is contributing some portion of the effort. Interestingly, the General Accounting Office once tried to develop a method for conducting an evaluation of cabinet-level organizations as a whole, viewed over time. It called the evaluations its "general management reviews." The aim was to go beyond its usual methods of evaluating organizations, which generally consisted of two different kinds of evaluations: an examination of the organization's administrative systems, to determine whether they were in good shape, and program evaluations and benefit-cost studies of particular programs within the organization's jurisdiction. Instead of the limited views provided by these methods, the General Accounting Office wanted a picture of the organization's performance as a whole over a five-to-ten-year period—the kind of information that private investors have about firms in the private sector. Significantly, this effort failed. It failed partly because of technical difficulties: it was difficult to develop measurement tools for doing this work. But it also failed because of lack of congressional support: it was hard to find someone in Congress who was really interested in organizational performance as opposed to policy impact or program accomplishment. It was hard for elected representatives of the people to think about the value of public sector enterprises as organizations as distinct from policies or programs.

One might conclude from the foregoing that the only way to develop a bottom line for government is to somehow improve our methods of program evaluation and benefit-cost analysis. That might be true. The difficulty, however, is that such program evaluations are expensive to conduct, and only a few of any agency's organizations will be subject to serious evaluations in any given year. Moreover, by the time the information from such studies becomes available, the program has already been operating long enough to produce the effects that originally justified it. That means that it is hard to use this information in the short run to hold managers accountable for performance in real time as they are making decisions and spending resources.

The implication of these observations is that the public sector is currently stuck with two inadequate systems for measuring its performance. Its financial system, unlike the financial systems in private sector firms, cannot tell the agency much about the net value of what it is producing because it lacks the important piece of information that comes from individuals' directly valuing the products and services (and obligations) it delivers. On the other hand, program evaluations and benefit-cost analyses cannot be done comprehensively enough or quickly enough to make them useful to management in running organizations.

One possible answer to this dilemma would be to rely more on customer surveys of government clients. That is the line recommended by those who favor focusing on customer satisfaction. Such surveys might well be useful—even surveys of those who receive obligations from the government. The value of the information that comes in from customer surveys will be inadequate, however, for the reason noted above: namely, that the government is interested in more than customer satisfaction. It is also interested in knowing whether collectively valued results, encoded in policy mandates and mission statements, have been achieved, regardless of the satisfaction of the clientele.

A better answer might go something like this: First, government managers need to have detailed negotiations with their elected overseers about what constitutes value-creating performance and the terms to which they will be held accountable. Second, government managers need to construct and maintain measurement and reporting systems that make their operations transparent to their overseers on the dimensions of performance that concern them.

In all likelihood, this process would generate the need to collect information about many different dimensions of government performance. It would also put pressure on government to measure not only outcomes but also processes and activities. In evaluating the performance of a welfare program, for example, some overseers would be primarily interested in how well the clients were treated and whether their dignity and privacy had been respected. Some would be interested in determining whether the program had been successful in helping them make the shift to gainful employment. Others would be interested in the amount of money that had been lost to fraud. Still others would be interested only in the overall cost of the program.

To some, the idea of multiple measures of government performance, and measures that would cover not only outcomes but also outputs, processes, and activities, violates important ideas about how government programs should be evaluated. Instead, they feel, evaluations of government should focus on outcomes only, not outputs and processes, and should yield a single measure, equivalent to the bottom line of the private sector. Policymakers looking at multiple measures of performance will have to face the problem of how to add all the measures together to decide whether the program is valuable, all things considered; it will not be possible to isolate output and process to determine their effect on the achievement of desired results.

These objections are all valid: it is difficult to establish on an "objective basis" the (net) value of what government is doing. On the other hand, some real benefits are associated with constructing a scheme that has multiple measures covering costs, processes, and outputs as well as outcomes.

First, American citizens are interested in costs as well as in outcomes. Indeed, it is important to remember that the bottom line is a multiple measure: it includes both revenues and costs. It is converted into a single number only through a function that relates revenues to costs. In the public sector as well as in the private, we are not simply interested in maximizing the value of the output independent of cost; we are interested in maximizing the difference between the values of the resources used and the output generated.

Second, American citizens often place a value on the way government operates as well as the results it produces: we want to know that the government has distributed its resources according to some agreed-upon notion of desert, as well as need; and that it operates fairly and properly in its encounters with citizens, as well as producing outcomes. Third, those who authorize public activity often do so for different reasons, or they emphasize some values in a public policy decision over others. If authorizer A values effects x and y, and authorizer B values effects y and z, A and B can probably make a deal to authorize the policy, but they will evaluate the impact of the policy in different terms and will want different kinds of information about what the policy is producing. For all these reasons, multiple measures seem better than single measures; and measures that focus on costs, activities, outputs, and outcomes more useful than measures that focus only on outcomes.

Interestingly, this conclusion about what is necessary and desirable in the measurement of public sector performance is increasingly being embraced by private sector companies as well. The most sophisticated private sector companies are relying less exclusively on financial measures to guide their decisions and operations than they once did. They are, instead, increasingly employing a "balanced scorecard" that uses multiple measures distributed across the "value chain"—leading from fungible resources to concrete outputs, evaluated by customers not only in the short run, at the time of purchase, but also over the long run, as they maintain or abandon a relationship with the company. In this respect, the private sector is moving by choice toward a process that government must of necessity embrace because its financial scorecard gives it inadequate information.

Contracting Out

A third influential idea about public management that derives from market ideas is the notion that government should contract out more of its activities to nongovernmental producers. Again, there is much that is useful in this suggestion. It emphasizes the important difference between deciding that some goal is worth public financing and selecting public bureaucracies and government employees as the best way to produce it. It reminds us that the public might agree collectively on an important goal, and agree to tax and regulate itself to produce that result, but decide to use the money so raised to pay some nongovernmental agency to achieve that result.

Presumably, the decision to contract out would be a good one if the nongovernmental organization were capable of achieving the desired results more efficiently, more effectively, and with more responsiveness to clients than the government bureaucracy that was the principal alternative. Because government bureaucracies are often thought of as expensive, rigid, indifferent to the quality of service they provide to clients, and slow to innovate, it is not hard to believe that public services could be delivered more effectively and responsively by private organizations.

The private sector firms with whom government might contract include both nonprofit and for-profit firms. Both kinds of firms are private in the sense that they are legally independent of government control. They are publicly accountable through their boards of directors, whose only obligations are to act in accordance with the broad principles of corporate accountability. Unlike public agencies, they are not directly accountable to elected public officials who can direct and control their operations.

Of course, to the extent that they sign a contract with a government agency to produce particular results, using particular means, both nonprofit and for-profit organizations become accountable to the government for that portion of their operation that is covered by the government contract. The difference is that some kind of boundary exists between the state, on one hand, and the nongovernmental organizations, on the other. The nongovernmental organizations are free to do what they want with that portion of their resources that does not come from government. They are also free to refuse to do business with government and to seek revenues from other sources, such as the sale of products and services to customers in private markets or the solicitation of charitable contributions.

This "independence" from government is potentially useful and important to both sides of the contractual agreement. It gives both the nonprofit and the for-profit organizations a bit of latitude and discretion in deciding how they will do their work, without government oversight over all of the details. For example, both for-profits and nonprofits are free to experiment with new methods for achieving public purposes in ways that would be difficult for public sector organizations to do. They can "gamble" on new processes, using their own resources in ways that government might find reckless and irresponsible. This gives the private organizations a greater capacity to innovate in the general methods to be used in curing illness or providing job training.

These private contractors also have some discretion in adapting the way they respond to heterogeneous client populations. If they have contracted with the government to produce outcomes, rather than to deliver services in a uniform way, they are free within the bounds of their contract to deliver different services to different individuals as is necessary to achieve the results. They are not necessarily bound, as a government bureaucracy might be, to treat all clients alike.

Nongovernmental organizations have this freedom to innovate and adapt to heterogeneous clients at least in part because their operations are not wholly accountable to politics and government but only in that part of their operations that is covered by the government contract. In contrast, a public bureaucracy would be entirely accountable to politics and government. As a result, when the government agency tried an innovation that failed, or when it responded differently to different cases, it would be vulnerable to charges of reckless incompetence and unfairness.

To many, the independence of the nongovernmental organizations (even when bounded by a contract with the government) is the problem, however, not the solution. They worry that, in the discretionary spaces left to the private contractor, the private contractor will make choices that would depart from the values and aims of the society and its surrogate, government, and that to that degree, some important public value will be lost. They worry, for example, that a for-profit firm contracted to provide job training programs will respond by recruiting the candidates who are easy to train and ignoring the others. Such conduct would be fully consistent with a public contract that paid the private firm for socially desired outcomes (for example, successful placements). It would also be consistent with the private firm's desire to maximize its profits because it would allow the for-profit firm to keep its costs low while achieving its contractually mandated results.

This conduct might not be consistent with the goal of the public, however, who might think it more publicly valuable to train the hard-core unemployed than those who were only temporarily unemployed. They might have this view on the prudential ground that training the hard-core unemployed would reduce future problems and government payments more than training those who might be able to improve their circumstances on their own and would not, in any case, be as significant a problem. Alternatively, they might have this view on the justice ground that the worst off are most deserving of assistance. In either case, the public would not have gotten what it valued from the private firm. Another common worry that applies more to contracting with nonprofit organizations is that such organizations might display favoritism toward clients with the same religious commitments or ethnic origins as those who initiated or sustained the nonprofit organization. The fear is that any discretion left to those who use government assets will end up being used for purposes that are important to those actors rather than for purposes that are important to the public.

There are only a limited number of ways of coping with this "agency" problem. One can try to write rules that reduce or guide discretion so that the agents can be held accountable for producing what the public wants; or one can rely on the judgment of the agents one hires to carry out the purposes. The first is, in many ways, the bureaucratic solution. The reason that government has so many rules is precisely because its demands for accountability are so high. The public wants to be sure that every scrap of public money and public authority it has granted to a public purpose is used efficiently, effectively, fairly, and justly to produce the desired results. The public quite rightly worries that if the people who spend the government's money and authority are given too much discretion, they will abuse it.

They will steal. They will become lazy. They will try out their own uninformed ideas about how to accomplish the assigned task. They will express their unreasonable prejudices. To control these problems of fraud, waste, and abuse, governments write detailed policies and procedures and enforce them through close supervision—all of which increase the costs and reduce the flexibility of government operations.

The second option, relying on the discretion of the agents one hires, might be realized in government operations if Americans could somehow trust the professionalism and commitment of government employees. There was a time when we did—when we thought that government employees were not mere bureaucrats but public servants professionally trained for their jobs and morally committed to pursuing public rather than their own individual purposes. Now, however, because Americans no longer trust their public officials and have found the limits of trying to control officials' behavior through rules and direct supervision, attention has shifted to a different kind of agent to pursue our public purposes—not a bureaucrat but a government contractor from the nonprofit or for-profit sector.

In terms of dependence on the discretion of the private contractor, there might be important reasons for the government to prefer contracting with a nonprofit rather than for-profit enterprise. A nonprofit organization, for example, does not seek to maximize a financial return for its owners. Its "capital" is charitable capital and does not demand payment for its use. Furthermore, a nonprofit organization can often add voluntarily contributed resources of money, time, and material to its production processes, thereby reducing the price it would have to charge the government to achieve the same result. Finally, one might suppose that many employees of nonprofit organizations work for love of the cause as well as their paychecks; this might imply not only that the nonprofit would be less expensive but also that it would be more reliable in the execution of its duties. These features, if true of nonprofit organizations, would give them a cost and quality advantage over for-profit firms.

Indeed, the reason to be concerned about using for-profit firms as contractors is precisely that their goal is to maximize financial returns. This means that they will treat the performance standards set by government as a constraint and will use any discretionary room that is left to them in the contractual arrangements to maximize their financial returns. Thus, unlike a nonprofit organization, which has less reason to try to maximize financial returns, the for-profit firm will shift residual value in the operations to the owners of the organization rather than either the clients or the employees.

Of course, nonprofit organizations have their own characteristic vulnerabilities as agents of public purposes. Some worry that nonprofit contractors may behave in discriminatory ways, others that the nonprofit will be so serious in the achievement of its mission that it will be indifferent to the costs, spending more on achieving results it deems valuable than on the results the public values.

To address these concerns, government could rely once again on the strategy of trying to control discretion through rules—in this case, by writing more detailed contracts. However, these contracts come increasingly to look like the dense structure of policies and rules that we formerly relied on to control bureaucrats. The thickly structured contract may take away the very flexibility that was the original goal in shifting from directly producing government operations to contracting them out. The only thing gained is a temporary moment of freedom before the inexorable demands for public accountability reassert themselves and make their claims felt through the contracts that structure the relations between government and the organizations it is relying on to achieve its results.

Even if the benefits of contracting out are less than first imagined in terms of increasing the innovativeness and flexibility of government operations, contracting out might still be the best available option because it would allow the public to take advantage of competitive pressures to force cost reductions and quality improvements. In principle, of course, a government could structure competition into its own internal operations. It could, for example, treat different schools or different precincts of a police department as "profit centers," allocating both budget and responsibility to those schools and precincts that were performing well and taking away budget and responsibility from those schools and precincts that were performing poorly. It does not really do this, however, and would probably be prevented from doing so by the existing structures of political accountability and control.

The easiest way to take advantage of competitive pressures would be to put government activities out to bid. This would be particularly effective if private suppliers of the services government wanted to produce already existed. The government has long used this principle in buying things such as paper, desks, pencils, real estate, automobiles, and even vehicle maintenance. It has also used this principle for decades in contracting for such core government functions as the building of advanced weapons systems. It is now increasingly using this idea in the social services sector, as well.

An important question in setting up such competitive systems, however, is whether government agencies would be allowed into the competition. In one version of this idea, what was previously produced directly by government is put up for bid, and only private suppliers can bid for the work. This is commonly called "privatization." In another version, the work is put out to bid, and private contractors are encouraged to apply, but government agencies are also invited to bid for the work. This is commonly called "marketization." These two systems—privatization and marketization—could be evaluated along several different criteria: Which system is likely to make the most effective use of competition to drive down costs or increase quantity and quality for any given expenditure? Which is "fairer"? Which is politically more feasible?

A little reflection reveals that the marketization option is to be preferred to the privatization option on all grounds. Once the commitment to the use of competition has been made, there is no reason to restrict that competition to private suppliers. If former government bureaucrats are able to form enterprises that can do the job more efficiently, effectively, and fairly than private firms, then it would be to the public's advantage to allow them to compete. This would have the additional virtue of being fairer to government employees, who would otherwise be arbitrarily excluded from employment opportunities. To give special preference to private firms might advance the principle that the government should not take business away from private suppliers, but it would do so at a cost to the public if the public providers were, in fact, better than the private suppliers.

The key to successfully contracting out government business is the ability to say clearly, concretely, and completely what it is that the government wants to produce: that is, to define the value that the public is trying to capture through any given operation. This is, as it always has been, where the trouble lies. It is difficult for a collective to reach agreement on the precise attributes of public value that it wants to see produced in a given part of the public sector. Defining social utility functions in ways that they can be written into contracts is tough conceptually, analytically, and technically—and politically. The political problem will arise not from disagreement about the desired direction of change but from the difficulty to clearly define the relative importance of different attributes of performance.

To the extent that weakness shows up in our collective ability to define what we are trying to accomplish, an important vulnerability is introduced into the contractual system. Sloppiness in the definition of purposes will allow the private agents—whether nonprofit or for-profit—to advance purposes, using public resources, that the public does not necessarily want. It will also prevent competitive pressure from doing the work it is supposed to do because it will focus competition on getting better at things that are not necessarily valuable. On the other hand, to the extent that what the public wants can be clearly articulated, it may not be necessary to go to a contracting system. It may be possible to measure the performance of public sector organizations and hold them accountable for achieving the goals set for them.

The real key to producing more of what the public wants is not necessarily to be found only in new forms of administration. It lies instead in figuring out how to help politics and public policymaking become clearer in characterizing what the American public has collectively decided to produce. If that cannot be done, then no amount of administrative tinkering will save us; our ability to produce what we want will be limited, no matter what we do. On the other hand, if the goals and values can be clearly articulated, then all the tasks of managing to produce the desired result become much easier. We will know how to measure the performance of public sector organizations. We will know how to structure the competition among government agencies, nonprofit suppliers, and for-profit firms to ensure that costs are low in the short run and that they go down over the long run through the creation and adoption of important innovations. The problem in government management continues to be the difficulty of organizing politics to give a clear mandate of what is to be produced. That problem cannot be solved by pretending that "customer satisfaction" can best determine what government services should be produced or that "contracting out" will yield reduction in costs and improvement in quality when we have not been able to articulate what we intended to produce in the first place.

Conclusions

In the end, the most valuable idea that comes from the private sector is that government management should aim at the production of value:

government should use the valuable assets entrusted to it by its citizenry to produce things that are publicly valued. The mark of excellence in government management should be the same as it is in the private sector: namely, accomplishing established purposes as efficiently and effectively as possible and finding and exploiting the highest-value uses of the assets of government.

It remains maddeningly difficult to say what constitutes a valuable contribution of government, however. Two of the most important ideas that come to government from the private sector seek to provide an answer to that question. In one formulation, the goal of government is said to be the satisfaction of customers. That metric raises two questions: Who are the "customers" of government? What do they value? In the second formulation, it is recommended that the government establish the equivalent of a "bottom line." Yet as it turns out, the financial information the private sector uses to construct a meaningful bottom line is inadequate to the task of management in the public sector. The meaning of revenues raised by government agencies by levying taxes is different from the meaning of revenues earned by a private sector firm through its sale of products and services. Efforts to construct substitute measures have all had both conceptual and practical difficulties. We can be sure that contracting out can succeed only if we are able to clearly articulate what constitutes the value that the government seeks to produce through the contract. That is a necessary if not sufficient condition for contracting out to produce the improvements we hope for.

Thus the key challenge for government management remains what it has always been: to get some kind of secure and clear declaration from the citizens and their elected representatives of the value they would like government to produce. Paradoxically, the most important way to strengthen public management is to strengthen the quality of our deliberative political processes and to engage public agencies as intensely with that conversation as private sector firms are engaged in understanding their consumer markets.

Notes

1. It is easy to imagine that the application of these private sector management ideas might belong primarily to discussions about the means rather than the ends of government. In this view, management is seen as a discipline that is primarily concerned about

means, not ends—the how-to rather than the what. In reality, however, many of the most interesting and important private sector management ideas offer advice about choosing ends as well as means. For example, concepts of corporate strategy focus not solely on means but also on finding the highest-value use of the organization's existing assets or the best "fit" between an organization's existing capabilities and market opportunities projected into the future. These private sector management concepts explore how to choose ends wisely as well as the most effective means for achieving given ends.

Inevitably, some of this private sector management wisdom gets rolled into discussions about how government performance might be improved. For the most part, these commonsense management ideas have aligned themselves rather neatly with the same conservative views of the proper role of government that have animated the interest in the "privatization" and "marketization" of societies.

It would be possible, then, as part of our examination of the impact of "markets" on government, to examine private sector management ideas as ideas that have implications for the ends of government as well as the means. In this chapter, however, I resist the temptation to do so. I restrict myself to talking about those private sector management ideas that are focused primarily on enhancing government's capacities to achieve purposes it has accepted.

2. Of course, the concrete individuals who are customers of a private sector firm may also be investors or employees of the firm and therefore participate in the operations of the organization "upstream," at the governance end of the organization, and at the production stage of the enterprise as well as at the output stage. By definition, however, the customer is the person who is at the tail-end of the organization's production processes.

3. This is true even when the services are being paid for by the individuals with government-financed vouchers. Of course, if government pays for things through vouchers, the perspective of those running publicly supported organizations will change in important ways. Instead of looking upward to a government contractor with specifications to be met, they will look outward to individuals with vouchers to spend. In this respect, to the organizations providing services, government clients will look more like customers than they do under government contracts, because they will have money to spend and will be able to choose where to spend it. This, in turn, may have salutary effects on how hard the organizations work to satisfy the customers. The fact remains, however, that part of the financing of the clients' purchases comes from the collective and often comes with strings attached. Food stamps cannot be used to purchase liquor, for example; and vouchers for employment training may only be spent at accredited institutions. Those strings represent the shadow of the collective's ideas about the purposes to be served by this government spending as well as the shadow of the ideas of the individuals to whom the vouchers were supplied. It remains important that the publicly financed organizations satisfy the collective aspiration as well as those of the individual.

4. Of course, once we determined the extent to which an organization had achieved the concrete social goals set for it, we might try to convert these effects into economic value. That would allow us to compare the results of governmental activity directly with the financial costs of undertaking the effort. It would also allow us to compare the relative value of one government undertaking relative to another in a straightforward way. Although this possibility is attractive in theory, it has proved difficult to achieve in practice. Even when technical experts succeed in producing some agreed-upon estimates of the economic value of the benefits produced by governmental operations, the deliberative bodies that judge the

value of government operations have not been much influenced by these numbers. They have preferred in most instances simply to look at the concrete effects and decide whether or not to go ahead with the program.

5. The first two of these techniques rely on first defining the social purposes to be advanced by a policy or program and then finding the empirical means of determining the degree to which a particular policy or program achieved the intended goals. Finding reliable objective, quantitative measures of the "success" of a program often poses serious conceptual and empirical problems. It also turns out to be difficult to reliably attribute any observed changes in the measures of success that are chosen to the specific policy or program. The reason is that the important social effects have typically occurred both far down a causal chain and remote in space and time from the specific governmental action that was taken. In the space that lies between the government output and the observed social outcome, many factors other than the government's efforts can play an important causal role that either enhances or detracts from the impact of the government effort. The idea of benefit-cost analysis faces all the same difficulties as program evaluation and cost-effectiveness analysis but also imposes a third heavy burden: namely, the burden of taking some concrete effects of policies and programs and translating them into economic or financial value through some process of monetizing the value of what was produced.

13

ROBERT D. BEHN

Government Performance and the Conundrum of Public Trust

AMERICANS DON'T TRUST their governments. Both the scientific polls and our informal, sidewalk empiricism tell us so. When asked the basic question—Do you trust the government to do the right thing?—many citizens are answering no.[1]

Why? Thirty years ago, Peter Drucker, in an essay on "the sickness of government," took note of the "distrust of government" and offered one explanation: "the greatest factor in the disenchantment with government is that government has not performed." Moreover, Drucker concluded, this failure in performance was inherent to government. "The main lesson of the last fifty years," he wrote, is that "government is not a 'doer.'" Indeed, "the problem that government now faces," Drucker continued, is "the incompatibility between 'governing' and 'doing.'"[2]

As an alternative, Drucker offered his version of market-based governance, which he labels "reprivatization." Government should act as the "conductor," while nongovernmental organizations "would be seen as organs for the accomplishment of results." Drucker explained his choice of

The author thanks John D. Donahue, Shelley H. Metzenbaum, Bonnie Newman, Joan Goodman-Williamson, and the participants in the Visions of Governance in the Twenty-First Century Project's conference for their valuable comments and suggestions on a draft of this chapter.

the conductor metaphor: "The conductor himself does not play an instrument. He need not even know how to play an instrument. His job is to know the capacity of each instrument and to evoke optimal performance from each. Instead of 'performing,' he 'conducts.' Instead of 'doing,' he leads." Drucker's "doing" would be the responsibility of "institutions not run by government." Thus, he concluded, "the design of new non-governmental, autonomous institutions as agents of social performance under reprivatization may well become a central job for tomorrow's political architects."[3]

Drucker's call for government to stop being a "doer" and to become instead a "conductor" has obvious similarities to the suggestion made by David Osborne and Ted Gaebler that government should "steer rather than row." Osborne and Gaebler advocate for a government that is both market oriented and results oriented. They believe in "the superiority of market mechanisms over administrative mechanisms" and conclude that "if we applied market-oriented thinking to our public systems, we could accomplish a great deal." "The key to reinvented government," they argue, "is changing the markets that operate within the public sector."[4]

Indeed, market-based governance has become a central theme of what is known internationally as the "new public management."[5] Not all of the conceptions of the new public management emphasize market mechanisms, and some stress cost reduction more than performance improvement. Nevertheless, many contemporary efforts to rectify Drucker's sickness of government do employ market mechanisms to enhance the performance of government.

Drucker certainly considered the inability of government to produce results a serious problem. Indeed, because of this failure of government to perform, "we no longer expect results from government." Once, "we expected miracles," Drucker continued, "and that always produces disillusionment."[6]

Drucker's analysis suggests one possible way to reduce (if not eliminate) the disenchantment with government and thus to enhance the citizenry's trust in public institutions. By improving performance and producing results, government may be able to earn back the public's trust. After all, if our collective expectations for government's performance are so low, public agencies might, by producing a few significant results, build a reputation for producing miracles. In business and politics, winning means beating the expectations; and when playing this expectations game, prior expectations count as much as subsequent performance.[7]

If government could only improve its performance, people might trust it more. Maybe if the leaders and managers of public agencies could ratchet up the results that they produce for citizens, they might earn more trust. After all, what could do more for the public's understanding that government can do the right thing than for government to do some right things well—and do a number of different right things really well? Thus one of the implicit promises of market-based governance is that it will not only directly improve the performance of government but also, as a result, indirectly improve the public's trust of government.[8]

Four Reasons Not to Trust Government

Yet we Americans have never trusted our government. That is why we became Americans. As British subjects, we learned not to trust the Crown, the parliament, and the regents that they dispatched to govern us. So we revolted, setting up a government designed to prevent people whom we do not trust from getting away with too much.

Today, we do not trust government for at least four fundamental and different reasons:

—The people in government abuse their authority: "You can't trust 'em; they'll misuse their power."

—The people in government are corrupt: "You can't trust 'em; they'll line their pockets."

—The people in government exercise policy discretion ineptly: "You can't trust 'em; they'll make the wrong decision."

—The people in government don't perform: "You can't trust 'em; they'll screw it up."[9]

The failure of public agencies to perform up to the expectations of citizens is only one of several reasons why we don't trust our governments.

The causal connection between any of these four factors and the public's distrust of their government is complicated, even convoluted. After all, people do not somehow add up their scores on these four dimensions to decide whether or not they trust government; if government is behaving poorly on one of these dimensions, no amount of excellence on the other three will convince them that their government is trustworthy. Moreover, the recent decline in the public's trust of government (since the mid-1960s) has many other causes: macroeconomic transformations, technological innovations, political shocks, rising expectations, cultural upheavals, and social trends. Collectively, these have influenced the public's attitudes toward not just government but a variety of other social institutions—from businesses to churches—and the result, for the most part, has been less trust.[10]

Nevertheless, if all of these other factors contributing to the decline of trust in government were to be fixed or to disappear, the fundamental four would remain. We would still recognize that government can abuse its power. We would still uncover examples of governmental corruption. We would still be annoyed or distressed with the discretionary decisions that government makes. We would still be dissatisfied with government's performance.

At least, we would still be dissatisfied with the performance of some government agencies. After all, we are frequently (and often repeatedly) dissatisfied with the performance of some business firms, of some nonprofit social service agencies, of some churches, of some schools, colleges, and universities, and of the Boston Red Sox. We might hope, for example, that all businesses from which we buy goods and services would always be excellent performers, but we would never expect it. Similarly, we would not expect that every public agency would always be functioning at maximum efficiency and effectiveness. Still, if more would, the public's trust in government might ratchet up a notch or two.

The Abuse of Power

Government can abuse power. Public officials at all levels of government—from kings and queens to frontline bureaucrats and even unofficial hangers-on—can abuse government's power. Citizens know this. Some have experienced such an abuse of power (or think they have); quite naturally, they quickly come to distrust government. Nevertheless, even those who have never personally observed a government official exercising power abusively—even those who have never read or heard about a government official who exercised power abusively[11]—will not fail to understand how easy it can be for public officials to abuse the extensive powers they have. Children figure this out before they get to eighth-grade civics. So, naturally, mature citizens will worry that their government officials will exploit their authority.

Not only did Americans revolt against the abuse of governmental power; our resulting distrust of government was central to the way we framed our

Constitution. James Madison did not need a poll to know that the colonialists did not trust government; he himself did not. Thus, "to controul the abuses of government," he advocated "the necessary partition of power among the several departments." In "Federalist 51," Madison writes that "the great security against a gradual concentration of the several powers in the same department, consists in giving to those who administer each department, the necessary constitutional means, and personal motives, to resist encroachments of the others"—that is, "ambition must be made to counteract ambition."[12] James Madison did not believe in trust.

For this reason Madison created a divided government and established a system of multiple checks and balances. Because the various institutions of government will be ambitious, and because each will have the means to identify and call attention to the abuses and failures of the others, our Constitution ensures that one of Madison's departments will alert us to many of the others' abuses of power. Thus our constitutional system both institutionalizes our distrust and reinforces it.

The Bill of Rights explicitly identifies a variety of potential abuses of governmental powers and forbids our government to engage in them. Our government cannot tell us what to say or publish, dictate how or when we worship, take away our guns, or force us to quarter soldiers in our homes.

Nevertheless, government officials continue to abuse their power. Police engage in racial profiling; they shoot people who are (seen in retrospect, at least) perfectly innocent citizens; they physically abuse those whom they arrest. Superiors "ask" their subordinates to do them personal favors—from watching the cat, to picking up the laundry, to engaging in sexual relations.[13]

Today, many people do not trust the Federal Bureau of Investigation (FBI). Why? Because they believe that it abused its powers in the shooting of Vicki Weaver (Randy Weaver's wife) at Ruby Ridge, Idaho, in 1992 and in the deaths of eighty Branch Davidians in Waco, Texas, in 1993. When Timothy J. McVeigh bombed the Alfred P. Murrah Federal Building in Oklahoma City, he thought he was fighting a war against an illegal government that was abusing its power. We may dismiss the modern militia movement as a collection of unstable wackos and paranoid misfits; but they believe not just in the abstract potential but in the concrete reality of government's abuse of its power.

Moreover, other citizens also believe that the FBI abuses its power. Joseph Salvanti spent thirty years in prison for murder because the agency withheld evidence that could have exonerated him.[14] The attorneys for

Wen Ho Lee, the scientist at Los Alamos National Laboratory charged with security violations, accused the government of racial profiling. When Lee pleaded guilty to one count of mishandling nuclear secrets, federal judge James A. Parker apologized to him, declaring that the actions of the government had "embarrassed our entire nation."[15] Members of various minority groups have learned from experience not to trust their government, and no absolution from another "ambitious" branch of government will assuage these critics.

The Corruption of Public Officials

Government can be corrupt. Public officials of all kinds at all levels of government—from kings and queens to frontline bureaucrats and unofficial hangers-on—can use their position for personal gain. Citizens know this. Some have experienced such corruption (or think they have); quite naturally, they quickly come to distrust government. Even those who have never personally been asked for a bribe will not fail to understand how easy it can be for public officials to extract some personal benefit (often money or votes) in exchange for a government job, a government contract, a government permit, or some other governmental benefit. So, naturally, these citizens worry that government officials will use their authority to line their own pockets.

Corruption, of course, is just another way in which public officials abuse their power. It was not, however, the dominant concern of Madison and his colleagues. They worried less about public officials who used their powers for their own personal benefit than about public officials who used their powers to threaten the freedom of the citizenry. Dividing the "different powers" of government among different branches, writes Madison, "is admitted on all hands to be essential to the preservation of liberty."[16]

Toward the end of the nineteenth century, however, government corruption did become a public concern and a greater source of the citizenry's distrust of government. The Progressives—the visionaries and reformers of their day—distrusted their government not so much because it abused its constitutional powers as because it abused its authority to exercise the judgment inherent whenever a government official was able to fill a position, let a contract, issue a license or permit, make a regulatory ruling, or reveal or withhold some valuable information. Every time a government official can take such an action—every time a government official can exercise such judgment—he or she has the opportunity to extract a little personal benefit.[17]

To prevent such corruption, to limit such judgment, to keep public officials from personally benefiting from the exercise of such judgment, the Progressives and their heirs created a variety of laws and regulations—from the civil service system to sunshine laws—designed to inhibit corruption. In many ways, this accumulation of rules designed to formalize the process by which public officials exercise judgment and dispense or withhold favors has inhibited corruption. It is a tribute to the effectiveness of the Progressives and their descendants that today we are worried about the performance of government. For if corruption dominated our concerns, we would never get around to even noticing how well or poorly government was performing.[18]

Nevertheless, government corruption has not disappeared. At the beginning of the twenty-first century, corrupt public officials still make front-page headlines. In May 2001, the indictment of U.S. Representative James Traficant of Youngstown, Ohio, for bribery, tax evasion, and the obstruction of justice was reported across the country. Moreover, corruption is not a monopoly of big-city machines; small-town machines are guilty of it, too. In June 2001, in Cicero, Illinois, the mayor, the former public safety director, the former treasurer, and seven other individuals were indicted for looting the town's treasury of $10 million.

The FBI was once known as the most uncorrupt law enforcement agency in the country.[19] In 2001, however, FBI agent Robert P. Hansen was accused of selling public secrets to the Soviet Union, and agent James J. Hill was charged with selling classified information to organized crime. Such revelations remind us that the potential for corruption is a problem not just for random citizens who manage to get elected to public office but also for highly educated, carefully screened, thoroughly trained, and frequently scrutinized civil servants.

The Inept Exercise of Policy Discretion

Government can exercise policy discretion. Many public officials are supposed to exercise policy discretion. Legislators and elected executives have to exercise policy discretion; judges and justices make decisions and, thus, have to exercise discretion.[20] So do political appointees in the executive branch and on legislative staffs. It is the job of these public officials to make policy decisions and thus to exercise discretion. Still, we worry. We worry that government officials will exercise their policy discretion inappropriately, poorly, stupidly, or unscrupulously.

We worry about the discretion that public officials inherently exercise for two different reasons. We worry that they will engage in explicit quid pro quo corruption, trading legislative votes for campaign contributions or trading a regulatory decision for a relative's job (or an implicit promise of their own future employment). In addition to this worry about quid pro quo corruption, we also worry that, when making policy decisions, public officials will be swayed by ideology, friendships, interest-group lobbying, simplistic arguments, faulty analysis, or astrological alignments. Even public officials who reject any opportunity to personally benefit from their policy decisions may nevertheless exercise that discretion incompetently.

Government officials with the responsibility for macro, policy decisions can make poor choices. Citizens know this. Any citizen who follows the policy debates will, inevitably, disagree with at least some of the major choices made by government officials. Frequently, and quite predictably, such citizens will conclude that the responsible officials have exercised their discretion badly. Children may not figure this out. Engaged citizens, however, will conclude that they cannot always trust their government to make wise policy decisions.

When government officials decide to permit logging in a public forest, environmental interests accuse them of being venal; when government officials decide not to permit logging in a public forest, economic interests accuse them of being stupid. When public officials move budget allocations from defense to education, the advocates for a stronger military believe that government is being short-sighted; when public officials move budget allocations from education to the military, the advocates for children believe that government is being short-sighted.

Even if no public official ever abused his or her power, even if no public official ever engaged in quid pro quo corruption, citizens would still have reason to distrust their government. No one who makes government's policy decisions possesses the wisdom of Plato's philosopher king.

This reason for citizens to distrust government is more abstract and more subjective than the other three. It is not about a specific official's abuse of power or a specific official's corrupt behavior, and it is not about a specific agency's failure to produce a specific result. Rather, this is about public officials making (given our own personal values, analyses, and judgments) the right or wrong policy decisions. Yet the question often used to

THE CONUNDRUM OF PUBLIC TRUST   331

measure trust is, Do you trust government to do the right thing? And the exercise of policy discretion is, at the macro level, about doing the right thing.

Discretion, Corruption, and the Abuse of Power

Discretion provides the opportunity for the abuse of power, for corruption, and for poor policy decisions. If public officials were denied discretion, they could not misuse the power of their office, engage in corrupt behavior, or make any kind of policy decisions (moronic or wise). Thus, to analyze why citizens fail to trust government, we need to distinguish among these three consequences of discretion.

At the same time, however, we need to recognize that, in the minds of many citizens, these are not three distinct reasons for distrusting government. When pollsters ask people whether or not they trust government to do the right thing, they do not define what "the right thing" is. Pollsters don't ask, "Do you trust government officials to do the right thing and not abuse their power?" They don't ask, "Do you trust government officials to do the right thing and not line their pockets?" They don't ask, "Do you trust government officials to do the right thing and not make dumb policy decisions?" The question doesn't have any people in it; the question is just about some vague "government," not about government officials.[21] Yet it is the people who work in government, not some abstract, impersonal officialdom, who do the things that warrant our trust or foster our distrust.

The ambiguous way that the standard polling question about trust is asked (along with our human facility for interpreting the same words in multiple ways) permits people to respond with answers to very different questions. When they hear "trust" and "right thing," some may worry about the abuse of power. Some may worry about corruption. Others may worry about poor policy decisions. Still others may just blend everything together in their own minds without thinking carefully about what non-right things government officials might do. Some may at different times have had different, and specific, concerns about whether government officials were doing the right thing; thus, when asked about their trust of government, they may simply recall some recent incident (perhaps an example of corruption or a policy decision with which they disagreed) that suggests that government is not worthy of their trust.[22] The things that can be categorized as a misuse of discretion form less a crisp set than a fuzzy one. Thus so do the reasons why people might not trust government to do the right thing.

In attempting to design remedies (or amerioratives) for the public's distrust, however, we citizens ought to recognize that there are three distinctly different ways in which public officials can misuse their discretion. They can be personally corrupt, using their discretion for private gain. They can be officially evil, using their discretion not for any personal benefit but simply (and perhaps only implicitly) out of personal prejudice, operational convenience, or brutal maliciousness. They can be analytically deficient, using their discretion (again, not for any personal benefit) without having a complete and unbiased examination of the available evidence and analyses.

Government officials make thousands of decisions daily. They are constantly exercising discretion—sometimes soundly or brilliantly, sometimes imperfectly or defectively. Which is it? The judgment is, almost always, personal and subjective.

When should we conclude that a specific exercise of governmental discretion is so flawed that the agency or official does not warrant our trust? This, too, is almost always a subjective judgment. Cases of personal corruption may generate the most agreement among citizens (though we keep the judiciary in reserve precisely because we do not always have a perfect consensus). Some cases of the abuse of power may appear indisputable to you and me; to others, however, they may simply be the instinctual exercise under stress of officially (and appropriately) delegated discretion. Cases of policy discretion, however, are inevitably open to debate. Even when the benefit-cost analysis suggests that one alternative is overwhelmingly superior, the decisionmakers must still deal with the distribution of the costs and benefits and the questions about who should be compensated for what losses by whom, when, and by how much. As long as government officials have the discretion to make policy decisions, some citizens will disagree with those decisions and conclude that these errant choices provide further evidence that they should not trust their government.

The American system of governance is designed to generate multiple illustrations of the official misuse of discretion, each of which suggests that government does not warrant trust. If we as citizens, journalists, scholars, and candidates begin with the premise that, at a minimum, government needs to be carefully watched lest it somehow violate our trust, we will undoubtedly discover examples of (to our eyes) the misuse of discretion. Given the number of people in the United States who work in government, there will always be an adequate supply of public officials who, while exercising their discretion, abuse their power, behave corruptly, or make poor policy decisions.

The Absence of Performance

Government can perform. But not always. In fact, in the lexicon of talk-show hosts (and of many political candidates), government performance is an oxymoron. Public agencies of all sorts fail to perform up to our personal and collective expectations.[23] Citizens have experienced this lack of performance—either because the ambulance did not arrive quickly, or because the state park was not clean, or because the veteran's benefit check was not mailed on time.

Governmental units of all kinds—from a local school, to a municipal sanitation department, to a state or provincial environmental agency, to a national army, to a nation itself—can fail to produce results. Citizens know this. Some have personally experienced such a deficiency in performance (or think they have); often they quickly extrapolate from this experience to conclude that all of government is incompetent. The failure of a Division of Motor Vehicles to perform some of the basic, customer, service tasks mastered by most private organizations can damage all of government's reputation for competence. How can citizens trust an incompetent government?

The FBI's announcement that it had failed to turn over three thousand pages of documents to Timothy McVeigh's lawyers suggested that it was not even competent enough to manage a simple paper-tracking process. Moreover, though 54 percent of the public believed this failure was accidental, 32 percent thought it deliberate.[24] "The public has been losing confidence in the FBI," observes Republican senator Charles E. Grassley. Democratic representative David Obey calls the FBI "something close to a failed agency."[25] No official statement, however, quite captures the decline in the FBI's reputation for performance like the cartoon in the *New Yorker* in which a television newscaster announces, "China now says it will withdraw its opposition to the missile-defense shield if the F.B.I. builds it."[26]

Government's inability to produce results—its "lack of performance"— has certainly been one of Peter Drucker's big themes: "In every country, there are big areas of government administration where there is no performance whatever—only costs." Thirty years ago, Drucker was particularly struck by the ineptitude of America's urban governments, which he derided as "impressive" for their "administrative incompetence." In other Western democracies, however, Drucker found "the same lack of performance" and "the same triumph of accounting rules over results."[27]

Similarly, writing about the federal government, Derek Bok has observed that "Americans have little regard for its performance." Yet looking at specific indicators of society's (if not directly government's) performance, he found that "on the basis of some sixty to seventy specific objectives of importance to most Americans, the United States has made definite progress over the past few decades in the vast majority of cases." At the same time, he noted, such progress in the United States has, in general, lagged behind that made by Great Britain, Canada, France, Germany, Japan, and Sweden: "In roughly two-thirds of these cases, the United States has performed less well than most of the other nations since 1960. In roughly half of the cases, our record is actually at or near the bottom of the list." Thus, Bok concluded, "although the results do not justify the overwhelming negative impressions that most Americans currently hold about their government, they do paint a disappointing picture."[28]

Others who share the concern for the performance of government expressed by Drucker and Bok suggest that improving performance will contribute to improving trust. For example, in the first report of his National Performance Review, Vice President Al Gore wrote of "our twin missions: to make government *work better and cost less,*" which would help in "closing the *trust* deficit."[29] When Congress enacted the Government Performance and Results Act, it did so, in part, to "improve the confidence of the American people in the capability of the Federal Government, by systematically holding Federal agencies accountable for achieving program results."[30] President George W. Bush's "management agenda"—"a bold strategy for improving the management and performance of the federal government"—emphasizes that government should be "market based" and "results oriented." "What matters most," says the president, "is performance and results."[31] Although he never uses the word "trust," he stresses that government should work hard to ensure that the taxpayers' "money is spent wisely"—that the federal government should be "responsive to the people's needs, and responsible with our people's money."[32]

Similarly, a panel of the National Academy of Public Administration has concluded that "better government performance is a key to rebuilding public trust." Thus, the panel recommends, "governments at all levels should explicitly adopt and aggressively adhere to a concept of service and a culture of performance and results."[33] In his book *Trustworthy Government*, David Carnevale writes that "faith in public institutions will be restored when they perform better."[34]

The Complex Interconnections between Performance and Trust

Government performance affects the public's trust in government. Conversely, the public's trust in government can affect government's performance.[35] After all, as Joseph Nye observes, such performance depends on "the willingness of the public to provide such crucial resources as tax dollars, the willingness of bright young people to go into government, and voluntary compliance with laws." The consequence of these interconnected, causal relationships can be, he argues, "a cumulative downward spiral" in both trust and performance: "Without critical resources, government cannot perform well, and if government cannot perform, people will become more dissatisfied and distrustful of it."[36]

This suggests that ratcheting up performance will not be easy, for it will require a simultaneous ratcheting up of trust. Because each improvement in one requires an improvement in the other, the steps will be incremental. A small improvement in performance can create a small improvement in trust, which can provide the resources and flexibility for another small improvement in performance, which can.... Any upward spiral in trust and performance will take time.

Donald Kettl has examined what he calls "the global public management revolution," which he defined to include the use of "market-style incentives to root out the pathologies of government bureaucracy." He suggested that "public confidence is a lagging indicator of reform." Improved performance, he argued, will not produce quick changes in public trust. Indeed, "it might take long and sustained government improvement to register with citizens and to be reflected in higher confidence in government."[37] Kettl noted that the public's "confidence in government hinges on many things"; yet "it will be hard to reduce the confidence deficit without also tackling the performance deficit."[38] Still, if improved trust lags improved performance, and if improved trust is required for improved performance, we will need many time-consuming iterations to ratchet up both performance and trust.

The Paradox of Great Performance, Less Trust

Meanwhile, some of the core components of market-based governance have the potential to actually undermine public confidence in government. After all, most of the market- and results-oriented suggestions for improving the performance of government require increasing the discretion exercised by public officials—and by individuals in private sector organizations with which government has contracted. It is precisely this discretion that contributes to the other three causes of the public's distrust of government.

For example, Lydia Segal warns that "unless the new public management addresses the potential for corruption, it may unleash scandals that will generate pressure for top-down controls." She argues that "increasing discretion while decreasing oversight will only give employees additional opportunities for abuse with lower risks of detection."[39] George Frederickson also believes that the new public management "will multiply the possibilities of corruption" while reducing the capacity of government agencies to manage themselves and their contracts. Moreover, Frederickson suggests that "the logic and the effects of the new managerialism move democratic government further away from the possibility of an influential and selfless public service."[40]

Even if the new public management were to improve the performance of government, reasons Alasdair Roberts, it still might not improve the public's trust. Roberts calls this "the paradox of public sector reform," for "the result may be a government that works better, costs less—and is nonetheless distrusted." Specifically, he worries that "many of the new methods of service delivery now being established by governments deliberately abandon institutional arrangements that have been used to reassure the public that public authority would be exercised appropriately." For example, market-based governance and other reforms are explicitly designed to reduce political control over actual service delivery; as a consequence, however, they also give those with operational responsibility an opportunity to abuse their power, to behave corruptly, or to exercise too much policy discretion. As a consequence, writes Roberts, such "reforms might simultaneously improve performance and corrode public trust."[41]

Kenneth Ruscio would agree with Roberts. To Ruscio, trust depends on "a confidence in institutions and procedures." Indeed, he argues, "political trust may actually depend on more rather than less structural and procedural complexity." Why? Ruscio explains that "by virtue of their particular design, certain institutions make us more willing to trust others in a political setting by protecting us against the harm that can arise from a violated trust." How might public officials violate our trust? Again, there are four possibilities: by exploiting their authority, by lining their pockets, by making the wrong decision, or by not producing results. Ruscio, however, appears to worry more about the first three—about the poor exercise of government's discretion—than about poor government performance. To promote trust, he emphasizes not results but "institutional design"— indeed, "institutional complexity."[42]

Furthermore, if better results are achieved through market-based reforms that employ formal, contractual exchange relations between public agencies and nongovernmental service providers (rather than relations that emphasize implicit trust), it may not be possible to use such reforms as evidence of government's competence. Even when performance is enhanced, what possible lesson might citizens (and opinion leaders) draw from a public service that was once provided, unsuccessfully, by a traditional government agency but is now provided—with much better results—by a nonprofit or for-profit organization under contract with the government? As usual, there can be multiple explanations. Some citizens might conclude that government officials had gotten smarter, had invented an innovative way to deliver services better, and thus deserved more trust. Others, however, might assume that government officials had only stumbled onto (or were forced into) this contracting strategy and that the new success of the nongovernmental organization only proved that public agencies are (inevitably) incompetent. Still others might conclude that if they want to deal with government they need a formal quid pro quo, not something as amorphous as trust.[43] "Detailed contracts align expectations when trust is weak," observes Craig Thomas, "but such contracts also signal the absence of trust by one or more parties to the contract."[44]

Communicating Performance Data and Performance

Nevertheless, improved performance might help to enhance the public's trust of government. This, however, will not happen automatically. Even if the results produced by government were to increase dramatically, citizens might not personally experience enough of these improvements to notice. Consequently, whenever a public agency has been able to accomplish significantly more, the agency's leadership needs to explain to citizens when, where, and how performance is actually improving.[45]

After all, as Joseph Nye and Philip Zelikow note, "large parts of the public are demonstrably ill-informed about many aspects of government performance."[46] Bok reports that public opinion surveys "cast doubt on whether the public is well enough informed to make reliable judgments about the government's performance." Moreover, he continues, such surveys also suggest that "people tend to evaluate the work of government officials and agencies much more highly if they have direct contact with them than if they know about them only secondhand."[47]

"Many citizens become aware of local government services only after they fail," observes Evan Berman, who suggests several "public administration strategies to reduce public cynicism." In particular, "to enhance the reputation of local government for competence and efficiency," Berman advocates both "good performance and effective communication of that performance." Noting that "ensuring public trust is not a simple task," he argues that public trust requires citizens to "believe that government serves their needs, that they can affect decision-making, and that government is able to deliver."[48]

Blaine Liner and his Urban Institute colleagues make a similar recommendation for state government. "Providing regular information to a state's citizens about the progress being made in addressing problems important to those citizens," they write, "seems very likely to increase people's interest in, confidence in, and support of, their state government." Yet the Urban Institute team "found few attempts by state governments to communicate with their citizens about the outcomes of state government activities." Consequently, they offer a variety of suggestions "to improve communications about outcomes, potentially improving accountability and trust in government."[49]

Regina Herzlinger offers a similar communication strategy. Herzlinger asks, "Can public trust in nonprofits and government be restored?" and responds with a proposal to "increase the *disclosure, analysis,* and *dissemination* of information on the performance of nonprofit and governmental organizations, and [to] apply *sanctions* against those that do not comply with these requirements." Such an approach, she argues, "would certainly increase public trust in these organizations and probably improve their performance as well."[50]

Publishing raw performance data is hardly a communication strategy. The data never speak for themselves. Data become information only when interpreted through some analytical framework; and different frameworks can produce different interpretations. Consequently, public agencies or governments that wish to enhance the public's trust in their ability to produce results that citizens value need a sophisticated communication strategy—one that permits an intelligent, realistic interpretation of both enhanced performance and needed improvements.[51]

Operational Trust

Citizens can express their trust in their government verbally or operationally. "Trust is a complex, multifaceted concept," observes Thomas, with "cognitive, emotional, and behavioral components."[52] Consequently, citizens have at least two ways to express their trust for their governments: verbally, with their words, and operationally, through their deeds. Citizens can report, to friends and pollsters, that they trust (or do not trust) their government to do the right thing. They can also demonstrate their trust in government by cooperating with it: by paying their taxes, by obeying the laws, by voting, and by neither abusing public officials nor trying to bribe them. There is little reason to expect that the trust (or distrust) that citizens explicitly report with either thoughtful reasoning or impulsive emotions will perfectly match the trust (or distrust) that they implicitly reveal through their behavior.[53]

Indeed, if we watch what citizens do rather than what they say, we may be surprised to discover that Americans exhibit significant quantities of behavioral trust. They voluntarily pay their taxes—and do so more voluntarily than citizens of many other nations.[54] When the 2000 presidential elections created ambiguous results, and one of the country's dominant political institutions, the Supreme Court, made its decision, the nation accepted it. American citizens did not riot in the streets. American citizens were not even surprised that people did not riot in the streets—though Americans would also not have been surprised if citizens of other nations did riot under similar political circumstances.

In the aftermath of the terrorist attacks on the World Trade Center and the Pentagon, what did Americans do about airport security? We unprivatized it. The private sector, Americans decided, was not doing an adequate job. It was time to turn this important function over to the federal government.

Trust in government, argues Ruscio, is not and should not be personal trust. Rather, political trust depends upon the design of institutions that can balance discretion with accountability. Such political trust, he argues, rests "on a confidence in institutions and procedures rather than a host of private virtues or commonly shared values."[55]

We pay our taxes not because we trust the people who manage or work for the Internal Revenue Service or our state Department of Taxation or our municipal tax office. How many citizens even know the name of the director of the Internal Revenue Service or of their municipal tax assessor? No, we pay our taxes because we trust the institution that collects them. We trust that this institution has been designed to ensure that the people who work there will treat all citizens (including ourselves) fairly—that it has been designed to prevent employees from exploiting their authority or lining their pockets.

Similarly, we accepted the Supreme Court's decision on the 2000 presidential election not because we trusted these nine individuals. (Again, how many citizens can name all nine justices? How many can name the chief justice? How many can name even one justice?) We accepted this decision even if we agreed more with the logic of the Florida court. We accepted this decision even if we thought the nine justices exercised their inherent policy discretion ineptly. Certainly, we were told by numerous commentators how poorly reasoned the Supreme Court's decision was.[56] No, we accepted the decision because of our long-run faith in the design of our complex, judicial system—and, more specifically, in the design of our institution for the final resolution of all legal and political disputes: the Supreme Court.

Why did we think that the federal government would do a better job screening airline passengers for weapons than the private sector had done? Airport security is certainly not one of those few "inherently governmental functions"—a job that we implicitly accept ought to be done by a public organization rather than a private one. Certainly, it is not an inherent monopoly. Before September 11, 2001, a variety of different private firms were providing airport security, and no one complained that this was wrong or even inappropriate. Yet after these terrorist attacks, we citizens quickly decided that government would do a much better job ensuring the safety of airline travel than business did, would, or even could. And Congress responded amazingly rapidly—drafting, debating, redrafting, again debating, and still passing the Aviation and Transportation Security Act of 2001 within sixty-six days.

Why? Because we citizens trusted the federal government to create an institution that we could trust. We didn't really know what that institution would look like or how it would function. In fact, Congress debated whether to give the assignment to the Federal Aviation Administration, or to the Department of Justice, or to some new unit within the Department of Transportation. Indeed, even when Congress acted to create a new Transportation Security Administration within the Department of Transportation, to be headed by a new under secretary of transportation for security, we had no idea how this organization, or this person, would function. Nevertheless, when confronted with a significant problem of public safety, Americans instinctively decided that they trusted the federal government more than the private sector.

Realistic Expectations

Trust in government is difficult to create. After all, as Thomas notes, "our instrumental knowledge about building, maintaining, or recovering public trust is quite limited."[57] It is not at all obvious that improving the performance of government agencies will improve the public's trust in government. It might help, it might not. It might help some, but not very much.[58]

Does all of this mean that we ought not to worry about government's performance? Does the identification of multiple sources of the public's distrust of government—of which inadequate performance may be one of the least important—suggest that we can discard the effort to improve the performance of public agencies? Does the complex necessity of simultaneously (and slowly) ratcheting up both performance and trust suggest that the task is too difficult to contemplate?

No. The magnitude of the challenge, however—combined with the uncertain connection between performance and trust—suggests that we should be a little more realistic about the changes in public attitudes that market-based reforms, enhanced performance, and better communications will produce. Even if our federal, market-based environmental policy were significantly reducing pollution in our water and air, even if our state, contracted-out Division of Motor Vehicles were to require of us only five minutes to get a driver's license or register a vehicle (all the while improving the safety of our highways), even if our municipal, voucher-financed school system were turning out high school graduates, all of whom were becoming productive employees and responsible citizens—even if we citizens were personally familiar with all of these performance improvements, we would not immediately become completely trusting. We would still have ample reason not to trust our government. If, for example, the performance of the local school system, the state Division of Motor Vehicles, and federal environmental policy were all to improve significantly, would minority citizens who have experienced racial profiling tell pollsters that they now trust their government?

To enhance the performance of government, we ought to experiment with the full array of leadership strategies, managerial tactics, and market-based reforms.[59] At the same time, we ought to be a little less giddy about what improved performance can do for public trust. As Thomas writes, "producing trust in government at a macrolevel may indeed be extraordinarily difficult in a heterogeneous society such as the United States."[60] Thus we ought to expect few miracles. Whether we are hoping to enhance our personal accumulation of financial assets with some high-performing stocks or to enhance the public's accumulation of trust with some high-performing agencies, we ought to be wary of irrational exuberance.

Nevertheless, we ought also to devote significant energies to improving the performance of public agencies. After all, we think that the public's trust in government depends upon government doing the right thing.[61] And improving performance is certainly the right thing to do.

Notes

1. The Pew Research Center for the People and the Press words its trust question this way: "How much of the time do you think you can trust the government in Washington to do what is right? Just about always, most of the time, or only some of the time?" In 1958, 16 percent of the respondents said "just about always," and 57 percent said "most of the time"; by 1998 those numbers had dropped to 5 and 29 percent, respectively ("Deconstructing Distrust: How Americans View Government; Overview," Pew Research Center for the People and the Press, March 10, 1998 [http://208.240.91.18/trustrpt.htm (February 2, 2002)] and "Deconstructing Distrust: How Americans View Government; Survey Methodology," Pew Research Center for the People and the Press, March 10, 1998 [http://208.240.91.18/trustque.htm (February 2, 2002)]).

For data on the decline in the public's trust in government, see Gary Orren, "Fall from Grace: The Public's Loss of Faith in Government," in Joseph S. Nye Jr., Philip D. Zelikow, and David C. King, eds., *Why People Don't Trust Government* (Harvard University Press, 1997), pp. 77–107.

In recent years, some polls have found an upturn in some of the data. For example, every two years, the National Election Studies at the University of Michigan asks Americans, "How much of the time do you think you can trust the government in Washington to do what is right—just about always, most of the time, or only some of the time?" The just-about-always answer dropped from a high of 17 percent in 1966 to 2 percent in 1974 and has fluctuated between 2 and 4 percent ever since. The most-of-the-time answer dropped from 62 percent in 1962 to 19 percent in 1994; since then, however, it has increased steadily to 40 percent in 2000 (National Election Studies, "Trust in the Federal Government 1958–2000" [www.umich.edu/~nes/nesguide/toptable/tab5a_1.htm (September 2001)]).

Then came September 11, 2001. The *Washington Post* reported that between April 2000 (when it took its last such "trust" poll) and September 25–27, 2001, the percentage of people who trusted the government in Washington to do the right thing "just about always" jumped from 4 percent to 13 percent, and the percentage who answered "most of the time" doubled from 26 to 51 percent. Yet the terrorist attacks and the subsequent anthrax alarm had not demonstrated an increase in government's performance. If anything, they had exposed failures in both government's intelligence-gathering capacity and its ability to respond to threats. *Washington Post* (www.washingtonpost.com/wp-srv/politics/polls/vault/stories/data092801.htm [February 2, 2002]).

2. Peter F. Drucker, "The Sickness of Government," *Public Interest*, no. 14 (Winter 1969), pp. 3–23, pp. 4, 7, 17.

3. Ibid., pp. 4, 7, 17; pp. 18, 19, 22. Through reprivatization, Drucker seeks to implement the same distinction between policy and administration that was advocated by Woodrow Wilson and Frank Goodnow a century ago (Woodrow Wilson, "The Study of Administration," *Political Science Quarterly*, vol. 2, no. 2 [1887], pp. 197–222; Frank Goodnow, *Politics and Administration: A Study in Government* [New York: Russell and Russell, 1900]). Yet this politics-administration dichotomy is based on the fallacy that the implementation of policy is inherently not political (Robert D. Behn, *Rethinking Democratic Accountability* [Brookings, 2001], pp. 50–51).

4. David Osborne and Ted Gaebler, *Reinventing Government* (Reading, Mass.: Addison-Wesley, 1992), pp. 28, 299, 307, 308.

5. For example, Sandford Borins, *Innovating with Integrity: How Local Heroes Are Transforming American Government* (Georgetown University Press, 1998), offers five "key ideas" of this "new paradigm," two of which concern market mechanisms and improved performance: "public sector managers must appreciate the value of competition and maintain an open-minded attitude about which services belong in the private, rather than public sector"; and "organizations and individuals should be evaluated and rewarded on the basis of how well they meet demanding performance targets" (p. 9). B. Guy Peters, *The Future of Governing: Four Emerging Models* (University Press of Kansas, 1996), defines four new models of governance, the first of which is the "market model," for which "the operative assumption appears to be that the best or even the only way to obtain better results from public-sector organizations is to adopt some sort of a market-based mechanism to replace the traditional bureaucracy" (p. 21). Donald F. Kettl, *The Global Public Management Revolution: A Report on the Transformation of Governance* (Brookings, 2000), writes of a "global public management revolution" containing "six core characteristics," two of which are "marketization" ("How can government use market-style incentives to root out the pathologies of government bureaucracy?") and "accountability for results" ("How can governments improve their ability to deliver what they promise?") (pp. 1, 2).

6. Drucker, "The Sickness of Government," p. 5.

7. If the expectations game works in business and politics, why can't it work in government, too? The strategy is quite simple: To win, you have to beat the expectations. Thus, winning requires a two-prong strategy: Obviously you need a strategy that will beat the expectations. First, however, you need to set the expectations low enough so that you have

a chance to beat them. It is much easier to win the expectations game if expectations are low. Given the current state of the public's expectations for government's performance, many public agencies ought to find it easy to win at this game.

8. The implicit promise that market-based governance will directly improve government's performance is based on the assumption that private sector organizations (because they are disciplined by the market) perform better than public sector organizations. For example, just imagine the public ridicule that would be heaped upon the Federal Software Administration if it produced a word-processing program (let's, hypothetically, call it "Word") that consistently failed to put footnotes on the proper page.

9. I have converted the do-you-trust-government question into a do-you-trust-government-officials question by focusing on four untrustworthy things that these officials sometimes do. However, at least two other untrustworthy actions might be added to the list: fifth, the people in government do not tell the truth ("You cannot trust them; they will lie to you"), and sixth, the people in government do not behave virtuously ("You cannot trust them; they will follow a depraved moral code"). These actions are not unique to government, however. They are more personal than institutional; all citizens can do these things in their private lives. Thus, I have chosen not to examine them in detail.

10. See Joseph S. Nye Jr., Philip D. Zelikow, and David C. King, eds. *Why People Don't Trust Government* (Harvard University Press, 1997), for thorough analyses of the various factors contributing to the public's declining trust in government.

11. For those people over the age of ten, this is surely a null set.

12. James Madison, "The Federalist 51," in Alexander Hamilton, James Madison, and John Jay, *The Federalist Papers* (Bantam Books, 1982), pp. 261–65, pp. 262, 261, 262.

13. As these three examples illustrate, the abuse of power is not limited to public officials. People who work in the private sector can abuse the power they exercise over their subordinates. Indeed, nongovernmental organizations can be mistrusted for the same four reasons: they also can abuse their power, be corrupt, exercise policy discretion ineptly, and fail to perform. When we discover a private sector organization whose people have done one or more of these four things, however, we have a choice: we can stop doing business with the organization. We cannot, however, stop doing business with our government.

14. Wayne Washington, "Freeh Defends FBI, Despite Its Woes," *Boston Globe,* May 17, 2001, p. A2.

15. "Statement by Judge in Los Alamos Case, with Apology for Abuse of Power," *New York Times,* September 14, 2000, p. A25.

16. Madison, "Federalist 51," p. 261.

17. The official may not be able to withhold a license, for example, but he or she can often delay its issuance, and such a delay can cost the citizen money or time, or both. So even if the public official cannot deny a citizen a job, a contract, or a permit, the official can still impose a cost on the citizen and is thus able to extract some benefit. This personal benefit from corruption need not, however, be cash. An official seeking to hire someone or to let a contract can simply choose a friend, someone with whom he or she will enjoy working.

18. See Behn, *Rethinking Democratic Accountability,* chapters 1 and 2, for a discussion of how our efforts to prevent corruption in government can inhibit its performance.

19. To create the FBI's reputation for incorruptibility, J. Edgar Hoover focused his law enforcement efforts on criminals (such as bank robbers) who would be less likely to tempt

his agents. During Prohibition, Hoover carefully kept the FBI from having any responsibility for enforcing Prohibition (Eugene Lewis, *Public Entrepreneurship: Toward a Theory of Bureaucratic Political Power* [Indiana University Press, 1980], p. 106). And Hoover refused even to admit that organized crime existed, let alone to assign agents to investigate it, in part because he feared that it could corrupt his agents (Curt Gentry, *J. Edgar Hoover: The Man and the Secrets* [W. W. Norton, 1991], p. 238).

20. If the judicial branch did not exercise judgment in making its decisions, all nations would have long ago adopted Max Weber's "modern judge who is a vending machine into which the pleadings are inserted together with the fee and which then disgorges the judgment together with its reasons mechanically derived from the code" (quoted in Reinhard Bendix, *Max Weber: An Intellectual Portrait* [University of California Press, 1960], p. 421).

21. Usually the question is about "the government in Washington," but this leaves open the question of whether this government in Washington is the Congress, the Supreme Court, the president, the Environmental Protection Agency, or the Indian Health Service.

22. The terms *trust, government,* and *the right thing* may not even have the same meaning today as they did fifty years ago. The dictionary definitions have remained constant, but the way respondents to polls have interpreted these words may have changed.

23. Of course, such performance expectations might have been created not by those accused of failing to produce but by legislators or other advocates who have an obvious incentive to promise that their latest policy proposal will—if implemented faithfully, intelligently, and competently—create a big jump in performance.

24. Cheryl W. Thompson and Claudia Deane, "FBI's Ratings Suffer in Light of Blunders," *Washington Post,* May 22, 2001, p. A3.

25. Roberto Suro, "Mission Unfinished: Louis Freeh Tried to Change the Culture of the FBI: His Successor Will Face the Same Task," *Washington Post National Weekly Edition,* May 21–27, 2001, p. 29.

26. *New Yorker,* May 28, 2001, p. 52. Fifty years ago, this would not have been funny. Fifty years ago, no one would have thought of making a joke about the incompetence of the FBI. In July 2001—just two months after the appearance of this cartoon—the FBI reported that 449 of its guns plus 184 laptops has been lost or stolen over the previous eleven years, further damaging the agency's reputation for operational competence (Dan Eggen, "FBI Lacked Inventory Controls, Panel Told," *Washington Post,* July 19, 2001, p. A18).

27. Drucker, "The Sickness of Government," pp. 12, 7, 8.

28. Derek Bok, "Measuring the Performance of Government," in Nye, Zelikow, and King, *Why People Don't Trust Government,* pp. 55–75, pp. 55, 61, 63, 65. See also Derek Bok, *The State of the Nation* (Harvard University Press, 1996), especially chapters 18–20.

29. Al Gore, *Creating a Government That Works Better and Costs Less: Report of the National Performance Review* (U.S. Government Printing Office, September 7, 1993), p. i.

30. *Government Performance and Results Act of 1993,* P.L. 103-62, sec. 2(b)(1).

31. Office of Management and Budget, *The President's Management Agenda* (U.S. Government Printing Office, 2001), p. 1.

32. From President Bush's radio address, August 25, 2001 (www.whitehouse.gov/news/releases/2001/08/print/20010825.html [September 2001]).

33. The Panel on Civic Trust and Citizen Responsibility, *A Government to Trust and Respect: Rebuilding Citizen-Government Relations for the Twenty-First Century* (Washington: National Academy of Public Administration, 1999), p. 17.

34. David G. Carnevale, *Trustworthy Government: Leadership and Management Strategies for Building Trust and High Performance* (San Francisco: Jossey-Bass, 1995), p. 12.

35. The causal interactions between citizens' trust in government and government's performance can be quite complicated. To earn the cooperation of citizens, government may need to convince citizens that it does indeed do the right thing, which may cause citizens to cooperate more with government, which may enhance government's ability to perform, which citizens may interpret as doing the right thing, and so on.

36. Joseph S. Nye Jr., "The Decline of Confidence in Government," introduction to Nye, Zelikow, and King, *Why People Don't Trust Government*, pp. 1–18, p. 4. This interconnection between government performance and public trust is also noted by John J. DiIulio Jr., Gerald Garvey, and Donald F. Kettl, *Improving Government Performance: An Owner's Manual* (Brookings, 1993): "Efforts to improve government performance are inseparable from improving public perceptions of government" (p. 78).

37. Kettl, *The Global Public Management Revolution: A Report on the Transformation of Governance*, pp. 1, 56–57.

38. Donald F. Kettl, *Reinventing Government: A Fifth-Year Report Card* (Brookings, 1998), p. 36.

39. Lydia Segal, "The Pitfalls of Political Decentralization and Proposals for Reform: The Case of New York City Public Schools," *Public Administration Review*, vol. 57 (March–April 1997), pp. 141–49, p. 147.

40. H. George Frederickson, "Public Ethics and the New Managerialism," *Public Integrity*, vol. 1 (Summer 1999), pp. 265–78, pp. 276, 274, 267.

41. Alasdair Roberts, "The Paradox of Public Sector Reform: Works Better, Trusted Less?" paper prepared for the annual research conference of the Association for Public Policy Analysis and Management, New York, October 29–31, 1998. Roberts is talking not just about market-based governance but about an array of reforms that he calls "a new pragmatism."

Barbara Ferman has a different take on what she calls "the policymaking-implementation gap," arguing that "the gap between policy intent and implementation outcomes may not be so bad after all" (Ferman, "When Failure Is Success: Implementation and Madisonian Government," in Dennis J. Palumbo and Donald J. Calista, eds., *Implementation and the Policy Process* [Greenwood Press, 1990], pp. 39–50, pp. 39, 49). This is because, she suggests, "implementation is another check in the American system of government" (p. 39). Yes, Ferman admits, the implementation process "can be a source of delay and diversion of objectives, but it also protects against the concentration and abuse of power. Moreover, the delay factor can be beneficial to the extent that it guards against the commitment of egregious errors by allowing more time for analysis and testing" (pp. 39–40). To Ferman, "the policy/implementation conflict is another example of the Madisonian victory" (p. 49).

42. Kenneth P. Ruscio, "Jay's Pirouette, or Why Political Trust Is Not the Same As Personal Trust," *Administration and Society*, vol. 31 (November 1999), pp. 639–57, pp. 641, 652, 654, 652.

43. Of course, the high-performing nongovernmental organizations with which government contracted relied heavily on internal trust to create their effectiveness (see Francis Fukuyama, *Trust: The Social Virtues and the Creation of Prosperity* [Free Press, 1995]). This lesson, however, is apt to be lost.

44. Craig W. Thomas, "Maintaining and Restoring Public Trust in Government Agencies and Their Employees," *Administration and Society*, vol. 30 (May 1998), pp. 166–93, p. 188. Ruscio disagrees. "Our intuitive understanding," he writes, "is that institutional complexity, elaborately codified rules, or complicated procedures are indications of weak norms and low levels of trust." Ruscio carefully distinguishes, however, between personal trust and political trust. Thus, he argues, the "conventional view" (such as that expressed by Thomas) "may be accurate only to the degree that we view trust in interpersonal terms" rather than as a political judgment (Ruscio, "Jay's Pirouette," p. 652).

45. Elsewhere I have written that one of the eight basic reasons to measure a public agency's performance is "to promote"—to "convince political superiors, legislators, stakeholders, journalists, and citizens that their organization is doing a good job" (Robert D. Behn, "Why Measure Performance? Different Purposes Require Different Measures," *Public Administration Review* [forthcoming, 2002]).

46. Joseph S. Nye Jr. and Philip Zelikow, "Reflections, Conjectures, and Puzzles," conclusion to Nye, Zelikow, and King, *Why People Don't Trust Government*, pp. 253–81, p. 256.

47. Bok, "Measuring the Performance of Government," p. 56.

48. Evan W. Berman, "Dealing with Cynical Citizens," *Public Administration Review*, vol. 57 (March–April 1997), pp. 105–12, pp. 106, 111, 110.

49. Blaine Liner, Harry P. Hatry, Elisa Vinson, Ryan Allen, Pat Dusenbury, Scott Bryant, and Ron Snell, *Making Results-Based State Government Work* (Washington: Urban Institute Press, 2001), p. 38. In particular, Liner and colleagues suggest annual reports and web pages that include performance measures (pp. 38–43).

50. Regina E. Herzlinger, "Can Public Trust in Nonprofits and Governments Be Restored?" *Harvard Business Review*, vol. 74 (March–April 1996), pp. 97–107, pp. 97, 100. Herzlinger's article focuses primarily on nonprofit organizations, with some discussion of municipal finance.

51. Craig Thomas offers some suggestions for any such communications strategy by emphasizing that those assigned to communicate with a particular constituency should possess human or professional attributes similar to those of this constituency's members: "Because individuals are limited in their abilities to process information, they often rely on relatively simple heuristics, such as personal characteristics and professional affiliation, to make judgments about organizational trustworthiness. Therefore, agency managers might try matching the personal and professional characteristics of employees with targeted groups outside the agency, or appointing individuals outside the agency to sit on [its] advisory boards" (Thomas, "Maintaining and Restoring Public Trust in Government Agencies and Their Employees," p. 187). For a description of one such communications strategy, see Robert D. Behn, *Leadership Counts: Lessons for Public Managers* (Harvard University Press, 1991), chapter 5, pp. 83–103.

52. Thomas, "Maintaining and Restoring Public Trust in Government Agencies and Their Employees," p. 166.

53. Of course, the two kinds of trust could be linked: a person who believes that government will do the right thing may be more inclined to cooperate with it.

54. Because different nations employ different kinds of taxes (some of which are easier to police than others) and because different nations collect their data differently, it is impossible to directly compare the voluntary compliance rates of different nations. Nevertheless,

the consensus of tax experts appears to be that voluntary compliance of U.S. citizens is higher than for many other nations (though not necessarily for those in Scandinavia).

55. Ruscio, "Jay's Pirouette," p. 641.

56. Alan M. Dershowitz, *Supreme Injustice: How the High Court Hijacked Election 2000* (Oxford University Press, 2001).

57. Thomas, "Maintaining and Restoring Public Trust in Government Agencies and Their Employees," p. 168.

58. If our sole objective is to improve trust, we might follow Ruscio's implicit suggestion and concentrate less on marketization and other strategies for improving the performance of government agencies and more on the design of governmental institutions to ensure that they warrant the public's trust.

59. Market-based governance is not the only macro-level strategy for improving the performance of the public sector. After all, many of the private sector's "market-based" organizations perform poorly. Many fail. Whether the organization is private, public, or nonprofit, it needs to internally employ nonmarket strategies (including the creation of trust) to drive its own performance.

60. Thomas, "Maintaining and Restoring Public Trust in Government Agencies and Their Employees," p. 188.

61. At least, this is how we phrase the polling question.

Contributors

All contributors are at the John F. Kennedy School of Government, Harvard University, unless otherwise noted.

Robert D. Behn
Visiting Professor, Kennedy School of Government, and Professor of Public Policy, Duke University

Cary Coglianese
Associate Professor of Public Policy

Georges de Menil
Visiting Professor, Kennedy School of Government and Professor in Economics, Ecole des Hautes Etudes en Sciences Sociales, Paris

John D. Donahue
Director, Visions of Governance in the 21st Century and Raymond Vernon Lecturer in Public Policy

Karen Eggleston
Assistant Professor of Economics, Tufts University

Peter Frumkin
Assistant Professor of Public Policy

Archon Fung
Assistant Professor of Public Policy

Elaine Ciulla Kamarck
Lecturer in Public Policy

Steven Kelman
Albert J. Weatherhead III and Richard W. Weatherhead Professor of Public Management

David Lazer
Assistant Professor of Public Policy

Mark H. Moore
Daniel and Florence Guggenheim Professor of Criminal Justice Policy and Public Management and Director, Hauser Center for Nonprofit Organizations

Frederick Schauer
Frank Stanton Professor of the First Amendment

Robert N. Stavins
Albert Pratt Professor of Business and Government

Virginia J. Wise
Lecturer on Law, Harvard University School of Law

Richard Zeckhauser
Frank Plumpton Ramsey Professor of Political Economy

Index

Abuse of power by government, 326–28, 331–33
Accountability, 1–25; extensive, 5–7; and Government Performance and Results Act, 334; intensive, 4–8; of new forms of government, 233–34, 253, 257–59
Acid rain, 177, 190, 191, 250. *See also* Sulfur dioxide allowance trading program
Adidas, 152
Administration of contracts. *See* Strategic contracting
Aerospace industry, 89, 91
Agriculture, U.S. Department of (USDA), 212, 213, 215, 216–17
Aid to Dependent Children, 110
Airport security, 4, 339, 340–41
America Works, 247, 258
Apparel Industry Partnership, 154
Armey, Dick, 3
Arnold, R., 45
Arrow, K., 46
Asquith, Herbert, 110

Aviation and Transportation Security Act of *2001*, 340
Ayres, I., 205

Babbitt, Bruce, 241
Baltimore, nonprofit payments in lieu of taxes, 82
Banking, transformation of, 238–39
Bardach, E., 258
Behn, R. D., 258
Belgium, old-age and survivors' insurance, 108
Berle, A., 7
Berman, E., 338
Bertrand, M., 45
Bill of Rights, 327
Bismarck, Otto von, 108–10
Blair, Tony, 122
Blood banks, 52, 54
Body Shop, 152
Bok, D., 338, 354
Bottom line: for private sector, 306–07; for public sector, 305–06, 307–13
Braithwaite, J., 205

351

Branch Davidians, 327
Brazil, government, 229
Budget, public sector: contracting out, 89; government work force scaled to spending, 269–71; transparency, 255
Buffa, D., 240
Bulgaria, mandatory private pension accounts, 121
Bureau of Labor Statistics, 272; National Compensation Survey, 276
Bureaucracy in government: and market-based environmental protection, 187; and public opinion, 227–31, 234–40; in Soviet Union, 229. *See also* Transformation of government
Bush, George H. W., 2, 190, 228
Bush, George W., 334

Caldeira, G., 135
California, energy crisis, 251, 252
Canadian HACCP program, 216
Carbon dioxide emissions, 178
Carnevale, D., 335
Castro, Fidel, 230
Census Bureau data: government outsourcing, 272; government pay scales, 277
Centers for Disease Control (CDC), 212
CERCLA. *See* Comprehensive Environmental Response, Compensation, and Liability Act
CFCs, 189, 190, 191
Chemical industry: disclosure per Toxics Release Inventory, 156–57, 158, 168, 178; vulnerability to social market forces, 164, 167
Chernew, M. E., 48
Child labor, 152, 154, 162, 167
Chile, mandatory private pension accounts, 120–21
China, government, 230
Clean Air Act Amendments of *1990*, 177, 181, 186, 188, 250

Clinton, Bill, 2, 228, 235, 241
Compensation of employees: public work force vs. private sector, 276–90; service contracting, 73–74
Comprehensive Environmental Response, Compensation, and Liability Act of *1980* (CERCLA), 178
Computer Sciences Corporation, 91
Considine, M., 244
Consumer activism. *See* Social markets
Contracting officer's technical representative (COTR), 91–97
Copyright, 132
Corporate social responsibility, 152
Corruption of public officials, 328–29, 330, 331–33
COTR. *See* Contracting officer's technical representative
Court opinions, publication of, 128–42
Cove, Peter, 258
Croatia: health-care system, 50, 55; mandatory private pension accounts, 121
Cuba, government, 230
Customer service approach to government, 297–305
Czech Republic, health-care system, 47, 49–50, 55

Death of Common Sense, The (Howard), 228, 234
Defense industry: development of, 246; strategic contracting with, 89, 90, 91, 96
Denmark, old-age and survivors' insurance, 108
Dentistry, 52, 54
Deposit-refund systems, 176, 233, 250
Developing countries, revolt against bureaucracy, 237–38
Diamond, P., 117
Disclosure of social environmental performance of corporations, 147, 156–57, 158

INDEX

Distrust of government. *See* Public opinion of government bureaucracy; Trust in government
Drucker, P., 323–24, 333–34
Duggan, M., 45, 50

Eastern European countries: health-care systems, 31, 45, 47, 50–51, 52, 54–55; old-age security, 117, 121. *See also specific countries*
Eco-labels for products, 156, 157, 160, 178
Education: charter schools, 67, 80–81; for-profit vs. nonprofit providers, 67, 80–81; voucher movement, 251, 252–53, 259
Emissions trading program (EPA), 177, 180
Energy-efficiency labeling, 178
Energy Star program, 156
Entrepreneurial government, 231, 232, 240–44, 254–55, 257
Environics International, 151
Environmental Defense Fund, 189
Environmental protection, management-based, 202, 218
Environmental protection, market-based, 16–18, 173–200; advantages of market-based instruments, 175, 250–51; ambient permits, 183; analysis lessons, 182; bureaucrats' position, 187; charge systems, 176; command-and-control regulations vs., 174–75, 185–87; control costs, 174, 189; deposit-refund systems, 176; design and implementation lessons, 179–81; emissions trading program, 177, 180; Energy Star program, 156; environmental activists, 185–86, 189; experiments and experiences, 175–78; fossil fuel subsidies, 178; government subsidy reduction, 178–79; hazardous waste liability, 178; "hot spots" due to taxes or tradable permits, 183; identification of new applications, 182–84; incentive lost to develop new technologies, 175; increase in use, 188–90; labor organizations and, 186; lead allowance trading program, 177, 179; market friction reduction, 177–78; municipal solid waste collection, 176; normative lessons, 179–84; positive political economy lessons, 184–90; product labeling, 156, 157, 160, 178; RECLAIM program, 177, 183; and social markets created by consumer actions, 146, 153–54, 163–64; sulfur dioxide allowance trading program, 177, 180, 181, 182, 184, 188, 189–90, 203, 233, 250; taxes as environmental user charges, 176, 182–83, 185–86; technology-based standards vs., 174; Toxics Release Inventory, 156–57, 158, 168, 178; tradable permits, 177, 179–84, 185, 187–88, 189, 190–91
Ethical consumerism, 151. *See also* Social markets
Ethical sourcing, 152
Ethical Trading Initiative, 155
European Union: health-care systems, 31, 52; as networked government, 232; revolt against bureaucracy, 237. *See also individual member countries*

Fair Labor Association, 154–55, 156
FBI. *See* Federal Bureau of Investigation
FDA. *See* Food and Drug Administration
Federal Acquisition Institute, 94
Federal Activities Reform Act of *1998*, 265
Federal Bureau of Investigation (FBI), 327, 329, 333
Federal Meat Inspection Act, 212
Fee-for-service health care vs. capitation system, 47

Feldstein, M., 115
Food and Drug Administration (FDA), 212, 214, 215, 216–17
Food safety: Canadian program, 216; critical control points for, 214–15; *E. coli,* 217; ease of inspection, 212–13; enforcement challenges, 214–16; federal laws, 212; HACCP plan, 212–18; heterogeneity of industry, 213; and management-based regulatory strategies, 208, 210, 211–17
Forest Stewardship Council (FSC), 153–54, 155, 160
Forestry: associational efforts for ecologically sound practices, 153–54; retailers' interest in environmentally responsible providers, 165; Sustainable Forestry Initiative, 154, 155
Fossil fuel, 178, 191
France: mutual aid associations, 106–07; old-age security, 108, 122; pension fund and life insurance company assets, 112
Frederickson, G., 336
Freeman, R., 151
Friedman, M., 145
FSC. *See* Forest Stewardship Council

Gaebler, T., 324
GAO. *See* General Accounting Office
Gap, 152, 164
Garment industry: sweatshop labor, 151–52, 154–55, 166–67; vulnerability to social market forces, 162, 164–65
Garnik, Barbara Kates, 251
Gasoline taxes, 186
General Accounting Office (GAO): criticism of FDA, 217; evaluations of cabinet-level organizations, 310
Gerdtham, U., 47
Germany: mutual aid associations, 106; old-age pensions, 108–10, 111, 122;

123; pension fund and life insurance company assets, 112
G.I. Bill, 233
Gingrich, Newt, 229
Global governance and networked government, 232, 245
Goldin, C., 284
Goldsmith, Steve, 244
Gore, Al, 228, 334
Government Performance and Results Act, 334
Government reform. *See* Transformation of government
Government work force, 21–22, 264–95; compensation and differential from private sector, 276–90; outsourcing, 265–75; scaled to public spending, 269–71; as share of total employment, 267–69; state employees, 266; statistics on, 266–67; unionized nature, 278
Grassley, Charles E., 333
Great Britain: entrepreneurial government, 242–44; insurance, 106–07; mutual aid associations, 106–07; National Health Service, 51; Next Step agencies, 242–43; pension fund and life insurance company assets, 112; pensions and old-age security, 108, 110, 113, 122; privatization of government functions, 228, 237; Railtrack, 4; revolt against bureaucracy, 235–36; Stakeholder Pension Schemes, 122
Guyana, government, 230

HACCP. *See* Hazards Analysis and Critical Control Points
Hallock, K., 45
Hansen, Robert P., 329
Hansmann, H., 45
Hart, O., 40
Hazardous waste liability, 177

Hazards Analysis and Critical Control Points (HACCP) protocol, 212–18. *See also* Food safety
Health care, public vs. private providers, 8–10, 29–65; benefits, costs, and purchaser's objectives, 36–38; blood banks, 52, 54; communicable diseases, 52; community benefits from public hospitals, 35; community hospitals, 53; comparative advantages, 43–44; competition and selection by patients, 48–49; conceptual framework, 36–39; cream skimming, 49; dentistry, 52, 54; endogenous differences, 39–51; fee-for-service vs. capitation system, 47; government purchase, 51–52; heterogeneity and selection by patients, 49–50; hospices, 52, 53; institutional characteristics and contract structure, 46–51; managed care, 52, 67; multidimensional quality, 48; nonprofit ownership and health-care purchasers, 44–46; nursing homes, 52, 53, 54, 77, 78; OECD ranking, 31–32; payment incentives, 46–48; performance differences, 34–36, 41–46; pluralistic delivery of, 52–55; postcontractual innovations, 40–41; preference trade-offs, 38–39; psychiatric hospitals, 52, 53; quality innovations, 43; quality of care, 34–36, 41–46, 77; risk adjustment, 49; risk selection, 49–50; sloughing by private hospitals, 35; soft budget constraints, 50–51; substance abuse, 52; upcoding by private hospitals, 35
Health care reform, 229
Heinz, John, 173
Herzlinger, R., 338
Hill, James J., 329
Hirth, R. A., 48

Home Depot, 153, 165
Human services contracting, 10–11, 66–87. *See also* Service contracting
Hungary: health-care system, 47, 50, 55; mandatory private pension accounts, 121

IBM, 264
Ikea, 153
Incomplete contracting, 29–30
Indianapolis, privatization of city services, 244
Industrial insurance companies, 107
Information technology: contractors evaluating work of other government contractors, 98–99; personal banking, 238–39
Innovation: as government objective, 253–55; health care, 40–41, 43
Inspections of food and food production facilities, 212
Insurance, development of, 106–07
Inter-American Development Bank, 238
Interfaith Council on Corporate Responsibility, 165
International Labor Organization and garment industry standards, 154
International Monetary Fund, 238
International Organization for Standardization, 204; ISO *14000*, 218
Italy, old-age security, 108, 122, 123

Japan, pension fund and life insurance company assets, 112
Johnson, Lady Bird, 250
Jönsson, B., 47
Joskow, P., 188

Katz, L., 282
Keeler, E. B., 34
Kelman, S., 189
Keohane, R. O., 258

Kessler, D., 36
Kettl, D. F., 89, 93, 98, 99, 335
Kluwer, 133–34
Krueger, A., 282

Labeling products for environmental compliance, 156, 157, 160, 178
Labor organizations: and environmental issues, 186; and government work force, 278
Labor, U.S. Department of, 152
Laboratories of Democracy (Osborne), 241
Latin America: old-age security, 117, 120, 121; privatization of state-owned enterprises, 237. *See also individual countries*
Lead allowance trading program, 177, 180
Leaded gasoline, 189, 190, 191
Lee, Wen Ho, 328
Legal information, 14–15, 128–42; bundling, 134–39; citation form, 132; copyright, 132; decrease in private providers, 133; history of private provision of, 129–34; key-number system, 130–31; LEXIS, 133, 135; private reporters, 129; regional division of West's reporters, 135–37; Reporter of Decisions, 130; supply-driven nature of, 134; Supreme Court opinions, 129, 131, 132; training of law students, 132–33; tying vs. bundling, 135; *United States Reports* and *United States Code*, 131; West Publishing Company, 130–33, 135; WESTLAW, 132–33, 135
Lesser, C., 258
Lewis, J., 244
LEXIS, 133, 135
Liebman, J., 115
Liner, B., 338
Lockheed-Martin, 247

Lowe's Home Improvement, 153, 165

Maastricht Treaty, 237
Madison, James, 327, 328
Managed care, 52, 67. *See also* Health care
Management-based regulatory strategies, 18–19, 201–24; advantages, 202–04; conditions for effectiveness, 204–08; division of labor between government and private actors, 207; enforcement, 208–11; environmental regulation, 202, 218; and food safety, 208, 210, 211–17; government use, 205–08, 219; HACCP protocol as, 212–18; heterogeneity of regulated parties, 207, 213; homogeneity of regulated parties, 206–07; at implementation stage, 210–11; performance-based regulation vs., 202–03, 205, 207, 218; at planning stage, 209–10; private behavior model, 205; technology-based regulation vs., 202, 205, 218. *See also* Food safety
Margo, R., 284
Market government, 233, 249–53, 255, 257, 259
Marketization of government functions, 318
Marymount University, Center for Ethical Concerns, 151
Maximus, 247
McClellan, M., 36
McEntree, Gerald, 266
McVeigh, Timothy J., 327, 333
Means, G., 7
Meier, K., 248
Metropolitan Insurance, 107
Metzmeier, K., 138
Military: work force size, 266, 268, 269. *See also* Defense industry
Militia movement, 327
Milward, H. B., 97, 245, 248

Mulroney, Brian, 236
Mutual aid associations, 106–07

National Academy of Public Administration, 334
National Performance Review, 334
Needleham, J., 35
Negative images of government spending, 12, 90–91
Networked government, 231–32, 244–49, 255, 257
New Deal welfare programs, 110–11
New Zealand, entrepreneurial government, 231, 242–44
Nike, 152, 164
Nonprofit institutions: educational, 67, 80–81; government outsourcing to, 313–17; tax advantages, 81–84. *See* Health care; Service contracting
Nye, J. S., 258, 335, 338

Obey, D., 333
Occupational Safety and Health Administration (OSHA), 218
OECD. *See* Organization for Economic Cooperation and Development
Oklahoma City bombing, 327
Old-Age Insurance (OAI) and Old-Age Assistance, 110–11
Old-age security, 13, 105–27; Britain's system, 110, 122; Chile's mandatory private pension accounts, 120–21, 122; compulsory insurance through private pension providers, 118–20; emergence of old-age and survivors' insurance, 108–10; financial markets as providers, 113–14; Germany's public pensions, 108–10; industrial insurance companies, 107; and inflation, 117; in Latin America, 117, 120, 121; and market failures, 114–16; moral hazard of guaranteed pensions, 116; mutual aid associations, 106–07; notational defined-contribution schemes, 123; OECD countries' pension fund and life insurance assets, 112–13; in postcommunist Europe, 117, 121; private pensions funds, 111–13; retirement annuities, 108; Social Security, 110–11; state provision of, 116–17; in western Europe and U.S., 106–11

Organization for Economic Cooperation and Development (OECD): governance issues of developing countries, 238; health-care systems, 31–32; old-age security reforms, 122–24; pension fund and life insurance assets, 112–13. *See also individual member countries*
Orricirio dos Santos, Jose, 229
Orzol, S. M., 48
Osborne, D., 231, 238, 240–41, 324
O'Toole, L., 232, 245, 248
Outsourcing: by private businesses, 264. *See also* Privatization of government functions

Passport administration, 254
Patel, J., 35
Performance-based contracts: service contracting, 75; strategic contracting, 95–96
Performance-based organizations (PBOs), 254
Performance-based regulation vs. management-based, 202–03, 205, 207, 218
Peters, B. G., 233
Peters, T., 239
Peterson, J., 232, 245
Philadelphia, reinvention of city government, 243–44
Pinkerton, J., 239–40
Poland: health-care system, 50–51; mandatory private pension accounts, 121

Pollution control. *See* Environmental protection, market-based
Poterba, J., 282–83
Prison management, 40
Privatization of government functions, 228, 229, 237, 265, 296–332; advantages, 317; authority of government, 302–05; competitive bidding, 317–18; contracting out, 313–19; customer service improvements, 297–305; definition of bottom line, 305–13; definition of public value, 318–19; delivery of government obligations, 301–02; estimating outsourcing, 272–75; independence from government, 314–15; legal information, 128–42; marketization vs. privatization, 318; nonprofits vs. for-profits as providers, 313–17; performance assessment, 311–12; public management, 22–23, 296–332; and size of public work force, 265–75
Progressives, 328–29
Project *88,* 173
Provan, K. G., 245, 249
Prudential Insurance, 107
Public opinion of government bureaucracy, 227–31, 234–40. *See also* Trust in government
Pure Food and Drugs Act, 212

Railtrack (Great Britain), 4
Reagan, Ronald, 2, 228, 235, 236
Reason Foundation, 266
RECLAIM program (Los Angeles), 177, 183
Reebok, 152, 164
Reed, Bruce, 249
Reed-Elsevier, 133–34
Reilly, Richard, 241
Reinventing Government (Osborne), 231, 238, 240–41

Reinventing government initiative of *1990s,* 99, 228–29
Rendell, Ed, 243
Reprivatization, 323
Retirement income. *See* Old-age security
Ritter, G. A., 109
Roberts, A., 336
Romania, mandatory private pension accounts, 121
Roosevelt, Franklin D., 110–11, 246, 254
Roosevelt, Theodore, 254
Rubinow, I., 107
Rueben, K., 282–83
Ruscio, K., 336–37, 339

SA*8000* (Council on Economic Priorities), 154–55
Salmonella, 216, 217. *See also* Food safety
Salvanti, Joseph, 327
Samuelson, P., 113
Sanmina-SCI, 264
Savoie, D., 236
Schmalensee, R., 188
Schroeder, Gerhard, 123
Segal, L., 336
Service contracting, for-profit vs. nonprofit providers, 10–11, 66–87; capitalization, 70–72, 80; competition, 68–69; cost data, 77–79; criteria for public managers' choices, 76–79, 84–85; employee compensation, 73–74; lobbying and access to power, 72; merger of nonprofits to enable competition, 80; normative constraints, 74–75; performance-based contracts, 75; policy options for preserving mixed market, 79–84; quality and effectiveness, 76–77, 79; scale and complexity limitations, 69–70, 80–81; tax advantages of nonprofits, 81–84

INDEX

Shleifer, A., 40
Silverman, E., 45
Skinner, J., 45
Slaughter, A. M., 232, 245
Sloan, F., 34
Slovenia, health-care system, 50, 55
Social markets, 15–16, 145–72; associational efforts to ensure compliance, 153–55; building institutions, 157–63, 169; comparability of social performance, 160; corporate responses, 151–52; and disclosure requirements, 147, 156–57, 158; eco-labels, 156, 157, 160; effect on firms, 148–49; emergence, 150–57; ethical consumerism, 151; government initiatives to ensure compliance, 155–57; intermediary associations, 160–62; limitations, 158, 163–69; operation of well-ordered social market, 147–50; preference articulation and transformation, 162–63; public as beneficiaries, 149; and public sentiment, 150, 163–64; regulation of, 148, 165–69; transparency needed, 158–59; vulnerability of firms, 164–65; wage and hours laws, 166–67. *See also* Environmental protection, market-based
Social Security Act (*1935*), 110
Social Security system. *See* Old-age security
Solid waste collection and charge fees, 176
Soviet Union: revolt against bureaucracy, 229, 247; weapons research, 247
Stakeholder Pension Schemes (Great Britain), 122
Stavins, R., 251
Strategic contracting, 11–13, 88–102; attractiveness of administration jobs, 96, 97; contracting officer's technical representative, 91–96; contractors used to evaluate others, 98–99; by Defense Department, 89, 90, 91, 96; documentation, 94–95; importance of, 89; job description of managers, 94–95; monitoring of labor-hour invoices, 95; negative images of government spending, 90–91; performance measurement, 95–96; skills needed for managers, 92–94, 96–97
Sulfur dioxide allowance trading program, 177, 179, 180, 181, 182, 184, 188, 189–90, 203, 233, 250
Supreme Court opinions, 129, 131, 132; and public trust in judicial system, 340
Sustainable Forestry Initiative (SFI), 154, 155
Sweatshop labor and garment industry, 151–52, 154–55, 166–67
Sweden, old-age security, 108, 123
Switzerland, old-age and survivors' insurance, 108

Taking Control: Politics in the Information Age (Winograd and Buffa), 240
Taxes: advantages of nonprofit service contract providers, 81–84; as environmental user charges, 176, 182–83, 185–86; gasoline, 186; unrelated business income tax, 82–83, 84
Technology-based regulation: vs. management-based strategies, 202, 205, 218; vs. market-based environmental protection, 174–75
Thatcher, Margaret, 2, 122, 228, 235–36
Thomas, C., 337, 339, 341
Thomson, 133–34
Tobacco industry, 163, 164

Toxics Release Inventory (TRI), 156–57, 158, 168, 178
Tradable permits for pollution, 177, 179–84, 185, 187–88, 189, 190–91, 233. *See also* Sulfur dioxide allowance trading program
Traficant, James, 329
Transformation of government, 19–21, 227–63; accountability and transparency, 233–34, 253, 257–59; developing countries, 237–38; entrepreneurial government, 231, 232, 240–44, 254–55, 257; Europe, 237; governance vs. government, 230–31; Great Britain, 235–36, 242–44; Latin America, 237; market government, 233, 249–53, 255, 257, 259; networked government, 231–32, 244–49, 255, 257; new forms, 231–34; New Zealand, 231, 242–44; presidential efforts, 228; public opinion of government bureaucracy, 227–31, 234–40
Transparency: of new forms of government, 233–34, 255–57; of social markets, 158–59
Trust in government, 4, 23–24, 323–48, 335; and abuse of power, 326–28, 331–33; communicating performance data, 337–39; and corruption of public officials, 328–29, 330, 331–33; erosion of, 235; and failure of government to perform, 323, 333–35; and government employees, 316; interconnections between performance and, 335; and market-based government, 324–25, 337; operational trust, 339–41; and policy discretion problems, 329–33; and realistic expectations, 341–42; reasons against, 325–26; resurgence after September *11*, 227
Trustworthy Government (Carnevale), 335

Unemployment Insurance, 110
Unions. *See* Labor organizations
United Mine Workers, 186
United Students against Sweatshops, 155
Upcoding by hospitals, 35
Urban Institute, 338
USDA. *See* Agriculture, U.S. Department of

Veterans Health Administration, 34
Vishny, R., 40

Wagner, Adolf, 109
Wal-Mart, 165
Weaver, Vicki, 327
Welfare reform, 247, 249
Welfare-to-work services: accountability, 258; creation, 247; for-profit vs. nonprofit providers, 67, 77, 247
West Publishing Company, 130–33, 135; WESTLAW, 132–33, 135
What Comes Next (Pinkerton), 239–40
Winograd, M., 240
Wirth, Timothy, 173
Worker Rights Consortium, 155
World Bank: and development of state capacity, 237–38; and pension systems, 121

Zeckhauser, R., 35
Zelikow, P., 338